JEWISH
ODESA

THE MODERN JEWISH EXPERIENCE

Marsha L. Rozenblit and Beth S. Wenger, editors

Paula Hyman and Deborah Dash Moore, founding coeditors

JEWISH ODESA

Negotiating Identities and Traditions in Contemporary Ukraine

MARINA SAPRITSKY-NAHUM

INDIANA UNIVERSITY PRESS

This book is a publication of

Indiana University Press
Office of Scholarly Publishing
Herman B Wells Library
1320 East 10th Street
Bloomington, Indiana 47405 USA

iupress.org

Manufactured in the United States of America

First Printing 2024

Library of Congress Cataloging-in-Publication Data

Names: Sapritsky-Nahum, Marina, author.
Title: Jewish Odesa : negotiating identities and traditions in contemporary
    Ukraine / Marina Sapritsky-Nahum.
Other titles: Negotiating identities and traditions in contemporary Ukraine
Identifiers: LCCN 2024006900 (print) | LCCN 2024006901 (ebook) | ISBN
    9780253070104 (cloth) | ISBN 9780253070111 (paperback) | ISBN
    9780253070128 (pdf)
Subjects: LCSH: Jews—Ukraine—Odesa—History—21st century. |
    Jews—Ukraine—Odesa—Social conditions—21st century. |
    Jews—Ukraine—Odesa—Social life and customs—21st century. | Odesa
    (Ukraine)—Ethnic relations. | Jews—Ethnic identity. | National
    characteristics, Ukrainian. | Nationalism—Ukraine—History. | BISAC:
    HISTORY / Jewish | SOCIAL SCIENCE / Anthropology / Cultural & Social
Classification: LCC DS135.U42 O357 2024 (print) | LCC DS135.U42 (ebook) |
    DDC 947.7/2—dc23
LC record available at https://lccn.loc.gov/2024006900
LC ebook record available at https://lccn.loc.gov/2024006901

I dedicate this book to my parents, Valentina and Victor Sapritsky, who showed me how to care deeply about the world and the people we encounter. I am forever grateful for their gifts of kindness and love.

This book is also for my grandmother Mira (Gorelik) Sapritsky (1927–2003) and my great-aunt Valentina Tzirlina (1930–2022), whose lives, imbued with strength, wisdom, and courage, shaped me as a woman, a scholar, and a person. They continue to inspire me beyond their days. The dates of their passing mark the duration of this project, as if one set the course and the other was there to oversee it until the end. I miss them both immensely.

I also dedicate this book to all the Ukrainian women, children, and men who have lost their lives in this treacherous war and to those brave souls who have shown such tremendous resilience and unimaginable strength to fight for their freedom and to find meaning and joy in life.

CONTENTS

PREFACE

In the opening of *Unorthodox Kin: Portuguese Marranos and the Global Search for Belonging*, author Naomi Leite reminds us that anthropologists, like everyone else, live in a temporal flow: our findings from the field reflect what has already passed and is becoming history.[1] And so it is, if not more so, with this ethnography. It covers the two decades after Ukraine's independence, a crucial period of the longer and ever-evolving trajectory of post-Soviet Jewish life and Ukrainian Jewish history.

Many of the events collected here reflect the fieldwork I did in Odesa between 2005 and 2007. These events should be read as helping us better understand the dramatic changes that followed the 2013–14 Maidan protests (including the deadly fire in Odesa), the ongoing war between Russia and Ukraine in the Donbas region since 2014, and the full-fledged invasion of Ukraine by Russian forces in February 2022, a tragedy that is ongoing as I complete this book. No one knows how or when the war will end—or what the outcome will be for the country's Jewish population—but the ways they experience the war and understand themselves might be anticipated in the pages here.

As a result of Russia's unprovoked attack on Ukraine, more than half of Odesa's Jewish population has fled to become refugees in neighboring countries. Although some Jewish Odesans have returned, others remain on the move, and the city's Jewish communities have been greatly reduced, with some ceasing to exist all together. Rabbi Shlomo Baksht of the Litvak congregation closed the doors of his synagogue and evacuated most of his congregants to Romania. Yulia Gris of the Progressive Jewish congregation facilitated the move of her community to Poland and Germany, where she resides to this day. In the first weeks of the war, Rabbi Avraham Wolf of the Chabad congregation evacuated part of his congregants to Germany, including most students and children from the orphanage, while he himself remained in Odesa to serve those who could not or would not leave. He and his wife continued to travel back and forth between their various groups of congregants for the duration of a year, until the majority of the group returned to Odesa. Some Jews chose destinations with the help of their religious leaders, others followed family and friends, and many went where they could find any support or assistance. To this day, Odesa's Jewry is spread among Ukraine, the neighboring European states, the United Kingdom, Canada, the United States, and Israel. Again, as in Soviet times, Odesa has only one synagogue in operation, and it provides a home to all remaining Jews in the city.

The Israeli Cultural Centre and the Jewish Agency have closed their facilities. The Jewish Distribution Committee (JDC or the Joint, as it is known in Ukraine and the Former Soviet Union [FSU]), which operated remotely for the first six months of the war, reopened in September 2022. Three of the women leading Migdal, a Jewish community center, and the head of Mazl Tov, the Jewish early development center, stayed in Odesa. Along with staff who remained, they aided many in evacuation and also assisted the families with children who have not left as well as the refugees flooding into the city from affected areas nearby. Together, these women organized weekly lunches at the city's sole remaining kosher restaurant—both to help the business and to support the remaining Jews by connecting them with a community.

Many young Jewish men volunteered to serve in the Ukrainian forces and the territorial defense of their city, while others launched volunteer initiatives to deliver meals, groceries, medicine, and other essential goods to residents, soldiers, and the increasing number of refugees. The war has fractured the previous forms of Jewish life in the city, but it has not eliminated the sense of community for those who remain there. Jews, like others, are learning to live in their "new normal," with daily sirens and the very real fear of invasion. Jewish holidays have been celebrated throughout the war to mark the Jewish calendar, and Purim, Passover, and Rosh Hashanah services organized by the Chabad congregation have brought Jews of all walks of life together in great numbers. Many of the city schools reopened in September 2022, including the Chabad Jewish schools, with approximately one-fifth of the prewar student body currently enrolled. With the help of electric generators and bomb shelters, where many lessons take place during air raids, many schools in Odesa have managed to stay open. Day by day, Odesa, now painted in blue and yellow throughout, feels more alive than in the earlier months of the war. But, although the cafés, restaurants, beauty salons, and some shops have reopened, there are constant reminders that war is here: the absence of many familiar faces, the influx of refugees, the presence of the military on half-empty, curfew-regulated streets, the sandbags and antitank equipment on those same streets, the roaring sirens throughout the day, destroyed buildings, and the loss of life.

In the first month of the war, I spoke with one elderly Ukrainian Jewish refugee in Berlin who, seeing great irony that he was taking refuge from Russian soldiers in Germany, told me he feared that Jewish life in Odesa and the rest of the country would never be the same. Everything that had been painstakingly built in the thirty years of post-Soviet life would either be physically destroyed in areas directly hit in the war or would vanish as so many Jews fled the country. Some members of the younger generation seemed to nurture the hope of an eventual return to their communities, but almost all had no clear sense of their future.[2] The Jews who remained in Odesa were more optimistic about the resilience of the Jewish people, often citing biblical and historical stories of Jewish survival and triumph. Rabbis also noted that the internal displacement of Jews meant new communities were being formed in places that previously did not have Jewish life. Families and lives have been fragmented on physical, social, economic, mental, and psychological levels as people face the loss of any form of life as they had come to know it.[3] But Jews in Odesa and those across modern borders have also become united in their support for Ukraine and vocal about their solidarity with the larger Ukrainian society. Ukrainian Jewry indeed stands a real chance of becoming an important part of Ukraine's civil society in a way that was not certain prior to the war. Putin has done more to unite Ukrainians of all backgrounds, Jews included, than any Ukrainian leader.

This book comes to life at a time when the topics of Jewish-Ukrainian relations, Ukrainians' connection to the Russian world, and the role and dynamics of Ukrainian nationalism are all highly politicized. Publishing an ethnography of a place that has since become defined by the starkly different reality of war brings the risk that my words might be used for different ends from those I intended. The book presents a cultural moment two decades after the dissolution of the Soviet Union, before Ukrainian relations with Russia deteriorated, and before Russia launched a war in Ukraine to pull it into a greater Russia under the pretext of "liberating," "disarming," and "denazifying" its neighboring state. I want to be, and must be, true to the stories entrusted to me by my interlocutors and friends during *that particular time*. It was, again, a period embedded in the longer trajectory of post-Soviet reforms and developments in Ukraine, and the events of that time are important and relevant for understanding this complex present.

Like other researchers who write about dramatically changed environments, such as anthropologist Tone Bringa, who described a mixed Muslim/Catholic village in central Bosnia before and after the 1990s Balkan War, I have had to deploy both present and past tense as I work to capture the processes of conti-nuity and change.[4] As we know, identities are never stable, static, or bounded; they are always evolving, adapting, and transforming in the midst of daily life. In the early years of my fieldwork, I looked to Odesa as a case study of Russian-speaking Jewry in a post-Soviet urban city that was historically famed for being Jewish. Although I was carrying out research in modern-day Ukraine due to Odesa's specificity as a city, I hadn't considered myself a scholar of Ukraine. I myself had left the Soviet Union as a child of nine and was raised in a secular Jewish environment, but I often wondered what remained of the world we left behind when my family moved to the United States. This book grew out of my desire to understand Soviet Jewish history more deeply and to learn about developments that followed the dissolution of the USSR. I chose Odesa as my field site because I was interested in the process of religious, specifically Jewish, revival that took place after the end of the Soviet regime, generated largely by international organizations in a place that had a long history of evolving Jewish identities and traditions. I wanted to comprehend the variety of views, compet-ing ideas, and practices of Judaism and Jewishness that evolved and to explore how Jews were reacting to the new models of Jewish life and expression as well as how the city's character was being transformed as a result of those reactions.

At that time, most of my interlocutors did not identify themselves as Ukrai-nian Jews. If anything, they saw themselves as Jews living in Ukraine and as part of the larger ex-Soviet Jewish population connected by the Russian lan-guage and by Russian-speaking Jewish initiatives across the globe. This was the case for many ex-Soviet Jews who grew up in the Soviet Union, especially those who had emigrated before the collapse of the USSR or shortly after: they regarded themselves as "Soviet" or "Russian" based on the fact that they grew up in the Soviet Union or with Soviet values, primarily spoke Russian, and identified with Russian culture.

More recently, both Ukrainians and Jews have been described as marginal-ized subjects whose cultures were repressed in certain periods of the Soviet regime. Odesa, however, is a Russian-speaking city in Ukraine with historical links to the Russian Empire. And it is also a place where Ukrainian identi-fication is undoubtedly ascendant. Everyone I know in Odesa is supporting Ukraine in the war, even if they are divided on how to express their loyalty. Most disapproved of gestures like trying to erase Pushkin from Odesa's history because he was a Russian writer, but others understood and even supported efforts to *de-Russify* the city. The more rockets fell on the city, the more the desire to part from all things Russian grew. At the end of December 2022, the statue of Catherine II, the city's founder, was removed from its prominent place overlooking the Black Sea. One woman told me that although she was pained by these transformations, she understood others who saw these monuments as memories of a traumatic past, comparing their feelings to a rape victim who is left with physical reminders of their aggressor.

My hope is that this book can help readers understand the tension between the city's historically rooted identification with Russia and the rise of a Ukrainian identity. It is true that as I struggle to bring this work to a close, I ask myself how I can write about Odesa at a time when a devastating ongoing war threatens unforeseeable effects. Are my conclusions valid, given today's unfolding reality? How can I speak about the notions of cosmopolitanism and tolerance when we stand witness to the bombings of civilians by the country that historically birthed Odesa? I am pained by this reality, but I am also confident that a picture of Odesa captured a decade and a half before the country it is part of was invaded can reveal the stakes of identity formation for the city and its Jewish population.

A sign that hangs in my office, a gift from a dear friend as a goodbye token during my 2014 visit, reads, "It's nice here but I love Odessa." That sign stands as a reminder, not only of my own love for Odesa but also of the unconditional love held by Odesans around the world for their native city. I hope that the people whose voices are heard in the pages that follow, as they relay the stories of their own lives, families, communities, and homes (real and mythical), will feel that my description represents their reality, even if some do not agree with my interpretations and analysis.

There have been many ends of "Old Odessa," but the city and its people provide numerous historical lessons on how different people can live and thrive together. More importantly, it shows many examples of how they can heal in the aftermath of conflict.[5] My wish is that this book will provide guidance for understanding a crucial period in the city's history and offer ideas that can help bring about peace in the future.

ACKNOWLEDGMENTS

This book defines nearly half of my life. It is a great pleasure to express my deep gratitude to the many people and institutions that contributed to its making. The idea behind this project began with a desire to understand the reality of post-Soviet Jews who, given the chance to leave, remained in post-Soviet society. I wanted to know how their Jewish identity and community life were shaped by forces of migration, philanthropy, Jewish revival, and the greater sociopolitical changes that were unfolding then in an independent Ukraine. I was drawn to Odesa by its rich Jewish history, its famed cosmopolitanism, its humor, and its southern flair, all of which makes so many people fall in love with the city. Today, my deep connection to the place is defined by the Odesans I met at home and abroad. While working on this book, I have watched many of the children I knew grow into adulthood, the young adults I knew form their own families, and, sadly, the elderly I knew pass from this life.

I want to thank all the Odesans who welcomed me so warmly into their homes; shared their life stories, reflections, and memories around the kitchen table; and proudly showed me *their* Odesa—introducing me to their favorite places, streets, and buildings and bringing me into their families and circles of friends. I will always cherish your kindness and openness, and I hope my analysis and interpretations here reflect and honor your voices.

Emma Gansova, my Odesa mama, took me under her wing both as a supervisor at the Odesa National University and as a dear friend. I miss her wit and bubbly personality every day. Mila Volkova, who left this world so unexpectedly, always treated me with such love and attention and put on a feast every time I came to visit her, which was often. The remarkable women who head up Odesa's Jewish community center, Migdal—Kira Verkhovskaya, Tanya Boyko,

Polina Blinder, Ina Naydis, and Yulia Maksimuk—made me feel like a part of their Migdal family. They taught me much about Jewish life in Odesa and openly shared their personal journeys in Judaism. I grow as a person whenever I am in their company.

Anna Misiuk and Mark Naidorf welcomed me into their home and spent endless hours sharing their stories about historical and modern-day Jewish Odesa. I am profoundly grateful for their wealth of knowledge, support, and patience to tend to my many questions. Mikhail Rashkovetsky, Vladimir Chaplin, and Nusia Verkhovskaya from the Odesa Jewish Museum were instrumental in my work. I am grateful for their time, insight, and ongoing friendship. I also want to wholeheartedly thank my dearest friends, Kazatzker, Oks, Izu, Volk, Markovskaya, Moldovansky, Nos, and Zubrik, for making my days in Odesa so memorable. With them, I became an *Odesitka*.

My great appreciation goes to the many families from the Or Sameach and Chabad communities who welcomed me into their homes for Shabbat meals, as well as Rabbi and Rebbetzin Wolf, Rabbi and Rebbetzin Bacht, Rafael Kruskal, and Rabbi Yulia Gris, who opened the doors of their congregations to me and always made me feel like I belonged.

At the London School of Economics (LSE), my academic home throughout the making of this book, which emerged out of my dissertation, I am grateful to my PhD cohort of anthropologists, especially Irene Calis, Sarah Grosso, Hakem Rustom, Ankur Datta, Hans Steinmuller, Judith Bovensiepen, Katie Dow, Elizabeth Frantz, Marcello Sorrentino, Andrew Sanchez, and George St. Claire. As my PhD adviser, Stephan Feuchtwang guided me through the crucial years of coursework, research, and writing, and his mentorship was instrumental in the making of this manuscript. Indeed, his extensive knowledge, empathy, and deep concern for the world have shaped me as a scholar and an individual. Stephan's wife, Miranda, has also become a good friend; I cherish the time we spend together and our Shabbats. Our common friend Beverly Brown was incredibly helpful in the final edits of my dissertation.

As my master's supervisor and then as mentor during my postdoctoral fellowship, Matthew Engelke was immensely supportive, always expressing great interest in my work and helping me sharpen my ideas and make connections to the wider field of religious studies. In many ways, my deep interest in the anthropology of religion comes from being his student. Rita Astuti has been a supportive friend and colleague throughout my years at the LSE. I started my teaching career as Rita's teaching assistant, learning from her what it means to teach with your heart. Mathijs Pelkmans has been my mentor in the Anthropology Department for many years, and I am extremely grateful for his steady encouragement, sound advice, and guidance. At University College London (UCL), Ruth Mandel has been a wonderful adviser and a supportive friend. I am also grateful to my dear friend Nicholas Lackenby for always finding time to read my work.

Many colleagues and friends around the world gave me strength when I needed it most and helped me structure my ideas more clearly. Tanya Richardson assisted me in making my first contacts in Odesa and has been a dear friend ever since. My copy of her book *Kaleidoscopic Odessa*, much scribbled in and marked up, was a key text in my understanding of the city. I had great pleasure sharing my Odesa days with Abel Polese. Life is never dull with Abel, and I am always impressed by his lightness, infectious curiosity, and desire to teach all he knows to others. I also enjoyed meeting the late Patricia Herlihy and John Doyle Klier, whose earlier works on Odesa and our conversations together shaped my knowledge of the city's past.

Steven Zipperstein kindly read numerous drafts of my history chapter, highlighting necessary amendments and calming my fear of being an anthropologist writing history. I am grateful for his ongoing support and interest in my work. Larissa Remennick provided valuable commentary on the parts of this book that I presented to the public and always encouraged me to write more. The late David Shneer read early drafts of my chapter on migration, and our correspondence remains extremely meaningful to me.

I also want to acknowledge Zvi Gitelman, who has dedicated his career to understanding the different tenets of Soviet and post-Soviet Jewish identity. Zvi was always there to answer my questions. Throughout the years, I have learned a great deal from our interactions, collaborations, and personal correspondence. I particularly enjoyed our walks together in the streets of old Jewish Odesa during his visit to the city. Fran Markowitz's first manuscript, *A Community in Spite of Itself*, was an inspiring text, and Fran herself became an inspiring mentor. Always supportive, always encouraging, she pushed me to add that extra oomph to my writing and to believe in myself. I am deeply grateful for her guidance and friendship.

I have had the pleasure of developing parts of this book in various collaborations with Efraim Sicher, Mirja Lecke, Vera Skvirskaya, Caroline Humphrey, and Tom Selwyn. Efraim's read of my last draft was extremely valuable, and I am deeply grateful for his input and corrections. Throughout the years, I have benefited from rich discussions about Jewish studies and anthropology with Dani Kranz, who has a sharp eye for connecting ideas to a world outside of academia. I thank Jessica Roda for suggesting the bold title of this book. Vladislav Davidzon persuaded me to write for the wider public and I thoroughly enjoyed all our collaborations dedicated to Ukraine. Catherine Wanner, who read parts of this book in the making and always expressed a deep interest in my research, offered many words of encouragement, and her constructive feedback has made its mark throughout these pages. Sarah Zukerman Daly helped me organize my last edits and reach the finish line by caring for our combined eight children and taking me on walks.

I am grateful to the acquisition editors of Indiana University Press, Anna C. Francis and Gary Dunham, and the editors of the Modern Jewish Experience series, Deborah Dash Moore and Marsha Rozenblit, for believing in this work. I am equally grateful to those anonymous readers whose thorough and careful readings and constructive feedback strengthened its quality. Eliza Frenkel helped me with transliteration, and Barbara Peck and Daniel Listoe provided crucial copyediting support, often going beyond the call of duty to see this project through.

This book would not have been possible without various institutions and fellowships I received along the way. The initial fieldwork was made possible by an American Councils for International Education's Title VIII Research Scholar Fellowship. At the LSE, I received the Alfred Gell Memorial Studentship of the Department of Anthropology. I was fortunate to receive a doctoral scholarship and a fellowship grant from the Memorial Foundation for Jewish Culture and a junior faculty grant from the Brandeis-Genesis Institute for Russian Jewry.

Above all, I am most fortunate to have the support of my entire family. You are my village and pillar of strength. I thank my sister, Anya El Wattar, and brother, Ilya Sapritsky, and their beautiful families for their unwavering presence. My in-laws, Nicole Nahum, Isabelle Saltiel-Nahum, Candice Nahum-Enrici, and their families were there to take care of my boys when I needed it most. My parents, Valentina and Victor Sapritsky, have always nurtured my quest for knowledge and my passion for adventure. My husband, Stephane Abraham Joseph Nahum, has been my everything: enduring my absences for research and writing, welcoming a constant flow of Odesans into our home, reading multiple drafts of my chapters at all hours of the night, and most importantly believing in me. His love has made this project a reality.

Our four beautiful sons are my proudest achievement and source of boundless joy; their hugs and inspirational talks got me through some of my hardest days. Elaijah was born just after I finished the first draft of my dissertation, and I edited it with him in my arms. Isaac and Jeremiah, twins who arrived a year later, were a blessed gift. Needless to say, this book and, indeed, my career as a whole took on a different pace with three babies and only two hands. Our youngest son, David, who is defined strongly by his name, arrived to rule our kingdom four years later. By the time this book comes to life, my four boys will be joined by a long-awaited baby sister. Many scholars struggle to negotiate the demands of academia, family life, and other commitments, and I am no exception. But I wouldn't change a thing in the long, winding, and messy path to this book's completion.

A NOTE ON TRANSLITERATION AND TRANSLATION

It is always difficult to make choices about place-names in countries with shifting borders and complex language politics. In Ukraine, city names have changed often, depending on administrations, and spellings have shifted between Russian and Ukrainian, as well as Polish, German, and other languages. Beyond the most recognized spellings of Odesa (Ukrainian) and Odessa (Russian), in different national historiographies and academic texts, the city's name has also been referred to as Odessos (Greek), Odes (Hebrew), and Ades (Yiddish). The range of names speaks to Odesa's multicultural and multilinguistic cosmopolitanism.

Language choice and place-name spellings have become a very sensitive topic in the current political climate of the Russian-Ukrainian war, and attitudes vary greatly. I consulted many experts and international scholars on how to spell the name of the city in this book when I am referring to different historical periods, and I was offered many different approaches. There is no clear answer in this ever-evolving present. The traces that we leave on paper (creating a permanent mark for future readers) are often surrounded by complex tensions and competing perspectives.

In February 2024, I discussed the matter with one of the colleagues at the Museum of the History of Odesa Jews, where she was in the process of changing the display signs from Russian to Ukrainian and English. She admitted that removing Russian, her native language, from the signs had been "a very hard decision done with a heavy heart," but she thought the new signs better reflected the current reality. While continuing to conduct her museum tours in Russian, she recognized that the official labels had to be in the official language of the state. I decided then to follow the museum's approach. For the sake of

Figure Note.1. "Odessa, Ukraine!!!" on a banner written in Russian, spring 2022. Photo by and courtesy of Boris Bukman.

consistency, I refer to the city as Odesa throughout the text, except when quoting passages where it appeared in the original text as Odessa or when citing Russian speakers.

But it is important to note that the Ukrainian spelling Odesa does not mean that the Russian spelling Odessa has disappeared altogether from the urban landscape, even in this time of war. During my initial research, many of my interlocutors told me they did not wholeheartedly adopt the legal change of place-names. Although the Ukrainian spelling Odesa was used in most public spaces, thereby linking the city to the Ukrainian nation-state, I often heard people say, "I can't get used to seeing it spelled with one *s*. It just doesn't look right," or "I can't switch to Odesa with one *s*; it changes the pronunciation and meaning completely."

The linguistic entanglements of Ukrainian, Russian, and other languages that have always defined Odesa continue to define it today.

For Ukrainian, Russian, and Hebrew (modern Israeli spellings) transliteration, I mostly follow the simplified recommendations of the Library of Congress (omitting diacritical marks). For Yiddish, I have used the YIVO Institute for Jewish Research system. However, I deviate from those guidelines for words that are widely recognized in the English language: for example, I use Chanukah instead of Hanukah, Pesach instead of Pesah, and the *z* instead of the *s* for spelling words like *hametz, tzedakah,* and *tzitzit.* Otherwise, I follow the *Merriam-Webster* dictionary.

Except for public figures and persons who specifically asked to be identified by name, I have employed pseudonyms, using the most widely known English spellings, to protect the privacy of those who so graciously entrusted me with their stories. Unless otherwise indicated, translations are my own.

JEWISH ODESA

Introduction

A Jew in a Kippah

As my father and I walked in Odesa's Shevchenko Park one afternoon in 2006, we came across a group of children from a nearby Jewish kindergarten.[1] We sat down to rest and watch them play. "I know we're in Odesa," my father said, "but I can't believe these Jewish children are openly walking around the park in kippahs."[2] He knew what Odesa represented, but he had grown up in the Soviet Union, where public displays of religion were banned. As we sat talking, a little boy came up, having recognized me from previous visits. He said hello, asked how we were, and chattered on. At one point, he asked if my father was Jewish. We told him he was. He then pointed to my father's head and asked, "Well, why isn't he wearing a kippah?"

Taken together, my father's surprise and the boy's response reflect the profound changes Odesa has undergone since the fall of the Soviet Union. Contemporary Odesa—for locals as much as visitors, the young as well as the old—is a place where multiple orientations of Jewishness converge. Since the late 1970s and '80s, when Soviet migration policies began to loosen, more than seventy thousand Jews have emigrated from the city—an exodus that especially picked up after the eventual collapse of the Soviet Union, which opened up emigration to Israel, the United States, Germany, and elsewhere. For the approximately thirty thousand Jews who resided in the city at the time of my research, new opportunities for Jewish expression had emerged from multiple sources: a complex of migration patterns that interconnected Odesa to many points in the world; the widespread post-Soviet religious resurgence; and the social, cultural, and political transformations that characterized the Ukrainian state at the time.

This book is based on fieldwork I carried out between September 2005 and February 2007 and during follow-up visits in May 2014 and May 2019, as well

1

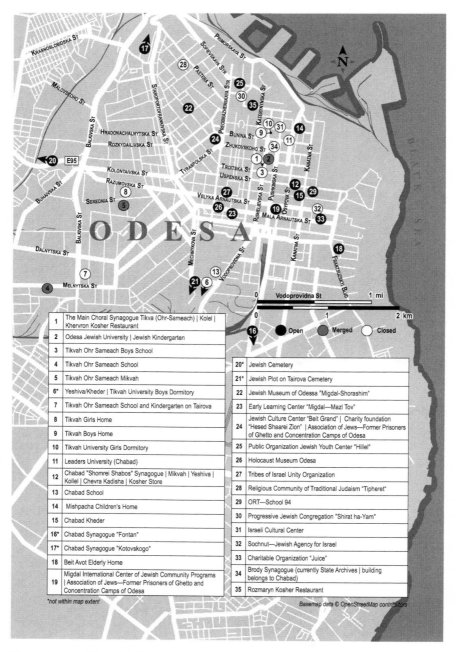

#	
1	The Main Choral Synagogue Tikva (Ohr-Sameach) | Kolel | Khervron Kosher Restaurant
2	Odesa Jewish University | Jewish Kindergarten
3	Tikvah Ohr Sameach Boys School
4	Tikvah Ohr Sameach School
5	Tikvah Ohr Sameach Mikvah
6*	Yeshiva/Kheder | Tikvah University Boys Dormitory
7	Tikvah Ohr Sameach School and Kindergarten on Tairova
8	Tikvah Girls Home
9	Tikvah Boys Home
10	Tikvah University Girls Dormitory
11	Leaders University (Chabad)
12	Chabad "Shomrei Shabos" Synagogue | Mikvah | Yeshiva | Kollel | Chevra Kadisha | Kosher Store
13	Chabad School
14	Mishpacha Children's Home
15	Chabad Kheder
16*	Chabad Synagogue "Fontan"
17*	Chabad Synagogue "Kotovskogo"
18	Beit Avot Elderly Home
19	Migdal International Center of Jewish Community Programs | Association of Jews—Former Prisoners of Ghetto and Concentration Camps of Odesa

#	
20*	Jewish Cemetery
21*	Jewish Plot on Tairova Cemetery
22	Jewish Museum of Odessa "Migdal-Shorashim"
23	Early Learning Center "Migdal—Mazl Tov"
24	Jewish Culture Center "Beit Grand" | Charity foundation "Hesed Shaarei Zion" | Association of Jews—Former Prisoners of Ghetto and Concentration Camps of Odesa
25	Public Organization Jewish Youth Center "Hillel"
26	Holocaust Museum Odesa
27	Tribes of Israel Unity Organization
28	Religious Community of Traditional Judaism "Tipheret"
29	ORT—School 94
30	Progressive Jewish Congregation "Shirat ha-Yam"
31	Israeli Cultural Center
32	Sochnut—Jewish Agency for Israel
33	Charitable Organization "Juice"
34	Brody Synagogue (currently State Archives | building belongs to Chabad)
35	Rozmaryn Kosher Restaurant

*not within map extent

Open   Merged   Closed

Basemap data © OpenStreetMap contributors

Figure Intro.1. Map of Odesa. (Locations marked "Closed" were closed after the 2022 Russian invasion.) Map by Johnson Cartographic LLC.

Figure Intro.2. Three students from the Jewish kindergarten sitting on the stairs of the Chabad Jewish school. Photo by author.

as my ongoing engagement with Odesans. In these pages, I explore the lived experiences and orientations of Odesa's Jewish residents in the decades after the dissolution of the Soviet Union: their shared and conflicting efforts to construct forms of Jewish belonging, to rediscover and negotiate historical and traditional expectations of Jewish life in the twenty-first century, and to cultivate and question the institutional forms of togetherness and community. To this end, the book follows the trajectories of particular Jewish Odesans of different backgrounds and generations as they discover, develop, and then redefine their sense of being Jewish in independent Ukraine. It illustrates how the discourse of Odesa as a cosmopolitan and Jewish city shapes their identity formation, their sense of the city as home, their interpretation of change, and their vision of the future.

The ethnographic picture I present reveals the complexity and diversity of engagement with this discourse among Jewish Odesans who understood that the city's unique historical and mythical narrative was both supported and disrupted by international efforts of Jewish revival, the larger processes of nationalism, and the unfolding of regional politics surrounding Ukraine and

Russia. These conditions contributed to an ambivalent and contested notion that Odesa represented what it meant to be a tolerant, open, effectively cosmopolitan city. And yet this city—both as a reality and an idea—does indeed operate as a source of meaningful identity, livelihood, and social relations. The ambiguous, contradictory, and challenging process of identity formation experienced by the Jewish Odesans I've interviewed and studied stands, I argue, as part of the desecularization experienced throughout the ex-Soviet Jewish world and beyond at that time.

While Odesa has been defined as "Jewish," cosmopolitan, and tolerant throughout its history; these features have also been questioned and debated by scholars from different disciplines writing about the city. Built as a key international port of the Russian Empire, it was shaped by a multiethnic and multireligious population from its earliest days. In the 1890s, it was home to a population that came from more than thirty countries, spoke around fifty-five languages, and adhered to a wide variety of religious beliefs.[3] Two related themes that run throughout this book are how the multiethnic and multireligious makeup of Odesa's population has fed into the idea of the city being "Jewish" and, as a result, how its Jewishness metonymically defines Odesa as a whole. This argument dovetails with the book's central focus on how Odesan Jews have oriented themselves to the new forms of Jewishness that have appeared in the city from the early 1990s, in a process broadly described as a "Jewish revival."

For the young generation of local Jewry involved in Jewish religious organizations, the orientation to Judaism has been not handed down but adopted. Only then is it brought into the family—a reversal of the traditional knowledge transmission seen in other parts of the ex-Soviet bloc two decades after the dissolution of state secularism.[4] Indeed, in some of the families I met in 2005, children enrolled in Jewish schools were the ones teaching their parents and grandparents about the "proper" ways to be Jewish. For some of those, like the boy who questioned my father's Jewishness because he wasn't wearing a kippah, religious observance has become a natural way of identifying oneself and others as Jews. This is not at all the case for older generations. Indeed, in the encounter between the boy of contemporary Odesa and my father, born in 1947 and raised in the Soviet Union, their mutual bewilderment at meeting as Jews is characteristic of Odesa today—multiple systems of meaning of Jewishness sharing a common designation.

Currently, more Jews born in Odesa are residing abroad than in Odesa itself, meaning that the idea of Odesa as a home for Jews is threaded through with movement and migration and with associated networks of relationships, attachments, information, people, and goods. In the context of Zionist or classical models of diaspora centered on a Jewish homeland, Odesa is part of the diaspora, and yet it is also the central point for a diaspora of its own. My study helps us understand how the Jewish population doesn't always orient itself toward a Jewish center as laid out in classical analysis of diasporic groups and how, in some cases, the center is defined within the so-called Jewish diaspora.

Jewish Odesans of different generations—residents, former residents, Jewish activists, those who returned after emigrating to Israel, and those who assumed a transnational way of life—described *home* and *belonging* using many references to places other than Israel. Instead, they were oriented by a constellation of destinations and communities. Stories of those who emigrated only to return show clearly that while many Jews found themselves maintaining their connection to Israel, they did not necessarily feel it was a home they could live in—or even, for some, an option for the future. Many returnees regarded Odesa as a home, some lovingly calling it "Odesa Mama," even as they understood it was undergoing change. Some experienced their return as a homecoming; for others, it was an encounter with something almost foreign.

The Jews in Odesa became increasingly connected to global Judaism through interactions with international Jewish organizations, philanthropy outreach, transnational media, migration and travel. But a significant transformation also took place at the urban level, as they built their own traditions in response to Ukraine's processes of nationalism and globalization. Similar to the historical representations of the Soviet past, which were negotiated among competing groups and emerged as "sites of cultural contestations" following Ukrainian independence—as described by the anthropologist and scholar of religion Catherine Wanner—Jewish Odesa became an arena of many new orientations.[5] In the nearly fifteen years since Ukraine's independence, there have been multiple efforts, initiated both locally and from abroad, to restore, shape, and stimulate forms of Jewish life via the formation of Jewish cultural and religious organizations. Each institutional form has competed for recognition, legitimacy, authority, and authenticity, and each has, in turn, shaped Odesa's Jewish spaces.[6]

Odesa: A Jewish City?

Located in the southern part of Ukraine, on the coast of the Black Sea, Odesa is the fourth-largest city in the country, with a population of just over 1 million and with 2.5 million people in the greater Odesa area. It is a major seaport and transportation hub for Ukraine and neighboring states and has commonly been recognized, by locals and others alike, as unique, special, and different as compared to other Soviet, Russian, or Ukrainian cities. Odesa has been called a "state within a state."[7] Historically, it maintained strong links to Russian-speaking culture and the ethnoreligious heterogeneity typical of borderlands and other port cities.[8]

Figure Intro.3. The Odesa port. Photo by author.

As an "imagined community," to use the famous term of the historian and political scientist Benedict Anderson, Odesans imagine themselves and are seen by others as a distinct *narod* (people).[9] They have been described as "a breed apart," known for their *joie de vivre*, sense of humor, southern temperament, resourcefulness, and entrepreneurial spirit; for their specific dialect of Russian (mixed with Yiddish and Ukrainian); and for being apolitical.[10] These qualities are attributed to growing up in a "cosmopolitan," "tolerant," and "ethnically mixed" city and also to the region's warm climate and the influence of its port-related commercial activity.[11]

A number of locals at the time of my fieldwork regarded their city as simultaneously European, due to the influence of its foreign rulers and architecture; Russian, due to its founding by Catherine the Great and therefore having been historically part of the Russian Empire; Jewish, due to the long presence of Jewish culture in the city; and Ukrainian, due to its being part of independent Ukraine. Odesa's historically multiethnic character is reflected in its street names: French Boulevard, Italian Street, Jewish Street, and Greek Square. Most of the streets were returned to their prerevolutionary names after 1991, as part of the city's initiative to "remove the imprint of the Soviet past from the cityscape and to inscribe a new understanding of history" and to "evoke Odessa's traditional plurality."[12] Others were renamed after prominent Ukrainian figures. Even so, most residents continued to use the Soviet, prerevolutionary, and new names

Figure Intro.4. Statue of Duc de Richelieu above the Potemkin Stairs. Photo by author.

interchangeably.[13] Street signs and most of the official inscriptions on the streets appeared in both Russian and Ukrainian at the time of my initial fieldwork.

Anthropologist Tanya Richardson notes regarding Odesans that "while on the one hand mixing [of cultures] is stressed, on the other, the important role Jews played in the city and the strong influence of Yiddish culture on the development of what is felt to be distinctively Odessan is virtually always cited."[14] Local scholars and guides of Jewish Odesa proudly describe the imprint of Odesa's Jews on the city and the impact that Odesa's Jews have made on the world. Odesa is often recognized as one of the important centers of the Zionist movement and home to many Zionist activists. Literary scholars cite Odesa as a "cradle of modern Hebrew literature" where Jewish intellectuals known as the "The Wise Men of Odesa" or "Sages of Odesa" (Leon Pinsker, Moses Leib Lilienblum, Ahad-Ha'am, Mendele Mocher Sforim, Semyon Dubnov, Joseph Klausner, and Haim Nachman Bialik) contributed to the intellectual debates about the future of the Jewish national culture.[15] Odesa is the birthplace of many prominent Jewish families like the Ephrussis, whom Edmund de Waal

Figure Intro.5. A sign, "Jewish Street," written in Ukrainian and Russian. Photo by and courtesy of Igor Oks.

describes in his memoir, *The Hare with Amber Eyes*. It was also the birthplace of Jewish gangsters like Benya Krik, the fictional hero of Isaac Babel's book of Moldovanka stories, *How It Was Done in Odessa*.

Jewish residents and others who admired the city's history joked about its "Russo-Yiddish-Ukrainian" tongue and praised the delicious Jewish Odesan cuisine. "In Odesa, everyone is a little Jewish and a little of everything else," said one of my friends. Many non-Jewish Odesans considered the city's uniqueness to be linked to the Jews. *"Evrei eto iziuminka goroda"* (Jews are the special character of Odesa), insisted a Ukrainian woman in her twenties when we discussed the character of her hometown in the summer of 2022. We see that when Odesans used the term *Jewish* to describe their city, they didn't literally mean that only Jews lived there or that they dominated the place in any significant shape or form (especially given their low numbers in the contemporary Ukraine).[16] Rather, this stereotype served as a metonym for the city's cosmopolitanism and tolerance, without cloaking its other characteristics (or inhabitants). Indeed, claims of Odesa as an international city, a multiethnic and multireligious city, a Russian city, a Ukrainian city, a Greek city, and a relic of the Ottoman Empire live alongside the idea of "Jewish" Odesa.

Figure Intro.6. Deribasovskaya Street in Odesa, 2007. Photo by author.

Odesa presents a unique urban context for studying cultural, ethnic, and religious orientations in the present-day Ukraine. The history and present-day images and realities of Jewishness have been built and rebuilt, and sometimes torn down, in Odesa. The city is an arena for the negotiation, representation, and reproduction of what it means to be Jewish. The sense of attachment that many Odesans feel toward their place of residence includes the physical qualities of "their" parts of the city as well as their own personal views of its history.

The recent shifts in its demographic makeup raise the question of whether Odesa can still be regarded as a "Jewish" city. And if so, what makes it Jewish today? Some scholars have declared that in the USSR and its successor states, Jews and other nationalities like Russians or Ukrainians were mutually exclusive categories.[17] The Soviet government classified Jews as one of more than one hundred *natsional'nosti* (nationalities or ethnic groups) within the Soviet Union. The separation of nationality from religion in the Soviet definition of a Jewish nationality suggests that the closest translation of the Russian term *evrei* is actually "Hebrew," not "Jew."[18] After 1932, all urban residents had to carry internal passports that specified, on the fifth line, their official *natsional'nost'*. Anyone with two Jewish parents was classified as a Jew, whatever his or her choices, feelings of belonging, language, residence, or religion. Members of mixed families could choose which *natsional'nost'* would be inscribed in their official documents. Since 1991, however, Jews are no longer bound by these

Soviet markers. Exposed to new components of Jewish identification, they face pressure from many sides on how, where, and whether to be Jewish.

My work details how ethnic categories or nationalities in Odesa were historically more fluid than elsewhere, more porous and intermixed, and more strongly influenced by the local city culture. On some levels, the same can be said about contemporary Odesa. But on another level, its ethnic and cultural categories—Russian, Ukrainian, Jewish—have become more definitive and more mutually exclusive, a point on which I elaborate later in this book.

According to the census conducted in 2001, approximately 62 percent of Odesa's total population identified themselves as Ukrainian, 29 percent as Russian, and only 1 percent as Jewish. All of the city's non-Russian minorities grouped together—Bulgarians, Moldovans, Belarusians, Armenians, Poles, and Jews—made up just over 4 percent of the population. Despite the abolition of internal passports labeling Ukrainian citizens by their ethnicities, the census categories at that time still categorized Jews as a separate "nationality" (ethnicity) in population surveys throughout the country. Many of the Jews I met spoke of being Jewish as their nationality. Statistics on the number of Jews in the region vary greatly, from the estimate of 12,500 declared in the 2001 city census to numbers as high as 45,000 concurrently provided by some community leaders.[19]

It's important to remember that many Jews choose not to be officially registered as such. Though they regard Jewishness as one of their identifications, they register as Ukrainian or Russian in a mark of allegiance to their nation-state or their language. I met several Jews who, despite their self-identification as Jewish, felt it more appropriate to label themselves as Ukrainian or Russian in official documents. The number of those receiving Jewish aid from various Jewish centers was higher than the official census data, indicating that the number of Jews in Odesa was closer to thirty thousand. This figure was most often recognized as correct by local scholars of Jewish history and by the Museum of the History of Odesa Jews. Official statistics for all of Ukraine are equally debated: based on the 2001 census, estimates of Ukraine's Jews range from 71,500, identified as the "core" Jewish population, to 200,000, in a total population of 43 million.[20] But these figures overlook the smaller communities of Israeli Jews, returnees, and transmigrants who travel back and forth. Furthermore, no recent census has been carried out in the country that reflects the annexation of Crimea, the war in the Donetsk region, and the most recent outflow of Ukraine's Jewish population as a result of the Russian invasion.

Ukrainian is the official language of the country, but during my initial research, and even on later visits, I rarely heard it spoken on the streets of Odesa. The Jewish families I visited all spoke Russian at home and with each other, although many increasingly used Ukrainian at work and in public spaces.[21] Government legislation passed in 1992 "stipulated that in all schools the history of Ukraine be taught in Ukrainian," but "there was some variation in how this was actually practiced."[22] It wasn't unusual to hear conversations in both languages, with questions posed in Ukrainian and answered in Russian, or for conversations to switch from speaking in Ukrainian in public to speaking Russian in private. This was often the case in the university seminars I attended with some of my interlocutors. Although Ukrainian was officially the dominant language in the media, especially after 2006, when President Viktor Yushenko signed a law stipulating that 75 percent of the content on radio and television had to be in Ukrainian, many Odesans continued to use Russian in social media and less-regulated public platforms.[23]

At the time of my fieldwork in the mid-2000s, most Odesan Jews I met identified with Russian-speaking culture, even if they also knew Ukrainian, held Ukrainian citizenship, and considered themselves civilly Ukrainian.[24] Many of the same individuals expressed a connection with Ukraine through family history or the fact that their city lies within Ukraine's state borders and that they are, as a practical matter, subject to Ukrainian laws and regulations. Their attachment to Russian culture did not mean that these Odesans considered themselves "Russian Jews" rather than "Ukrainian Jews." In different contexts, my interlocutors expressed a connection with both groups or with neither. They saw the Jewish history of the city as linked to the Russian Empire and later the Soviet Union. As anthropologists Abel Polese and Anna Wylegala note, in the case of Odesa, a "Russian speaker might not be Russian, might not identify at all with Russia and [yet] still be accepted as Ukrainian."[25] Depending on the circumstances, the terms *Ukrainian* and *Russian* were sometimes used interchangeably or replaced with *Odesan*. Odesa's mayor at the time of my fieldwork, Eduard Gurvitz, even supported "the idea of 'Odessan nationality' (*Odesskaia natsional'nost'*) as a kind of supra-ethnic identity."[26] It was not uncommon for my interlocutors to elevate their affinity with the city above their connection to the state.[27] Historian Roshanna Sylvester notes that "despite the fact that Odessa served as an incubator for both virulent Russian nationalism and Zionist activism, and that a series of pogroms marred the city's history, most Odessans took pride in their cosmopolitanism, asserting the primacy of local (and international) over national identity."[28]

Events from 2013 until today have made such relations even more complicated. Russia's annexation of Crimea, the simmering battle with Russia in the Donbas region, internal divisions within Ukraine—if to a lesser degree in Odesa—and then the 2022 Russian invasion of Ukraine have created new stakes for the ways Jews in Odesa identify themselves. The 2013–14 Euromaidan protests and counterprotests were violent and deadly—forty-eight anti-Maidan activists were killed in Odesa in May 2014. Moreover, those protests created a context in which even cultural orientations toward Russia could be politicized and disputed, as was the case with Ukrainian-Jewish relations as a whole, where the past (specifically World War II and the Holocaust) has been kept alive and enhanced—historian Paul Robert Magocsi and Jewish studies scholar Yohanan Petrovsky-Shtern refer to this process as "the politicization of the past."[29] Although I discuss Maidan and its aftermath in the epilogue, in the book I focus more on the formation of Jewish life in a post-Soviet pre-Maidan environment that wasn't so politically restrictive and that couldn't have foreseen the attack on Ukrainian sovereignty and the threats to its national viability that came with war.

At the time of my study, Jewish leadership in Odesa involved both local activists and multiple international Jewish organizations. The city had three active Jewish religious congregations, with several affiliated educational facilities. Two of the synagogues—sponsored by Orthodox congregations, Chabad Shomrei Shabbos and Tikva Or Sameach—have since the 1990s occupied structures originally built as religious institutions and used for other purposes during the Soviet era. They have the largest number of congregants, nearly 3,000 each.[30] The third, Emanu-El (renamed Shirat Ha Yam in 2016), sponsored by the Reform Jewish movement, was a community of some 120 congregants that functioned in a rented space during my study. Despite many years of authorities trying to return the famous Brody Synagogue building—once home to a thriving modern Jewish congregation and later turned city archives—the Reform congregation could not gain city approval or find necessary funding to take on restorations. In 2016, the building was officially granted by the city council to the Chabad congregation, who took responsibility for its future repairs. In 2012, the World Council for Conservative/Masorti Synagogues started operating its programs in Odesa. The affiliated Kehillat Tiferet congregation had about sixty congregants in its opening year; it organized educational programs and Jewish holiday celebrations for its community.

Odesa has two ritual baths (*mikvaot*), run separately by the two Orthodox congregations, as well as four kosher stores (two that are online) and four kosher restaurants. Strolling through the city center, you could find nonkosher restaurants that were named after famous streets in Tel Aviv, such as Dizengoff and Allenby.[31] Six hotels advertised their "Jewish Observant Friendly" (JOFY) services on the web.[32] There is a salon on Jewish Street where observant women go to style the wigs they bought at the huge Seventh Kilometer Market or ordered from Israel. The city has one old Jewish cemetery and two newer ones: one run by Chabad; the other, by Tikva Or Sameach.

In 2007, I visited Warsaw with a group of American Jewish families who were involved in a cemetery restoration project. I was surprised by the contrast: Odesa seemed much more Jewish than Warsaw, not only because of the sheer number of Jewish institutions but also in the vibrant zeal of the people and the visibility of public celebrations, Jewish holidays, and Jewish culture. I thought of the giant *chanukiah* (the nine-branched candelabra lit on Chanukah) displayed near the famous statue of the Duc de Richelieu (Odesa's governor in 1803) at the top of the Potemkin Stairs; the street musicians playing the popular Jewish song "Hava Nagila" beside a sign asking for spare change; the posters outside the Odesa Opera House advertising "Jewish Tours of Odessa"; the parade of men carrying beautifully decorated Torah scrolls on Odesa's Jewish Street; and Chabad congregants singing "Lekhah Dodi" at the welcoming of Shabbat with as much energy and enthusiasm as if it were their national anthem.[33]

Sporadically, episodes of anti-Jewish sentiment occurred in Odesa, sometimes involving violence and hooliganism. In 2006, during my fieldwork, stones were thrown through a window of the Chabad synagogue. The same year, one of my religiously observant friends was attacked and beaten on the street; he attributed it to his Jewish appearance. Shortly after I left Odesa in February 2007, 320 Jewish gravestones and a Holocaust memorial were vandalized and painted with swastikas and antisemitic slogans. Many people I knew, both Jews and non-Jews, considered these tragic attacks to be out of the ordinary for Odesa. The incidents were rarely discussed at length by either Jewish or non-Jewish Odesans; most residents adamantly supported the rhetoric of tolerance as one of the city's chief characteristics.

Odesa: A Cosmopolitan City

Tolerance and cosmopolitanism were indeed traits often ascribed to the city by Jewish Odesans. A key theme of this book is the way a discourse of Odesa as a cosmopolitan and Jewish city shapes the process of identity formation among Odesa's Jewry—their sense of the city as home, their interpretation of change, and their vision of their future. It was in this way that they spoke of the city's distinct Jewish history, for these terms dominate the wider historical perspective about its Jewish past while also playing a role in the way local Jewry see themselves and others (including foreign religious leaders) as either continuing or breaking away from these fundamental traits in the process of revival.[34]

In the chapters that follow, I demonstrate the complexity and diversity of different people's engagement with this discourse, but I also show how contemporary Jewish Odesans are becoming cosmopolitan—in the way that scholars today use this term to talk about cultural dimensions of globalization. Thus, Jewish Odesans are experiencing different dimensions of cosmopolitanism that delve into the historical realities of their city's multicultural and ethnically diverse past, where Jews felt themselves to be part of the modern world, and the contemporary ways Jews feel a connection to the world through a network of transnational organizations, tourism, and philanthropy.

My goal in the discussion of cosmopolitanism and tolerance in Odesa is not to debate whether Odesa was or is cosmopolitan or tolerant. Rather, I want to tease out what, when, and for whom something is or isn't cosmopolitan and what that trait means in different contexts. I also want to analyze the ways in which Odesa's Jews and religious leaders used these terms and wove them into their personal or public narratives to confirm, question, or authenticate their own place in Odesa's Jewish spaces. And I analyze the ways in which Jewishness is used as a metonym for cosmopolitan Odesa and the Odesa myth that lives on in the public imagination through stories, images, city tours, films, and conversations about the city.

When writing about cosmopolitanism as a feature of Odesa's past, historians, literary scholars, musicologists, and other academics highlight the multiethnic fabric of the city in the first half of the nineteenth century. This phenomenon was the result of Catherine II's initiative to welcome Turks, Greeks, French, Italians, Jews, and others to the new and bustling city on the periphery of the Russian Empire. An "entanglement of international culture" was created by the commercial and cultural exchange taking place in this free port city that looked to the Levant and the Mediterranean.[35]

Many scholars have pointed out that the Jewish presence played an important role in defining Odesa's modern and cosmopolitan experience. Describing Odesa in the late imperial period, Roshanna Sylvester writes that the Jewish experience was central to what it meant to be a modern Odesan.[36] Indeed, a potential causal connection between Odesa's cosmopolitanism and its thriving modernist movement across social and cultural spheres was at the heart of the 2021 conference "Odessa, Cosmopolitanism and Modernism," organized by the Israel Institute for Advanced Studies. But as literary scholar Mirja Lecke acknowledged in her opening notes at the conference, cosmopolitanism is a "contested notion, diverse in its layered historical meaning."[37] Jewish studies scholar Brian Horowitz points out that unlike cosmopolitanism as "commitment to a society in which national borders as well as internal ethnic and religious differences have less significance than universal values," Jewish cosmopolitanism in 1900s Odesa was "a specific kind of individual self-consciousness."[38] It meant "one's openness to people of other nationalities, to integration into non-Jewish society, and to a rejection of Jewish exclusivity."[39] In other words, the usage and understanding of the term "cosmopolitanism" in the context of Odesa's intelligentsia, unlike other meanings often ascribed to the term, didn't signify a harmonious coexistence of Jews and non-Jews, but rather it was "the Jew's self-conscious openness to non-Jewish elements, especially in public spaces."[40] Historian Evrydiki Sifneos expands the picture of cosmopolitanism in imperial Odesa by focusing on the intersection of different ethnic groups in the sphere of economic and social activities.[41] Anthropologist Caroline Humphrey suggests we think of "cosmopolitanisms" in the plural, pointing out that "the forms of cosmopolitanisms were very different at the beginning of the 19th century from those at the end."[42] In the specific context of Jewish Odesa, the pogroms that took place in the city in the late 1800s "erased a good deal of the city's cosmopolitan luster."[43]

Cosmopolitanism is often juxtaposed with nationalism. The idea, born in ancient Greece, has meant to define oneself as a citizen of the world. For some, like the Argentinian author Jorge Luis Borges, cosmopolitanism was regarded as a modern argument against the tyranny of "tradition," defined as narrow parochialisms and ethnocentrism.[44] In this exact way, Odesa was what historian John Klier dubbed "a kind of anti-shtetl," where Jews came when fleeing the traditional and distinctive way of life that had trapped them elsewhere in the Pale of Settlement, the area where Jews could legally reside from 1835 to 1917.[45] Cities, and port cities specifically, have been "a privileged site" for cosmopolitan lifestyles.[46] In Russia and the Soviet Union, cosmopolitanism was rejected "as a bourgeois, yet misconceived idea of international coexistence."[47]

Anthropologists have long explored practices of socialization among different cultures, ethnicities, religions, and people. The new vocabularies of "rooted cosmopolitanism," "vernacular cosmopolitanism," and "actually existing cosmopolitanisms" arise from a characteristically anthropological acknowledgment of diversity and attachments to place.[48] Based on the definition of anthropologist Ulf Hannerz's "genuine cosmopolitanism," I see cosmopolitanism primarily as an orientation toward, and willful interaction with, the other—or what Hannerz calls a "state of mind" and anthropologists Humphrey and Vera Skvirskaja describe as "a capacity for openness, an appreciation for others and the ability to stand outside the givens of one's own community."[49]

Some discussions of cosmopolitanism, including that of Hannerz, have been criticized for their elitist assumptions that travel and movement can be undertaken with ease and that encounters with other cultures are a matter of free choice.[50] Other critiques of cosmopolitanism "questioned the use of an enlightened notion of cosmopolitanism."[51] These critiques apply to our conversation about Odesa, as not all of the city's Jewish citizens could engage freely with

others in the fashion that Hannerz assumes to be true in genuine cosmopolitanism, and the cosmopolitan experiences I refer to are not all connected to an
elitist vision of culture, as some notions of cosmopolitanism assume to be true.
The "entanglement of cosmopolitan discourse," which includes the "demotic
cosmopolitan practices" observed by anthropologist Ruth Mandel in Berlin,
is also visible in Odesa's "shifting cosmopolitics."[52] In my analysis, I discuss
cosmopolitanisms in the plural, as suggested by the historian James Clifford,
noting "a complex range of interpersonal experiences, sites of appropriation
and exchange."[53] But looking beyond intellectual orientation, I also note the
need to see cosmopolitanism as practical coexistence and peaceful interaction
with different ethnoreligious groups—accepting and valuing the other's cultural capital, expressing concern for other humans, and rejecting a xenophobia
grounded in specific places. As scholar of comparative literature Ackbar Abbas
writes, "cosmopolitanism must take place somewhere, in specific sites and situations."[54] In this regard, twenty-first-century Odesa is, as Tanya Richardson
notes, "much *less* ethnically diverse than it was even before WWII, while its
economic and port status is more marginal than during the Soviet period."[55]
Indeed, historians of Odesa have noted an end of cosmopolitanism in different
times of Odesa's history.[56] With its fading maritime connection to the world
and changed demographics, Odesa has been described as a "post-cosmopolitan
city."[57] But we've learned that cities can wax and wane into and out of cosmopolitanism. Clifford, in particular, focused our attention on hybrid cosmopolitan experiences in what he refers to as "discrepant cosmopolitanism."[58]
Although Clifford focuses his discussion of discrepant cosmopolitanism on
the multiple identities, outlooks, and practices that remain in a state of flux and
are continually subject to redefinition, renegotiation, and contestation, authors
writing about Odesa have highlighted the different historical temporalities
that cast a shadow of doubt on the city's proclaimed cosmopolitan reality.[59]
Humphrey's work on pogroms in Odesa and Charles King's historical study
of Odesa's complex constitution of the genius and greatness and violence both
underscore how cosmopolitan cities can experience crucial periods of brutality
that challenge notions of lived cosmopolitanisms.[60]

The changes in sociality brought on by the Russian-Ukrainian war present
a new context for the timely discussion of cosmopolitanisms. As I describe in
the epilogue, the circumstances of war have both fragmented and solidified
different social classes, ethnic and religious groups, families, communities, and
Odesa's social networks of émigrés. It is obvious that the already-altered reality will continue to change with the turbulent currents of the war and Odesa's
cosmopolitan traits will be challenged by the growing anti-Russian sentiment,
the recast of historical memory, language politics, and the economic, social,

and political reality of postwar Ukraine. My research considers the historical dimensions of Odesa's cosmopolitan claims as well as their contradictions and limitations. It also shows that there are competing notions of what counts as cosmopolitan in any one place throughout a city's history and different ways of being cosmopolitan, as in experiences of staying, migrating, or being transnational. In other words, different groups and different generations within any one group draw on different historical truths to confirm, challenge, or debunk cosmopolitan claims about a place. In this process, some draw on universal connections of people and places and others draw on particular experiences and habits. And in this respect, different groups see post-Soviet transformations in Odesa as either asserting or challenging the city's core values of tolerance and multicultural urbanity. My research suggests that a place can be simultaneously defined as cosmopolitan and *not* cosmopolitan, thanks to divergent understandings of the term brought about by different generations being exposed to the afterlives of empires and also exposed to the transnational networks connecting Odesa's Jewry to destinations where family and friends reside.[61] Moreover, Jewish Odesans find themselves to be part of different communities simultaneously: as Jews, as Odesans, as Ukrainians, and as Russians or Russian speakers. These categories also take on new meanings in the unfolding of history and the ongoing war at the time of writing.

One can argue that Jews have historically been cosmopolitan by the sheer fact of being part of a global diaspora. During Stalin's regime, the term *rootless cosmopolitans* was often used as a synonym for Jews. In the context of post-Soviet Jewish Odesa, the religious landscape became dominated by Orthodox Judaism, and questions of tolerance, cosmopolitanism, and openness resurfaced in the contestations of various models of Jewish moral codes. This was especially evident in dialogue about Jewish education; in later chapters, I describe how some interlocutors feared that Jewish schools and cultural centers separated Jews from others, undermining the integrated quality of Odesa's diversity.

Some elderly Odesan Jews see the religious "revival"—or, rather, what they believe to be new Jewish traditions—as detracting from the city's cosmopolitan achievement of multiethnic social encounters, engagements, and relations. In their minds, that life was sustained, even in the time of Soviet ideology, under the rhetoric of international brotherhood or friendship between nations (*druzhba narodov*). Other Jews are less attached to those secular Soviet ideals and more critical of them. They celebrate religious freedom and the possibility to learn about traditions and openly practice Jewish rituals. And for many of the children raised in Jewish institutions—especially those in the Tikva and Chabad schools and orphanages—religious observance is now the norm.

But a new form of cosmopolitanism has also emerged through membership in Jewish organizations that has increased the possibilities for travel, migration, and return migration. If we link cosmopolitanism and secularism with modernization—as many elderly Odesans did when I spoke to them about these trends—it becomes apparent that the entanglements of religiosity and modernity are complex and much scrutinized in contemporary Odesa, where diverse meanings of cosmopolitanism traverse "different spatio-temporal dimensions of modernity" and different understandings of modernity.[62]

Main Themes of the Book

As an ethnography of Odesa's Jewish people and places, this book draws together theories of Jewish belonging, diaspora, and migration studies and critically applies the concept of a "religious revival" to analyze change and continuity in a historically Jewish city. In presenting a picture of everyday life in Jewish Odesa, it weaves together history, anthropology, and Jewish studies to depict the aftermath of the legacy of state secularization and Soviet rule. My research thus touches on the wide-ranging phenomenon of postsocialist identity formations and shifts in morality as a result of migration, state-building processes, and the local, national, and global developments that have altered the region.

This book focuses on the Jewish communities that remained in what is now independent Ukraine. However, my study also engages with the migration and return migration of Jewish Odesans, examining the city itself as a place of belonging for the larger Odesan Jewish diaspora now scattered around the world. I locate the analysis of the bond of people and place in relation to the critique of the concept of Jewish diaspora put forth by Jewish studies scholars Caryn Aviv and David Shneer and others, and I analyze the changed status and position of Russian-speaking Jewry within the larger Jewish world and global Judaism.[63] Since the end of the Soviet Union and the establishment of independent Ukraine, the Jewish voices featured in this book are no longer those that Elie Wiesel lumped together as "the Jews of silence."[64] These voices expand, alter, and enrich the stereotypical accounts of Jewish experiences in the USSR. The book thus opens a window on the processes of negotiating the identities and traditions that define Odesa, Ukraine, and the larger post-Soviet world today.

Soviet and post-Soviet Jewish research has become a distinct field within the larger realm of Jewish studies.[65] Its themes include issues of migration and resettlement, political and religious repression, religious and community vitality, and questions of Jewish identity. Recent anthropological work has likewise expanded the field's focus to include new dimensions of Jewish life.[66] For example, anthropologist Sascha Goluboff's ethnography introduces the idea of race to highlight how distinctions between nationalities, ethnicities, and racialized others were used in power struggles among Russian, Georgian, and Mountain Jews of Moscow's Central Synagogue.[67] Likewise, cultural anthropologist Alanna Cooper's book—part ethnography, part history, part memoir—draws attention to fractured identities among Bukharan Jewish communities in light of their internalized Soviet ideals, assimilation to Russian culture, and practice of customs native to the specific traditions, the authenticity of which are all challenged by foreign Jewish representatives.[68] But my work doesn't just document the limitations and problems of Jewish "revival"; it also includes testimonies of those who have welcomed new centers of Jewish life and new models of Jewishness, both globally constituted and locally implemented throughout Odesa, in official, semiofficial, and informal settings. Like anthropologist Magdalena Waligorska, I see revival as "a space of interaction," a contact point of various Jews and Jewish voices of authority.[69] In the context of Odesa, the use of the term *revival* was also questioned because it could mean a rebirth of Jewish traditions, a new way of defining Jewishness, and everything in between.

The type of negotiations I focused on from the mid-2000s in Odesa are specific to that time and place, but the questions they raise are not. Much like the "Muslim politics" Tone Bringa describes in Bosnia, "being Jewish" in Odesa was a negotiated concept defined by ordinary Jews, not solely determined by Jewish Orthodox doctrine or distinctively "religious" values.[70] Odesan Jews questioned what "being Jewish" meant, as Soviet markers of Jewish identity faded and various models of Jewish identification put forth by religious, Zionist, and cultural organizations replaced the symbolic production, control of institutions, and voices of authority on what makes people and places Jewish.

This is not a story of just one city or of a single ethnic or religious group. With the collapse of state secularism after more than seventy years of socialist ideology, religion resurged in public and private life, leading to important transformations in the lives of all ex-Soviet citizens. To date, the analysis of this religious resurgence in the FSU has mainly concentrated on the proselytizing religions and has tended to overlook the growth and development of Judaism and Jewish life. That's because active proselytizing and the conversion of non-Jews haven't been part of Jewish religious practice for many hundreds of years. This remains true of today's Jewish revivalist movements. In contemporary Ukraine, Jewish activists are making sustained, highly visible efforts to connect existing Jews to "their" traditions and history.

Studies of Odesan Jews can help explain how individual actors combine secular and religious practices and orientations in their daily lives and how these practices are influenced by the development projects of international representatives and institutions. Like other groups, Jews are constantly engaged in the process of creating and refining their bonds of solidarity and structures of moral understanding.[71] Therefore, one element of this study involves highlighting how Odesan Jews have come to identify themselves and the parameters of their communities in these new political, social, and cultural environments, and how their experiences compare to those of other ethnoreligious minorities in former Soviet states.

As with other ex-Soviet ethnoreligious minorities, the historical representation of Odesa's Jewry is surrounded by assumptions, manipulated truths, and simplistic explanations of social realities produced by Soviet and foreign media and scholarship. Such views have not only influenced scholars but have also shaped how activists on the ground have approached Odesa's Jewish population during this project of "revival." This book thus explores the dynamics of a revival that was accepted and welcomed by some but questioned and challenged by others. The latter regard the modes of Jewishness introduced by foreign activists as completely new, and see them as proposing a new way of being a Jew. As an elderly taxi driver said, while he and I watched a group of black-clad observant Jews cross the road in front of us, "Odesa's Jews never dressed so religiously. These are all tourists." Indeed, that group was a delegation from Israel, but many of the local Jews I knew in the city did dress the same way: over the years, more and more women started to cover their hair, wear wigs, and adopt more modest dress, swapping trousers for long skirts. And of course, historically, Odesa's observant Jews did dress much like those observant Jews we saw crossing the road. But to the taxi driver, the level of religiosity seemed foreign and inconsistent with his sense of Odesa and its mores.

In the chapters that follow, I look at the cultural, religious, Zionist, and philanthropic activists and organizations involved in Odesa's complex Jewish network. I also examine the various reactions to the models of Jewish life they have introduced, as Odesans actively negotiate identities and traditions: local and global, Jewish and non-Jewish, religious and secular. I consider what implications the different international projects of Jewish revival have for Odesa's historically proclaimed cosmopolitanism and Jewishness. While local initiatives in Odesa tend toward flexible cultural models of Jewish expression, the new authority figures associated with internationally driven projects have significant influence on the criteria by which Jewish identity is recognized. Orthodox religious organizations define a Jew as someone born to a Jewish mother or someone who converted to Judaism by Orthodox standards. Zionist organizations refer to the Israeli Law of Return, which allows Jews, along with their children, grandchildren, and spouses, to immigrate to Israel. Anyone who has at least one Jewish grandparent on either side of the family counts. These definitions challenge previous markers of Jewish identification in Odesa.

Those markers were not just the formal, Soviet-state designations of "Jewish nationality"; they were also the informal, cultural, and cosmopolitan markers that permeated Odesa: attachment to the Russian language and culture, the education of the intelligentsia, a certain cultural refinement, a form of wit and humor, and even the flavor of the city's signature cuisine.

This book explores discourses surrounding traditions. Often, traditions are viewed as customs and practices handed down from generation to generation.[72] However, my research problematizes this supposed natural flow of transmission and reveals the different ways the term is used locally in various contexts of everyday life. In relation to religion, a tradition is "something learned in order to participate in a faith, for example in Christianity, Islam and Judaism."[73] In the context of Jewish studies, tradition was often discussed in opposition to modernity, but many scholars have questioned this old opposition, identifying the "permeable boundary" between the two forces and going so far as claiming "traditionalism as itself modern" or even "beyond modern."[74] This argument is part of the larger observation that religion isn't merely an example of the tenacity of old ideas, and that this unidirectional view of religion's decline under the weight of modernity missed a great deal of its resurgent force.[75]

In Odesa, Jews used the terms *tradition* and *traditional* in different and sometimes contradictory ways. For some, being "traditional" was a place between religious and secular, where they followed some Jewish traditions that they had accepted committing to without fully dedicating themselves to being "religious." At times, a "tradition" was referred to as something prescribed by Judaism that might not have been the case in the Soviet context but that has been maintained by Jews throughout history. For instance, the practice that required a man to be circumcised before burial was regarded as a Jewish "tradition" but also a transgression of a Soviet "tradition" where Jews were, for the most part, not circumcised. Specifically in times of life cycle rituals, the question of which tradition to appropriate was complicated by the altered norms defined by the established Jewish authority. Although many assume traditions are long-standing, established, and authentic customs and practices, they involve continual negotiation and contestation that is grounded in questions of legitimacy. In the context of contemporary Odesa, Soviet, urban, and family traditions were part of the ongoing and dynamic process of Jewish identification that entered into the arena of debate.

In his famous essay "Inventing Traditions," historian Eric Hobsbawm writes that "traditions which appear or claim to be old are often quite recent in origin and sometimes invented . . . and this occurs more frequently when a rapid transformation of society weakens or destroys the social patterns for which 'old' traditions had been designed."[76] The collapse of the Soviet Union and the process of state-building in Ukraine, coupled with global efforts to revive religion after communism, transformed the meaning of Jewish identity and urban-Jewish culture in Odesa. Soviet experiences and expectations didn't disappear overnight, and even thirty years after the dissolution of the USSR, they still stand as a reference point for elderly Odesans. If we keep in mind Hobsbawn's definition of old and new traditions coming together in periods of transition, we can better understand modern history and religious studies scholar Galina Zelenina's description of the contemporary religiosity she observes among Moscow's Jewry as a case of a *new old religion*.[77]

Methodology

I have much in common with the people I met in Odesa, but I had never lived there, or anywhere in Ukraine, before beginning my fieldwork in 2005. Although my family is originally from Ukraine, Belarus, and Latvia, I was born and raised in Russia. I'm fluent in Russian and had a taste of living in the Soviet Union until 1991. That year, when I was nine years old, my father was offered a work contract in the United States as a physicist, and my family followed him there. I lived in the United States until I was twenty-three, when I moved to London to pursue a graduate degree in anthropology. I live there still. I've made regular trips back to Moscow since 1993, but I haven't stayed in Russia for longer than a summer since my childhood. My interlocutors in Odesa regarded me as someone foreign, due to my years of living abroad, but also saw me as "one of them" because of my Russian-speaking Jewish heritage and fluency in Russian. Ironically, the same aspects of my identity that once defined my insider status as a researcher (speaking Russian and growing up in the Soviet Union) came to define me as an outsider after Russia's invasion of Ukraine. Although I knew that my years-long relationships with friends in Odesa were sincere, and that we'd established trust in our conversations, I also understood that, in a way, I was part of a world that now defined their enemy.

Having been raised with an awareness that I was Jewish, I've had some of the same experiences as my interlocutors: being brought up in a secular Jewish environment; hearing family members tell stories about the prerevolutionary lives of ancestors; joining family gatherings where I heard the migration stories of relatives now living in Israel, Australia, and the United States; indulging in Jewish dishes on days that loosely marked the Jewish calendar; having an inscription in my passport that read "Jewish" and carrying a "Jewish surname." I was always drawn to the topic of Jewish identity and curious about the destiny of those Jews who remained in the ex-Soviet state and the unexpected return migration of Jews to Russia, Ukraine, and other destinations in the FSU. This book was born out of my passion for learning about this new era of Jewish life, embedded in withering structures of socialism and the birth of a Ukrainian nation, and open to the globalization, democracy, and streams of religious, cultural, and national revival movements engaged in rebuilding Jewish communities. Odesa has its own history, and I wanted to know how the processes of Jewish revival played out in a city considered to be unique in the Jewish history of the Russian Empire, the Soviet Union, and present-day Ukraine.

Like other Western researchers working in Ukraine and in other countries of the FSU, I've been accused—jokingly, but sometimes not—of being a spy. The fact that I was conducting ethnographic research on the local Jewish population offended some; they supposed that anthropologists should only study small, isolated indigenous populations somewhere far off. Occasionally I was subjected to analysis and critique.[78] To avoid this awkwardness, I occasionally referred to myself as a sociologist.

My affiliation with the Sociology Department of Odesa University, where I was supervised by Professor Emma Gansova, helped with my initial introductions.[79] Professor Gansova's untimely passing in 2020 left an unfillable emptiness in my life and in the lives of all who knew her. It was through the university that I met some of my first interlocutors. Hearing that I was interested in how Jewish life in Odesa had changed since Ukraine's independence, they were keen to tell their stories and to have me meet their families, friends, and Jewish activists in various Jewish organizations. The personal introductions that followed proved to be an efficient way to meet a diverse group of Jewish residents of different classes, ages, and orientations. Most of them had some connection, even if tangential, to organized Jewish life in the city. Through the "snowball" method, I met the students and teachers at Migdal, the Jewish community center where I regularly attended lectures, occasionally conducted interviews, and, for six months, taught English to Jewish youth. At the same time, I taught English to toddlers in a Jewish nursery at the early childhood development center, Mazl Tov.[80] Through these classes, I was able to engage students, parents, and grandparents, all of whom helped me understand both the Jewish and the non-Jewish spheres of Odesan society. During the last three months of my fieldwork, I also attended weekly religious classes sponsored by the Student Union of Torah for Russian Speakers. I regularly spent Shabbats with religious families who kindly invited me for Friday night dinners or Saturday lunches. Most of my friends were affiliated with one of the two Orthodox congregations, though I also made frequent visits to the Reform community, where I was always welcomed with open arms.

Most of my interlocutors were somewhat aware of Jewish activities in the city, even if they didn't directly participate in any Jewish programs. Through several university students and my participation with Jewish philanthropy groups visiting the city, I met other Jews who weren't affiliated with specific communal structures of Jewish life, perhaps because they didn't know much about those organizations or simply because they avoided them. Some Jewish families either weren't aware of their Jewish roots or placed little emphasis on this aspect of their history. It was harder for me to locate such individuals because most of them weren't interested in discussing Jewish subjects and weren't socially connected with the more aware and active Jews who made up a large part of my interlocutors. More formal interactions with the city's academics, intellectuals, and leaders of various Jewish organizations gave me insight into present-day and historical issues of Odesa's Jewish development.

At the start of my fieldwork, in June 2005, and at the end, I spent a total of two months in Israel, interviewing Odesans who had left Odesa and those contemplating a return. In the years since, I have also visited a number of Odesan families who have relocated to Israel, Europe, and the United States.

My methods of gathering data varied depending on the situation and the individuals. Most of my data were collected in Russian, which served as the primary language of communication for nearly all the people I met. On a few occasions, my interlocutors chose to speak English to practice their language skills. I didn't encounter any Ukrainian-language Jewish social activities in Odesa; all the Jewish programs I attended were conducted in Russian. But Ukrainian often appeared on displays and in public Jewish memorials. I met a number of Jewish youths who spoke fluent Ukrainian, mostly as a result of their education (it had been the official language of instruction since the 1990s), but others who were educated in Russian-language schools did not. A few among their parents' and grandparents' generations spoke Ukrainian; others struggled with even the basic phrases needed to deal with the state bureaucracy. I met a few elderly Jews who knew basic Yiddish, but none who could converse freely in that language. Hebrew was only used to communicate among Israeli Jews, in religious services, and occasionally among returnees.

For most of the early phase of my fieldwork, I conducted informal interviews and engaged in ordinary discussions with those Odesans who agreed to make time for me. A main part of my early research included observation, which naturally turned into participation. This wasn't always easy. For example, Orthodox Jewish settings are designed to prevent the interaction of men and women during prayer and most rituals, so at such times I could engage only with the women in the congregation.[81]

It was also challenging at times to maneuver among the one Reform and two Orthodox congregations as well as the many Jewish organizations in the city. People would make assumptions about my beliefs based on my choice of

activities. Some read me as close to Israel; others, as aligned with the Orthodox community; and still others, as part of the Reform congregation. These
interpretations weren't unexpected, based on my interactions with different
groups or congregations in the city, so I had to make decisions about where I'd
celebrate holidays and share in the welcoming of Shabbat and which programs,
trips, and other activities I'd participate in. To some extent, my choices affected
which social circles I was invited to join and which I'd be excluded from—and,
consequently, what material I was able to gather. However, I was fortunate to
build genial relationships in most of my disparate social circles. Whenever possible, I tried to clarify my role as an objective observer in religious participation
and institutional associations.

I attended a variety of ceremonies and life cycle rituals, such as the wedding
of an Odesa friend that took place in the city of Dnipro (see chapter 4). I viewed
many videos and photographs of other friends' weddings that had occurred
before my arrival. I attended a circumcision (bris), a ceremony for the redemp-
tion of the firstborn son (*pidyon haben*), and an engagement ceremony (*erusin*)
as well as numerous Shabbat services and celebrations honoring the major
Jewish holidays. I didn't witness any burials in Odesa, but I did visit the Jewish
cemetery with friends to pay respect to their family graves and to hear stories
of their deceased relatives. Some informants invited me to their homes; others
were more reserved. When I was welcomed as a guest, I was able to have deep,
candid discussions over informal meals in the kitchen with friends and their
families. These conversations served as "small doorways into a complex system
of meanings and values, ideologies, identities and life strategies" that I try to
make sense of in this book.[82] Throughout my time in Odesa, I met regularly
with five elderly Jews and their families and collected their life histories in great
detail; these make up the body of chapter 2.

I sometimes recorded my conversations with my interlocutors; at other times,
I took notes. Sometimes, I simply listened. My interviews with leaders of various
Jewish organizations were arranged and conducted with a degree of formality;
these I recorded. I often used my evenings to augment my notes with material
I hadn't been able to jot down at the time. I made short videos and took many
photographs—another useful way to capture the details of Odesan life—some
of which appear in this work. Because I lived on my own, I was able to welcome guests to my apartment for meals and tea. Over time, many relationships
flourished into friendships. Personal invitations from friends, walks around the
city, and shared family celebrations became part of my Odesa experience.

Conducting research in Odesa after the Orange Revolution and again after
Maidan, I was privileged to be a witness to the complexities of my interlocutors' "changing life-scapes" amid the structural transformations of independent

Ukraine.[83] Most of my interlocutors were educated individuals who reflected on their own experiences and history and on current events and provided a high level of analysis. I've tried not to speak for them but rather to give prominence to their stories. And I've worked to present every social actor within the context of his or her particular background and the setting of the interview or conversation, to reveal to the reader each individual's "distinctive mix of insight and blindness."[84] Except for the individuals who were public figures and asked to be included with their real names, all names in the text are pseudonyms to protect the privacy of those who so kindly shared their thoughts and stories with me.

Book Outline

The first two chapters focus on Odesa's history and legacy. Much of this background centers on the myth of Odesa as an open, cosmopolitan, and Jewish city perceived as a "distinct place" within the Russian Empire, the Soviet Union, and present-day Ukraine. These two historical chapters provide the background needed to understand Odesa today; they also challenge the picture of a single, monolithic Soviet Jewish experience by recognizing the influence of specific urban cultures on the development of varying Jewish orientations.

Chapter 1, "Historical Background: The Lost, the Revisited, and the Re-created," lays out the backdrop necessary to understand the Jewish presence in the Russian Empire and the Soviet Union generally and the qualities of Odesa, in particular. This introduction to the city's historic past sets the stage for contemporary developments affecting the Jewish population of present-day Odesa, especially the multiple and often conflicted responses to international efforts to revive the Jewish life of the city. The chapter highlights the diverse experiences, loyalties, and orientations of Jewish Odesans and the often complex trajectories of their lives. This material helps counter much of the earlier literature on Soviet Jewry influenced by crude anti-Soviet stereotypes. It challenges conventional truisms that were based on a negative and monolithic picture of Soviet Jewish experiences and gives due attention to the specificity of urban cultures like Odesa's on the development of varying Jewish orientations.

The subject of contested history and memory is expanded in chapter 2, "Remembering the Past and Making Sense of the Present: Narratives of Elderly Jews," a detailed account of Odesa's older generation of Jews. The accounts of elderly Jews I interviewed reflect on their experiences and consider how they judge their present-day status as individuals, family members, professionals, residents of Odesa, and members of its Jewish population. This ethnographic portrait comprises four families whose stories reveal some of the complexities, contradictions, and contingencies of living through Odesa's Soviet period and its aftermath. I explore how members of this generation carry the past and make sense of the present, including the question of migration confronted by many elderly Jews as their children and grandchildren move abroad.

The next three chapters address the processes of Jewish cultural and religious revival that have been part of Odesa's reforms since the breakup of the Soviet Union. Chapter 3, "Jewish Revival: Opportunities and Tensions," describes the new forms of "being Jewish" through which Odesan Jews now identify themselves—forms brought in by the foreign emissaries and international organizations that have in large measure formed the Jewish revival in the city. These new voices of authority have reshaped the contours and content of Jewish identification; the chapter explores how these ideological agendas are internalized, negotiated, and contested by Jewish residents as they selectively appropriate new visions and practices of Jewish life.

Chapter 4, "From *Evrei* to *Iudei*: Turning or Returning to Faith," focuses on the idea of religious adherence to examine how some local Jews enact a religious Judaism in their lives and how they negotiate these values and meanings with nonobservant family members and friends. Jewish leaders, religious scholars, and some academics in the field have often treated religious practice as a "return" to previously abandoned practices, but as this chapter illustrates, most Jewish Odesans who welcome Judaism into their routines—whether occasionally or daily—are exhibiting new patterns of living imbued with new values.

Chapter 5, "Asymmetric Cultural Encounters: Jewish Philanthropy Missions and Revival on Display," details the visits of foreign donors, known as "missions," that are designed to give sponsors a sense of their investments in building up the city's Jewish life. This chapter opens up questions about the relevance and feasibility of Jewish outreach projects and development and explores how foreign missions intended to unite Jews around the world may indeed separate the givers from the receivers of Jewish philanthropy.

The final two chapters examine how the Jewishness of Odesa has been shaped and reshaped by historical patterns of migration. Chapter 6, "Jewish Is a Mode of Transportation: Between Home, Homeland, and Diaspora," explores how the present-day Jews of Odesa think about emigration and remigration (that is, the return to Odesa from Israel or elsewhere) in terms of *home* and *diaspora*. The complexity and fluidity of these concepts are illuminated by the individuals presented—those who remained, those who are leaving, and those who've recently returned from Israel—and their relationships with Odesa, Israel, and other possible places of belonging. The conventional wisdom that Israel is the homeland is broadened and enriched by the attachments felt by local Jews toward their life in Odesa and to other places where family and friends reside. This chapter shows how the concepts of home and diaspora are not fixed or absolute for those in Odesa, who are now part of a larger global community of ex-Soviet Jewry.

The image of Odesa as a "Jewish" city and a home to Jewish humor, cuisine, language, music, and literature is the theme of chapter 7, "Odesa: A Jewish City?" By examining the intertwined discourses of myth, history, and individual realities that simultaneously reproduce and contest Odesa's trope of Jewishness, this chapter demonstrates how locals draw on the Odesa myth to reaffirm it as a "Jewish city" for many purposes: as a claim to partial ownership of cultural traits, as a strategy of empowerment, as a way to maintain long-distance ties, and in some cases as a tactic for challenging global Judaism and Ukrainization.

In the conclusion, I argue that Jews in contemporary Odesa, like other minority groups, face the challenge of redefining themselves in a new cultural and political environment. Under these circumstances, the myth and reality of the city's character—its Jewishness, its Greekness, its Russianness, its Ukrainianness, and so on—serve to valorize and protect Odesa's distinctive nature.

It is impossible to write about Ukraine today without acknowledging the region's political upheavals and the political and social challenges they present for Odesa generally and for its Jewish population in particular. The war with Russia in the Donbas region, expanded through Russia's 2022 invasion, has created much animosity toward the Russian state, although relations with the Russian people, culture, and language are more nuanced. This book's epilogue therefore sheds light on how, as the political situation fluctuates, Jewish Odesans and leaders of religious organizations are positioning themselves within the changing array of alliances, loyalties, and identities.

1

Historical Background

The Lost, the Revisited, and the Re-created

This chapter aims to illustrate how, along with Odesa's development as a cosmopolitan city, the Jews of Odesa historically experienced periods of social and economic thriving alternating with dark stretches of hostility, discrimination, horror, and, later, rebirth. Both czarist and Soviet rule saw the development of social practices distinct to Odesa—with its vital commercial port and open, multiethnic population. The city's internal dynamics and the political, social, and economic influences that concentrated there helped cultivate a rich and diverse range of liberal identities among its Jewish citizens.

While the many Jews in Odesa experienced a dynamic process of modernization and transformation in their communities in the nineteenth century, efforts aimed at further Jewish integration persisted, and indeed the twentieth century's violence and brutality demonstrate the limitations of their acculturation. For some, modernization meant adopting a secularized identity: a sizable community of Jews in Odesa had left behind religious practices as they acculturated. For others, it meant bypassing Jewish identification altogether and taking up other meaningful identities that they felt brought higher status, whether at home or abroad. When Jews in Odesa altered their practices, beliefs, and self-identity, they were often prompted by the perception that social and economic adaptation was necessary to be successful in business. As historian Steven Zipperstein shows in his seminal book on the subject, by 1881, "religious traditions began to fade" and "all that truly mattered was business."[1] "The commercial history of Odessa *is* the history of Odessa," wrote Ukrainian historian A. A. Skal'kovskii about the city during the same time period.[2] Along with commercial activities, during the nineteenth and twentieth centuries, Jews became increasingly involved in Odesa's literary, musical, artistic, and scientific life. Cultural change among the city's Jewry was also driven by ideas of Jewish enlightenment, sometimes in support of Soviet ideology and sometimes out of the sheer necessity of survival.

The goal of this chapter is to analyze the history of Odesa's Jewish population by taking account of the sociopolitical events of the Russian Empire and the territory of Jewish settlement in the Pale, as well as those in the Soviet Union and later the Ukrainian state. To understand the position of Odesa's Jews, we must understand that the area that is present-day Ukraine was, in the seventeenth and eighteenth centuries, divided between Russia, Poland, and the Ottoman Empire; in the nineteenth century, divided between Russia and Austria-Hungary; and in the twentieth century, except for a short period of independence after World War I, for the most part integrated into the Soviet Union with smaller territories partitioned between Poland, Czechoslovak Republic, and Romania. In other words, Ukraine has been on the edge of various empires for centuries.[3] While the Jews of the newly acquired areas of the Russian Empire after the partition of Poland spoke Yiddish and other languages, the tsarist regime's policies of integration encouraged Russification (such as the establishment of Russian-language schools in 1844 for Jews and other minorities). Czar Alexander II saw these policies "as a key condition towards further sblizhenie (rapprochement) between Jews and Russians."[4] Jews who were involved in trade found Russian helpful in business affairs, and proponents of Jewish equality and adherents of Haskalah, the Jewish Enlightenment movement, endorsed acculturation as a modernizing force. Odesa, as I later discuss, was part of the territory conquered and developed by the Russian Empire in the late eighteenth century, and the city and its Jewish population have historically been shaped by processes of Russification that continued to dominate language politics in Russia in czarist and Soviet periods. These earlier developments help us understand how Odesa and its Jewish population remained predominantly Russian speaking in independent Ukraine. In the current context of the Russian-Ukrainian war, the cultural affiliation with Russia of Odesa and the larger territory of "Novorossiia" has been manipulated to justify Russia's territorial claim to large parts of Ukraine and is a crucial part of Putin's propaganda rhetoric that paints Odesa as a "Russian city" and ignores Ukrainian political and cultural sovereignty. This chapter and the next also document how for many Jews in Odesa, their connection to Russia and the Russian language was a strong element of their identity and one that has been affected by the trauma of the Russian-Ukrainian war.

To maintain its focus on the history of Odesa, this chapter provides only a brief summary of the multifaceted history of Jews in the greater region.[5] And while my book primarily considers Odesa some two decades after Ukraine's independence, the city's earlier history provides important reminders that the transformations defining contemporary Odesa are part of a long process of negotiation of lifestyles, traditions, loyalties, and identity politics. All these historical complexities and contradictions of Jewish relations with host societies and the influences of such encounters are relevant to recent events.

In presenting this history, I start by analyzing the way Jewish history in the region has been cast. My analysis is in line with the efforts of other scholars who seek to go beyond the "old paradigms of conflict and hostility" in the realm of Jewish-Ukrainian relations.[6] I look beyond the "bleak portrait of Jewish life" to highlight the importance of urban contexts in the Jewish encounters with imperial Russia, the Soviet Union, and independent Ukraine.[7] As other authors have demonstrated, the local distinctiveness of cities with large Jewish populations, regarded as "Jewish cities" in the Pale, expands our understanding of Soviet Jewish experiences. Odesa's past also frames the experiences of Jews in the early twenty-first century, which are at the core of this book.

To understand Odesan Jewry before Ukrainian independence, we must question and challenge conventional histories of the prerevolutionary Jewish experience and revisit Jewish realities within the Soviet Union. The opening of archives and resulting research carried out in the last three decades in the former Soviet Union have allowed historians to produce more synthetic accounts of the history of the Jews in this region and to correct the overly sentimental and excessively negative view of their past that was prevalent in previous accounts.[8] Needless to say, Russia's war against Ukraine has influenced and will continue to change interpretations of the past away from ideas dominant in Soviet and Russian-centric framing of historical narratives and will shift toward a more specifically Ukrainian experience, however modern that understanding is.

Revisiting the long history of Jews in Odesa underscores how that history contributed to Odesans' identity during the transformations that came in the post–Orange Revolution period. Oral histories presented in this historical background and in the following chapter sometimes support and sometimes challenge the collective memory of Jews in the Russian, Soviet, and Ukrainian contexts. This complex and contradictory historical account helps us envision Odesa as it was perceived by those who, despite the option of emigration, chose to stay in their city; those who left and returned; those who still contemplate a life abroad; those who identified as Soviet socialists above all; and those who, even in Soviet conditions, nonetheless sustained a Jewish identity. Through the diverse historical voices, we strive to keep in view the plurality of ideology and social practices that Jewish citizens of Odesa exhibit, given their differing loyalties to socialist values and Soviet life.

Recasting History

This section recasts history by exploring Odesa's placement in and out of the Pale. Much of the focus on Jews in imperial Russia has been defined by the central role of the Pale of Settlement, a swath of territory officially established in 1835 and lasting until 1917. The Pale of Settlement was the only area within the Russian Empire where Jews were free to reside permanently. While they needed no special permission to live here, movement within and travel to areas outside the Pale of Settlement were regulated by a passport system required for all but nobility.[9] The regulation of movement for most Jews in the Pale was long thought to have created "the least integrated of all the European Jewish communities," set off as "quintessential outsiders and scapegoats."[10] Overly simplified and negative images of communities in the Pale of Settlement were reinforced by literary works depicting poor Jews fleeing Russian pogroms at the turn of the century.[11]

A different school of thought cast the Pale of Settlement under the czars as a condition of Jewish preservation—a sanctuary within which Jews held to their rites, rituals, and traditions. Indeed, Yohanan Petrovsky-Shtern's *The Golden Age Shtetl* highlights the diverse experiences of Jews living in traditional communities from 1790 to 1840, when the shtetls of eastern Europe were "economically vigorous, financially beneficial, and culturally influential." He describes this as a space where "Polish, Jewish and Russian joined effort" and a "proud place with a fascinating social tapestry."[12] Nostalgic and romanticized descriptions of traditional Jewish society were a familiar motif among Jews before 1914.[13] Although Odesa, as previously mentioned, was regarded as a kind of anti-shtetl, some American Jewry contemplating their identity after World War II also romanticized the Russian Jewish past as evidence of a "spirituality, wholeness, and communal cohesion" that was later undone by Soviet rule and further destroyed by World War II.[14]

For other writers, Jewish identity under the Soviets had purely negative associations: Jews in the Soviet Union knew they were Jewish only because of daily discrimination. These perceptions were supported by interviews and memoirs of some Jewish activists, dissidents, and refuseniks.[15] But they are often contradicted by ordinary Jews, many of whom strove for assimilation on their own initiative and who, if they left the Soviet Union, did so for a variety of complicated and personal reasons.[16]

From yet another perspective, Soviet Jews were one of the most successful ethnic minorities in the Soviet Union because of their ability to survive and live as strangers.[17] As historian Stephen Kotkin said of those who participated in building socialism under Stalin, while there was a variety of reasons for doing so, "participate they did."[18] Historian Mark Steinberg and anthropologist Catherine Wanner describe how Soviet socialism, though often coercive, nonetheless "provided a type of moral community, a sense of integration, order, and shared values" to its people that many ex-Soviet citizens later mourned.[19] Caroline Humphrey describes the Soviet collective as a "moral universe of comradeship" where real warmth flourished in many social spheres of multiethnic collectives.[20] And anthropologist Alexei Yurchak writes that "for a great number of Soviet citizens, many of the fundamental values, ideals, and realities of socialist life (such as equality, community, selflessness, altruism, friendship, ethical relations, safety, education, work, creativity, and concern for the future) were of genuine importance, despite the fact that many of their everyday practices routinely transgressed, reinterpreted, or refused certain norms and rules represented in the official ideology of the socialist state."[21] It was in this context, historian Yuri Slezkine argues, that the Soviet Union offered Jews a place in the collective efforts at modernization and mobilization, a unifying project that created the conditions for consciously abandoning shtetl ways and becoming a highly educated, Russian-speaking, and predominantly urban minority.[22]

Other historians are more wary of the idea that the Soviet regime was responsible for transforming Jews from "quintessential outsiders to consummate insiders," arguing that reforms practiced by the czarist regime and Jewish elites were already setting the path for modernity.[23] As Petrovsky-Shtern reminds us in his description of Jewish life in the shtetl, "the dichotomy of modernity and countermodernity only poorly convey the vagaries and travails of Jewish experiences throughout its history." Questions of inclusion and exclusion and modernity versus tradition have remained important points of discussion in all periods of Odesa's Jewish history, as they were in the other places of present-day Ukraine where Jews dwelled.

Following the 2022 invasion of Ukraine by Russia, I have had to think carefully about the way I describe Jewish history in the region, relying on credible historians but also remaining aware of our long-standing tradition of looking at the history of Jews through the colonial lens of Russia, Poland, and other empires. In the conclusion of this chapter, therefore, I raise the topic of Jewish history as a part of Ukrainian history and Ukrainian-Jewish relations as a topic of historical exploration, issues that I pursue further in the epilogue.

The First Jews of Ukraine

Jews likely settled on the northern shores of the Black Sea as part of Greek colonies in the early centuries of the Christian era.[24] Among those early settlers were Crimean Jews and a sect of Karaites—followers of Karaism, a branch of Judaism that rejected the Oral Law. During the Middle Ages, the Jewish presence and influence in this territory—later absorbed into the Russian Empire—grew as Jews moved to the region from Byzantium, Crimea, and the short-lived nomadic kingdom of Khazaria, which existed between the Volga and Dnieper rivers and western Europe.[25]

Within Khazaria, Jews played an important role in international trade between the caliphate in Baghdad and the Byzantine Empire. But the expansion of the princedom of Kyiv into the Khazar region in the years 966–69 brought an end to Khazarian prosperity and reduced the Jewish population's influence in the region.[26] Despite evidence from medieval legends, historians have questioned or ignored the role of Khazaria's Jews in the formation of Jewish communities in Ukraine. Jews in Crimea engaged in trade prior to the establishment of the grand duchy of Kyiv (Kyivan Rus) in the tenth century but left little imprint on the later communities established in the region after the Mongol invasion in the mid-thirteenth century.[27] When Lithuania annexed Kyiv in 1320, Jews in the region were granted certain rights, and they grew in numbers and prospered, only to be expelled from Kyiv and Lithuania in 1495 and then allowed back in 1503.[28] Prior to the influx of Jews from the land of Ashkenaz (the territory inhabited by Yiddish-speaking Jews, extending from Amsterdam to Zhitomir) in the sixteenth century, Kyivan Rus had a very small community. After the dissolution of Kyivan Rus, Jews found themselves under three states: Lithuania, Poland, and the Crimean Khanate.[29] Jews living in Lithuania and Poland had the status of *servi camerae*, or servants of the royal chamber, who were given religious freedom and allowed to engage in moneylending, currency exchange, and tax collecting.[30] In the sixteenth century, the Grand Duchy of Lithuania and Poland became one polity, and as part of the Polish-Lithuanian Commonwealth, "Jews enjoyed a high level of legal and communal autonomy."[31]

But the status of the Jews also brought with it resentment from the wider society that resulted in deadly attacks on Jewish communities. Paul Magocsi and Yohanan Petrovsky-Shtern argue that because of the close economic ties between Jews and Polish magnates, the social tensions between the Orthodox Rus' and Polish populations and later rebellions against the Polish nobility resulted in attacks on and killing of Jews. The social unrest in the Polish-Lithuanian Commonwealth culminated in the 1648 uprising by the alliance of Zaporozhian Cossacks and Crimean Tatars led by Bohdan Khmelnitskyi, the hetman (military commander) of the Zaporozhian Cossacks, against the armies of the Polish-Lithuanian Commonwealth, bringing about the massacre of Polish nobility and Jews. This event is recorded in Jewish cultural memory as the Catastrophe of 1648–49—a heavy blow to eastern Jewish communities of the time. Jewish populations in Tulchyn, Nemyriv, and Polonne were decimated.[32] An estimated fourteen thousand to eighteen thousand Jews residing in the area were murdered, nearly a thousand converted to Orthodoxy, and others fled as refugees.[33]

As a result of Jews fleeing persecution during the Crusades, the Black Death in Germany, and expulsion and forced conversion in Spain, by the early seventeenth century the Polish-Lithuanian Commonwealth still benefited from an inflow of Jews from elsewhere. By the eighteenth century, the commonwealth had the largest Jewish community in the world, having grown from 10,000 at the end of the fifteenth century to around 750,000 (out of a total population of 14 million) by 1764.[34]

Jews in the Russian Empire

It was only in the late eighteenth century that a large Jewish population became established in the Russian Empire. Before the partitions of Poland in 1772, 1793, and 1795, during which Catherine II (1762–96) annexed the homelands of a large majority of Jews of the Polish-Lithuanian Commonwealth, only a small number of Jews had lived within Russia's borders.[35] As a result of the Russian Empire's late eighteenth-century expansions, it came to control the destinies of approximately one million Jews of the former Polish-Lithuanian Commonwealth.[36] By 1820, after the Kingdom of Poland was added to the new territories of the Russian Empire, the Jewish population increased to approximately 1.6 million, and by 1880, it had reached 4 million, constituting the largest concentration of Jews in the world.[37] By the end of the nineteenth century, Russia's Jewish population had grown to more than 5 million. In the words of Simon Dubnow, the leading chronicler of Russian Jewry in the early and mid-twentieth century, "the country which had stood in fear of a few thousand Jews was now forced to accept them, at one stroke, by the tens of thousands and, shortly afterwards, by the hundreds of thousands."[38]

While Empress Catherine held, in part, to the traditionalist doctrine embodied in the Russian church and her predecessors who displayed hostility to Jews, she was also influenced by the rationalist doctrines of the European Enlightenment and mercantilism. She thus attempted to "transform" her Jewish population into "useful subjects" by ensuring that Jews were, for the first time, invited to join the ranks of the three guilds of merchants and townsmen.[39] This allowed them to practice their religion and granted them permission to

participate (both as voters and as candidates) in local municipalities.[40] During
the eighteenth century and the first half of the nineteenth, it was not government policy to Russify the heterogeneous population of the empire.[41] For the
Jews, this meant that the *kehilot* (Jewish self-governing councils) continued to
preside over internal Jewish affairs.[42] This period, from the partition of Poland
to the death of Alexander I in 1825, was understood as a time when Jews were
largely left alone and able to manage their own affairs.[43]

   But the integration of Jews into the social, political, and economic spheres of
the empire presented new demographic and cultural challenges to the czarist regime. The Russian majority still viewed Jews as outsiders and regarded them with
suspicion, owing to religious differences and their links to the old Polish Kingdom.[44] The freedoms experienced by Jews in trade, religious practice, and politics
during Catherine's early years were soon curbed as a result of the upheavals that
followed the partition of Poland and the fear roused by the French Revolution,
not to mention such internal stresses as the complaints of Moscow merchants and
the church.[45] Jewish activity was restricted, first in the economic sphere and then
politically, until the autonomy of Jews was severely constrained.[46] Catherine's
edicts of 1791 and 1794 limited where Jews could live and implemented double
taxation for the region's Jewish merchants and townsmen.[47] Essentially, Jews under Catherine's rule were incorporated into existing social estates but maintained
the autonomous structures established in Poland-Lithuania and endured hostility
from those who saw them as harmful to the social order.[48]

   Alexander I, who followed Catherine after the brief rule of his father, Paul,
created the Committee for the Organization of Jewish Life. It devised a program for "Jewish reform," and it and many similar organizations that followed
promoted access to state schools and universities for Jewish children and
granted Jews the right to open their own secular schools using German, Polish, or Russian as the language of instruction. Other reforms required Jewish
members of municipalities to wear European-style clothes, limited Jewish economic activity, and restricted conversion.[49]

   The policies toward the Jews pursued by Nicholas I and his successors developed in similar ways. Again, there were attempts to make Jews loyal subjects
while mitigating their purported negative impact on society. According to
Yohanan Petrovsky-Shtern and Antony Polonsky, this was the basis of the decision to confine the Jews to the Pale of Settlement.[50] During Nicholas's reign,
attempts to incorporate Jews into the multiconfessional and ethnically diverse
empire failed.[51] Also, drafting Jews aged twelve to twenty-five in the military
and establishing both state schools and two rabbinic seminaries greatly undermined traditional Jewish leadership, increased social stratification, and created a real chasm between a minority of Jews like the *maskilim* (supporters of

Haskalah, the Jewish enlightenment) and the majority, who did not trust the government and perceived them as hostile.[52]

The Pale of Settlement

According to Russia's first statewide census, held in 1897, 5.2 million Jews resided within the Pale of Settlement, making up 4 percent of Russia's total population.[53] The Pale of Settlement was composed of territory in Lithuania-Belarus and Moldova, much of Ukraine, New Russia (or Novorosiya), and east-central Poland. Thus, the Pale was geographically, ethnically, and culturally diverse. Each of these different sections of the Pale, as well as the Polish region outside the Pale that was a major area of Jewish settlement, had a distinct historical background, ethnic composition, Jewish population, and urban and rural composition, plus different cultural elements and levels of industrialization. These factors affected the acculturation of Jews in each area.[54] The different areas within the Pale not only fostered diverse processes of cultural development throughout their histories but also attracted different types of Jews and provided different living conditions.[55] Zvi Gitelman describes how Jews in different parts of the Pale of Settlement started to diverge in their attitudes toward Jewishness during the last years of the nineteenth century: "The vast majority remained firmly rooted in their traditional primordial identities, something which was as much part of them as their own skin, assumed, unquestioned and perhaps unexamined. Others examined their Jewishness and found it wanting. They turned to enlightenment in an attempt to synthesize Jewishness and modernity, or they abandoned Jewishness altogether for Christianity and Russian culture or for socialism and 'internationalist' culture."[56]

Most Jews at the turn of the nineteenth century had been living in traditional, religiously observant communities and communicating primarily in Yiddish; the men worked as craftsmen or ran independent businesses, and most were poor. By the end of that century, a noticeable contingent of the Jewish population had started to depart from traditional values, abandoning some or many traditional religious rituals as they rose to higher ranks of business or established themselves in various professions.[57] The most successful Jews to benefit from "selective integration" (the process by which the Russian Empire hoped to disperse certain categories of "useful" Jews into the hierarchy of Russian society) were the Russian Jewish financiers who made their fortunes through military contracts and wholesale grain sales.[58] Others to follow profited from the state liquor monopoly, banking, and railway construction. Among the most prominent and well-known Jewish families at the time were the banking families of the Ephrussis, the Galperins, and the Guenzburgs; the railway magnates Samuel Polyakovs and Abram Varshavsky; the Kiev sugar king Iosef Brodsky; and the urban contractor Yakov Faibishenko. But we must not forget that most Jews in the Russian Empire of that time were poor and thus considered "unproductive"; they were, therefore, unfit for the social transformation embedded in the idea of "selective integration" that Benjamin Nathans describes.[59]

In the late nineteenth century, the Pale of Settlement "saw the appearance and increasing ascendancy of ethnic and national conceptions of Jewish self-identification, in particular Zionism" and diaspora nationalism.[60] Some Jews supported socialism and idealized the notion that the differences between Jews and non-Jews would be overcome in the new socialist world. Concurrently, Orthodoxy developed as *mitnagdic* (opposed to Hasidism), Hasidic followings grew, and Yiddish advanced as a literary language along with Modern Hebrew.[61] In cities like Odesa, Jews could therefore be part of various modern Jewish movements and, at the same time, partake in the growing economic, social, cultural, and literary spheres that departed from traditional Jewish life and strict religious observance.

Jews in the City of Odesa

It was once remarked that "if a Jew from the Pale of Settlement doesn't dream about America or Palestine, then you know he'll be in Odessa."[62] The city was founded in 1794 after the second Russo-Turkish war, when Russian forces led by Don Joseph de Ribas—a half-Spanish, half-Irish military commander under Catherine II—conquered the Ottoman fort of Khadzhibei, in the province of Novorossiia.[63] From the start, Odesa was a strategic warm-water port.[64] Catherine II offered incentives to attract settlers. The promise of individual freedom lured runaway serfs and other new arrivals, who received sizable land grants and other generous inducements in the form of monetary loans, exemption from taxes, and relief from military service. Russians, Ukrainians, Greeks, Albanians, Moldavians, Armenians, Bulgarians, and Germans settled there. Catherine's policies promoted trade, allowing foreign merchants from Greece, Italy, Galicia, and other parts of the world to establish brokerage houses in Odesa. While the Greek merchants, followed by Italians, French, German, and the British, predominated in the early years of Odesa's economic growth, after the 1870s Jews dominated the import and export markets in all mercantile activities.[65]

Catherine made it easy for Jews to move to the region of Novorossiia. Driven by "mercantilist considerations," she welcomed Jewish settlers who could boost the local economy.[66] Her governor general, the Duc de Richelieu (1803–14), and his successors, including the Count de Langeron (1815–22) and Michael Vorontsov (1822–56), further stimulated migration to the region by advancing Catherine's policies. What made Odesa important in the history of the Jews in the periphery of the empire, where most Jews resided, was that, unlike a traditional shtetl, it was the only town that had a largely middle-class character until the second half of the nineteenth century.[67]

Odesa's rapid growth in the nineteenth century placed it among the fastest-growing cities in Russia—comparable to Chicago and San Francisco in the United States. "In the period of 1800–92 alone, the population [of Odessa] increased by an astonishing 3,677 percent compared to rates of 220 percent for Moscow, [and] 323 percent for St. Petersburg."[68] During this time, Jews constituted the second-largest group of immigrants, surpassed only by Russians. In 1892, the city's total population reached 404,000—roughly 50 percent Russians (198,233), 31 percent Jews (124,511), 10 percent Ukrainians (37,925), 4 percent Poles (17,395), and 6 percent other foreigners (25,751).[69] By 1897, nearly a century after its founding, Odesa was home to 138,935 Jews, who composed a third of its total population.[70] The 1897 census also showed that 32 percent of the population spoke Yiddish and nearly 50 percent spoke Russian, while 5.6 percent of Odesans relied on Ukrainian as their native tongue.[71] For Jews, Odesa became a kind of sanctuary outside the borders of the Pale where they had rights unattainable in other parts of the country and could reside freely in any neighborhood.

While the earliest migrants to Odesa were mostly unmarried men looking for work and a new place to start their lives, later arrivals came with their families, attracted by the potential they saw in Russia's grain trade and the new Black Sea port. Odesa's status as a free port (1819–59) fueled prosperity driven by the trade in grain and other export goods, which were exempt from an otherwise heavy tax burden.[72] By 1900, "Odessa was ranked as Russia's number one port for foreign trade . . . handling the shipment of nearly all the wheat and more than half of the other grains exported from Russia."[73] The city also derived commercial success from the railway network that, beginning in the 1860s and 1870s, connected Odesa to the Caucasus and facilitated the delivery of goods across the country.[74] Unlike other areas within the Pale, where competition in trade and industry led to anti-Jewish sentiment on a political level, Odesa's ruling elite welcomed competition in trade and labor and thrived on the city's lucrative achievements. Indeed, Zipperstein suggests that one of the reasons for the city's tolerant attitudes toward Jews is that in Odesa, unlike elsewhere in Russia, Jewish policy was not framed with the implicit goal of minimizing Jewish economic competition and alleged exploitation.[75] But at the same time, there was economic rivalry among the middle-class merchants, and competition between Greeks and Jews in the grain trade was one of the factors in the pogrom of 1871.[76] While Jewish immigrants to the city ranged from laborers, tailors, wagoners, and cleaners to thieves, prostitutes, hawkers, and hooligans, many Jews were active in Odesa's commerce and valued for their commercial trading skills.[77] Starting with the export of salt, Jews came to monopolize the production of various trade stuffs including starch, refined sugar, tin goods, chemicals, and wallpaper and to dominate trade in commodities such as silk, cotton, wool, hardware, iron, and shoes.[78] By 1842, Jews owned 228 businesses in Odesa; some ten years later, 477 of the city's Jews belonged to one of the three merchant guilds.[79]

Importantly, Odesa had no Jewish quarter, nor was Jewish residence ever restricted, which "reflected the city's tolerance and testified to the wealth of relatively large numbers of Odessa's Jews."[80] Wealthier Jews settled in the center of the city; those who were poorer concentrated in Moldovanka and later Peresyp, which exposed them to the cultural practices of their Italian, Greek, Romanian, Bulgarian, Russian, and Ukrainian neighbors. Certain areas of the city where Jewish residents and their communal institutions were concentrated served as centers of Jewish life.[81] It may not be appropriate to describe Odesa as a "melting pot" as there was relatively limited interaction between ethnic groups outside the marketplace, but the city did enjoy a cosmopolitan sociality from the outset.[82]

Because Odesa was a new city, there was no established Jewish community or rooted Jewish traditions to define the place. Thus, from the beginning, it was dominated by "integrationalists, *maskilim* and a secular and Russifying Jewish elite."[83] The fact that Jews in Odesa lived far from any other major center of Judaism and were deeply engrained in the city's commercial culture, and that the city contained such varied ethnic and religious life, had a profound impact on Jews' engagement with traditional Judaism.[84] For example, Jewish traders found advantages in using the Russian language and following a looser code of religious observance.[85] Thus, the city became associated with indifference to religion. Popular Yiddish sayings arose to describe the city and its Jewish citizens, like "seven miles around Odessa burn the fires of hell" (in reference to the changing canons of tradition in Jewish education) and "to live like God in Odessa."[86] Zipperstein writes: "In an effort to adapt their social positions to their new economic standing, some Jews, a decade before the Galician immigrants (who arrived in Odesa around the 1820s), had already abandoned certain religious rituals and practices and tried to make themselves appear less distinct and foreign to the non-Jews."[87]

The Jews from Brody and elsewhere in Galicia (then in Habsburg, Austria, and now western Ukraine) had come to dominate the grain trade, becoming the wealthiest of Odesa's Jewry. They were more liberal and progressive in their religious observance than most, and by taking a leading role in the functions of middlemen, factory owners, managers, and agents, they worked closely with the Greek and Italian merchants who still controlled most of the grain export in the 1830s.[88] For the Brody Jews, the terminology of the German-based eighteenth-century Jewish enlightenment movement Haskalah was pervasive and acceptable. Although they were mostly driven by economic and social opportunities rather than ideas of enlightenment, like other *maskilim*, they were eager to connect Odesa's Jewish population with the greater world they inhabited, without necessarily abandoning their Jewish identity. As early as 1826, immigrants from Galicia had opened a modern Jewish school, the first of its kind in all of Russia, to provide education in both secular and Jewish subjects.[89] Fifteen years later, Odesa became home to one of the first major modern synagogues in the Russian Empire, organized by Jews who officially declared themselves as "enlightened."[90] The Florentine Gothic building of the Brody Synagogue proposed by the Milan-trained architect Francesco Morandi was built between 1863 and 1868 and became famous for its men's and boys' choir and the organs installed in 1909 above the Torah ark. Seats were sold to members of the congregation.

According to local lore, even non-Jewish Odesans attended services here, which were conducted by German-born Rabbi Simeon Leon Schwabacher, Odesa's official rabbi from 1860 to 1888. Worshippers were drawn by the musical prayers conducted on Shabbat and on Jewish holidays. By the 1850s, "Haskalah ideas had expanded beyond the confines of *maskilim* circles and had touched the lives of many other Jews in the city."[91] In Odesa, Jews could enjoy a cultural life enriched by artistic performances from around the world. "Jews flocked to the opera house and were said to nearly monopolize its seats, usually those in the hall's least expensive sections."[92] By the 1860s, many sat in the more expensive stalls and "even Jews with side curls attended."[93] The love of music and theater was so notable that some characterized Odesa as "the musical city of the empire."[94] Describing the "cosmopolitan soundscapes of Odesa" in the early 1900s, musicologist Anat Rubinstein notes, "the city's musical soundscape was an amalgam of Russian, Jewish, and Ukrainian musical genres and foreign influences that were brought in from Italy, Greece, and other countries."[95]

Indeed, because of its coastal location, migration, trade, and other activities associated with the port, Odesa was more open to wider cultural developments than the rest of the Pale of Settlement. Throughout its history, the city nurtured numerous violinists who would become world famous, including Mischa Elman and David Oistrakh. Even in the economic decline of the empire's later years, Odesa became associated with music (classical and popular, especially

Figure 1.1. Brodskaya (Brody) Synagogue, later used to house city archives and officially given to the Chabad Lubavitch congregation by the city council in 2016. Photo by author.

jazz), film, theater (especially comedy), and, until the consolidation of Stalinism in the early 1930s, journalism and fiction.[96]

Much of the socializing in early nineteenth-century Odesa took place in cafés and coffeehouses with "graceful verandas or tables simply placed under plantains and acacias on shady, picturesque streets." Because of its "similarities with the French capital, . . . Odesits, typical of their tendency towards exaggeration, liked to call their city 'Little Paris.'"[97] And Odesa continued to present enormous economic opportunities for Jews and others.[98] The city's Jews quickly earned the reputation, both within and beyond the city, as an increasingly assimilated, modern, Europeanized, and Russified Jewish community whose range of institutions and tenor of communal life were self-consciously becoming more and more modernized and enlightened.[99]

Jewish acculturation to Odesa's progressive atmosphere only continued in the second half of the nineteenth century. Jews there benefited from the Reform schooling introduced by the *maskilim* but also attended non-Jewish institutions more often, and some received their education abroad. Thus, by midcentury, Zipperstein observes,

ninety percent of the city's Jewish-owned shops were . . . open on the
Sabbath; Jews carried money on Saturdays [and] chatted in cafes, and when
rushing off to morning prayer, put out their still-smoldering cigarettes on
the synagogue's outer walls. Neither fathers nor sons went to synagogue
regularly; religious observance in general was erratic, and the same individual might fast on a minor holy day and then desecrate the Sabbath. . . . Even
in the 1830s pious Jews were spotted in the local opera house, despite the
religious prohibition against listening to women sing, and large numbers of
Jewish children were in attendance at the modern Jewish school . . . despite
widespread Russian Jewish fear of secular education. By the 1850s, prayer
in the major synagogue was designed along self-consciously *maskilim* and
"Germanic" lines.[100]

Odesa's cultural and economic conditions provided grounds for a uniquely
Odesan way of being Jewish. In 1886, every third student at Odesa University
and more than 40 percent of all medical and law students were Jewish.[101] By
1890, Jews made up 68 percent of all apprentice lawyers on the Odesa judicial
circuit.[102] There were also many Jews in medicine (30 percent), engineering
(30 percent), and politics (nearly 50 percent of local Duma representatives).[103]
    Culturally, in addition to the arts, there were literary societies, libraries, and
publishing houses.[104] The city was the birthplace of a modern Jewish press in
Russian, Yiddish, and Hebrew.[105] In the 1860s, it was the main hub for Jewish
periodical publications. Famous journals *Razsvet* (Dawn), *Sion* (Zion), *and
Den'* (Day) appeared in Russian; *Ha-Melits* (The Advocate) and *Kol mevaser*
(The Herald) were published in Hebrew; and Yiddish and *maskilic* books were
promoted widely by local publishers. This climate attracted prominent Jewish
writers who produced work in Hebrew, French, and Russian, among other
languages.[106] Recent studies bring our attention to the idea of "Ukrainian
Odesa" in literature of Jewish and non-Jewish writers.[107] As was the case in
Saint Petersburg, Odesa's Society for the Promotion of Enlightenment (the
second-largest branch in the country) was active in spreading Russian language, culture, literature, and learning among Jews and "providing substantial
ideological buttressing."[108]
    In many accounts, we can see the connection between emancipation and
Russification. One Odesa-based newspaper declared in the 1870s, "If one can
speak of a center of the Jewish intelligentsia where self-emancipation is becoming a reality, this without doubt is Odessa."[109] Among the prominent Odesa
figures were the author and playwright Sholem Aleichem (Solomon Naumòv-
ich Rabinovitch); writer Mordekhai Ben-Ami (Mark Rabinovitch); one of the

founders of modern Yiddish and Hebrew literature, Mendele Mocher-Sforim (Sholom Abramovitch); the physician, political activist, author of the famous pamphlet "Autoemancipation," and head of the Odessa Committee (officially known as the Society for the Support of Jewish Farmers and Artisans in Syria and Palestine) Leon Pinsker; philosopher and publicist Ahad Ha'am; the Yiddish poet Haim-Nahman Bialik; the writer, editor, and publisher Yehoshua Hana Rawnitzki (pseudonym Eldad); and Talmudic scholar and Hebrew author Rav Tsa'ir (Rabbi Chaim Tchernowitz), who, in the early 1900s, founded his own yeshiva, which attracted a number of the city's Jewish cultural luminaries. Many of these intellectuals used Russian more than Yiddish or Hebrew, preferring its practical benefits and prestige. Of those who "converted to the Pushkin faith," Slezkine writes, "young Jews were not just learning Russian the same way they were learning Hebrew: they were learning Russian in order to replace Hebrew, as well as Yiddish, for good. Like German, Polish, or Hungarian in other high-culture areas, Russian had become the Hebrew of the secular world. . . . If the Russian world stood for speech, knowledge, freedom, and light, then the Jewish world represented silence, ignorance, bondage, and darkness."[110]

Polonsky explains that many young Jewish gymnasium and university students were indeed attracted to the Russian intelligentsia and embraced their values by rejecting the Jewish backwardness and provinciality they saw in their own families. He gives the example of the poet Osip Mandelstam, who believed that his mother saved him from "Judean chaos" and the "talmudic thicket" through her love of Pushkin.[111] However, this use of Russian should not be exaggerated. The Jewish intelligentsia of the time spoke many languages, including Polish and German, and some still communicated in Yiddish.[112] In the early twentieth century (1911–12), only about 35 percent of Jewish students claimed that Russian was their primary language, and more than 40 percent claimed a good knowledge of Hebrew. Nor did the use of other languages mean that Jews drifted away from their Jewish identity or completely deviated from Jewish topics. Only 16 percent said they had no interest in Jewish matters.[113]

In a similar vein, not all Jewish residents were analyzing this process of modernization in ideological terms. Many of the city's Jews took advantage of new trends, adopting them into their pattern of living for practical reasons. But even if Odesa was not a center of traditional religious practice—like Vilna or Lviv—most Jews practiced Judaism.[114] Even those at the outer edge of assimilation still partook in Jewish practices, at least nominally.

By the beginning of the twentieth century, the city was home to some seventy synagogues and prayer houses, each requiring the presence of at least ten men for daily prayer. Most of the synagogues occupied small rented rooms or spaces donated by city landlords, but ten of them were in specially built structures.[115] Among the more famous congregations were the communities of the large Orthodox synagogue Beit Hakneset Hagadol (established in 1795–96) and the Brody Synagogue, the first choir synagogue in Russia (1840). Generally, Odesa's prayer houses were subdivided by professions, and congregants adjusted their working hours for observance.

In the early nineteenth century, Odesa "was the most 'un-Jewish' of Jewish cities from the traditional point of view, and the most 'Jewish' from the perspective of non-traditional Jewish life and attitudes."[116] Traveling by train through Poland and Galicia in 1898, Vladimir Jabotinsky, a writer and Zionist activist, writes in his journal, "I had not seen either the side-curls or the kapota, nor such wretched poverty. Nor had I seen gray bearded, old, and respected Jews, taking off their hats when they spoke to the gentile 'squire' in the street."[117] Unlike in other centers of Jewish life in the Pale, in Odesa "the less traditional Jews, *maskilim* and acculturated Jews were the standard bearers of their community."[118] Women's participation in Jewish education was also three times as high in the southwest of the empire, mostly because of the role of Odesa.

While some distinguished Hasidim, like the tzaddik (righteous religious leader) Dovid Twersky, were joyfully welcomed when visiting the city, "Hasidic wonderworkers were isolated and scorned, approached only by the poorest, most unfortunate women; and so they viewed the city as the source of 'neither gold nor fame,' indeed as an 'empire of hell.'"[119] According to Osip Rabinovich, an Odesan notary, journalist, and editor of the Russian-language Jewish newspaper *Razsvet* (Dawn), writing in the 1860s, "Hasidism perhaps still flourished in tiny isolated townlets, but not in large cities like Odessa. All of Jewish Odessa . . . had shown an unmistakable willingness to move forward with the times."[120] Indeed, the Brody Synagogue had become "the model for Jewish prayer in the city, and the older Beit Knesset Ha-Gadol was transformed in its image."[121]

Odesa continued to grow economically throughout the nineteenth century, with the abolition of serfdom and commercialization of agriculture.[122] Jews came to control 70 percent of the grain export, and Jewish brokerages were handling more than half of the city's total export. At the dawn of the twentieth century, Odesa's 160,000 Jews constituted more than 30 percent of the city's 511,000 inhabitants, forming an integral part of its economy and society. The economic opportunities were often illusionary for the many impoverished Jews, and of course the city had a great deal of Jewish poverty.[123] At the turn of the twentieth century, one-third of the city's Jews signed up for Passover relief (food distribution organized by Jewish philanthropic organizations around the Passover holiday). Jews were present in all spheres of society, including the underworld. For an analysis of ethnic markers in Odesa's crime, see an important article by

Gerasimov.[124] They owned many of the brothels in Odesa.[125] Jews were also involved in smuggling illegal and radical literature, and many Jewish students were prominent in Odesa's populist circles at the end of the nineteenth century.

In the late 1800s, Odesa had become the fourth-largest city in the Russian Empire (after Saint Petersburg, Moscow, and Warsaw), but it had started to decline in production and trade.[126] Political pressures were also mounting. The infamous and reactionary May Laws (also known as the Temporary or Ignat'ev Laws of 1882) were implemented to limit Jewish activity and economic advancement and guarantee that Jews could "no longer exploit non-Jewish neighbors."[127] These laws were also a way to appease Russians who might turn to revolutionary activity. Jews could no longer reside in villages, and they were forbidden from purchasing land outside the towns—and from working on Sundays, which hindered their economic advantage over Christians.[128] These laws weren't fully implemented in Odesa, and Jews from the countryside within the Pale continued to migrate to the Black Sea area.[129] Although Jews departed from their traditions to assimilate into Odesa's society, Jews and gentiles did not mix socially.[130] Jabotinsky noted that while growing up in the 1880s and 1890s, he didn't have a single close gentile friend, but he would reminisce poetically about the joyous days in a lighthearted city by the sea where inhabitants "babbled in a dozen languages."[131]

Tragically, anti-Jewish sentiment also grew in nineteenth century Odesa and the city experienced anti-Jewish pogroms and riots in 1821, 1849, 1859, 1871, 1881, and 1905 (which greatly influenced the development of the Jewish nationalist movement in the city as well as Jewish migration from the city and the empire).[132] These upheavals mainly resulted from a growing commercial rivalry and animosity between Greeks, who had previously dominated the grain trade, and the Jews who were taking over important positions in the industry.[133] But as Humphrey explains, "sometimes, it was wealth, or privilege or perceived economic advantage that was attacked, rather than 'Jews' as such."[134] However, the pogrom that swept through the city in the context of the Russian Revolution of 1905 was of a different order: some 400 Jews (and 100 non-Jews) were killed; approximately 300 people, mostly Jews, were injured; and more than 1,600 Jewish houses, apartments, and stores were damaged.[135] At that time, no other city in the Russian Empire experienced a pogrom comparable in destruction and violence.[136] Nearly 50,000 Jews left the city.[137] In this way, Odesa fit a predictable pattern of the empire more generally. The worsening situation of the Jews and the radicalization of the larger Russian society provoked a large-scale emigration— between 1880 and 1924, more than 2 million Jews fled the Russian Empire to Palestine, Argentina, and South Africa, but mostly to the United States.[138]

While there was an outflow of Russia's Jews from the rest of the country, Odesa recovered the post-1905 population losses, and its Jewish population continued to grow well into the twentieth century. Prior to the 1917 revolution, the city became home to a great many revolutionary and political organizations, turning it into one of the most active centers of Zionist activity in the empire. It was after the 1881 pogrom that Leon Pinsker wrote his famous pamphlet "Auto-emancipation," arguing that "anti-Semitism was a disease endemic to Europe" and urging Jews to immigrate to Zion.[139] Pinsker's call was taken up by other Odesan activists, including Jabotinsky, whose "revisionist Zionism" was committed to a Jewish homeland on both banks of the Jordan River (not in Uganda, as others proposed).[140] Many Zionist efforts were initiated by the Palestine Committee founded in Odesa in the 1880s, which worked to relocate Jews from the Russian Empire to the territories of what eventually became the State of Israel. In the early 1900s, Odesa was commonly known as the Gateway to Zion for the frequent voyages made from its port to Jaffa, including the famous 1919 crossing of the SS *Ruslan*, which arrived in Jaffa carrying 617 Jews from Russia and was considered the beginning of the third aliyah (Jewish migration to Israel). Until 1927, ships conveyed many Jews from all over Russia to Palestine.[141]

Between 1917 and 1921, when the Soviet regime came to power, the city changed hands nine times and suffered a major outflow of its population.[142] These turbulent conditions presented Ukraine with the rare opportunity to declare independence, which lasted from 1918 to 1921, when the three-way civil war between the Whites, the Reds, and the different national forces ended with the consolidation of Soviet power in much of the territory of the former Russian Empire, including Ukraine.[143] In the short-lived independent Ukrainian state, Jews were granted full national-cultural autonomy and allowed to establish their own houses of education and receive social benefits from the government, which issued its currency (the *karbovanets*) with a Yiddish inscription on the banknote as a way to win Jewish support in its struggle for independence.[144] While the Russian civil war brought heightened anti-Jewish violence elsewhere, Odesa largely escaped that fate.

Soviet Years

The 1917 revolution and the Soviet consolidation of power introduced freedom of speech, press, and assembly for all citizens, and Jews received an array of political and civil rights. Integration was encouraged by the abolition of all previous czarist restrictions, and Jews experienced upward mobility as a result of full-fledged citizenship.[145] Jews constituted part of the Soviet ruling elite and became part of the Russian-speaking intelligentsia. They were no longer defined as a religious minority but as one of many Soviet nationalities. Some Jews eagerly embraced the idea of a classless society. The Soviet regime allowed them to participate in the socialist society without prior discrimination and quotas. This sense of equality brought many Jews eager for mobility to the front lines of Communist Party activity.

In the aftermath of the WWI, Soviet Jewry made up the third-largest Jewish community in the world—in 1926, more than 2.6 million claimed Jewish nationality. That number rose to over 3 million by 1939, and historians estimate that in both years of the census, an additional 300,000 Jews claimed another nationality.[146] The 1926 census shows that Odesa's population at the time was 39 percent Russian, 36.7 percent Jewish, and 17.6 percent Ukrainian.[147]

In the interwar period, Soviet Jews officially had full equality, and intermarriage, which had previously required conversion, became more frequent. By 1936, approximately 42 percent of Jewish marriages in the Russian Federation, 15 percent in Ukraine, and almost 13 percent in Belarus were exogamous.[148] But while there was integration in the Soviet order, independent Jewish political organizations outside the Communist Party were banned, and religious Jews and their institutions were stripped of any meaningful way to contribute to Jewish life. In Odesa, there were campaigns against Jewish schools, synagogues, and other religious and cultural organizations.[149] This is not to say that state policy toward Jews was consistent, nor that all Jews accommodated themselves to the Soviet project. Indeed, as policies vacillated and were sometimes contradictory, many Jews found other ways to express their Jewishness.[150] All Soviet men and women were making such accommodations in some way: "Living in socialism according to the perceived rules made for its share of surprises . . . new categories of thinking suddenly appeared, old ones were modified; nothing stood still."[151]

As historian of East European Jewry Elisa Bempòrad points out, the transformation of core Jewish life occurred at a slower pace in historically Jewish centers in the Pale than it did in the Russian interior.[152] This was certainly true for Odesa, a city on the edge of the state. Even as organized Jewish life was closing under pressure from the government, members of Odesa's large Jewish population, approximately 180,000 to 200,000 in the interwar years, were still making their mark on city life, first and foremost on the Odesan language, regarded as a mixture of Ukrainian, Russian, and Yiddish. The city's Jewish density fostered in its Jewish residents self-confidence and comfort about their Jewish identity, an atmosphere shared by other towns and cities with a similar demographic, like Minsk, Gomel (Homel), Berdichev, Zhitomir, and Vinnitsa, where Jews accounted for more than 30 percent of the population.[153]

Soviet policy toward the Jews initially focused on their assimilation into the new socialist world. Lenin's early policies sought to integrate Jews into society by supporting a specifically socialist Jewish identity; this integration effort included the promotion of Yiddish language and culture and the creation of the *evsektsiia*, the Jewish section of the Communist Party.[154] However, Stalin's

Great Turn of 1929–32 was marked by an intensification of terror, often directed at the Jews.[155] Stalinist pressure banned religious practice, closed religious institutions, and repressed Zionist activity and Hebrew education. Jews became persecuted as members of the intelligentsia and as "rootless cosmopolitans." They were among the many Soviet citizens (estimated between 600,000 and 2 million) who lost their lives in Stalin's terror campaign of the late 1930s. But in the midst of the extraordinary purges, Bemporad reminds us, ordinary life continued for Jews in the Soviet Union; even in the years of Stalin's atrocities, Jewish identity was an evolving project, at once political, social, and cultural.[156]

If the Jews in the greater Soviet Union "seemed much more Soviet than the rest of the Soviet Union," the reintroduction of internal passports in 1932 concentrated the nature of the challenge: how to assimilate culturally while legally categorized as alien or "other."[157] Being legally defined as a Jew, as inscribed in one's passport under the heading "nationality," exposed Jews to quotas, limitations, and other official and unofficial tactics of discrimination and antisemitism. Political scientist Volodymyr Kulyk notes that "the category of 'nationality,' which was introduced during the 1920s policy of 'indigenization' with the aim of establishing ethnicity that may not have been congruent with current language practice as a result of tsarist Russification, later came to be reclassified as primordial and, therefore, unchangeable, to be determined by the nationality of one's parents (unless they had different nationalities)."[158] As a result, Jewish citizens took various routes to obscure their backgrounds or to highlight their assimilation and thereby avoid conflict: many Jews changed their names; in mixed families, children were registered according to the nationality of the non-Jewish parent; and some families simply never revealed that they were Jewish.[159] A number of Jews I met in Odesa in the mid-2000s had only recently learned of their Jewish lineage. It is in this context that Bemporad emphasizes that many Jews "attempted to walk a fine line between accepted Soviet behavior and social norms and expressions of Jewish particularity."[160]

In the absence of a more traditional basis in religion, Soviet Jews had their own markers of identity, linked to Russian culture and Soviet reality and later constrained by Stalin's terror. But many Jews also embraced the Soviet ethnic Jewish identity and regarded themselves as Soviet citizens beyond all.

World War II and the Odesa Massacre

In June 1941, Germany invaded the USSR. The "Great Patriotic War," as the eastern front in World War II became known in Russia, took the lives of 27 million Soviet citizens and left vast numbers permanently maimed. An estimated 1.4 million Jews perished among the 5.5 million (or by some accounts 7 million)

killed as a result of Nazi policies in the territories that made up Ukraine (including Transcarpathia and Crimea). Nearly 350,000 were evacuated out of
Odesa by the Soviets.[161] By some estimates, 80,000 to 90,000 Jews remained
in the city when it was besieged by Romanian troops, allies of Nazi Germany,
in August 1941.[162] The attack lasted seventy-three days. Ion Antonescu (prime
minister of Romania at the time) wrote, "The War in general, and the battles in
Odessa in particular, proved beyond the shadow of a doubt that *the Jew is the
devil* . . . hence our enormous casualties. Without the Jewish commissars, we
would have been in Odessa long ago."[163]

When Odesa finally fell to the Romanian troops on October 16, 1941, it was
declared the capital of Transnistria. Romanian officials ordered all Jews to
present themselves for official registration.[164] Between three thousand and four
thousand Jews were taken directly to jail, where most were tortured, and then
driven to the seaside and shot.[165] After the retreating Soviet armies bombed the
headquarters of the Tenth Romanian Division, killing General Ion Glogojanu
on October 22, 1941, the mass killings of Jews intensified. "I have taken steps to
hang Jews and Communists in the public square in Odessa," reported General
Constantin Trestioreanu, Glogojanu's successor.[166] (An explosion in Kyiv a few
weeks earlier had resulted in thirty-three thousand Jews being shot by German
SS and Ukrainian guards in the ravine at Babyn Yar.)[167]

The Romanian forces killed 15,000 to 20,000 Jews in Odesa in reprisal, most of
them shot or hanged in the streets of the city.[168] Hundreds of dead bodies were
left hanging along Aleksandrovsky Prospect, one of Odesa's central streets.[169]
Romanian officials "ordered the execution of the remaining hostages"; "close to
19,000 Jews were gathered into four barracks on the outskirts of Odessa and then
shot or burned alive."[170] Thousands of other Jews were crammed into jails, where
many died in horrific circumstances. The rest of Odesa's Jewish residents were
ordered into Slobodka, the newly created ghetto on the outskirts of town.[171] The
Romanians didn't create extermination facilities in the region, but they did create an array of camps and ghettos where Odesa's Jews and many non-Jews and
Roma from Bessarabia and Transnistria were sent.[172]

Some non-Jewish Odesans risked their lives to hide Jews in their homes or
help them escape the city with forged documents.[173] But some members of the
local police and ethnic German volunteers who formed their own SS police
collaborated with the Romanian regime, helping the occupiers in their execution of Jews and others.[174] When Romanian officials issued an order that "those
guilty of hiding Jews would be put to death," most of Odesa's remaining Jews
were forced into the ghetto—for the first time in history, restricted from living
in any other parts of the city.[175] In the winter of 1942, tens of thousands were
deported to the Berezovka region in Transnistria, specifically to three camps:

Bogdanovka, Akhmetchetka, and Domanevka. The evacuation began on foot and in horse-drawn carts in below-freezing temperatures. Those who tried to escape or who fell from exhaustion, hunger, or illness were shot on the spot; as a result, bodies lined the streets.[176] In Bogdanovka, all Jews were shot by Romanian and Ukrainian police. Thousands of Jews were shot at Akhmetchetka and Domanevka, and many died en route or during imprisonment from typhus or starvation as a result of neglect.[177] Those who survived were forced into slave labor by an official decree passed in December 1943 by Transnistria officials, which specified that all Jews between the ages of twelve and sixty had to work in specific jobs and that no work assignments (with the exception of special permission) were to be made in the city of Odesa.[178]

Charles King points out that killing Jews was not the primary goal of the Romanian troops as they headed east, but "being a Jew became a surrogate for being an enemy of the state" and "the lines between Communist, Jew, partisan, refugee, and simple inconvenience were hazy and often nonexistent."[179] Sometimes Jewishness depended on blood, and other times, it depended on faith. Despite the initial goals of Romanians' collaboration with the Nazis in the region, the execution of Jews became a plan and a reality. During the Romanian occupation from October 1941 to April 1944, an estimated 120,000 to 150,000 Jews perished in Odesa and in the region's death camps.[180] In only four days, 48,000 Jews were murdered in the Bogdanovka camp, "a record unsurpassed . . . even by the death factories of Majdanek or Auschwitz."[181] In Akhmetchetka, 4,000 captives died of hunger. Most of the 18,000 Jews in Domanevka were also exterminated.[182]

From the time of the Romanian invasion in October 1941 to the day of the city's liberation in April 1944, "the beautiful city of Odessa was transformed into a nightmare of terror, blood and pain."[183] Eighty percent of the Jews who had remained in Odesa were annihilated.[184] One Odesan later wrote, "The Jews who died in the first days of the occupation were the fortunate ones."[185] In the greater Odesa region, the prewar Jewish population was reduced by 40 percent,[186] and in total, Transnistria (the name given by the Antonescu regime to the territory of Ukraine between the Dniestr and the Southern Buh rivers occupied by Romanian troops) became the graveyard of some 250,000 Jews and 12,000 Roma, with many of the Jewish victims having been deported from Bukovina and Bessarabia, and many of the Roma victims coming from Romania proper.[187]

Postwar Odesa

After the war, many surviving Jewish Odesans remained silent about their experiences, fearing that their survival would be interpreted as evidence of collaboration with the Germans or Romanians. Indeed, many Odesans had denounced others at the onset of the Romanian invasion. What would become known as the Holocaust, as I discuss in chapter 5, was overshadowed by the dominant narrative of Soviet suffering under Nazi brutality. For example, a monument erected not far from Odesa to commemorate the Jews who perished in the area was never unveiled, on the grounds that "Holocaust memorials must not honor Jews as such, but only Soviet citizens in general."[188] In this way Jewish tragedies were downplayed, as were Jewish achievements, and mostly left unmentioned in official Soviet accounts of the war.[189]

Odesa's population after the war rose with those returning from the front or from evacuation; some moved to the city on work placement orders or seeking to escape an even more miserable existence elsewhere. Legally and illegally, many newcomers occupied the houses of those who never returned. For Jews, life in postwar Odesa was undoubtedly difficult, although it's a matter of debate whether they suffered the same level of persecution as Jews experienced in Moscow. Jews in Russia's capital, for instance, were targeted in Stalin's purges in the late 1940s and early 1950s against "cosmopolitan" intelligentsia as well as in the so-called Doctors' Plot, when Jewish doctors were arrested and charged with plotting the murder of party leaders.[190] Scholars have speculated about the planned deportations of Jews organized by Stalin in 1953, but those allegations remain undocumented. As author Joseph Rubenstein argues in his book *The Last Days of Stalin*, it's impossible to reach a definitive conclusion about Stalin's ultimate plans, and yet it's obvious that the antisemitic campaign was gathering momentum in the press and the mood of the population.[191] Indeed, at the time of the Doctors' Plot, two hundred Jewish students were summarily expelled from Odesa University.[192]

Following Stalin's death in 1953, many of the charges accusing Jews and others of acting against the state were dropped, but the overall climate of censorship remained in place, as did the anti-Jewish quotas. The official Soviet policy toward Jews was "characterized as an attitude of silence" and "mild discrimination," which had, to some extent, become normalized.[193] Under Nikita Khrushchev and Leonid Brezhnev, Jews remained without much upward mobility, as compared to the prewar era.[194] They became experts in the "rules of the game," including rules that were unspoken yet no less real.[195] For example, Elena, whose story appears in the next chapter, achieved higher education and a career of her choice by using a Ukrainian name to mask her Jewish lineage. Others spoke of dealing with the system through bribery.[196] For Soviet citizens, "ordinary actions undertaken as part of daily life had the effect of realigning, even if only slightly, what might be called the landscape of possibility."[197]

Although antisemitism was undeniably part of their experience, for many Jews it was simply accepted as a facet of everyday life and, in effect, normalized.[198] A few middle-aged Jews like Marina, whom we meet in chapter 7, claimed that they never experienced discrimination at all; in their view, this was due to Odesa being a "Jewish city." Others declared that discrimination made them work harder and enhanced the sense of survival necessary in many life circumstances.

Despite the changes in policy toward Jews that took place under Stalin's successors, Soviet Yiddish culture never recovered its prewar vibrancy, partly because by the late 1950s, barely 20 percent of Soviet Jews declared Yiddish as their mother tongue.[199] But one must not assume that the abandonment of Yiddish for Russian led to a disappearance of Jewish culture. As historian Jarrod Tanny demonstrates, the city's myth has always had a very strong influence on the image of Odesa as a "Jewish city": "Yiddish idioms and inflections pervaded the Russian spoken in Odessa, and the writers, musicians, journalists, and comedians from the city infused their work with Jewish characters, humor, and folkloric motifs."[200] Odesa's history illustrates a Jewish culture surviving and growing after the transition to Russian language had taken place, although it was severely damaged in Stalin's anticosmopolitan campaign.[201]

Emigration became possible for Odesan Jews in the 1970s and again in the late 1980s and early 1990s. Some emigrants were fleeing discrimination, but many were simply looking for a better life abroad. Some of the ex-Soviet Jewish immigrants I met in the United States and Israel during my fieldwork and on other occasions drew a distinction between the role of the state's socialist ideals and the ordinary lives of its citizens. Similarly, in literary scholar Maurice Friedberg's interviews of former residents of Odesa who left the city in the 1970s, most of his interlocutors "spoke of their native town with surprising warmth, affection, and considerable nostalgia."[202]

Such nostalgia can be explained by the fact that Jews in Odesa and elsewhere were unlikely to analyze their lives solely through the lens of being Jewish and more likely to do so by examining the full array of positions they held in both their personal and professional lives. For instance, a person's career served as a significant marker of identity during Soviet times: your work history was so integral that it appeared in almost any official document.[203] On numerous occasions, elderly Jews I was interviewing would proudly pull out their work history books to tell me of their life achievements.

Conclusion

It's impossible to explore questions of identity without encountering invocations of the past. A person's claim to being a *korenoi Odesit* (native of Odesa) or a *nastoyashi Odesit* (real Odesan) is strongly bound up with that individual's connection to Odesa's history and geographic location. The term *korenoi* actually means "rooted" in Russian. Locals often used the term "real *Odesit*" to compliment long-term visitors and nonnative residents who exhibit the qualities of an Odesan attitude to life, who know and appreciate the city's social and historical settings, and who enjoy the Odesan language, cuisine, and even humor. After I'd been in Odesa for a while, my friends sensed my attachment to the city in the way I used Odesan expressions or bargained for goods as the locals do. Half-jokingly, they'd call me "a real *Odesitka*."

Two decades after the dissolution of the Soviet Union, Odesa is no longer Soviet; it is problematically Russian, barely Jewish, and increasingly Ukrainian. But this kaleidoscopic recombining of Odesa's different histories has always been part of the city's life. These historical entanglements are in large part what are traced as the rest of the book unfolds and show how the process of the social, economic, and political transformations witnessed in Odesa and the larger Ukrainian nation—including historical narratives that are often edited to justify political action—play out there. As an elderly couple I knew in Odesa would say, the city's Orthodox rabbis and Ukrainian politicians both "recast the story of the city" to paint it in colors that served their purpose. Similar to the political elites of newly independent states like Ukraine, who "generate a sense of common territoriality and shared history in order to consolidate political communities," Odesa's religious leaders were engaged in struggles of community formation and contested identity.[204] For Odesa's Jewish intelligentsia, being part of their city's historical narrative and knowing its history helped them define their particularities and separate themselves from others. This was evident in the ways in which local religious Jews distinguished themselves from the foreign religious emissaries who occupied the high ranks of Jewish organized life but weren't necessarily recognized as leaders. These newly observant Jews felt that although the foreign emissaries knew more about how to be a "proper Jew," they knew much less about the city's own Jewish history, and thus couldn't truly represent their community.

During my time in Odesa, I saw history being disputed, defended, invented, and manipulated in conversations and in cultural displays presented at different times and for different audiences. The history this chapter recounts is always part of whatever new story is being told. A sense of history and a sense of place are vital for our understanding of what was lost, what is revisited, and what is being re-created in Odesa, as it is elsewhere in the world.[205]

2

~~~

Remembering the Past and Making Sense of the Present

Narratives of Elderly Jews

The story of older Soviet-era Jews has most often been told from the perspective of the Jewish activists, dissidents, and refuseniks who garnered attention in the West. This chapter, in contrast, focuses on Odesa's oldest generation so as to better trace the multiple changes in familial practices, senses of identity, and social orientations from the prerevolutionary time to today. To this end, it presents the lives and family histories of four elderly individuals—Olga, Viktor, Elena, and Nina—as they remember their pasts and their family histories and make sense of the present they were witnessing in Odesa. Such articulations of memory come with their challenges.[1] Still, oral histories have been instructive for understanding life in societies where public expression and personal opinion were suppressed—and, in particular, for accessing "Soviet subjectivity," "post-Soviet subjectivity," and "selfhood."[2]

Anthropologists studying the everyday life of societies have used oral histories to produce "thick descriptions" of ordinary experiences as well as major events such as the Holocaust "from below."[3] Using the "oral memoirs" method defined by oral historian David Dunaway, which involves having the subject tell his or her story as the author adds explanations and footnotes, I approach the life histories presented herein as faithful representations of Soviet experiences that, taken together, portray part of the structure and workings of society.[4] Similar to other scholars using oral history, I see value in letting people speak for themselves, as we try to understand the more nuanced, sensitive, layered, and contradictory historical experiences.[5]

I used the "flexible interview approach" outlined by oral historian Alessandro Portelli and embedded in Grounded Theory, where questions arise dialectically from the answers in what Portelli calls "thick dialogue."[6] Whenever it was possible, I recorded the stories and transcribed them afterward, but at times,

I had to jot down notes by hand. However, there were also moments during unrecorded interviews when I wanted to be fully present for my interviewee, paying attention to their words, body language, velocity of speech, and the silences in the room, so I just listened. I later wrote up these conversations from memory, verifying any gaps on my next visit. Because different environments allow for different levels of intimacy, I conducted interviews at the interviewees' homes, but I also included informal conversations that arose while walking on the street, tending to daily errands, going to the market, and talking around the kitchen table. At these times, my interlocutors felt more comfortable sharing details of their stories that would have been obstructed by a recording device and the formality of an interview.

My goal in seeking out my interlocutors' narratives was to understand the events, stories, and people that shaped their Jewish identity as they were being raised in Soviet Odesa. I wondered how they related to the socialist state apparatus, values, and conditions of everyday life in that specific urban context and how they judged post-Soviet transitions on both a sociopolitical and an economic level—specifically, the process of a Jewish and religious revival in contemporary Ukraine. The narratives that follow are indeed infused with the social dynamics that emerge from old courtyards and houses, family graves and state documents, and even climate and soil—the textures of everyday life in the city through which their Jewishness, with varying intensities, passed privately through generations or openly across borders. In this way, they offer a deeper understanding of Jewish life in the Soviet Union, providing counterpoints to what some scholars have called a "negative Jewish identity" determined by state-sanctioned discrimination and antisemitism.[7] The stories, similar to the interviews of shtetl survivors in Vinnytsya collected by historian Jeffrey Veidlinger and his research team, help us to "move away from stereotypes and generalities in order to understand in greater detail the specifics of daily life and social interactions in specific locales."[8]

Olga, Viktor, Elena, and Nina regarded themselves as secular members of the Russian-speaking intelligentsia, educated and raised in the "Soviet house of culture."[9] In this way, they sound similar to the Russian-speaking Jews interviewed by sociologists Edna Lomsky-Feder and Tamar Rapoport in Israel, for whom the intersection of language, sensibility, and social status was central to their self-identity as Jews from the former Soviet Union.[10] They are individuals, but they were also members of a collective; thus, when their stories are triangulated with other stories and other sources, we build a more in-depth picture of that Jewish intelligentsia. The stories in this chapter focus neither on those who defied the Soviet system and wanted to leave nor on those who felt completely assimilated, and indeed, scholars have criticized such images of the Soviet Jew as a "dissident intellectual" and of an "assimilated Soviet Jewish intelligentsia."[11] Rather, my interviewees thought of themselves as Jews, always, taking different paths to the reality of a Soviet framework.

I am not suggesting that their stories represented Odesa's intelligentsia as a whole or the elderly Jewish population holistically. As we know from the previous chapter, not all Jews were members of the intelligentsia. Steven Zipperstein notes that Jewish intellectuals were only marginally shaping the city's Jewish story in the early nineteenth century, but in Soviet Odesa, Jews did represent a high percentage of the city's white-collar workers and cultural elite.[12] I focused on this group for several reasons. First, it has been well documented that Jews in the Soviet Union made up a large percentage of the Russian-speaking intelligentsia, and although we know that Odesa's Jewry represented different strata of society, many of the elderly Jews I met self-identified as intelligentsia. Second, concentrating on this particular group of Soviet-born Jewry helps the reader understand where skepticism and critique of religiosity comes from and highlights a Jewish identity linked to the Russian literary and cultural world. Similar to the elderly Jewish woman Vera Chmeleva, the protagonist of the Regina Maryanovska-Davidzon film *Forgotten Fall*, the Odesan Jews who shared their oral histories also reveal a post-Soviet reality of a generation whose ideals have lost their importance. They too are forgotten by the state and are skeptical of political, economic, and religious reforms.

I was introduced to my oldest informants in 2006 by my friend Margarita, an energetic octogenarian philosophy professor. She insisted that I meet her dear friends as soon as possible because they were members of a now-dwindling social stratum, the type of Jewish Odesans I wouldn't just "meet on the street." Margarita felt that the days of that "Odessan Jewish intelligentsia" were numbered due to emigration, post-Soviet changes in the city, and the birth of what she called a "new type of Jew" in Odesa. When I questioned her on what made new Jews "new," besides their age, she replied that her older Jewish friends didn't feel the need to prove they were Jewish or to shout it out. The new Jews, she told me, had something to prove, and many who had only recently discovered their Jewish descent didn't have their family history to fall back on. Margarita believed that Viktor and Olga, a married couple with intricate family histories, could give me a more nuanced understanding of Jewish belonging in the Soviet era and tensions apparent in the relationship between old and new Jews in the city.

Viktor Feldman and Olga Notkina

When I met them, Viktor was eighty-nine and Olga, eighty-two. I spent more than a year getting to know them. Occasionally I would accompany Olga on her daily errands, but I usually went to their apartment, which they called "the birdhouse" (*golubiatnik*). It lacked the substantial wooden doors and neatly tiled hallways of others in their building and had no Jewish paraphernalia, whether mezuzah, menorah, or scripture.[13] Rather, a stack of Russian-language city newspapers was piled by the front door for disposal. A tiny kitchen connected the bedroom and bathroom. The bathroom had no door, just a curtain. In the bedroom, books spilled from dilapidated wooden shelves that leaned against faded wallpaper.

I sometimes felt that Olga and Viktor needed rescuing from these dire living conditions—a feeling that was undone by our long, intimate conversations, which revealed their sense of pride in where they were and how they lived. I often cried after our interviews as I reflected on the strength of their character and ideals and on the powerful sense of the past evoked by their stories. Viktor was slender, with a full head of gray hair and thick black glasses that always seemed to slope toward the right side of his face. Olga was small and fragile, with shining pale-blue eyes, and always neatly dressed. She passed away in March 2007, shortly after I left Odesa, and Victor died a year after that.

At the time of our talks, Viktor was housebound, only able to maneuver through their tiny space with the help of a cane. Olga, however, managed to attend at least two cultural events a month, mostly book signings and meetings with authors organized by the Odesa Literature Museum. For her, these outings were part of maintaining the routine of "seeing and being seen," and keeping Viktor up to date on city affairs. For the last ten years of her life, at times with Viktor's assistance, Olga also volunteered at Gmilus Hesed, the welfare center for elderly Jews, giving lectures on the history of her native city.

Both Olga and Viktor were historians, by education and disposition. They met at the library of Odesa University, where they worked for more than fifty years as specialists in various collections. Both had published extensively in Russian, and in 2006 they released their last book, *Together with Them* [*Vmeste s nimi*]—a work about their colleagues at the library, whose memory they were intent on keeping alive. They were proud to be able to tap into their knowledge of literature and history, to "turn on their brains" in conversations with members of the city's intelligentsia who came calling with questions about Odesa's past. As we sat at their small kitchen table, they would punctuate their narratives with references to books written by friends, pulling volumes off the shelves to contest each other's claims about the city's various "golden eras." "We're standing on the edge of a cliff," Olga told me, "and as soon as we're unable to answer a single question, we are gone."

When Olga and Viktor spoke of Ukraine's growing nationalism and the processes of Ukrainization that could be observed across the country, they believed these trends lacked momentum in Odesa. Distrusting the politicians, they blamed them for being corrupt and following their own agendas rather than the voice of the people. Likewise, they distrusted the city's Jewish religious leaders, saying that the rabbis who had come in to establish major synagogues were trying to turn Odesa Orthodox in its practice of Judaism. For Viktor and Olga, and some others of their generation, Odesa was never Ukrainian or Orthodox. Where some saw a post-Soviet revival of a repressed or lost Judaism, they saw a contemporary struggle for power.

Olga always allowed Viktor to start our discussions, waiting to speak until she thought he needed to be corrected or until I directed a question specifically to her. She wasn't prone to open up about personal matters unprompted.[14] Because Viktor was difficult to interrupt and Olga respected his role as the "voice of the family," his life story dominates their narrative.

A fourth-generation *Odesit*, Viktor was born in 1917, the year of the Bolshevik Revolution. He was raised in what he described as a "very Jewish house" next to the Jewish Burial Society, though with neighbors of different ethnicities. His paternal great-grandfather, Shimon, was a blacksmith by trade; carrying nothing but "a small sack and a pair of boots over his shoulder," he had arrived from a village near the current border with Belarus. Viktor's father, also named Shimon, was an optician by training. He worked for a pharmaceutical company, UROTAT, distributing medicine and medical supplies throughout southern Russia. Viktor's mother, Rahel Gendler, was a physician whose family had moved to Odesa from the Bryansk region of central Ukraine in the early 1900s. Partially educated in Switzerland, Rahel spoke fluent German. In 1911, shortly after she met Shimon, he was arrested and imprisoned for participating in an unauthorized meeting of social democrats. Following a trial, he was sentenced to a two-year deportation to the coast of the White Sea. Rahel sought to accompany him and wrote to the governor of Odesa to request permission to marry Shimon on the prison premises. It was granted, and there in the presence of a rabbi, the two were married in a Jewish religious ceremony.

Shimon and Rahel spent their first two years of married life in the Vologodskaia region, where Rahel launched her career in medicine. She worked as a doctor and continued to do so after their return to Odesa in 1913.[15] In one of the city's poorest neighborhoods, Moldovanka, she served as doctor for the needy (*vrach dlia bednykh*), attending to those who couldn't afford private care. Viktor described his parents as "revolutionaries in support of liberating reforms in their country." At home and in their professional lives, they always spoke Russian. Viktor said, "I could understand Yiddish because of my grandfather, but I never spoke it. My exposure to Hebrew was also minimal, as I never attended a *kheder* [religious school for boys], and it wasn't a language of conversation in my circles of friends."

Shimon died suddenly in 1922, and Viktor was partly raised by his paternal grandmother. "Grandma [*babka*] Feldman" was an observant religious woman from what Viktor described as "a good family." As Viktor recalled, "Catching me in the courtyard, she used to drag me into the synagogue, which I tried to avoid at all costs." His paternal grandfather, Pavel, was a shopkeeper (*magazinchik*) involved in the production, delivery, and sale of grain. He was, Viktor said, a religious Jew (*iudei* in Russian) but one who lived a "tailored" observant life: "My grandmother used to scream at him, 'You are not a Jew, you are a goy,' as he would heat up a little piece of pig fat [*salo*, a traditional Ukrainian delicacy] and dip his bread into the melted greasy puddle.[16] He would shout back even louder, 'I am a working man and I need to eat. God would not get mad at me for a little piece of pig fat.'" According to Viktor, his grandfather was far from exceptional among the Jews in Odesa, who, he claimed, regularly transgressed Jewish dietary laws (kashrut). The culturally diverse and delicious food sold at Odesa's famous Privoz market often lured Jews to eat nonkosher items. Pavel frequently attended the synagogue, but as Viktor remembered, he treated it as a gathering place for discussing social affairs rather than a holy house of worship. "He used to call the workers at the synagogue 'God's thieves' [*Got Ganoven* in Yiddish] because, in his eyes, they didn't work for their bread."

Viktor didn't remember his parents observing kashrut, Shabbat, or daily prayer (although his father, like his grandfather, had a reserved seat at the synagogue) and said that they did not wear the traditional Jewish attire that was common among his grandparents' generation. While Viktor acknowledged that his parents did not build their lives around the canons of religion, he made it clear that they kept to some traditions, perhaps mostly to please their elders. However, the rituals that remained were, for the family, hollowed of their religious content. Recalling Passover celebrations at his house in the early 1930s, Victor explained: "While my grandmother was alive, we always celebrated Pesach. For her, my mother would clear the house of any yeast products, buy unleavened bread [matzo], and cook her favorite Jewish dishes for our ritual festival meal [seder]. My grandmother would invite the whole family and ask my uncle to say the blessing over the wine as she sat graciously looking over our table. After her death, I don't remember celebrating anything." As Elissa Bemporad points out, by the second half of the 1930s, the social networks and family ties in Soviet Jewish families were expanding as Jewish identity moved from a religious one to an "ethnic" element in the larger Soviet project.[17] With this shift, Jewish religious rituals increasingly moved into the domestic sphere, where they cross-fertilized with a host of adjacent beliefs and practices.[18]

Viktor spoke of his secular education at a Russian-speaking gymnasium in Odesa. The year he started school, he said, Soviet national policy had begun to focus on raising ethnic awareness among the country's minorities, and a secular Yiddish education was supported and encouraged. The Soviet Union was the only country in the world with a state-sponsored system of Yiddish language schools, here designed to become an effective alternative to traditional religious-based education and to raise a generation of devoted Soviet citizens.[19] Throughout Ukraine in the 1930s, more than ninety-five thousand children were studying in more than eight hundred Yiddish schools (many in Vinnytsya province).[20] Odesa was an outlier. In the mid-1920s, 77 percent of its Jewish high school students, like Viktor, attended Russian schools.[21]

Viktor remembered that a city representative once came to their house and asked his mother why her son wasn't attending the local Jewish school. She answered, "I see no future in him applying himself in Yiddish. He lives in Russia, and I want him to be educated in Russian." This was common, as many Jewish parents wanted their children to avoid the stigma of speaking Yiddish-accented Russian.[22] Historian and Yiddish scholar Anna Shternshis also notes that "Jewish parents often preferred Russian schools because they felt that such an education would give children more opportunities in the future."[23]

The key point, Viktor emphasized, was that "education was always a necessity in my family, but religious subjects were viewed as backward and not in any way progressive." In his days, he explained, only Jews from small shtetls (*mestechkovye*) still wanted their children educated in a *kheder*.[24] "Jews in my circle of friends strived to receive education in one of the city's gymnasiums and apply their knowledge in universities, military academies, and music conservatories. . . . This was the case for Odessa."

Viktor's mother was fascinated with scientific theory and regarded religion as "simply silly." As Viktor described her, "She was of a different generation [from her parents], interested in Pavlov and the theory of relativity. . . . Even if they sometimes did it in a primitive manner, they [people of his mother's generation] tried to explain everything around them. . . . Darwin and Pasteur were more like gods to them than anyone else." Like his mother, Viktor had interests and affiliations that went far beyond a traditional Jewish life—or rather, his Jewish life had come to include new aspects of identification with the growing Russian-speaking intelligentsia. He studied many secular disciplines at school.

In the early 1930s, Viktor majored in history at Odesa University and joined the Communist youth league, the Komsomol, regarding it as a great honor at the time. "From an early school age, I was told that there is no God, and all religious leaders were crooks," he said. In the second or third year of his university studies, the faculty board of the history department decided that future Soviet educators had to be preachers of atheism. Shaking his head to show his distress over that long-ago pronouncement, Viktor recalled: "They sent us a young man who started giving lectures on the harmful nature of religion. At first we listened, but we were already historians, so when we realized that to him, Pontius Pilate and Rameses were, if not relatives [of each other], close friends, we just stopped paying attention. And then I started thinking, *Exactly what is it that I don't believe in?*" Viktor's curiosity drove him to commit a "terrible crime" for which, he pointed out, he could have been expelled from the Komsomol: "I found a Bible, some evangelical literature, a Koran in Russian translation, and a Jewish encyclopedia. . . . I spent close to a month familiarizing myself with so-called evil. I must say that I did not become religious. . . . I was left with the impression that these were collections of stories—some better, some worse—about cosmology and human morals . . . told by different people around the world, none of which I found close to my nature or explanatory of the world as I envisioned it at the time."

Viktor made it very clear that while his own immediate environment was secular, the city's Jewry as a whole had not simply abandoned religion. Speaking of his college years, he recalled that some religious rituals remained in place despite the atheist reforms: "I remember when, in the early 1930s, they started closing all the synagogues and churches in the city, and no one protested . . . yet at the same time, everyone insisted that the deceased would still be buried in their separate [Christian, Jewish, Armenian, Tatar, Karaite] cemeteries and according to their [respective] traditions. This was the practice all the way until the war."

At age twenty-four, Viktor was drafted into the army for what is known in Russia as the Great Patriotic War, leaving behind his young wife, a Jewish woman named Valentina, and their newborn son, Senya, who were evacuated to Azerbaijan. His experience of the Nazi invasion was entwined with stories of life in the Soviet Army. He recalled the horror of losing close friends and also recalled, with great pride, Soviet victory. Though antisemitic Soviet propaganda after the war portrayed Jews as cowards, Viktor stressed that many officers serving in the war were Jewish, including his two first cousins, who earned medals.[25] When Viktor spoke of the war, he dwelled on the astonishing number of Soviet casualties and their leaders' lack of concern for human lives. "In the Soviet Union," said Viktor, "homeland [*Rodina*] was spelled with a capital *R*, but person [*chelovek*] was spelled with a small letter *ch*."

Because of impaired eyesight, Viktor was demobilized after a year of service and reunited with his family. In 1945, following the Soviet liberation of Ukraine and the death of his wife, Valentina, Viktor and Senya returned to Odesa. Viktor managed to get a work placement at the private collection of Mikhail Voronzov, located at the public library of Odesa University. At that time, employment was needed to receive coupons for bread, so this job saved his life in many ways.

It was through this position that he met Olga, who would become his second wife, and it was there that Viktor began his long career as a historian.

In all our discussions, Viktor never acknowledged that antisemitism affected his own self-identification as a Jew. But he did recognize the role the Soviet regime played in driving anti-Jewish propaganda and in persecuting those whose passports revealed their Jewish identity:[26]

> When I was a little boy, there were some elements of antisemitism around. . . . At times there were fights between boys on that exact subject, but it didn't play a central role in my life. It wasn't until the Soviet regime actively supported antisemitic policies that we really experienced what that word meant. It wasn't systematic; rather, it was hidden behind the façade of the Soviet "friendship of nations" [*druzhba narodov*]. At first, we were all equals, and then in the late 1930s, and even more so after the war, it became impossible for a Jew to be admitted to any prestigious educational institution, because they all had quotas. You had to really prove yourself.

As he saw it, though, Odesa was more liberal and tolerant than other cities in the Soviet Union: "The city always had a rather large percentage of Jews who were visible in every layer of society. . . . They lived and worked among other nationalities, speaking one language [Russian]. My courtyard, for instance, was phenomenally international: one of the boys, Pavel Gau, was German, another boy was Greek, Borya Hadjim was a Karaite, and there were others. This living situation was very typical of Odessa, which never had a segregated Jewish quarter." Discussing antisemitism at the political level, Viktor described Stalin not as an antisemite but as a politician who used antisemitism:

> Similar to Lenin, [Stalin] was a man without principle, acting in his own interest and following one rule: divide and rule. . . . And during that time in history [the late 1930s], he realized, while keeping his finger on the pulse of the nation, that there was some turmoil in the country, and someone had to be blamed . . . so it was in his interest to find the guilty. . . . Hence he blamed the Jews, the intelligentsia, cosmopolitans, and other "know-it-alls." . . . Believe me, Jews were not the only ones who suffered from his brutality.

For Viktor, the Soviet treatment of Jews was contradictory: one day bringing them into the Soviet project, the next excluding them as other. Jews, said Viktor, were persecuted not necessarily because they were Jews, but because they belonged to a wider group of people whose loyalties, in the Soviet leaders' view, were questionable—and this at a time when scapegoats were politically expedient. But Viktor was always careful to distinguish the atmosphere of the

Soviet Union in general from his experiences growing up in somewhat more liberal Odesa.

Viktor never spoke about the Holocaust, even by using other terms to describe the more than 100,000 Jews who perished in the city during the Romanian invasion in 1941. That may have been because Jewish losses were not differentiated from Soviet casualties by the Soviet regime, and "because a half century of Soviet propaganda emphasized the city's defenders and downplayed its foreign occupiers and local collaborators."[27] Olga's recollections of antisemitism were sharper than Viktor's. She described being evacuated with her mother to a small town in northern Kavkaz during the wartime occupation of Odesa. "Some of these rural people were driven by fear and wouldn't open their doors to Jews," she said. "Others, driven by ignorance, regarded Jews as barbarians." She described a conversation with the woman who owned the house where Olga and her mother lodged: "There were hardly any Jews there. We were living with a woman who asked me one day, 'Jews, Jews, who are these Jews that people keep talking about? Have you ever seen one?' 'Yes,' I said, 'I have. They're just ordinary people. . . . For instance, if someone asked you who you are, what would you say?' 'A Russian,' she answered. 'Well,' I said, 'they would just say "a Jew."' 'Thank you for your clear explanation,' she said. 'I thought they were some kind of half-animal, half-human creature [*poluzveri*].'"[28] Olga pointed out that Odesa's general population, long exposed to Jews and Jewish practices, was far less susceptible to propaganda that relied on ignorance and mythology.

A third generation Odesitka, Olga was born in 1923 and raised in an atheist Russian Jewish family. Her father, Yehuda Notkin, worked as an engineer, and her mother, Polina Dreisden, taught literature in a city school. Both were supporters of the Bolshevik Revolution and of the Soviet regime that followed. Although Olga's grandparents' generation was religiously observant, her parents, like Viktor's, didn't follow Jewish religious law (halakha). "They were open about their Jewishness," said Olga, "but I don't remember them practicing religion." After graduating from a Russian-speaking girls' gymnasium, Olga too enrolled in the history department at Odesa University, where she studied until the beginning of the war.

Much of Olga's story echoed the themes of Viktor's. Her parents regarded their secular orientation and Russian education as a new benchmark of social acceptance and achievement, and contrasted that orientation with the family's earlier religious practices and beliefs. This same mix of values was passed on to Olga at an early age; like Viktor, she grew up surrounded by the Russian language and what she saw as its rich literature. At the same time, being a Jew was a proud fact for Olga's parents, something she also internalized as a child.

Following in her parents' footsteps, she connected her Jewishness with communist beliefs. She also joined the Komsomol during her school years, finding like-minded friends and, later, colleagues. Olga's passion for history and books was probably one of the reasons she and Viktor came to share their lives. They had no children together, but Olga treated Senya as part of their family.

For Viktor and Olga, leaving Odesa was never an option, even as they spoke of the city's state of decline. They saw how the process of Ukrainization was altering their city, which they regarded as rooted in Russian history and culture, with a cosmopolitan outlook. They were suspicious of the city's Jewish religious organizations. They adamantly rejected the claim of contemporary Jewish activists who said they were restoring the lost and destroyed Jewish life of Odesa. They felt that the rabbis (a term they used loosely to speak of religiously dressed Hasidic men) were pushing the Jewish population toward a new religious identity and connecting them to a set of new values: attending services at the synagogue, making donations to a specific congregation, observing Jewish laws of kashrut, choosing a Jewish spouse, educating children in religious schools, and disaffiliating themselves from Soviet secular holidays.

Viktor and Olga defended the view that Odesa's Jews *voluntarily* gave up religious values, even when I raised the fact that Soviet propaganda and fear of persecution played a role. Jews in Odesa were much closer to Russian culture, Viktor and Olga insisted, in "the language they spoke, the books they read, the theater they attended, the food they ate, the clothes they wore, and, on the whole, their philosophy of life or mentality [*mentalitet*]." At the same time, neither would argue that by adopting Russian culture, they or other Jews in the city had thereby ceased to be Jews or had become purely Russian. Rather, they identified themselves as Russian *and* Jewish. These categories, although legally exclusive of one another in the Soviet Union, were combined in their self-identification as Soviet Jews and specifically as part of the social class that was Russian-speaking intelligentsia.[29] In this group, they included "highly educated and cultured professionals such as teachers, professors, artists, doctors, engineers, architects, and other white-collar professionals." This ideal of belonging to the intelligentsia is central to the construction of the ethnic identity of Russian Jews, say sociologists Tamar Rapoport and Edna Lomsky-Feder, a "prism through which Jews consider and evaluate both themselves and others."[30]

Indeed, when I met Senya, a scientist then in his midsixties, at Viktor and Olga's apartment, he defined himself as Jewish by the standards of education, worldview, and career, which aligned him with other members of the intelligentsia. Senya didn't seem to object to the development of new Jewish institutions throughout Odesa as much as his father and Olga did, and he was openly curious about religious holidays like Chanukah and Simhat Torah, mentioning the elaborate celebrations he saw on the streets of Odesa. His immediate family all lived in Odesa, but some of his distant relatives had moved to the United States. One day, he said, this might be an option for himself or his children, depending on the state of affairs in Ukraine.

Many of my interlocutors also classified members of the intelligentsia as "cosmopolitan"—that is, people whose circle of friends included many different nationalities, not just Jews. In such circles, they contended, relationships were based on personal interests rather than loyalty to a specific religious or national group. Viktor and Olga believed that the new Jewish religious leaders were undermining this Odesan accomplishment by speaking and acting against assimilation. They questioned the motivations of younger Jews who had recently taken on a religious identity.

Friendships formed in Soviet times, Viktor and Olga explained, carried particular moral weight because they were valued for their own sake—not, as today, driven by economic motives.[31] "We were friends because we enjoyed each other's company. Now it's much more about what someone can do for you or what you can do for them. Why do you think people really belong to those Jewish organizations?" When I asked about their affiliation with Gmilus Hesed, the center for elderly Jews, they said it served as a social platform for discussing and commemorating Odesa's history. They distinguished participants like themselves, who were seeking communication and dialogue with other Odesans, from those who used Jewish networks to receive economic benefits.

Viktor and Olga described the assimilation and Russification that had taken place earlier in Odesa as a "natural process of cultural development [*razvitie*]" and viewed those who adopted these practices as culturally developed [*razvitymi*]. Rather than seeing the Jews of their generation as subjects suppressed by the Soviet regime, Viktor and Olga asserted that they voluntarily and enthusiastically accepted Russification and assimilation, viewing them as a way "forward" that would reap greater opportunities in education, professionalism, and self-development. They acknowledged the role of state authorities in perpetuating Russification and assimilation but viewed this fact as secondary to the self-chosen path of most of the Jewish population in Odesa—a city whose distinct history played a significant role in the speed and absorption of Russian language and culture among both its Jewish and non-Jewish populations.

While Odesa's particularities created a distinctive cultural setting that was conducive to assimilation, my informants viewed Russian culture as, on the whole, much "richer" than Jewish culture or "local" (Ukrainian) literature and, thus, more attractive to the greater part of the population.[32] As Olga put it: "Of course, we realized that Tolstoy and Dostoyevsky were three heads taller [much more talented] than Sholem Aleichem [the Ukrainian Yiddish writer best known for his tales of Jewish village life, which inspired the musical *Fiddler on the Roof*].... In my fifty years of working at the library, no one came to reread Sholem Aleichem or [Nobel Prize winner and Ukrainian] Mikhail Sholokhov's *And Quiet Flows the Don*. But they did come to reread Tolstoy's *Anna Karenina* and *War and Peace*."

For that generation, and indeed until quite recently, the world of Russian literature was more readily available than Jewish or Ukrainian writings. It was actively popularized during various periods of Soviet rule as the state promoted Russian language and literature as part of its "civilizing" and "modernizing" projects from the 1930s, sowing suspicion about much of the Jewish, Ukrainian, and other national literatures before banning them altogether.[33] Viktor and Olga agreed that this happened but insisted that Jews (and others in the intelligentsia) preferred works by Russian authors in any case. "People always say Odessa was a very Jewish city, but it was a Russian Jewish city," Viktor declared, putting an emphasis on the connections Jews had to Russian language and literature. He braided together the two seemingly disparate developments of Jewish nationalism and assimilation by stressing the role of the Russian language, not only among his circle of the intelligentsia but also among active Jewish nationalists prior to the Bolshevik repression on Zionist activity.

> Although Odessa served as a center of Zionism, it was also a center of Haskalah [the Jewish "enlightenment"], and assimilation followed on all fronts. These processes weren't mutually exclusive.... I remember there was a family in my courtyard, we called them *palestinofily* [lovers of Palestine]. Their daughter Nusia used to drag us to different Zionist clubs she organized around the city.... They were very active in support of the Jewish homeland, but at home they still spoke Russian. [And] Vladimir Jabotinsky, ... one of the leading figures in Zionism, not just in Odessa but a Jewish activist known to the world, ... [wrote] his novel *The Five*, which describes his life in Odessa, ... in Russian, not Hebrew or Yiddish.

As Viktor explained, Odesan Jews of his generation lived in a Russified environment, and thus, the Russian language and Russian culture came naturally into their lives. "Prior to the revolution, all Jewish boys of course went to a heder and were taught Hebrew, but the same families went to Russian theaters, cursed in Russian, and drank vodka in Russian style." Viktor emphasized that, like the city's other minorities, Jews simply adapted to their environment, learning Russian for the purposes of employment, education, and communication with the larger society. "It's not that we became Russian because we spoke and read Russian. Rather, we became Russian Jews, and with time Russian culture became dominant in circles of the intelligentsia, absorbing everything else. Among my friends, Yiddish was simply considered a dialect."

Viktor's perspective on Jewish acculturation shed some light on our discussion of Odesa's present-day Jewish "religious revival," which Viktor didn't view as progressive. Members of their grandparents' generation had defined themselves, and were identified by others, as members of the Jewish faith, but the elements of religion fostered by that generation were fading. The next generation growing up in czarist Russia—that of Olga's and Viktor's parents—was, as Viktor put it, a "different generation"; they looked away from a traditional Jewish world toward the greater Russian-speaking and, later, Soviet society. Jewish identification, as Viktor and Olga inherited, observed, and came to define it, was inextricably linked with the Russian-speaking intelligentsia, with being Odesan, and with their past affiliations with the Soviet political movement.[34]

More than the other elderly Jews I met, Viktor and Olga aligned themselves with the values of the Soviet state, although they certainly recognized the shortcomings of Soviet leaders and the atrocities committed. Olga said, "During my entire life, I never changed my name on any of my documents, as many other Jews did to avoid discrimination. At the same time, I never handed in my Communist membership card after the USSR collapsed, as many rushed to do. This is all part of my life, and as they say, 'You can't take words out of a song, for it will lose its rhythm.' This is my story, and I am extremely proud of every part of it."

Elena Martyanova

As Olga indicated, many Jews presented themselves as something other than Jewish in the Soviet system, seeking to avoid both state and social antisemitism. This was the case for Elena Martyanova, who was sixty-five when I met her in 2006. Petite and elegant, she often wore simple yet tasteful attire and had light golden hair. She seemed much younger than her age. She was born and raised in a secular working-class Jewish family in Kherson, a small city in southeastern Ukraine. In 1961, at the age of twenty, she moved to Odesa to attend its Pedagogical Institute (where she majored in linguistics) and fell in love with the "warm climate, atmosphere, and people." She also fell in love with Konstantin, who was nine years older and from a Russian and Polish family. They were married in a civil ceremony in 1971 and had two children, Dmitry and Ilya. The family lived in a fifth-floor, two-room walk-up allocated to them by the Soviet cooperative.

Like others of their generation, Elena and Konstantin pursued careers that were chosen early. Fluent in French and proficient in English and Italian, Elena had spent most of her professional life as an interpreter for Intourist, the Soviet travel agency.[35] Thus, unlike many Soviet Jews, she had traveled extensively through Europe and parts of North Africa. In the last two years before retirement, she taught social science at the Medical Institute of Odesa, not far from the Political Technical Institute where Konstantin taught political science and sociology for more than thirty years. While Konstantin had been a member of the Communist Party, which he considered unavoidable for anyone wanting a career in academia, Elena never joined. She understood Konstantin's pragmatism but regarded the party's "pretty slogans" as "lies" (vran'e).[36]

Their younger son, Ilya, moved to the United States and earned a PhD in biology at Dartmouth College. Dmitry, now an Israeli citizen, settled in Moscow with his Russian wife, Sveta, but regularly traveled to Tel Aviv. A successful businessman, Dmitry was supporting the entire family. When I met them, Elena and Konstantin lived in a spacious four-room apartment across from one of the city's main parks. It was a property far more expensive than what their combined state pension of 800 grivnas per month (about US$160) would have afforded them, but Dmitry had purchased it for them. The cost of living in Odesa had gone up since independence, and they felt the difference. "I don't know how people manage today on just their minimal pension; look at the prices for everything!" Konstantin exclaimed. "You have to have your own business [delo], or good children to support you." Elena elegantly added, "It all depends on your appetites"—and she observed that many people's appetites had changed significantly.[37]

As we walked through the apartment, they showed me pictures of their sons displayed behind the glass doors of tall, neat bookshelves. Konstantin's small decorative Russian Orthodox icons of Jesus leaned against hardbound volumes of Russian and translated classics. Ceramic plates showed the names of cities they'd visited—Jerusalem, Rome, Madrid. A Jewish calendar in the kitchen, courtesy of the synagogue, displayed the month of Nissan, year 5765 (2004–2005). When she saw my eyes land on the calendar's image of Shabbat candles, Elena said, "It was a gift," as if needing to justify ownership of this Jewish object. Like Viktor and Olga, they kept no other Jewish paraphernalia, but their connections to Israel were evident in the family pictures and other souvenirs around the house.

Behind her charm and indelible smile, Elena spoke of her childhood as "dark and difficult." She was born in Starinobrad, Tajikistan, during her family's wartime evacuation. Her mother, Eva Ninburg, was born in 1922 in Nikolaev (Mykolaiv), a small town northeast of Odesa, and was the youngest of twelve children. Elena's grandparents had provided the family with a prosperous and joyful life before the 1917 revolution, when they lost their land and house. While some extended family immigrated to the United States, Elena's grandparents and their children remained in what later became the Soviet Union. Life was difficult. All but three of Eva's sisters died of hunger, as did Elena's grandfather. The young Eva was placed in an orphanage because her mother couldn't provide for her; there she at least got one meal a day and basic care. Some years later, Eva returned to her family, but the fragmentation of her mother's family, and the fact that Eva had been sequestered in an orphanage, left her cut off from Jewish family traditions and other elements of Jewish life. Elena didn't know whether her grandparents had ever been religious. "My mom never talked about it," she said, "but she herself was an atheist."

Elena's mother had completed only ten years of school before the war started, and that was her only formal education. As Elena recalled, "She was a very smart woman. She didn't have a proper education, but she was wise and well read. That gave her understanding, understanding of life [*ponimanie, ponimanie o zhizni*]." After her studies in Nikolaev (Mykolaiv), Eva met Elena's father, Mendel (Mikhail), a young engineer of Jewish descent. They married in a civil ceremony and had their first daughter, Lilia, in 1940. Elena was born a year later. Like most men in the town, Mikhail was drafted into the Soviet army in 1941 to fight against the Romanian-German invasion. He was demobilized after receiving a serious head wound, which left him paralyzed for the rest of his life. Elena regretted never learning much about him: "I get so mad at myself for never taking the time to ask about his life. Back then it didn't seem that interesting. But also, I have to say, I was very afraid of him. He was a sick man. He had *mania presledovaniia* [persecution mania] . . . and then when he ended up in a mental institution, the subject was taboo—my mother never talked about it. She never talked about their experiences during the war, either. It was all too bitter for her to revisit. She passed over these subjects in silence [*Eta tema obhodilas' molchaniem*]."

After the war, the family moved to Kherson, near Nikolaev (Mykolaiv), where Eva found a job as a typist at a military base. She supported two daughters and an invalid husband on meager earnings and the housing that came with the job: a single small room on the base. But after a couple of years, Eva was accused of being an enemy of the state (*vrag naroda*) and fired because she was a Jew. Then a town commissar took pity and gave them shelter in a tiny 150-square-foot room in his basement: "It was a horrifying room, where I lived until I was sixteen years old and where my mother and sister lived for many years after I left. . . . The ceiling was so low you could touch it simply by raising your hand. . . . Our bathroom, our potatoes, coal, and firewood, our bed . . . and my paralyzed father . . . all in this cramped space. . . . Although back then, we were grateful even for that."

The Russian commissar who took them in was, according to Elena, "a very good man." But despite his respect for her mother, he couldn't help her keep her post. "It wasn't up to him," Elena explained. "Everything was decided higher up [by state politicians]." To Elena, her mother's unfortunate fate was nothing out of the ordinary: "It was [in the early 1950s] a time of repression, the Doctors' Plot, and so on. Jews were being laid off everywhere." As Viktor and Olga continually stressed, Jews in Odesa had different experiences from Jews elsewhere in the USSR, and indeed, the hardships Elena's family experienced in Nikolaev (Mykolaiv) were more typical. As a result of her treatment, Eva's political views turned "anti-Soviet," and she saw the state as a "false illusion of human equality." Elena's son Ilya wrote of his grandmother: "a very skeptical person by nature, who couldn't afford to rely on any self-evident truth in the form of higher authority—be it God or the Communist Party."

During the war, Elena's father used forged documents to change his nationality of record from Jewish to Ukrainian, a risky but common practice. With a birth certificate that included a Jewish mother and Ukrainian father, Elena chose the latter as her official nationality when she obtained her passport at age sixteen. "My whole life I passed as a Ukrainian. I don't know how my father managed to pull this off. My mother never told me. But it helped me get into the university in Odessa on the first try and get a placement with Intourist—at the time, a highly competitive organization where I doubt I could ever have worked as a Jew." Elena recognized that the decision to register her as Ukrainian was based on making her life "easier and safer" than that of her parents. "I think my mother wanted to protect me from everything she had to deal with in her life. I felt that she almost wanted to save me from the suffering she'd seen. I know it was done with the best intentions."

Elena graduated top of her class with a degree in French and entered her chosen career, and thus it could be said that she fulfilled her family's hopes that she would find full acceptance in society. That acceptance, however, was never without the shadow of her family history: "I still knew I was Jewish, despite what my passport said. I felt this [Ia eto chuvstvovala]. When I was younger no one called me a Jew, but I was always waiting for it to happen. I remember once, at a summer camp, I was sitting next to a friend who had an 'obviously' Jewish face [vyrazhennoe evreiskoe litso] when a drunken man stumbled up to our group, pointed at my friend, and started screaming, 'Zhidovka, you dirty zhidovka [kike, you dirty kike].' I just sat there in silence, but his words wounded me deeply."[38] While Elena, like Viktor and Olga, came to regard herself as cultured (kul'turnyi) and part of the Russian-speaking intelligentsia, and understood her Ukrainian identity as an assigned identification (propisannaia *lichnost'*), her Jewishness remained fluid. It played various roles in different periods of her life as circumstances changed.

During Elena's primary school education, her Jewishness wasn't an issue, as Jews constituted a majority in her class; in university there were occasional antisemitic slurs; and later, whenever she was among friends and coworkers where few were Jewish, she didn't speak about her family's roots. Possessing the status of Ukrainian nationality freed Elena from official anti-Jewish discrimination, and her sensitivity to antisemitism impacted how she allowed herself to be seen and accepted. As another elderly woman once told me, in Soviet times "Jewish" was a synonym for *being different*, as in: "You don't drink? What are you—Jewish?"[39]

When talking to people in Jewish organizations, I heard what they said about people with histories like Elena's: some elderly Jews disdained and mistrusted newly proclaimed Jews who had previously passed as Russian or Ukrainian. Others, however, were less judgmental, understanding that people had their own reasons for choosing to live as a non-Jew in Soviet times and as a Jew today. In our conversations, Elena was adamant that religious belief played no part in her upbringing. "Both my parents were atheists. My mother used to ask me, 'How could anyone believe in God after what happened to the Jews during the war?'"

When Elena and I discussed the renovation of religious buildings that was then going on in Odesa, she recalled an occasion when she was walking with her mother and sister past an old church that was being restored. "We girls wanted to peek inside, but our mother simply refused to join us. She waited outside." Elena went on to explain, "She didn't believe in religion or religious institutions, not even enough to set foot in one of its man-made manifestations." Her grandson Ilya wrote to me: "My grandmother was vehemently opposed to religion (not only Judaism but religion in general) because she had to cope with the not-so-bright reality around her and could not waste her time on fairy tales and utopian beliefs." At the end of her days, before her body surrendered to a long battle with cancer, Eva asked to be cremated and interred in Kherson, where she'd lived most of her life before joining Elena in Odesa.[40] Elena and her sister carried out this wish after Eva passed away in 1993.

In her late sixties, retired and living in an independent Ukraine, Elena openly and freely discussed her Jewishness. Elena's two maternal aunts had shared many stories about her Jewish ancestors, since they had grown up in a family environment that her mother, born too late, hadn't shared. Elena regarded her aunts' stories as "fairy tales" that allowed her to imagine a different reality from her everyday life. Moreover, in her own stories about a purportedly irreligious family, she discovered what Galina Zelenina calls "subconscious observance"—rituals saved and passed down in Soviet families without being regarded as markers of religiosity.[41] "On Pesach," Elena told me, "I remember my mother making the most delicious matzo. She also baked what she called Haman's Ears [triangular 'ear-shaped' pastries traditionally made for the holiday of Purim]."[42] Eva was using her mother's recipes for these, though she did not then pass them down to Elena. Perhaps, Elena speculated, this was simply because she was the younger daughter and cooking had always been her sister's responsibility.

In another conversation, as we were walking past the Jewish community center, Migdal, Elena said, "I remember the time my mother took us to see the Yiddish theater that came on tour to Kherson. I was young and couldn't understand much. It was all so foreign to me: women with covered heads speaking those funny words [in Yiddish]. My mother explained that it was a performance of a Jewish wedding." Then later, at her kitchen table, Elena told me she considered herself Jewish, but "I'm interested in Jewishness as a culture [*Ia interesuius' evreistvom kak kul'tura*]." She paused, then added, "I don't believe in God [*v boga ia ne veriu*]." Planning to immigrate to Israel, she was taking Hebrew lessons at one of the Orthodox synagogues and at Migdal, but for her this was quite separate from religious belief, which she kept at arm's length. On this topic she told me that throughout her teaching career she'd encountered students from religious backgrounds who questioned her atheist position. One student asked her, "Elena Michaelovna, do you not believe in God?" When Elena said no, he asked, "Well, who do you believe in, then?" "I looked at him," Elena recounted, "and said, 'I believe in you. I believe in humans [*Ia veriu v tebia. Ia veriu v cheloveka*].'"

In Elena's opinion, many religious people do good things because they're afraid God will punish them if they don't. "I try to do good deeds [*dobro*] because I'm a human being [*chelovek*], because I'm a cultured human being [*ku'lturnyi chelovek*], a well-mannered human being [*vospitannyi*]. And I believe that as a human being I have to act with dignity [*dostoino*], try to help others, grow as a person, and not cause harm to others. This is how I was raised, and how I was always taught to behave, without a religious presence in my life. Religion doesn't make you a better person, as religious leaders like to suggest; they have it all backward." She pointed out the many religious conflicts being waged around the world and went on to tell me of religious people who put on a front of being good humans but, in reality, "only want good things for their own people." Elena had little contact with Odesa's Jewish organizations and, based on insights from the Hebrew classes she was then taking, she was skeptical of the Jewish "born-again" believers and members of other faiths, questioning the motives for their newfound religious affiliation. Her skepticism was less politicized than that of Olga and Viktor and linked more to her own humanistic view and upbringing. But Elena and others in her generation had trouble understanding how someone becomes a believer "overnight" and disputed the assumption that being religious gives you better values and makes you a better person.

Elena and Konstantin tried to teach their sons the importance of being good people first and Jewish, Ukrainian, or Russian second. Registered as Russian in their passports, the boys learned of their Jewish roots only at school age, and each then explored the subject in his own way. Elena told me that one day when Dmitry was seven, he came home from school and, laughing, asked her, "Mom, do you know what OEE means? It means *ostorozhno edet evrei* [be careful, Jew behind the wheel]," he said with a stretched grin. Furious, Elena asked, "What's so funny? Is it the 'be careful' part that's making you laugh?" "No," he replied. "The 'behind the wheel' part?" "No," came his answer. "Was it the word 'Jew'?" Dmitry lowered his head. Calmly, Elena then said, "Why is the word 'Jew' funny to you? It's just a *natsional'nost'*, like Russian, Ukrainian, or English. Are those funny to you as well?" "No," he answered. She asked him, "Do you want to see a Jew?" She pointed a finger at his small round face. "You are a Jew, I am a Jew, your aunts and your cousins are Jews." "But why am I a Jew?" Dmitry asked, puzzled. "Because I am a Jew," Elena answered. She concluded the story by describing how, when that seven-year-old boy grew up, he was the first in her family to apply for Israeli citizenship and to move to Israel.

Of course, it must be added that like many others who left the former Soviet bloc after its collapse, Dmitry's emigration had not been due to a Zionist or religious calling or to the urge to relocate to a historic homeland; nor was it indicative of a heightened Jewish identity on his part. Rather, as his mother said, "He was going *na bum* [with no expectations] to try life in another country and, I think, to secure another citizenship and country of residence in case running a business in Russia became too difficult."

Elena told me that her younger son, Ilya, grew very passionate about his Jewish roots. "I tell him everything I remember," she said. Living in the United States, Ilya has become a member of Hillel, the international Jewish youth organization. Both Elena and Konstantin approved of this, although they seemed to regard it mostly as a strong network of friends who support their son and other international students during their study abroad. On the whole, Elena felt that her sons' respective places of residence further enriched their Jewish orientation—which she welcomed, as a secular cultural Jewish ideology that she herself shared.

And indeed, Elena and Konstantin ended up moving to Israel as well. Elena's exposure to Odesa's organized Jewish life consisted of her weekly Hebrew classes. She thoroughly enjoyed learning languages and believed that the free Hebrew lessons would help her settle in as one of the *olim hadashim* (newly arrived immigrants) in Israel. Konstantin had opted not to learn Hebrew, preferring to rely on his wife's linguistic talents. Elena visited Odesa's Israeli Cultural Center, where their family documents were under review for emigration, sometimes to attend scheduled appointments and sometimes for the free lectures on various topics of Israeli life.[43] She expressed a certain degree of discomfort at being in religious Jewish establishments, because of the contrast between her atheist beliefs and their "Orthodox and stuffy atmosphere." Even so, she regarded the simple presence of these establishments as a positive step in post-Soviet society. She often asked me how I viewed the religious congregations in the city; she was curious about the rituals and traditions practiced on religious holidays and on Shabbat but too shy and uncomfortable to join in the events organized around the city. During her Hebrew lessons, she occasionally picked up and read Jewish newspapers, but she never subscribed to them.

Besides her son, a number of Elena's family members—her sister, two cousins and their extended kin—had also immigrated to Israel. This brought Elena closer to an Israeli-centered Jewish identity and exposed her to the Israeli life that would become her own. When I asked Elena why she and Konstantin hadn't emigrated sooner, she answered, "We had good jobs and a good life here. We saw no reason to leave." She explained that her family members had left Kherson and Nikolaev (Mykolaiv) mostly for economic reasons, with hopes of a better life for their children. "Kherson [where her mother had lived] was just a dead city. You'd walk down the streets and there was nobody and nothing. In Nikolaev [the city her sister's family left] at the time, shipbuilding had collapsed, causing more people to be unemployed than employed. My sister . . . saw no prospects for her children, having herself lost her accounting job at a state factory." Elena's comments were consistent with other research that reveals mostly economic motivations for the post-Soviet wave of migration.[44]

Elena often expressed her great admiration and love for Odesa and her sense of comfort there. "I became a true *Odesitka*," she'd say. "We'll have a hard time leaving—we have such wonderful friends here, and everything is familiar and dear to us [*rodnoye nam*]. Odessa is our home." Nevertheless, when I saw Elena in Netanya, Israel, in the spring of 2009, she had adjusted to her new life. She was enjoying her new freedom to travel as an Israeli citizen, and she shared her feeling of liberation in living openly as a Jew—something that had seemed more difficult in Odesa, even in the post-Soviet environment. Israel offered a new beginning, where having a Jewish orientation no longer cast a shadow from the past.

Nina Malahova

Nina Malahova's life also involved emigration. Unlike Elena, she had left Odesa for Israel in the 1990s with her youngest son but returned after many years. Like the others, Nina strongly identified with being an Odesan. I first telephoned Nina to pass on a greeting from our mutual friend, the anthropologist Tanya Richardson, and Nina suggested we meet during one of her weekend outings with the Odesa Walking Group.[45]

Every Saturday for years, Nina and about twenty other Odesans had attended free walking tours of "Old Odessa" led by Valerii Netrebsky, a middle-aged man who was half Russian and half Jewish. His audience was mostly middle-aged or older, natives and members of the intelligentsia, and fairly knowledgeable about the city's history. They gathered to walk through Odesa's historical sites, listening, learning, and commenting on Netrebsky's guided tour. These walks had become part of my regular routine, too, and I was able to build relationships beyond the walks with some members of the group. Although they were open to answering my questions during the walks, most preferred to keep their distance. Nina, however, welcomed me immediately. Friends often described Nina as "poetic," due to her romanticized outlook on life—not to mention her actual love of poetry. She was tall and medium-framed, with yellowish hazel eyes and light brown wavy hair, which she wore short, parted, and tucked behind her ears. Her voice was already soft, but she muted it further by always covering her mouth when she spoke, as if afraid that someone might overhear her conversation. An artist by education and profession, Nina sewed her own dresses, knitted her own berets, and decorated almost every square inch of her apartment with her own stained glass, ceramics, and the watercolors she'd painted during her first years at the Odesa Art Academy. Over the course of a year, from 2006 to 2007, I conducted numerous interviews at Nina's home, joined her on routine trips to the market, visited her family graves with her, and engaged in many informal conversations during our walks through the city.

Nina's apartment was on the ground floor and consisted of a single main room and a narrow corridor leading to a small kitchen and bathroom. It was part of a *kommunalka* (communal apartment) that had been split into four small units, each sold separately. The lack of space wasn't an issue for Nina, but she feared the dark and found the place gloomy and depressing. Nor did she like that she could hear every word of her neighbor's conversations through the paper-thin walls—and so, she assumed, could the neighbor hear hers.

Whenever I visited, she'd immediately turn on the radio or her old television set to mask the sound of our voices. When we met, Nina had lived in the apartment for close to six years, and during the time I knew her, she was always trying to sell it.

Nina was born Rosalina Leihter in Odesa, in June 1934. A fourth-generation Odesitka of Jewish descent, she grew up in an upper-middle-class family whose status in the city declined gradually during the Soviet period, and more drastically with the Nazi occupation. When I met her, she was a retired art teacher and artist; occasionally, she showed her work in exhibitions around the city but never offered it for sale. "I don't have the facilities to create something new, and this is all I have to show for my years of work," she told me, pointing to a display of ceramic plates decorated with colorful nature images.

Nina was living on a small monthly pension of 400 *grivnas* (about US$80), supplemented by slightly larger sums paid periodically by the German government as compensation for being a ghetto survivor. She was often concerned for her health and worried about being alone if her children permanently left Odesa. "In Israel they really take care of the elderly," she said, "but here no one does anything." And yet, despite her appreciation for life in Israel, she had no regrets about her decision to return to Odesa. "This is where I feel at home. My whole family is here [buried at the Third Jewish Cemetery], and my whole life is here."

One wall of her living room, which also served as her bedroom, was hung with a collection of black-and-white photographs of her family that she often referred to when telling me stories. Next to the family pictures was a faded sepia photograph of her old house, and above that a small wooden icon of Jesus, draped with a beige plastic rosary. Nina, as I later learned, was a congregant of Odesa's Evangelical church. She didn't present her religiously Christian and ethnically Jewish orientation as a major contrast, though she was aware that others might think otherwise.[46] All these pieces of Nina's life found their order and connection in the stories she told me throughout our friendship.

Nina's mother was born Tauba Komar in 1905 to a middle-class Odesan Jewish family. Her ancestors migrated to Odesa in the mid-nineteenth century. Tauba's father had a well-paying job in the textile industry, and her mother, Rosalina, stayed home with the children. Of the nine children she bore, only six survived to adolescence: Tauba, her two sisters, and three brothers. The children received their primary and secondary secular education in Odesa. Tauba attended the state gymnasium where, along with the standard subjects, she mastered many foreign languages and developed a passion for classical music and piano. Upon graduation, she enrolled in Odesa's nursing school, where she finished the course with high honors and began a career in medicine.

In the early 1920s, Tauba met Osip Leihter, and married him in 1924 in a civil ceremony conducted in the Odesa City Hall. Four years later, they had their first daughter, Frida (later known as Galina). Rosalina—much later known as Nina—arrived six years after that.

Osip was born in Odesa, one of five boys of Jewish parents, Yakov and Frida Leihter. He was a craftsman by education. Following his father's death, Osip and his brother Iogan were responsible for the family's metal workshop. After the Russian Revolution, when the state confiscated private property, Osip and Iogan managed to hold onto the shop by hiding its operations. Meanwhile, they took jobs as manual laborers at a German-owned factory called Gena, where another brother, Ruvin, had started working as a first-class engineer after completing his education in Munich. In the late 1930s, the eldest Leihter brother, Sasha, immigrated to the United States and was never heard from again. Lev, the youngest, worked as a teacher. After he married a non-Jewish woman and converted to Evangelical Christianity, Lev was ostracized by his father and, to a lesser degree, by the rest of the family, according to the stories Nina heard.

Among Nina's parents' generation, intermarriage occurred on both sides of the family, albeit not without straining family relations. Nina recalled that her grandparents didn't approve, viewing those who "married out" as "abandoning their traditions." Neither Tauba nor Osip was especially religious in their Jewish identification. Although Nina believed that her father was most likely educated in a *kheder*, she didn't recall any religious practice in his daily routine. "They were all circumcised, I know that. And [Nina's uncle] Iogan was religious—or so it seemed to me back then. He always dressed in black and walked around with a prayer book. But my father didn't believe in God. . . . My mother never even spoke about religion because she wasn't religious herself—and also because it was prohibited." Prior to the revolution, the Leihter family had owned two houses on Primorskaya Street, near the sea in one of Odesa's most prestigious neighborhoods. One of these properties was confiscated by the Soviet regime; the other was taken over by neighbors and vandalized during the Nazi occupation. When I was interviewing her, Nina was still paying visits to her old house, though it was a mere concrete skeleton. She told me she liked seeing the trees her father and grandfather had planted, the yard where she remembered celebrating her birthday, and especially the scent of the seaside air, which infused her memories of the playground of her early years.

Nina's family didn't join the flood of Odesa's evacuees in 1941. Osip and Tauba refused to believe the Germans would invade their city. Her uncle Ruvin, who had lived in Germany more than four years, would say, "It's all a conspiracy against the leaders of civilization," meaning the Germans. Nina's parents were reluctant to abandon their property and Osip's workshop. "We didn't know what would happen to our house and all our things once we left. We had so many valuables," said Nina, listing their book collection, their white piano, bicycles, workshop machinery, and so on. Similarly, many Jewish families had a hard time abandoning a home and property; they made the choice to remain in the city instead of evacuating.[47] Nina's family stayed in Odesa but went into hiding.

> When the Nazis invaded Odessa, we had nowhere to run. Ships leaving the port were overcrowded with people, screaming children, crying mothers. . . . I remember watching one ship go up in flames as the Romanians started bombing the port. At first we hid in the city's underground catacombs, but due to the damp and dark atmosphere we couldn't stay more than a few days.[48] The Romanians were looking for Jews everywhere, and they relied on the aid of local Russians and Ukrainians. When Romanian soldiers were coming to our courtyard, my mother would hide my father and his brothers in the basement and tell my sister and me to sit silently in our room. There were signs everywhere telling Jews to gather at what they called "meeting points," which mostly turned out to be ghettos. We'd heard rumors that if we went, we would never come back alive, so we kept hiding. Then one day when I was standing on our balcony, I saw a Romanian soldier walk up to one of our neighbors, a young boy, and ask him, "Where are the Jews?" In silence, the boy pointed a little finger at the balcony where I stood. That day, my whole family was rounded up and taken to Slobodka. We'd thought of it as a meeting point, but as I later found out, it was our first ghetto.

In their first week of imprisonment in 1941, Nina's uncle Ruvin, who walked with a limp, was shot "like a dog" in front of Nina's eyes. Osip became very ill and lost his strength; he could barely walk after a month of hard labor in the ghetto. Tauba, Nina's mother, tried desperately to find a way for her family to escape the barbed-wire enclosure. She finally bribed a guard with money her sister-in-law had smuggled in, and Nina's family managed to flee into a nearby forest. For two months, they hid in the woods, surviving on raw and frozen winter potatoes and melting snow. Nina told me she would "never forget the coldness of those nights and the hunger of those days." Exhausted, they were once again captured by the Nazis and transferred to another ghetto, this one in Chechel'nik, a small town in the Vinnytsia region. Osip died a few months after arriving and was buried somewhere Nina has never been able to locate. Less than six months later, Tauba managed to secure a false passport that iden-tified her as a Ukrainian named Tatiana Semenovna Larushkina. With this document she was able to escape with her daughters to a nearby village. There they hid for three years, until the Red Army liberated that region.

When the war was over, Tauba and her daughters returned to Odesa. All of the Leihter brothers—except perhaps Sasha, who had immigrated to the United States—had been killed in the war. Two of Tauba's siblings had survived: Theodor and Klavdia. "We came back to nothing," Nina said. "My family had always considered themselves a lot better than the parochial [*mestechkovye*] Jews around; we held our noses really high in the air. But after the war, our noses were so low they were buried underground." The family house had been vandalized, robbed, and taken over by others. "We were able to live in one of the rooms of our old house, but the rest were occupied by neighbors or complete strangers. Often, we'd see our belongings in other people's apartments, but my mother gave us strict orders not to say a word."

Veidlinger writes that many returning from evacuation found that "in their absence their homes had been occupied by neighbors or others in search of shelter" and, invariably, "their property had been plundered."[49] Many had assumed that evacuees would never return, and that their property was free for the taking. Describing the return of evacuees in Odesa, historian Rebecca Manley notes that Jews were at a distinct disadvantage and faced particular difficulties in reclaiming their properties and belongings.[50]

Nina explained at length how her mother never told anyone where they'd been; the previous three years remained a secret.[51] In that sense, like Elena's mother, Tauba treated the subject of the war as taboo and surrounded it with silence. Nina said of her mother:

> She would often answer questions about where we'd been for the past
> couple of years with a simple answer: "evacuation." She never said anything
> more, and at times she said less. I think she felt guilty that we'd survived
> when others didn't, and at the same time, she was scared that others would
> consider us traitors [*predateli*] who must have protected our lives by
> acting as spies for the Germans. This was Stalin's conspiracy against Jewish
> survivors, whom he labeled "enemies of the state." Following my mother's
> ways, we never talked about our time in the ghetto. Can you imagine living
> through that and never ever talking about it?

Tauba kept her Ukrainian name, Tatiana Larushkina. After the war Frida adopted the name Galina, and Rosalina became Nina. The practice of changing one's name, as Sheila Fitzpatrick points out, wasn't unusual for Jews in the Soviet Union; it was a way to "Russify" their identity and separate themselves from the "backwardness" of distinctly Jewish names, thus escaping their "dangerous" status as "enemies of the state."[52] The three women lived together until

Galina married and moved to Saint Petersburg. Tauba went back to work. It's notable that she chose an environment where silence was part of her daily routine: she worked as the head nurse and a teacher of young children in an orphanage for the deaf and mute. Nina, just ten years old when the war ended, started secondary school. She became a Young Pioneer of the Soviet Union, and later took the Komsomol oath. She went on to continue her education at the Odesa Art Academy, specializing in applied arts.

Nina married and divorced twice and had a son from each marriage—Yura and Kostya. She raised both on her own as she taught art and worked as an artist. And then, at the end of 1989, aged fifty-five, Nina immigrated to Israel. The decision to leave Odesa was one she had to make alone; it involved a lot of "back-and-forth thinking and contemplation." Like many others in her circle, Nina wasn't sure of her future in Odesa, which she described as "gloomy and bare" at that time, but she still considered it her beloved city (*rodnym gorodom*). As we walked down Pushkin Street one day, she stopped to recall how, a few days before leaving Odesa, she'd picked up a handful of earth from this very spot and carried it in a bottle all the way to Israel. "I wanted to take a piece of my home, a piece of my Odessa, with me."

From the start of our conversations, it was clear that Nina's decision to emigrate was not a matter of making aliyah (immigration to Israel). She did not see her move through a Zionist lens. She described her emigration from Odesa as "leaving home," but she did tell me she was comforted by the idea of going to a place where no one would call her *zhidovka* (yid).

Having never traveled abroad, Nina had little knowledge of life outside the USSR. Yura had decided to stay in Odesa (he later immigrated to Germany), but her younger son, Kostya, would go with her. Before leaving Odesa, she attended information meetings organized by the Jewish Agency (Sokhnut) to learn about Israel's housing, social security program, citizenship, and employment.[53] But she didn't have much sense of what "Russian" immigrant life would be like in the "Holy Land," unlike later migrants who had the benefit of letters and phone calls from those who preceded them. The question of where they were going seemed secondary to the question of departure per se. "Whether we would stay in Israel forever wasn't decided, but it seemed unimaginable that we'd ever be able to return [to Odessa]."

Nina and Kostya, then nearly eighteen, sailed from Odesa to Haifa, where Israeli state representatives welcomed them with instant immigrant visas, a prerequisite to applying for Israeli citizenship.[54] Beyond the welcoming, there were challenges. Nina had great difficulty finding employment and struggled with other social problems associated with an immigrant's life. "I was terribly homesick. Whenever I heard the word 'Odessa' I'd have hot flashes and my eyes would light up. If I learned someone was from Odessa, I'd go out of my way to meet them, talk to them, invite them for tea." After nearly four years in Israel, Nina's overwhelming nostalgia, and a certain curiosity about other options, led her to book a monthlong return visit to Odesa.

When she arrived back in the summer of 1993, it seemed to her that Odesa hadn't much changed. "It was still rather gray," she said, "but life was slightly jollier." She told me with excitement how she had visited the Privoz market, a place she'd greatly missed and where she felt at home. She reflected that it was in this city that she had been born and had spent most of her life; it was here that her family graves spoke of her history, allowing her to imagine life as it was, prior to her own generation, as told in the stories of her parents. It was a place where everything was familiar—the language, people, climate, architecture, even the trees. In Odesa, she didn't have to prove herself as an artist, as a person; she could just be. This visit was very important to her.

Five years later, in 1998, Nina's economic situation in Israel worsened and she made up her mind to return to Odesa permanently. "I came back to a changed Odessa," she said, "but I still came back home." She didn't miss Israel. "On the contrary," she said, "I've started to see my life here in Odessa very differently, and I've developed a new love for this city through my weekly walking tours." Besides occasional visits to Gmilus Hesed, the center for elderly Jews, Nina did not take part in the city's Jewish activities, nor did she identify herself as being Jewish through any of the new avenues available to Jews in Odesa. Her two sons had taken divergent paths. Yura shared his mother's secular and nonaffiliated Jewish orientation as part of the Russian-speaking intelligentsia, while Kostya (whose story is told in chapters 4 and 6) had started to partially observe Jewish religious commandments.

As in Viktor's and Olga's families, Nina's immediate relatives were educated Russian-speaking Jews who enjoyed their social status in Odesa. But this world was only a faint memory for Nina, whose early recollections were overshadowed by her arduous and terrifying experiences during Nazi occupation. Nina's silenced Jewish identity and her official Ukrainian documentation made daily life easier after the war, as they had for Elena. Nina didn't deny her Jewish roots, but nor did she call attention to them. She avoided talking about Jewish subjects not because of her Soviet convictions, as with Olga, but because of the fear and horror brought by the Holocaust, a taboo subject.

Conclusion

The stories of these four elderly Jews of the intelligentsia give us a set of reference points and identifiable themes that they themselves saw as central to

understanding their lives and family trajectories: the impact of the Soviet period, Holocaust trauma, and observations on Jewishness, Russianness, and
Ukrainianness. These themes reflected their understandings of self and of their
families; their relationship with Odesa and their thoughts about it being a
distinctive place with its own history; and their sense of the present-day sociopolitical atmosphere. They thus chart orienting points for inquiry through
Odesa's altering social, political, and cultural landscape.

Viktor and Olga spoke of the changes in Jewish values and orientations,
both in their own families and in the greater Odesan Jewish population, which
they saw as "progressive." They viewed Odesa's accomplished and "assimilated"
Jewry as a product of that specific urban culture. For them, this was one of the
great modernizing achievements of their time. They felt that the newly arrived
Jewish educators were trying to reverse this progressive trend by inculcating
the younger generation with the patterns of a traditional Judaism that Viktor,
Olga, and their families had voluntarily relinquished.

Elena's story focused on her hidden Jewish identity, the hardships of WWII
and the Holocaust, and the Soviet antisemitism endured by her parents. But
Elena also relayed more positive memories of Jewish cooking, family stories,
teaching her children about their Jewishness, and learning Hebrew herself as
she made plans to move to Israel. The main themes of Nina's story were the
tragedy of losing family members, the family's property, and its social status in
Odesa, as well as her departure from, and return to, Odesa.

No single interpretation of Jewish lives in the Soviet Union could reveal
a complete picture of Odesa's Jews; there are too many ambiguities and am-
bivalences embedded in memories and representations of Jewishness. For instance, when Olga recalled experiencing the war and anti-Jewish sentiment, she
stressed the distinctive nature of her native city. She explained how discriminatory policies were offset by "personal relations," which "determined more than
state politics." In support of this observation, other life histories collected in
Ukraine in the early years of independence suggest that an individual's place
of residency and generation had the most impact on the extent to which they
followed Jewish traditions.[55]

In contrast, we hear Nina's story of Ukrainian and Russian collaborators in
Odesa and her family's betrayal by a neighbor child. Both Nina and Elena expressed ambivalence about the Soviet system. Elena blamed it for marking her
mother as an "enemy of the state" simply because she was a Jew. Nina criticized
Stalin's regime for treating her family as "traitors," along with other survivors of the Nazi occupation. Although Nina herself joined the Komsomol, and
Elena understood her husband's membership in the Communist Party, neither
woman expressed much admiration for Soviet days. Olga and Viktor, however,

deeply identified with and embodied many of the values that sustained the Soviet system.

Each of these older informants had adopted secularism for different reasons. For Olga and Viktor, it signified identification with the modernizing project of socialism, while Elena's mother had denounced God for undeserved Jewish suffering. All the narrators proudly described the social status they achieved as members of the Russian-speaking intelligentsia and as individuals of cultured backgrounds who had enjoyed careers in art, tourism, and academia. In all cases, Jewishness was one of their inherited identifications—one strand of their being—but by no means the only lens through which they judged their experiences or the experiences of others. There were other social roles and allegiances that also defined their relationship to the state and to their city, family, friends, and colleagues.

These reflections also display a range of views about contemporary Jewish life in Odesa. Viktor and Olga, for example, questioned the sincerity of newly observant Jews and shunned the foreign rabbis and Jewish emissaries who came to Odesa. They participated in organized Jewish life but on their own terms, along with selected "like-minded people" who regularly convened at Gmilus Hesed or the Odesa Literature Museum. Elena had only recently approached the city's Jewish organizations, and mainly used them as education centers for her future life in Israel. She welcomed Odesa's cosmopolitanism, tolerance, and openness to religious freedom, but like others in her generation (and perhaps especially because she'd previously had to hide her Jewish identification), she wasn't comfortable in groups that were exclusively Jewish or in very religious settings. After Nina's long absence from Odesa, she had reached out to Odesan groups, not exclusively Jewish ones, where she and others shared a passion for walking and discussing Odesa's history. She, too, was a member of Gmilus Hesed, which provided medical and other benefits, but unlike Olga and Viktor she didn't take much part in the club's activities.

Soviet-era Jews are often depicted as being highly assimilated, secular, and nonobservant; some see the category as one "largely emptied of its cultural content," with few, if any, key markers of Jewishness.[56] After seventy-plus years of Soviet leadership, the tragedies of the Holocaust, and massive migration, Jewish identity in the Soviet Union has been described as "an ethnicity without an ethnic language; without Judaism as a religion or a way of life; without major cultural markers such as rituals, education, and public performances; without community organization; and even without deep historical roots and memory."[57]

Russian ethnographer Igor Krupnik defends this portrait, a contrast with the situation of Jews prior to the 1917 revolution, when the Russian Empire's

Jewish population was seen as a religious community, as opposed to Soviet Jews and their "largely hollowed Jewish identity."[58] One goal of this chapter is to counter this academic construction, which has long been due for careful examination and criticism. In the Western imagination, the figure of the Soviet Jew came to be defined, as literary scholar Sasha Senderovich points out, by its ambivalence toward traditional Jewish religious and cultural practices.[59] Zvi Gitelman has problematically referred to the Soviet Jew's "thin culture."[60] While Senderovich attempts to look at the Soviet Jew as imagined in Soviet historical and cultural contexts (especially novels, short stories, literary sketches, and films) before it became a figure that needed to be "saved," I use the medium of oral histories to challenge narrow visions of Soviet Jewish experiences embedded in emptiness and repression.[61] Paying attention to how these Jews raised in the Soviet Union have talked about the changing nature of their Jewishness shows how memories of family history and of achievements and hardships have endured, connecting many Jews to a much more complex but no less substantial Jewish orientation.[62] The cases of Viktor, Olga, Elena, and Nina demonstrate that Soviet and post-Soviet Jewishness—though it may be subtle, nuanced, privatized, and internal—is far from "hollowed." As literary scholar Harriet Murav reminds us, questions of Jewish belonging can't be approached "with a fixed template of what Jews and Jewishness are" because the markers of ethnoreligious distinction, particularly in the context of Soviet life, were redefined more than once.[63]

Sociologist Herbert Gans's notion of "ethnicity without content" emerged from his observation of the "symbolic ethnicity" of American immigrant communities (including Jewish ones).[64] Jews in the Soviet Union were exposed to different pressures and opportunities of assimilation than the groups Gans describes and have come to regard themselves as Jewish, mostly along secular, ethnocultural lines without practice or participation in Jewish ethnic or religious culture. They have immersed themselves in the larger Russian, Soviet, and local (here, Odesan) culture, and they have found identity constructions more rewarding than devoting themselves exclusively to their old Jewish culture—which, with the passage of time, had little meaning apart from pleasing the older generations.[65]

As the previous stories show, evolving historical circumstances forced Jews in the Soviet Union, as well as those in America and Europe, to develop their own set of markers (both positive and negative) to recognize one another and define themselves as Jews. For most (urban) Soviet Jews, these markers were mainly concentrated on the value of education (predominantly reading), career achievement, and participation in the activities of the Russian-speaking intelligentsia; they also took the negative form of enduring quotas and other forms of antisemitism. As Markowitz concludes, "To have lived a Jewish life [in the Soviet Union] is to have suffered."[66]

It must be understood that for these Jews, the values of education, career success, and the activities of the Russian-speaking intelligentsia were seen *as Jewish values*—a distinctively urban-Jewish way of living and approaching the world. Other ethnographic studies of ex-Soviet Jewry demonstrate that Jews engage in "contradictory but always meaningful and contextual processes of identity formation" as they combine the supposed mutually exclusive categories of Russian (Ukrainian or Georgian) and Jewish.[67] Literary scholars Larisa Fialkova and Nina Yelenevskaya point out that many of the Russian-speaking Jews they interviewed in Israel "spoke about some elements of the Jewish tradition that had been preserved in families despite all the obstacles. But the meaning of the tradition had undergone significant changes, often remaining obscure even to those who tried to observe it."[68]

Collecting the life histories of elderly Odesan Jews is one of my most cherished experiences. Through their stories, I saw how the lives of middle-aged and younger Jews had been shaped by family and historical lineages. Many of today's middle-aged Jews constitute a generational link between very different values and ways of being Jewish. Their own children have often departed from the orientation of their grandparents or have enriched their secular intelligentsia values with new orientations and behavior patterns linked to Judaism, Jewish culture, and Jewish history. The following chapter moves on to the generations after Viktor, Olga, Elena, and Nina and to the recent and highly visible developments on Odesa's Jewish frontier.

3

Jewish Revival

Opportunities and Tensions

Without the old Soviet restrictions on public display of religiosity, Jewish activity became an increasingly visible part of Odesa's urban landscape since Ukraine's independence. Soon, it pervaded the city's culture. On my first visit to Odesa, I encountered not only the Museum of the History of Odesa Jews but also kosher restaurants, traditionally dressed religious families in the streets, Jewish newspapers for sale, street signs directing drivers to the two Orthodox synagogues, and public Jewish festivals and life-cycle ceremonies. During important Jewish holidays, I saw religious objects such as the sukkah and *chanukiah* along with advertisements for Jewish cuisine.[1] Less obvious was the work of Jewish activists who promoted Odesa as a city with a long and textured history of Jewish habitation. Their work was devoted to "uncovering and popularizing the cultural history of Odessa" through publications, organized talks, tours of the city's Jewish landmarks, and contributions to Jewish cultural organizations.[2]

Since Ukraine's independence, the city council has turned over public buildings that historically belonged to the city's Jewry for use by Jewish organizations. What was once called the butchers' synagogue now houses the Jewish community center Migdal. In another location, Migdal's staff also run Mazl Tov, a Jewish early development center. The Glavnaya (Main) Synagogue belongs to the Litvak Orthodox congregation Tikva Or Sameach, and the former tailors' synagogue is occupied by the Chabad Lubavitch congregation. The famous Brody Synagogue was officially handed over to Chabad in 2016, but the building still serves as the state archives.[3] Students received a stipend to take synagogue-sponsored classes, a practice that has attracted an increasing number of young Jews.[4]

According to Migdal, almost 80 percent of the city's Jewish population prior to the onset of the 2022 war was affiliated in some way with at least one of

Figure 3.1. A sukkah outside the Chabad synagogue. Photo by author.

Figure 3.2. An advertisement for Jewish food week posted at an Odesa café. Photo by author.

Figure 3.3. Jewish men from the Chabad congregation in procession from Rosemarin kosher restaurant after the completion of a Torah scroll. Photo by author.

Odesa's Jewish organizations. A number of these organizations are devoted to caring for the elderly, who are often seen as the "lost generation"—exhausted by their age and secularized by their Soviet upbringing. Other organizations serve the "middle generation," whose members are valued for their contribution in raising their children as Jews. But most programs focus on the youngest generation, seeing them as future decision-makers on such questions as observance and migration and as the cultural transmitters of all that is taught to them in the various environments of Jewish education. While the cultural emphasis is distinct from the spiritual orientation of the city's religious congregations and their supporting organizations, as well as separate from the Zionist ideology of Israeli-sponsored programs, the initiatives of these various organizations tend to intersect. For example, Odesa's Jewish historians and journalists often write for newspapers published by the city's two Orthodox Jewish congregations and for the *Migdal Times*, a magazine produced by the Jewish community center.

This range of organizational activity reveals a vast project of Jewish revival, taken on independently by many separate actors since the end of the Soviet era, to cultivate the Jewish religious and cultural presence in Odesa. The impetus for these distinct groups to pursue this common goal was the assertion that Jews in Soviet times were prevented from connecting to Jewish life by anti-semitism, Soviet repression, and state secularization policies—hence the mission to restore a "lost" Jewishness. However, the varying ideas of "Jewishness" that have entered the rhetoric and cultural representation of Odesa have come through the work of international institutions and private donors, most from the United States, western Europe, and Israel but also, in more recent years, from Ukraine, rather than from the city's Jewish population itself.

The processes of ethnic, religious, and cultural makeover such as those occurring in Odesa are often referred to in popular and academic literature and by activists as *revivals*. The term presumes that what is being "revived" was once part of the cultural milieu; in other words, it's a bringing back to life of a previous culture and set of traditions. The notion of revival implies the existence of historical roots to be recovered and cultivated; it implies the rejuvenation and restoration of forgotten or abandoned elements of a past life. But in Odesa and elsewhere, ethnic, national, and religious revival involves significant innovation, invention, and investment rather than a return to the past. As writer Ruth Ellen Gruber notes in her discussion on monuments to the Jewish experience in eastern Europe, the process of actual physical restoration and reconstruction of Jewish heritage exists in parallel "to the way we reconstruct (or construct) things, in our minds and on the ground, to create new realities rather than 're-create' past models."[5]

The city's Jewish population has long been exposed to competing ideologies and external points of reference. Describing the history of Jewish Odesa, John Klier writes, "Odessa was a town without 'native' Jewish traditions, where new Jewish traditions had to be created."[6] Vladimir Jabotinsky also notes in his journal, "Odessa did not have any tradition, but it was therefore not afraid of new forms of living and activity."[7] At the beginning of the nineteenth century, for example, newly arrived Jews, mostly from Germany and Austrian Galicia, as well as other areas of the Pale, were instrumental in setting up Odesa's most influential religious congregations (as described in chapter 1). Likewise, Odesa's Jewish affairs from 1860 to 1888 were largely controlled by the city's chief rabbi, Aryeh Schwabacher, a German Jew who spoke neither Russian nor Yiddish.[8] One could say that the one main tradition being replicated by the current wave of revival is that of external interventions shaping Odesa's Jewry.

It is in this light that we can better understand the tensions created by what the diasporic community understood as Ukraine's post-Soviet "rabbinic revolution," a stage of development that called on, reanimated, and recast many of the older institutions of Jewish life in Ukraine.[9] Together, these institutions, established throughout the country in places with sizable Jewish communities, created a "full-fledged communal infrastructure consisting of burial societies (*khevra kadisha*), which renewed traditional burial rites at specially allocated cemeteries; rabbinic courts to resolve divorce and conversion issues; kosher kitchens and canteens for the elderly and poor; and *matso* bakeries and butcheries to prepare kosher products."[10] What is being revived in Odesa, therefore, is the possibilities created by outside influences. Even if those influences may be, in part, shaping deeply rooted Jewish institutions and building up Odesa's Jewish life according to existing models of Jewish identification, they should be understood as not merely unearthing and illuminating suppressed relics of the past but rather introducing new dynamics and expectations about the meaning of Jewish life.

This is to say, outside ideologies, representatives, institutions, and practices have long been internalized, negotiated, and disputed in the everyday life of Odesa's Jewish population. Jewish belonging in Odesa hasn't been definitively demarcated by the new voices that are claiming authority and structuring aspects of the revival. Rather, different meanings of Jewishness—both those deeply embedded in the Jewish forms of living in the city and those envisioned as *new*—have been recognized and contested in the various forums of Jewish life. Jews in Odesa may have accepted foreign offers of aid and assistance, but they are still adopting, adapting, questioning, and contesting the discourses and practices that have arisen in the wake of Ukrainian independence.

Historian Mark Bassin and literary scholar Catriona Kelly point out that ideologies (and traditions) don't just "exist"; they are constantly reinterpreted and debated.[11] And as the contributors to their edited volume, *Soviet and Post-Soviet Identities*, emphasize, the relationship of Soviet and later post-Soviet subjects "was not one of unquestioning replication or helpless 'cultural inertia,' but a dynamic process" in which people "constantly reassessed their heritage and its significance as a model for the present, and a guide to everyday behavior."[12]

In this way, what Jews in Odesa experienced after independence reflects the kind of cultural transformations that played out across states of the former Soviet Union. Suppressed ethnic, religious, and national identities did not simply emerge—they were generated and now serve as vectors of ideological contestation. In the words of Bassin and Kelly, "the former Soviet Union can be treated as a variable laboratory of identity construction and manipulation, within which identity operates in different ways and at various levels."[13] Identity narratives in the former Soviet states are, of course, defined by a number of factors outside of national identity, including gender, age, sexual orientation, religion, and geographical region.[14] Religious, ethnic, and national groups in the region are also shaped by various processes of revival. Active arenas for local and international initiatives exist throughout the former Soviet Union among Jewish populations who were thought to have lost, forgotten, never learned, or abandoned their Jewish traditions under the Soviet modernization project.

Investments in a Jewish Revival

Following the immediate breakup of the Soviet Union, newly independent states saw the influx of transnational influences and a greater allowance of religious expression.[15] In particular, they became active arenas for foreign aid and philanthropic initiatives to save, rejuvenate, or relocate Jewish life. As anthropologist Rebecca Golbert observed of Jewish youth in Ukraine's capital, Kyiv, such interventions helped remake "identities and allegiances from a wide range of old and new cultural models emanating both from within and outside the geo-historical borders of Ukraine."[16]

Those international interventions had roots in the 1970s efforts to save Soviet Jewry from the oppression of living under the Soviet regime. In that Cold War context, pressure from American Jewry and others lobbying to "Let Our People Go" eventually forced Soviet leaders to allow some Jewish families to emigrate.[17] After the fall of the USSR, the efforts to restore what was imagined as long forgotten, forbidden, or abandoned—including Jewish education, religious institutions, and cultural activities—were tied with efforts to create paths for emigration.

In 1991, foreign organizations saw that Odesa's Jewish population of some sixty-five thousand had no overarching community structure.[18] A handful of short-lived underground organizations had operated under the Soviet Union, and a small number of elderly Jews occasionally attended the city's sole functioning synagogue, although there was no rabbi, just a *starasta* (eldest member of the community). Most of the Jews I met in Odesa in 2005–7 had only faint recollections of the synagogue's limited activities during that time. Their strongest memories were of visiting its bakery to drop off flour for making matzo for Pesach. Anna, who worked at the Odesa Literature Museum, said she was never told why her father would wait outside while she ran into the small wooden house to give the baker a sack of flour. Only after he died did she realize that her father's membership in the Communist Party kept him from showing an affiliation with anything Jewish.[19]

The contemporary religious authority in the city can be traced to the time just before independence, when Ishaya Gisser, a native of Odesa who had immigrated to Israel several years before, returned to rekindle Jewish life. Shaya (as most people called him) hadn't received his *semikha* (rabbinic ordination), but Odesa's Jewry consider him the city's first contemporary rabbi.[20] Filling the long-standing void in religious leadership, he founded a congregation called Shomrei Shabbos, and in 1992, he persuaded the city council to grant it the old tailors' synagogue, which at that point had long been used as a mere warehouse. Though the congregation was limited to some two hundred people, it was said to have felt like a *full* synagogue.

I met a few of Shaya's first students, some of whom still observe the Jewish commandments. To them, the early 1990s was a time ripe for heightened Jewish self-identification (*nastoiashchego pod'ema evreiskogo samosoznanie*). Describing their first encounters with Judaism in Odesa, they used such phrases as "true enthusiasm," "true interest," and even "true fanaticism." Their affiliation was driven by an intense interest in learning what had previously been forbidden or unspoken. Of course, at the time of independence most state-organized youth movements had ceased to exist, which meant that reasons for affiliation also included "lack of another collective," desire for an "escape from the deep-felt instability," "something new," and a "chance to meet interesting people."

Among my interlocutors, those who either had been affiliated with Shaya's activities or knew him through other social networks felt strongly that he understood and represented the authentic Odesan Jew. Unlike later rabbis in Odesa, he was a native *Odesit*. Evgeniy, a journalist and art collector in his late sixties, praised Shaya for "helping people, not just Jews," and admired the open, humanitarian dimensions of Shaya's "Odessan character." As Evgeniy's friends from the "old days" recall, Shaya never wanted to work under foreign authority and avoided all official affiliations. Although he identified himself as a Lubavitch Hasid, Shaya refused to follow the agenda of the Ohr Avner Foundation, which was funded by the famous billionaire Lev Leviev—who, among others, sponsored the work of Chabad Lubavitch, a branch of Hasidism in the former Soviet Union.[21]

In 1993, Rabbi Shlomo Baksht came from Israel and established the Litvak Orthodox congregation, Or Sämeach, later renamed Tikva Or Sameach. He recruited religious families from Israel to teach in a private Jewish religious school, the first to operate in this period of revival.[22] Rabbi Baksht's community eventually reclaimed the original Glavnaya (Main) Synagogue, which had been used during Soviet rule as a gymnasium for Odesa University.[23]

Aided by foreign donations, Baksht went on to establish an extended network of Jewish schools, including the first Jewish university in Odesa, as well as a home for needy and homeless Jewish children called Tikva.[24] According to an employee of the congregation, Tikva Or Sameach had close to one thousand members by 2006.[25] Leaders of Tikva thus make a powerful claim for its role in a religious revival: "Tikva has . . . been a pioneer in the revitalization

Figure 3.4. The main prayer hall of the Tikva Or Sameach Litvak synagogue. Photo by author.

Figure 3.5. The Litvak synagogue. Photo by and courtesy of Igor Oks.

of Jewish life in Odessa, reaching into the heart of the Jewish community, re-building Jewish identity destroyed by decades of persecution and communist rule."[26]

Rabbi Baksht's community pursued this revival primarily through Jewish education in the teachings of the Torah and the Talmud. This has historically been the case for Litvaks, Jews who followed the *litvish* (Lithuanian) tradition (which also expanded into Belarus), "favoring the analytical and rationalist approach to Jewish lore over the mystical one endorsed by Hasidic rebbes."[27] One interlocutor explained that some Jews regarded Baksht's congregation as "the strictest and most closed and conservative" of the two Orthodox communities that emerged. Though many followers admired Baksht for his dedicated teaching of the traditions, some Odesan Jews saw him as "distant" from the local Jewish population, partly because he commuted between Odesa and Jerusalem, where his family remained.

By 1998, Shaya Gisser could no longer sustain his independence against the pressures from outside Odesa, so he left the city. When I asked observant Jews associated with Shaya why and how he had left, many told me he had no choice. One woman said, "He couldn't compete financially with the money and influence of foreign donors or with the Israeli rabbis who had the resources and personnel to build up the infrastructure for Odesa's observant Jews." In my interview with Shaya in June 2020, he explained that he could not agree to align his programs with the demands of investors: "I made everything with my own hands, and I wanted the investors to support the programs we built. I didn't want to follow their agenda. I acted on my ideals, but I was not a manager." Shaya was succeeded by a Chabad Lubavitch rabbi, Avraham Wolf, who transformed the Shomrei Shabbos congregation by aligning it with the Chabad Lubavitch movement.[28]

Rabbi Wolf, aided by his donors and some ten religious Israeli families, echoed Rabbi Baksht's initiatives by setting up educational facilities and programs to raise religious awareness among local Jews. According to figures provided by the secretary of the Chabad synagogue, the congregation had as many as six thousand members in 2006, based on the number of subscribers to the Shomrei Shabbos newspaper, though only 10 percent of them might have attended services on high holidays. I saw around seventy or eighty men and an average of thirty to forty women at the service on my own Friday visits to the Chabad synagogue and two hundred to three hundred people in the gender-separated halls during the holidays.

Wolf's community was usually regarded as "more relaxed" than the Tikva Or Sameach community, though no less Orthodox, and Wolf himself was widely admired for being "more open" and "more involved" with the greater

Figure 3.6. The main prayer hall of the Chabad Shomrei Shabbos synagogue. Photo by author.

Jewish population than Rabbi Baksht.[29] The Chabad congregation also runs an orphanage for children who are homeless or otherwise at risk. In a similar tone to Tikva, Chabad's message links its revival to the efforts and hard work of its current rabbi. The announcement on its website reads, "With great toil and effort, Chabad Shlichim [emissaries] established a vast communal infrastructure and today, Jewish life in Odesa has been reborn. Under the leadership of the Lubavitcher Rebbe, Rabbi Menachem M. Schneerson, the past decade has seen the reawakening of Judaism in Odesa from total spiritual hibernation. The Rebbe's emissaries, headed by Rabbi Avraham Wolf, the Chief Rabbi of Odesa and southern Ukraine, have spearheaded a wave of activities dedicated to saving the lives and souls of tens of thousands of people."[30]

At the same time, Wolf and his wife, Chaya, were sometimes criticized for being too socially active with the city elite, such as potential donors and supporters, and overlooking the "problematic social pasts" of congregants who had served time in prison. When interviewed by the journalist and writer Vladislav Davidzon in 2015, a Chabad congregant, Yoel, explained that accepting people with troubled pasts was a "prerequisite for establishing a functioning community when the majority of Odessan Jewry is to be found in New York, Haifa,

Montreal, and Berlin." Such acceptance was seen as a way to "integrate the community's base of potential donors."[31]

The fact that the congregants included men with prison tattoos startled one of my friends from abroad on his visit to the Chabad synagogue. But some local congregants have come to see it as normal, even presenting Odesa's history of Jewish "gangsters" to explain that this too is Jewish Odesa. Many Chabad congregants admired Rabbi Wolf for welcoming Jews whatever their background. Others, however, felt the Jewish leadership was crossing a moral line in their affiliation with what some called "Jewish bandits." Gossip spread during the years of my initial research as both rabbis, each claiming the status of chief rabbi of the city, acquired properties, bought cars, and expanded their programs.[32] While some appreciated the fact that Rabbi Wolf was "business-oriented" and thus helpful in connecting people, others condemned this materialistic behavior in moral terms.

In the mid-2000s, Odesa also had a small and much less visible Reform (also called Progressive) congregation, led by Yulia Grishenko (widely known as Julia Gris). Originally from Bryansk, a city close to the Ukrainian-Russian border, she started serving as a religious leader in 2001, when her congregation was founded with the backing of the US-based World Union for Progressive Judaism. Her Temple Emanu-El (renamed Shirat Ha Yam in 2016) congregation was housed in a basement space in a building where faded letters on the façade still spelled out the word "store" (*magazin*). Whereas the Chabad and Litvak communities had managed to reclaim Odesa's historic synagogue buildings, Yulia's efforts to take over the building of the Brody Synagogue—the first synagogue designed along modern lines in Odesa and one of the first in the Russian Empire— faltered due to a shortage of funds for renovation and a lack of support among city authorities. In the mid-1800s, the Brody Synagogue was "the model for Jewish prayer in the city," but Yulia's community in 2007 was a mere hundred or so.[33] By 2021, the Progressive congregation was said to have two hundred permanent congregants. While the Progressive congregation operating in Odesa at that time had no tangible relationship with the Brody congregation in prerevolutionary Odesa, Yulia, like other religious leaders in the city, felt her congregation was "rooted" in Odesa's Jewish history and the important historical imprint of modern Jewish ideology of the place. On numerous occasions she shared with me her disappointment in the city council for not supporting her congregation's claim to the Brody Synagogue, which was, at the time it was built, considered modern and thus, she argued, "progressive."

Overall, Reform or Progressive Judaism has not been as successful as Orthodox Judaism in building up Jewish communities in the FSU. In his 2007 article "Why Chabad Excels in Russia, and Why Reform Judaism Doesn't," historian and Jewish studies scholar David Shneer writes, "While most American Jews were chanting 'Let My People Go' in order to 'save' Soviet Jewry, Chabad was already building an underground infrastructure for Jewish life in the Soviet Union. When Communism fell apart, Chabad was ready to inherit a post-Communist Russia."[34] Beyond their organization and leadership, Shneer explains, Chabad rabbis rarely leave their posts and see their *kiruv* work—bringing other Jews closer to true Judaism—as a mission. Furthermore, their vision of a unitary, authentic Judaism is understandable to many Russian Jews who might have been seeking a clear system of belief after the fall of communism.[35]

Some religious Jews I spoke to did not take the Reform movement seriously; they called it "easy" or "simplified" Judaism. One man in his thirties told me a joke on the topic as he explained the differences between the congregations: "In an Orthodox wedding, the mother of the bride is pregnant; in a Conservative wedding, the bride is pregnant; and in a Reform wedding the rabbi is pregnant." Knowing of these rumors, Yulia blamed the propaganda on Orthodox Jews who regarded the Reform movement as a foreign and recent American invention. Commenting on the same phenomenon in Russia, Galina Zelenina notes that "historically Reform Judaism is not an American but a European invention, and in big cities of imperial Russia, the Jewish public was more used to reformed German-style practices (such as having a choir and organ music during religious services) than to Hasidic rituals, so it would be more accurate to speak of the expansion of the shtetl-born, provincial Hasidism into metropolitan spaces that from prerevolutionary times had been occupied by modern Judaism, and not of planting an American invention on Russian-Jewish soil."[36]

There were even rumors that Yulia wasn't really Jewish at all and that she wasn't officially trained as a rabbi.[37] It was not uncommon among religious Jews to discredit someone's authenticity on the basis of kinship or education. Sadly, Yulia suffered on both fronts.

I suspect that some challenged her Jewishness as a way of saying that she was not Jewish in the traditional sense. When I asked my friend Lina why she thought Yulia was not Jewish, she quipped, "Because she is Reform." Yulia dismissed all the rumors and talk of her legitimacy (as a Jew and rabbi) as hearsay. She saw these comments as an effort to undermine her place in Odesa's religious landscape. At the same time, she understood that the traditional image of a Jewish rabbi in the former Soviet states was, historically, a bearded man. Indeed, Odesa was not unique in its tension between the traditional and the Reform. Similar disputes and attempts to prevent rabbis from Progressive Judaism took place in Kharkiv, Dnipropetrovsk, and other cities in Ukraine.[38]

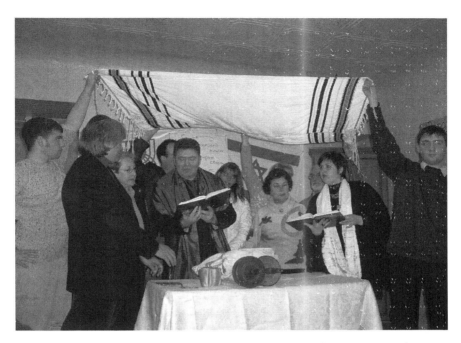

Figure 3.7. Receiving a new Torah scroll from an American delegation at Temple Emanu-El. Photo by author.

The Role of Religious Organizations

Given the firm divisions between synagogues in Odesa, this popular joke will come as no surprise: "How many synagogues does one Jew need? Three. One that is his, one that is not his, and one that he will never go to." Indeed, at the time of my initial research in 2005–2007, there were very few "floaters" (people who attend services and programs at both Orthodox congregations).[39] In fact, relations were strained among the three religious leaders: they interacted on few occasions and agreed on little, apart from the Orthodox refusal to recognize the Reform community. But in only a generation, the three synagogues, their communities, and the organizations behind them had established a firm network of new Jewish institutions throughout Odesa. In addition to holding Shabbat services and celebrating Jewish holidays and life-cycle rituals, each synagogue took over former Soviet-built retreat centers for extended *Shabbatons* (communal Shabbat ceremonies). The programs of the Reform community were admittedly far less developed. It had a youth club, classes on Judaism at the synagogue, annual camps, and communal Shabbat celebrations as well as a Facebook page. In 2006, the kindergarten the Reform community opened on the city outskirts was its first attempt to organize formal education.

The Orthodox communities each established its own mikvah (purifying bath), syndicate of (girls' and boys') schools, children's home, kheder for junior rabbinic study, yeshiva for senior rabbinic study, and kolel offering postgraduate rabbinic study for married men. They also created youth clubs and organized a range of social activities. Both Orthodox communities were publishing weekly newspapers in Russian, distributed free at the synagogue or by subscription, and sponsoring hour-long weekly television programs dedicated to Jewish lessons. Eventually they both published websites dedicated to their activities in the city.[40]

The religious organizations also offered crucial material benefits for their congregants. As my interlocutors explained, you are "provided for" if you're accepted and if you accept the values attached to being Jewish.[41] This recalls anthropologist Melissa Caldwell's focus on the pragmatic factors that contribute to religious revival in Russia, where missionaries and other foreigners find lucrative opportunities both for themselves and their congregants in a new religious landscape.[42] On numerous occasions, I heard Rabbi Wolf point out to donors that there were no homeless people begging outside the synagogue. That had been the case in the 1990s, he recalled, and it's still true outside many churches. Here in the synagogue, Wolf declared, "All those in need are taken care of."

In Odesa, affordable, even free travel abroad was available for Jewish young people—usually to Israel but sometimes to the United States. The synagogues' low-cost, high-quality summer camps taught youngsters Jewish history and traditions and exposed them to Israeli culture. Jewish youth could attend programs sponsored by the Student Union of Torah for Russian Speakers, which often took place on the synagogue premises or sometimes in the private homes of Israeli emissaries; those students received a monthly stipend of seventy-five US dollars. Odesa's Jewish schools had become known for their strong academic curricula, but they also offered students nutritious meals and other forms of care.

In addressing the daily needs of their communities, these new organizations were working to fill the void left by the loss of Soviet state welfare programs. Faith-based organizations, especially those linked to the West, turned the prosperity of their donors, and their philanthropic efforts across the globe, into specific benefits and security for their congregants.[43] Subsidized food, medicine, and home care were given to those in need, if they were members of the religious organization. Unfortunately, seeing these resources provided to Jews by international Jewish organizations prompted a new wave of anti-Jewish sentiment. This appears to be part of a wider phenomenon in which ethnic differences and social hierarchies are used to explain economic and social imbalances. I occasionally heard non-Jewish Odesans complaining about their Jewish neighbors receiving packages from Jewish centers when no such benefits were available to them and expressing their envy of Jews' travel and emigration opportunities, including the possibility of European or Israeli citizenship.[44]

Here we see how a sense of exclusivity created by benefits and resources reserved for members of an exclusive community runs up against older concepts of rightful social distribution. An important legacy of the Soviet era is the socialist assumption that the welfare system provides for all on equal terms.[45] But in contemporary Odesa, being a Jew is no longer an undesirable identity—instead, it gives one privileged status.

New Challenges to Jewish Identification

With the aforementioned privileged status came a much stricter application of the laws of the halakha, which determine membership in the Orthodox community. Again, in the Soviet Union, the state defined Jewish identity as a secular nationality. As historian and Jewish activist Mikhail Chlenov points out: "The new awareness of *halakha* that developed in the Soviet Union in the late 1980s, as a result of migration, led to the creation of new terminology: '*halakhic* Jew,' for those born of a Jewish mother and a non-Jewish father; '*non-halakhic* Jew,' for those born of a Jewish father and a non-Jewish mother; and a 'full Jew,' for people born of two Jewish parents."[46] Due to the high rate of intermarriage between Soviet Jews and non-Jews, the proportion of "full" Jews in the overall Jewish population is, by this definition, relatively small.[47] One of the chief rabbis of Odesa told me, "If you meet a Jew whose parents are both Jewish, it's probably an accident."[48]

Halakhic status is usually affirmed by one's passport and birth certificate or by documents showing the Jewish "nationality" of one's mother or maternal grandmother. Soviet-era passports were therefore reviewed carefully by synagogue personnel to eliminate forgeries, and paperwork was sometimes sent to Israel for a final consultation on those who lacked official documentation, usually as a result of World War II and evacuation. Many elderly informants told me of their distaste at having to present documents to prove themselves Jewish. Raisa, a woman in her eighties, described how angry it made her: "I feel like we have to prove our Jewishness to them. Do they think they're more Jewish than we are?" Indignantly, she added, "We never ask them for documentation." Raisa wasn't alone in finding the identity check a "degrading" process. For those with only Jewish fathers, the result was exclusion from the Orthodox community when they had previously identified and been recognized by the state as Jewish.[49]

Religious leaders insisted that such checks were essential. I heard of cases where documents had been forged in applications to Jewish schools and universities. Such stories are even presented in a positive light, as "the best advertisements for Jewish congregations." As one member of the Tikva Or Sameach synagogue put it, "Back in the old days, people forged documents to hide their Jewish identity. Now they forge them to create one." Documents showing Jewish descent were essential for inclusion in the network of services previously described: emigration; children's admission to Jewish religious schools; religious life-cycle ceremonies such as marriage, circumcision, and burial; membership in many Jewish clubs; social and economic benefits; and subsidized travel to Israel.

A number of my friends in Odesa recalled that people had submitted forged documents to get into the Jewish summer camps they'd attended in their teens—though none of them claimed to have done this themselves. As twenty-three year old Karina said, "It used to be that you didn't have to submit your actual passport for proof of identity. A photocopy was enough, until they realized that many people were writing 'Jewish' under the heading 'nationality,' having masked their Russian, Ukrainian, or other legal status." When I questioned this, Karina explained: "At that time [the early 1990s], there wasn't much to do in Odessa. Jewish children came back raving about their experiences at camp, [so] of course others wanted to go too."

The case of Sasha, an entrepreneur who was twenty-eight when we met in 2006 at the Chabad synagogue, offers a different example. He told me he had always considered himself Jewish, having been raised as a Jew by his father and other relatives. The fact that his mother isn't Jewish was never an issue. But even though he was an active participant in his synagogue, others saw him as an outsider, and he became more isolated as the Chabad community expanded its activities. Comments I heard among Sasha's peers confirmed his suspicion that he was seen as a non-Jew. Sasha told me the following story to describe his relationship with the rabbi:

> I am very close to Wolf and I really respect him, but certain things aren't right. I know the synagogue recently formed a youth club. They don't say it's only for halakhic Jews, but that's exactly the point of it: to separate them from the nonhalakhic Jews so they'll have pure Jewish marriages. Believe me, I know how it works. I know some of my friends asked if I could join the club and the rabbi didn't respond positively. It hurts me. The rabbi sees me [at the synagogue] almost every Friday for Shabbat and the holidays, and he

knows everything I do for him. I know he's happy I'm there, but I now know
the boundaries. I thought about *giur* [conversion], but I don't want to live a
religious life . . . I sin too much.

Similar issues are raised by anthropologist Alanna Cooper in her research on
Bukharan Jews.[50] She documents a number of such "fragmented identities" in
Uzbekistan, where in cases of intermarriage it was common to register the child
according to the father's nationality.[51] These people aren't accepted as Jews by
the Orthodox Jewish organizations now in charge.[52] "You can no longer respond
to the question 'Are you Jewish?' with a simple 'yes' or 'no.' Now the answer is, 'It
depends on who you ask.'"[53] The same is true in Odesa.[54] Amid the transformations in Samarkand that Cooper describes in the late 1990s, Chabad Lubavitch
plays a major role in teaching practical halakha to local Jewry, which includes
the *brakhot* (blessings) on their food, *benching* (blessings after meals), davening
(praying), and wearing a yarmulke and tzitzit (undergarment with fringes). The
vision of Chabad, as voiced by Menachem Mendel Schneerson (the Rebbe), is
that "Torah and the Mitzvoth [religious commandments], the Jewish way of
life which has remained the same throughout the ages and in all places, is what
binds Jews and defines them as 'one people.'"[55] Strict boundaries of who is a Jew
based on halakha left many outside the border of this community.

In some cases, acts of rejection turned Jews away from Jewish life altogether.
In other cases, disappointment led them to withhold loyalty and trust and to
decide that formal conversion was too difficult, unrealistic, or impractical in
their present family and life settings—as was the case with Sasha.[56] I met only
a few Jews who had completed an Orthodox conversion and thus had been
welcomed by the Orthodox congregations.

While the use of the halakha to define Jewish identity excluded some children of mixed marriages, for others it presented opportunities. Among my
interlocutors who'd recently learned of their Jewish roots, the initial inquiry
was most often prompted by possible migration, membership in a Jewish organization, or applying for a job at a Jewish institution, where one was directly
questioned about one's Jewish connection.[57] Vika, a sixteen-year-old student
at the Chabad girls' school at the time of our meeting in 2006, told me her
family's story: "My aunt married a Jewish man and they decided to immigrate
to Israel. During the visa application process, she needed to present her documents, so she went to the archives to try to find something. As it turns out, we're
Jewish—from Polish Jewish roots! My ancestors were from a family of rabbis,
and they were religious. Around that time, my mother was looking for a job
and saw a posting for one at the Jewish kindergarten. There she saw the care
provided to Jewish children, and she transferred me to the Jewish school." For

Vika, this discovery and her mother's choice to enroll her in a Jewish school led her to further pursue Jewish religious education and then to become partially observant.

Other Jewish youth who discovered their heritage later in their lives had similar reactions as Vika and were keen to explore their Jewishness and enroll in Jewish programs. Like those described by writer Barbara Kessel in her book, *Suddenly Jewish*, newly discovered Odesan Jews professed to have always felt a connection to Jews. As one woman Kessel interviewed reported, "My identification with the Jewish world is so strong that I often forget what a long path I had to take to come here."[58] For the youth I met in the context of religious schools, their newfound Jewish identity opened doors, but there were others for whom the discovery of Jewish ancestry didn't spur a call for identity searching. And conversely, as Sasha's case demonstrates, Jewish heritage on the "wrong" side, as deemed by halakic standards, caused some Jews who had always identified as such to have to engage in identity proving.

Israeli Organizations and the Law of Return

Those who are denied Jewish identification by the religious rules of the halakha may still seek recognition of their Jewish status through other Jewish organizations in the city that extend their programs to those who fall under the Israeli Law of Return. Such organizations include the Sokhnut, the agency of the Israeli government that helps Jewish immigrants, and the Israeli Cultural Center; the Migdal Jewish community center and programs funded by the American Joint Distribution Committee (JDC or simply the Joint); and the World Association for the Promotion of Skilled Trades, originally founded in Saint Petersburg and now headquartered in the UK.[59] These groups draw their boundaries in accordance with the criteria for Israeli citizenship, which begins with simply having one Jewish grandparent. Individuals who meet those criteria, as well as their spouses, are regarded by Zionist organizations as potential repatriates to Israel.[60]

While the religious organizations mentioned here tried to facilitate the revival of a religious life and communities in Odesa, as they did throughout the FSU, the Sokhnut and the Israeli Cultural Center (established and operated by the Israeli embassy) "worked toward dissemination of information about Israeli national culture and encouraged repatriation to Israel." The Joint, which was also interested in the revival of local communities and encouraged their establishment, worked to build Jewish programs according to American standards of voluntary, social, nongovernmental, and not necessarily religious lines of organization.[61]

In the political Zionist movement, a person's connection to Jewishness is first and foremost built on the idea of a Jewish nation in Eretz Israel (the Land of Israel). Since the establishment of the state of Israel in 1948, it is expressed most vividly in the act of making aliyah. In Odesa, immigration rights have mostly been publicized through the immense outreach program of the Sokhnut, whose primary mission is to connect (or "reconnect," as its leadership states) local Jews to Israel. Naturally, this meant drawing on the large pool of Odesans who, whatever their relationship to Jewishness, were able to participate in the city's Jewish life and were regarded as potential Israeli citizens.

The Sokhnut thus further reconstitutes the identity of Jews in Odesa, stressing their place in the diaspora and underscoring the implicit assumption about the bond between a people and a territory, where Israel is assumed to be the home of the Jews—a *proper* place for a people."[62] Israel is not alone in offering such "ancestral" rights: other nonnative groups in Russia—Greeks, Germans, Poles—are legally entitled to return to their ancestral homelands and to gain an alternative citizenship, a much sought-after privilege.[63] In my time in Odesa, I did not come across any non-Jews seeking to marry a Jew in order to leave Ukraine, but many of my friends told me this was common in the late 1980s and early 1990s. While Greece, Germany, and Poland welcome back their former people and their descendants, no other country's efforts to regroup its "native" population can compare in scope to those of Israel. Maintaining or increasing Israel's Jewish population is crucial in the realm of politics, economics, and state security and to preserve the Jewish majority over a fast-growing Arab population.[64]

Since the mid-2000s, the number of people moving from Odesa to Israel has dwindled.[65] But the Sokhnut centers continue to operate around Ukraine, mainly as informational organizations publicizing various study-abroad, travel, and internship programs. The centers also run summer camps in and around Odesa, where Jewish youth learn about Israel through its music, food, traditions, and history. The retreat centers are decorated with Israeli flags and other symbols of Israeli material culture, and Israeli teachers trained by the Sokhnut seek to create a sense of belonging among those who have the right to belong. Active participants in the Sokhnut who have recently made aliyah often return to teach at the summer camps. There is also a number of staff members long affiliated with the center who work as local teachers or leaders of small collectives. Some said they experienced some guilt about telling others to go to Israel while not moving there themselves. Diana, a leader of one of the Sokhnut's sponsored programs, told me, "It just looks bad to work for a Zionist organization for so long and not move to Israel." While Diana had considered relocating, her father's poor health and her career as a translator for the European Commission kept her in Odesa. Her choice to remain reflected her effort to balance the Zionist narrative with her loyalty to family and work.

Those who had spent time in Israel were aware that life there presented hardships that the Sokhnut presentations fail to mention. Some of them expressed guilt and discomfort at taking part in what they called the Sokhnut's "brainwashing." When I spoke with Ira, a Russian-speaking Israeli who'd worked at the Kyiv branch of the Sokhnut and had made aliyah five years earlier, I asked her what she meant by "brainwashing." She replied: "They would tell you that everyone's waiting for you in Israel, that life is great, and you'll have a beautiful future there. They didn't tell you about the problems and the issues you could have. . . . Most of them have never been to Israel or anywhere abroad. After years of sending off students, I felt that I simply couldn't stay any longer." Like many others who had left their families to pursue Zionist ideals, Ira was quite cynical about the Sokhnut's activities. The vaunted "gold mountains" were nowhere to be seen; the beautiful life described by the Sokhnut was never to be experienced.[66] While some worked through a difficult period of adaptation, it was not uncommon for disenchanted young people to choose return migration (see chapter 6).

Community Building: The American Dream

Each of the religious and Zionist organizations influencing Odesa had its own agenda and mode of Jewish expression. US philanthropic organizations were broader community-building projects that followed a more flexible (Reform) structure of religiosity and Zionism and were modeled on the Jewish community center (JCC) projects across the United States.[67] In the summer of 2006, I accepted an invitation to participate in a focus group organized by the Joint to discuss the future of Odesa's new $4 million JCC, now officially named the Jewish Community Campus, or Beit Grand. Program leaders hadn't yet reached a consensus about the center's function, and the Joint sought to understand what local Jews wanted from it. The interviewer posed this opening question to me and the five other focus group members: "What reaction would you have to a place called the Jewish Cultural Center?"

Katya, a twenty-six-year-old architect, thought the title sounded rather "exclusive," and too close to the names of other Jewish organizations in the city. The fact that you had to present documents proving Jewish descent to become a member, she said, underscored the sense of exclusivity—a feeling that was already widespread in the city and would be further inflated given the scale of this new campus in the city center.

When someone pointed out that there are non-Jews who participate in Jewish organizations, Katya asked, "Yes, but how many?" Dasha, Katya's roommate,

Figure 3.8. The Jewish Community Campus, Beit Grand. Photo by author.

of Russian descent, said that although she wasn't Jewish, she was glad to participate in Jewish activities. But while the few events she'd attended with Katya were "interesting" and "cool," she did feel left out of certain ceremonies and discussions, such as those related to free travel to Israel under the Law of Return. Katya asserted that some non-Jewish Odesans are familiar with Jewish activities in the city and welcome them, but they're in the minority. Most of the participants agreed that although Odesa always had a Jewish presence, it never stressed any sort of ethnic "purity."

Alex, a twenty-three-year-old IT specialist, said that he didn't even know which of his friends were Jewish—and though he himself was Jewish, he didn't feel the need to declare it to everyone. "But if I said to my friends, 'Let's go to the Jewish Cultural Center,'" Alex continued, "we'd all be wondering which of us was Jewish, and what that meant." According to Alex, such centers create divisions among people and pose questions about "who you are and who you're with, based on just your nationality rather than your interests." In his eyes, Odesa was a city where people of different backgrounds mixed with one another and weren't separated on the basis of nationality.

After some more discussion, the focus group leader asked, "How would you feel about the integration of non-Jews in such an organization?" Everyone agreed that the center should be open to non-Jews, but no one had clear ideas on how to regulate membership or what non-Jews would find attractive in the programs. Katya and Alex again brought up the issue of separating activities and people into the bracket of "Jewish," saying that this would increase social divisions. All the participants agreed that although the city has Romanian, Greek, German, French, and English cultural centers that are open to all, a Jewish cultural center would mean something different—but no one could really explain why. Since the institution's official name was still undecided, some participants suggested it be called the Israeli Cultural Center.

David, a twenty-six-year-old observant Jew who at the time lived in Jerusalem and was visiting his family in Odesa, responded, "There's already an Israeli Center in the city. This project will be a Jewish center, not an Israeli one." When the focus group ended, David left with some disdain, clearly feeling at odds with the group. I caught up with him to talk, and he explained that he wasn't used to hearing Jews be so critical of their own culture: "I'm a religious person, and for me a Jewish organization is a natural part of life. It's where you meet other Jews and maybe find a Jewish wife."

Beyond the focus group, I heard much dissent among Odesa's Jewry about this new home of Jewish life. Some believed that many Joint employees had enriched themselves by pocketing investors' money. Others said the building was redundant since the city already had a Jewish center, Migdal, and that it was too big—"twice as large as the Jewish population itself." Leaders of local programs complained about having to share space with the commercial businesses that would be renting part of the building to help cover its costs. Some potential participants were affronted by the high prices of the programs to be offered. One visitor expressed shock at learning that employees of the new organization didn't even know that the Museum of the History of Odesa Jews is located on the same street, directly opposite the new center. But the fundamental question among the Jewish population was what would another Jewish center say to Jews in Odesa about the commonalities and differences among themselves and with others? In this way, Beit Grand brought to light a general apprehension that funds from foreign donors to promote Jewish activities and events didn't necessarily help Jews in their daily lives. Some felt the project lacked a connection with Odesa as a place, with its values of diversity in Jewish practice and close interethnic relations. Because so many of the city's families are of mixed origin, some felt that such projects should be sensitive to the role of non-Jews in Jewish institutions.

These conversations reminded me of what Viacheslav, a middle-aged man who ran a math club in the early 1990s, said about the potential fall of Odesa's cosmopolitan ethos. He used the example of the rise of Jewish schools: "It used to be that everyone in Odessa had at least one Jew in their class. They knew what Jews looked like and who they were, either through close or even distant interaction with them. In my own classroom, when I was a student, I had Ukrainian, Albanian, and Greek friends. Children in Jewish schools are surrounded only by other Jews. This limits their sociality with others." According to Viacheslav, both Jews and non-Jews would suffer from this lack of everyday interaction: each group would see the other as fundamentally different, which would erode the city's multinational character. Viacheslav said that in his math club, "No one asked each other, and no one cared if the others were Jewish. We were all interested in math and problem solving. We came together because of our interests, not because of a superficial tie based on our nationality." He also stressed that the Jewish schools fail to teach *Odesika* (Odesan history and culture). Although Jewish subjects are taught, along with a secular curriculum, the religious values adopted by the children in Orthodox Jewish settings do privilege a transnational and transhistorical bond to the Jewish people.

Viacheslav's account of the cohesiveness among students of mixed backgrounds in his classroom was similar to stories told by older Jews in the city. But like many recollections, these may be somewhat romanticized. Certainly, people revealed more about painful episodes of being called *zhid* or *zhidovka* in the schools they'd attended previously. But besides the conflict-related reasons for attending Jewish schools, many students I met described their experience at a Jewish school as "interesting" and "exciting." Karina, a seventeen-year-old student at the Chabad girls' school, spoke of the thrill of learning a new language (Hebrew), being in a milieu that often included foreign teachers, and interacting with foreign students visiting Odesa. She welcomed the chance to learn about her religion and heritage and spoke proudly of herself as a Jew.

While Viacheslav didn't mention the new transnational relations being forged in the classrooms of religious Jewish schools, this aspect of the schools was especially valued by Karina and a number of other students I met. Many students in Odesa's Jewish religious schools were indeed gaining access to the large network of Jews overseas. Like the Ukrainian Jewish youth in Kyiv described by Golbert, they were experiencing "transnational orientations from home" and being linked into cross-border networks, relationships, institutions, experiences, and lifestyles—without even having to travel.[68]

Anna Misuk, a local historian and employee of the Odesa Literature Museum who'd been involved in various Jewish projects since the early days of perestroika, frequently mentioned that contemporary Jewish life in Odesa was increasingly isolated from the city's wider social environments. She made an interesting analogy between learning a new language and learning new ways to be Jewish:

> When people are fluent in a language, they can make up words and speak incorrectly, but they know when it becomes nonsense. When you're

learning a new language, you don't have the same comfort and security in your understanding of what you can and cannot say. This type of "disloyalty" [to the rules] is unknown to many people today. A nonfluent speaker or a novice, similar to the newly observant Jews, isn't as secure in his or her language skills and thus often relies on other authorities, such as books and the advice of assumed-to-be experts, to make their judgment. Before, when Jews were exposed to various ways of being Jewish, they understood that their transgressions didn't take away their Jewishness. In other words, they were no less Jewish for having stepped outside Jewish Orthodox law—especially in Odessa, where Jews lived in a relatively liberal manner. Today, when Jewish education is mostly directed at bringing assimilated Jews into the religious Jewish world—thus stripping them of all that's condemned as non-Jewish—a stricter trend of observance follows.

During her years of working for various Jewish initiatives, Anna had met young people who now judged and valued their Jewishness on the basis of religious or traditional principles. These newly "literate," rule-bound young Jews were sometimes prone to ostentatious displays, such as refusing to ever set foot in a church. Anna questioned this: to her, it was obvious that Jews don't lose their Jewishness by entering a church, any more than they could easily gain it by entering a synagogue. Newly observant Jews, like new language learners, felt less comfortable making such judgments. In Anna's view, since they'd only recently taken on an identity filled with new terminology, symbols, and laws in which they weren't yet fluent, they lacked the inner authority of "just knowing."

Anna both endorsed Jewish education and worried about it. She welcomed the openness of learning in the post-Soviet environment and the opportunity to explore explicitly Jewish topics. She was also concerned that such teaching would adversely affect how Jews related to other Jews and to non-Jews. The current narrowing of interethnic contact in Odesa was, for her and others, a departure from the historical achievements of the city's uniquely cosmopolitan way of life. With the boundaries between ethnoreligious groups becoming more clearly delineated, Anna believed there was a perceptible increase in intolerance—such as the spray-painted swastikas that sometimes appeared in the city.

Conclusion

Anthropologists have long investigated tradition and "related notions of authenticity as symbolic, interpretive constructions in and of the present through the invocation of links to a meaningful past."[69] In a postsocialist reality, writes anthropologist Ludek Broz, revival "entails utilizing the past to advocate a particular vision of the future."[70] Under conditions of marked social and cultural change, the ideology and rhetoric of tradition are understandably more apparent.[71] We have seen in this chapter how the processes of building up Jewish life in Odesa meant calling on destroyed or abandoned practices and institutions along with new values, practices, and orientations that weren't always easily absorbed. If there was revival, there was also negotiation and resistance. Moreover, the Jewish organizations harbored competing notions of what it was that needed reviving, which resulted in a lack of cooperation and even in rivalry.

Some local and newly arrived Jews believed that Odesa's rich Jewish history made it particularly open to such a project of revival. I interviewed many Jewish leaders and activists involved in organized Jewish life who earnestly saw themselves as rebuilding a lost and forgotten world of pre-Soviet Odesan Jewry and continuing the legacy of Jewish life in Ukraine. After all, nineteenth-century Odesa was home to a number of vibrant traditional communities, including the Glavnaya (Main) Synagogue, with its large congregation, and more than seventy smaller prayer houses, including followers of Hasidism. Observant followers of Chabad felt strongly that living as religious Jews in Ukraine connected them to the long history of Hasidim and righteous tzaddikim who once lived in the shtetls and cities of the Pale of Settlement, located in what is today the independent Ukraine.

Likewise, Odesa was also famous for the impressive modern congregation of the Brody Synagogue and for being one of the centers of Zionist activity, Jewish press, Jewish education, and Jewish philanthropy. Thus, a number of the city's organizations had taken up prerevolutionary names, such as the Jewish publishing house Moriah (a reference to the biblical land of Moriah translated as "the place where God worshiped" but also "land of Torah"); the Jewish sports community Maccabi (named after the Maccabees, Jewish warriors who fought Antiochus IV Epiphanes in the Seleucid Empire in 175 BCE); and the Jewish literary club Beseda (which means "conversation").[72] But it's arguable how much the new organizations can be considered historically Odesan. The Soviet system destroyed prerevolutionary Odesan Jewish institutions, so in this sense, there are few roots left to revive. Instead, the Soviet era produced secular markers of Jewish identity rather than religious ones; thus, as Tanya Richardson observed in Odesa in the early 2000s, the wave of religiosity seen at that time was regarded as alien "for some Odessan Jews who grew up in the Soviet era and who did not emigrate." For them, "the deeply religious communal life that is becoming increasingly dominant is in fact foreign to the city and to their own idea of what it means to be Jewish."[73]

My observation is that religiosity in Odesa is less "alien" than what Richardson describes and more accepted as a way of "being Jewish." However, recall that some secular Jews, especially the members of older generations that I interviewed in 2005–2007, were skeptical of the ardent observance they witnessed on Odesa's streets among the younger generations. Still others claimed to have always lived Jewish lives or described coming to Jewish observance by their own idiosyncratic path (as I show in the next chapter).

Such a range of Jewish identification indeed challenged the idea that international Jewish organizations were reviving or rebuilding Jewish Odesa. Although Jews in Odesa were more assimilated than the communities of Bukharan Jews living in central Asia, who historian Zeev Levin describes as being treated like "lost children," we can argue that the Jewish qualities of Odesa's past and present were behind the arguments of some Odesans, who said that they lived and identified as Jews in what they believed to be a Jewish city always.[74] In other words, many Jewish Odesans of the older generation felt they needed not to be "rescued" but rather to be left to continue along paths that they had established while navigating Soviet Jewish ideology and the cultural context of the Russian Jewish intelligentsia—or by the sheer fact of having been born and raised in the milieu of Odesa's Jewishness (food, language, literature, and myths).

At the same time, because most Jewish activists have emigrated from Odesa, and from the rest of Ukraine, outside Jewish organizations have taken a leading role in the city.[75] To see this, one need look no further than the relatively weak status of Odesa's Reform Jews today and the dominant position of the two Orthodox congregations, especially the stronghold of Chabad Lubavitch.[76] This "is an ironic renewal of Hasidism in a city that was always better known as a center for liberal Jewish traditions."[77] Although some scholars have linked the success of Hasidism in Ukraine to the historical importance of the area for the development of the Hasidic movement, Odesa was never regarded as the center of Hasidism. In fact Chabad, the most popular strand of Hasidism in present-day Ukraine, was born in the Russian village of Liubavichi and hence is far from endemic to the city.

Thus, it can also be argued that present-day missions of world Jewry are importing and imposing variants of Judaism that are new to Odesa. Indeed, I found the Jewish residents of Odesa divided in their views on any development said to represent them and in their understanding of what "Jewish" would mean. In the end, it's questionable how far we can generalize about any continuing Soviet imprint on the thoughts and behavior of Odesa's younger Jews. As Martin Horowitz, director of the Jewish Community Development Fund in Russia and Ukraine, points out, "the growth of at least two generations of Jewish youth who have experienced open celebrations of Jewish holidays,

Figure 3.9. Children at the Mazl Tov, the Jewish early development center, prepare for the Passover celebration. Photo by author.

attendance at Jewish schools, and an environment of open, public Jewish activity has produced a Jewish youth quite different in attitudes and sensibilities from its [Soviet-era] parents."[78] The imported Jewishness has become their own, and they associate their participation in Judaism with the participation of their ancestors.

Anthropologist Mathijs Pelkmans's edited volume, *Conversion after Socialism* (which mainly focuses on Christian and Muslim conversions), highlights the "problematic notion that religious life after socialism can be characterized as a *revival* of repressed religious tradition."[79] As he points out, in post-Soviet times "religion served new needs and was linked to new imaginaries." In the next chapter, we see how in the aftermath of state socialism, Judaism was introduced to Odesa's Jews as a religious system of beliefs, values, and practices and how these have been internalized in a variety of competing and conflicting ways.

4

From *Evrei* to *Iudei*

Turning or Returning to Faith?

The previous chapter illustrates the institutional dimensions and societal importance of Odesa's major synagogues as well as the role that visible Jewish celebrations, symbols, and rituals have come to play in the city.[1] This chapter, in turn, focuses on the personal testimonies of those whose relationship to Judaism was redefined in these new institutional and cultural contexts. The stories told here help us understand how and why some Jews responded to this emergent public Judaism and how religious ideas, institutions, and leadership influenced personal, kin, and social relations in the city. They demonstrate the sometimes-fraught relationships between newly observant Jews and their nonobservant family members and friends. And they show the general skepticism and doubt expressed within and outside some of Odesa's religious Jewish circles about the authenticity and sincerity of the newly observant or overtly religious practices. I argue that adopting a religious identity in twenty-first-century Odesa *became* a way for Jews to define their Jewishness by turning to, rather than returning to, religious practice and faith.

Throughout this chapter, I highlight the notions of "tradition" and the descriptions of what is "traditional" or "traditionally done" as conveyed by my interlocutors. In its general usage, *tradition* refers to "elements of historical continuity or social inheritance in culture, or the social process by which such continuity is achieved."[2] In some contexts, secular Jews used the term to refer to the collective social inheritance or collective identity, such as traditions that are "Odesan," "Soviet," or "Jewish," as they referenced beliefs, practices, habits, routines, institutions, or texts, among other things. But in the context of Odesa's religious Jewish population, the term *traditsionnyi* (traditional) demarcated a level on the hierarchy of observance. By claiming to be *traditional* in this way, they were demonstrating their knowledge of Jewish religious practices and partial commitment to some observances, which, they indicated, distinguished them from the secular as well as the fully observant Orthodox. In its practice-centered understanding of tradition, there is an assumed temporal continuity guided by precedent and convention, and tradition is construed as replicating what has been done before, regulated by the moral weight of public opinion, especially that of ancestors.[3] But in the case of Odesa's Jewry, traditions inherited from ancestors and learned in post-Soviet Jewish institutions sometimes showed themselves to be contradictory—the situated practice, ideology, and rhetoric about tradition may "serve as well for conflict as for the 'binding force' of acquiescence."[4] By claiming to be "traditional," younger Jews indicated their separation from their immediate family while establishing a connection with a more distant imagined community: the Jewish people. Moreover, in most families, children taught in various Jewish centers of activity educated their parents about the "traditional" ways of the Jewish people, as such, reversing the ancestral role in the inheritance.

For many Orthodox congregants who claimed to be "following traditions" or who described themselves as "traditional," such assertions served as claims to authenticity that rested on the historical reach of Orthodoxy (and Orthodox teachings to this day) and revealed the congregational politics between Orthodox and Reform in Odesa. Some elderly secular Jews, who had long internalized a Soviet theory of modernization, used the term *traditional Jews* to pejoratively refer to those who were "shtetl-like" and "backward." In this way, they challenged the local hierarchy of knowledge linked to Jewish observance.

Anthropologists have long pointed out such dynamics in the politics of tradition—traditional tales as instruments of divisiveness rather than unity and performed in defense of competing claims to status.[5] In Zvi Gitelman's analysis of the evolution of Jewish identities, he asks simply, "Is 'Jewish' an ethnic or a religious adjective?"[6] The Russian language supports this distinction by providing two words for "a Jew": *evrei* and *iudei*. The word *evrei* is used for a member of the Jewish ethnic group (Hebrews) or the Soviet-defined nationality (*evreistvo*); *iudei* identifies a Jew as "a follower of the laws and rituals of *iudeistvo* [the Jewish religion], or *iudaizm* [Judaism]."[7] This explains how a survey analysis of post-Soviet Jewish life conducted in the 1990s found that "Jews in the FSU do *not* strongly connect the Jewish religion with being Jewish."[8] Competing and contradictory qualities and content of being Jewish are not specific to Odesa, to Ukraine, or even to the larger territory of ex-Soviet states. Rather, individuals draw on entirely different domains to explain their sense of Jewish identification—ritual practice, ethnicity, shared history, secular culture, and common descent, for example—which reminds us of the extent to which "all expressions of social solidarity are, like the identities from which they stem, both socially produced and culturally inflected."[9]

In the Odesa that emerged out of state socialism, Judaism as a religion was a defining feature of Jewish identity. Even among my less-observant friends in Odesa, I witnessed how life cycle rituals (births, coming-of-age birthdays, weddings, and funerals) and Jewish celebrations were increasingly infused with Judaic markers. Many of Odesa's Jews had indeed begun to see their Jewishness through a religious lens, using vocabulary linked to Judaism, partaking in Jewish religious practices, dressing religiously, observing some religious commandments, and taking on Jewish names. Yet, it wasn't out of the ordinary for some to adopt religious practices without adopting the label "religious."

In light of this change of practice, this chapter questions the validity of the term *revival* in the context of religiosity more than two decades after state socialism. Although the number of religious communities in the city increased between the years 1991 and 2003, local sociologists saw religion and religious values as marginal to the overall public consciousness. This observation led them to conclude that while one might have spoken of a religious rise in Ukraine in the mid-1990s, by 2003 that was no longer the case.[10] Some scholars have argued that although there was a "general decrease in Jewish educational activity by the Jewish population" in Russia and Ukraine after the early 1990s, those who regularly attended religious programming expressed a "deeper interest" in these subjects than before.[11] Other studies support the view that this is not specific to Odesa and that *revival* is a problematic term to describe religiosity in the FSU for several reasons. In her research on Russian Jews in Moscow, Galina Zelenina casts doubt on the term *revival*, noting that because most of the underground religious Jews and those involved in the national movement had left, "the Jewish revival of the 1990s was carried out by new actors and organizations, and it produced new ideas."[12] In Kyrgyzstan, Mathijs Pelkmans finds a comparable phenomenon: although the number of mosques rose and people more readily asserted their religious affiliation, "it is questionable to what extent this meant more active participation in Islam, or Christianity for that matter."[13] Pelkmans reports, "I was more struck by the lack of interest most Kyrgyz displayed in religion than by a 'religious revival.'"[14] Similarly, in Odesa at that time, one's affiliation or even observance of some traditions didn't necessarily convey a religious belonging.

Defining the Borders of Religious "Community"

Orthodox Jews, most often, define themselves by their religious observance of Shabbat and the laws of kashrut and *nidah* (family purity).[15] But as social anthropologist Jonathan Webber points out, Orthodoxy "may mean different things in different contexts."[16] The Orthodox Jews I met in Odesa tended to label people as religious according to the standard of a commitment to observance rather than on faith (in the sense of *belief*). Thus, many of Odesa's Orthodox Jews used the words *religioznyi* (religious) and *sobliudaiushchie* (observant) or *sobliudaiushchie traditsii* (observant of traditions) interchangeably. Other ethnographers have described Judaism as an embodied religion that is articulated through practice and organically connected to the cultures where it is embedded.[17] Pelkmans notes a similarity among the mainstream Sunni Islamic communities and Orthodox Christians who use the label "religious" to refer to that commitment to practice instead of belief. But he draws a distinction with Protestants (especially Evangelical Pentecostals) for whom *religion* and *religious* are suspect terms to be avoided compared to the true marker of faith.[18]

It was not uncommon for Jews in Odesa to define themselves as Orthodox simply to mark their difference from Reform Jews. To locate themselves more precisely within the local sphere of Orthodoxy, they named their orientation as either Chabadnik (follower of the Chabad Lubavitch congregation) or Litvak (follower of the Lithuanian Orthodox movement, Tikva Or Sameach). As for the far fewer congregants of Progressive Judaism (Reformisty), they placed *belief* above the strict adherence to rituals of observance, observing them in their own ways. It must also be noted that there were Jews in Orthodox settings who claimed to be *veruiushchie* (believers) but not *sobliudaiushchie* (observants) and others who identified as not religious but felt more connected to the Orthodox community's approach, atmosphere, and ideology. Most Orthodox congregants were not observant but were aligned in their view that Orthodox Judaism was authentic Judaism.

According to the chief rabbi of the Progressive Jewish Congregations in Ukraine, Oleksandr Dihovnii, what defines Reform congregants as religious Jews is their "Jewish soul." This faith in Judaism guides their moral actions in life, and the ethical commandments are emphasized as key markers of Jewish identity. But in the Progressive perspective, rituals can be transformed to meet the needs of the present. In Rabbi Dihovnii's view, Jewish traditions are always evolving and are enriched with new meaning with every new generation. Based on this definition, members of Rabbi Yulia's Reform congregation whom I observed during my research identified themselves as religious even though they didn't follow strict commandments. Their practice of Judaism included participating in synagogue life and celebrating Shabbat and the Jewish holidays—events where men and women mixed, and there was singing and guitar music. They viewed these practices as symbolic activities important for their Jewish identity and regarded adherence to strict religious commandments as old ways of marking Jewishness that were no longer suitable for modern times.

In this way they saw themselves as more "modern" and continuing Odesa's long lineage of modern Jewish traditions.

Likewise, Jews affiliated with the wide array of religious institutions throughout the city did not feel that adhering to strict religious commandments was part of their Jewish identity. Many Jews used synagogues for social and educational activities. Many relied on the aid and welfare provided by the congregations; others came to see friends, meet potential partners, broker business deals, or catch up on the latest news and gossip. As mentioned earlier, many subscribed to the Jewish newspapers that are printed in Russian and distributed free of charge: the *Shomrei Shabbos* newspaper, for example, has six thousand subscribers. None of these facts necessarily reflect any particular pattern of observance. I met many students in Jewish schools, universities, after-school programs, and camps who followed the rules of religious conduct when they were within an institution but not when they were outside of it. The "proper" codes of behavior and dress were matters of institutional necessity, not rules for their private lives. Even the religious organizations understood that they could only teach and preach the importance of their rules and commandments, not dictate personal choice, and they therefore requested that at least in public, religious rules be observed.

Although religious leaders saw their congregants as part of their religious community—many Jews applied the term only to those who they knew lived by religious laws within and outside Jewish institutions—observance was often only partial among the majority of affiliated Jews in Odesa. Joseph Zissel, director of the Association of Jewish Organizations and Communities of Ukraine, said half-jokingly in an interview in 2019 that "the majority of Jews in Ukraine are not religious. But don't tell that to the rabbi. They think everyone is religious."[19] He estimated there were five to six thousand religious Jews in Ukraine. As for *which* observances might mark one as religious in Odesa, the question invited reflection. Vera, who was born in 1976 and saw herself as religious (and even taught Judaism), put it this way:

> First of all, it's difficult to say who exactly fits into that [observant] cat
> egory. Obviously, those who keep Shabbat, kosher, proper dress, mikvah,
> and so on. But as you know, in Odessa you meet people who observe these
> commandments in various combinations. Take me, for instance: kosher,
> Shabbat—but I wear trousers and not a skirt [as is demanded of women
> by the Jewish law, halakha]. I think that for many, my status is [therefore]
> questionable. Second, today there are a number of people who don't neces
> sarily demonstrate their observance of commandments publicly. They live
> by them, but you don't really see them doing it.

In other words, Jews who were religious in differing ways couldn't easily identify one another, but to most, those who observed Shabbat and laws of kashrut were generally regarded as religious.

Again, it's important to note that the three religious congregations were independent of one another, offering few joint events. Noting the rarity of multicommunal events, one of the employees of the Chabad congregation told me that the two Orthodox congregations were last brought together for the great cycle celebration of the sun (*birkat hakhama*), which occurs every twenty-eight years and took place on April 8, 2009. And while Odesa has never had and still does not have a Jewish quarter, observant Jews looking to buy property made it a priority to live within walking distance of their synagogue, which resulted in more concentrated Jewish areas surrounding the two congregations in the center of the city. This division carried over into gender distinctions within the congregations because women, unlike men, were not obliged to participate in public prayer. Exempt from such specific time-bound commandments, women could find themselves praying alone at home, without meeting one another as observant Jews. Jewish men, on the other hand, were brought together by the obligation to pray three times a day, preferably in the presence of a minyan and usually in the synagogue.[20] For a number of elderly Jews, and in some cases their children, avoiding public displays of traditions was also a relic of Soviet upbringing, when much of the observance of commandments, if practiced, moved into the private and domestic realms.

These varied orientations toward being Jewish are partly a matter of religious flexibility and partly the result of Odesa's changing religious environment. Many of the old ways of being identified as Jewish in Odesa, in Ukraine, and throughout the FSU are disappearing or have already faded from view. The Soviet passport designation of "Jewish" as a nationality, along with state-directed antisemitism and Jewish quotas in education facilities and workplaces, is no more. The idea that being Jewish was a secular, biologically inherited identity passed through either parent that for many meant belonging to the Russian-speaking intelligentsia has been eclipsed by rules of halakha and the practice of specifically religious Jewish rituals and traditions.[21] Thus, even those Jews who rejected the new religiosity, or whose observance was less public or visible, were defined by an environment of controversy, negotiation, and experimentation that has surrounded Jewish traditions since the late 1980s.

For instance, when my friend's father died in Odesa in 2006, the *khevra kadisha* required that his corpse be circumcised before they could give him a Jewish burial. While I was shocked to hear about this at the time, his daughter reassured me that all "halakhic Jews" had to be circumcised before they could be buried. "By tradition means by tradition" (*Po traditsii znachit po traditsii*), she concluded. She wasn't at all distressed. But a Jewish friend raised in Soviet Odesa who was now living in the US was deeply upset that a man who had lived as a Jew his whole life now needed a new confirmation and affirmation of his Jewishness, as defined by the Chabad rituals, to be buried as a Jew. It is apparent that having some old traditions like circumcision reinstated after a person's lifetime, as a correction to Soviet Jewishness, aroused ambivalent feelings among some close friends who questioned this transgression, especially without the person's consent. But kin who were educated in the new canons of Jewish practice accepted the practice as the correct and "traditional" ritual in the burial procedure.

From Secularism to Judaism: Motivations and Paths of Return

Because most of the older generations of Soviet-raised Jews I met in the mid-2000s grew up secular, very few could teach their children about Judaism. This meant that for many families, religious upbringing in postindependence Odesa had to take place outside the home. The newly observant Jews I met learned about religious observances through interactions with religious Jewish emissaries and Jewish organizations or through personal relations with an observant Jew. They were not recovering a previously abandoned or suppressed family practice, as implied by the term *ba'al teshuvah*, which is often used by religious leaders who consider newly religious Jews to be those who "repent and return" to Judaism.[22] Rather, most newly observant Jews described their journey as twofold: first, they rejected what they often called the "religious/spiritual emptiness" and "absence of knowledge" about Judaism and moved toward learning and eventually adopting a new value system strongly attached to faith in God and the practice of the commandments (such as keeping Shabbat and so on); and second, they gave up their non-Jewish practices.

To be clear, many Odesan Jews did not move up a "progressive scale of observance," to quote the phrase used by Rebecca Golbert to describe young Jews in Kyiv who similarly "reject[ed] the institutional model of religious development."[23] Instead, as the stories that follow show, Odesa's Jews engaged in attachments to religiosity that were partial, indefinite, or interrupted or that had even been abandoned altogether. Along the way, many of them questioned their own commitment—and that of others—to religious practice and faith. I met observant Orthodox Jews who described a "process" that began with, say, no longer eating pork and moved on to accumulating religious responsibilities that led to daily observance of such rituals as prayers, dress codes, and dietary laws. But the steps were varied, and the process took longer for some than it did for others, with changes of direction and devotion. Some abandoned observance altogether.

Many of the foreign Jews working in Odesa described the new religiosity along the lines of a return and revival. They tended to see Odesa's religious Jews as part of the *ba'al teshuvah* movement, which brought Jews out of the darkness of communist reforms to modern-day religious freedom. Odesan Jews rarely described their personal trajectories as returning to traditions that had previously been abandoned by their elders, nor did they refer to themselves as *ba'alei teshuvah*. Instead, I saw that newly observant Jews were seeing themselves as pioneers by adopting customs that weren't familiar to or approved of by their parents or even their grandparents. Not surprisingly, in some cases, those secular family members repudiated these new religious practices as "backward," articulating the residual force of the Soviet modernization narrative.

As this new version of Jewish life took shape in Odesa in the early 1990s, it garnered much interest. Many Odesans told me they were drawn to the topic of religion, which had previously been banned. They also wanted to feel part of a meaningful community. Speaking to newly observant families, I often got the feeling that people had found great strength, courage, and meaning in their dedication to Judaism, and most important, they had found a community linked to Odesa and beyond. Their stories were infused with a sudden sense of the power of God and with a spirit of rebellion against their previous ignorance of Jewish history, traditions, and religion, the exploration of which was now emerging as a form of new, post-Soviet freedom. Vera, for example, described her early days of observance as being a form of romantic militancy, as if she were part of an underground movement: "It was more like a period of war than a time of normal living." Being observant "was very difficult then, but my memories of this period are very warm."

Vera's mother was Jewish and her father, Ukrainian. She grew up outside Kyiv, and her family had survived the Chernobyl catastrophe. She told me that in her early years, she was "very distant from Jewish life." But in 1990, she went to Odesa, where she had family, and enrolled in the university there. That summer, before school started, she was already wanting to change her life for something more meaningful and resonant, and yet she felt that she lacked the proper foundation to do so. The first step was an education: "At the end of that summer, an ad in the local newspaper announced that all Jewish girls over the age of twelve and all Jewish boys over thirteen could have a bat or bar mitzvah.[24] One of my cousins decided to take part in this ceremony. Then a small group formed of people interested in studying tradition, rituals, Hebrew, and so on. My cousin took me to one of these meetings. It was all very exciting then; everything was new and we were eager to learn." Still, Vera emphasized, "it didn't happen overnight."

> When I was first starting to observe, everything was difficult. What to eat, how to observe Shabbat and holidays, and combining them with my studies. I always had to find a way to get around something. I remember that first, my two cousins and I decided we would keep Shabbat. And then, with time, the three of us made the decision to keep kosher. We were living at home with my aunt, who didn't support our choices and viewed them as extremely radical. So that obviously made things more difficult. We kashered [made kosher] one burner on her stove and a few pots, and used only those to cook with.

The sense of doing something radical and demanding played into Vera's feelings of comradery through the discipline of maintaining strict adherence.

Maya, who was born in 1973, had a similar account. Though she grew up identifying as a Jew and had always had Jewish friends, it was only at university that she started practicing Judaism. "I was studying math, and many of my friends in the department were Jewish." She saw an ad promoting a synagogue's Chanukah celebration, and she attended with a fellow student named Slavik, who later became her husband. "We didn't really know what to expect," she said, "but we decided to try it. I had grown up playing chess and traveling to tournaments, and going to KVN [Klub Veselykh i Nakhodchivykh, the Club of the Merry and Resourceful, a student comedy club], but all these things were no longer happening. So this was something new, something interesting and intellectually stimulating. At the end of the night, we were invited to come back, and as you can see, we haven't left since." For them, Maya said, the process began slowly: "We started giving up some things, such as eating pork and shrimp, mixing dairy and meat, going out on Fridays. . . . With time, it became more natural to us and we took on more and more. It wasn't until we moved away from Slavik's parents' house that we started observing fully. Once you start doing certain observances it doesn't feel right to turn back. . . . Now it's just part of life." As Maya explained it, she and her husband had made a moral commitment, and establishing the practice as natural contributed to their growing observance. Maya and Slavik were among the first couples in Odesa to have a religious Jewish wedding ceremony with a chuppah, in 1993.[25] She showed me pictures of the ceremony and even a newspaper clipping—because Jewish religious weddings were so rare in Odesa then, their ceremony made the local news, and their chuppah is on display at the Museum of the History of Odesa Jews.

Some individuals explored other religions before choosing to live by the canons of Judaism. Dima, a biology student born in Odesa in 1973, shared this story of becoming observant when we met in Israel:

> I was always interested in religion. My mother is Jewish and my father is Russian. At one point in my life, I was intrigued by Catholicism and seriously entertained the idea of becoming a devoted religious man. . . . I first came to the old synagogue to learn Hebrew, thinking I might one day go to Israel, where some of my family had emigrated. There I met Shaya [Gisser] and we started talking. I never made it to Hebrew [class], but I decided to start studying with Shaya instead. There were probably only fifteen of us, and we met daily. This man [Shaya] was able to answer a lot of my questions about life and religion.

A number of observant Jews—and not just those associated with Shaya's pioneering initiative—called their decision to turn to Judaism a "religious awakening," a sudden moment of clarity that they needed to live a "morally right life."

Katya (born in 1991), a student at the Lithuanian Orthodox Jewish school Tikva Or Sameach, told me that despite her many years of Jewish education, she had never wanted to be a practicing Jew. She was often suspended from school for misbehavior, and no one, even she herself, ever thought she would become observant. But one night she had a dream that showed her she would be going to hell for all her mischief. When she woke up, she made the decision to live her life with the Vsevyshnii (the Almighty). That very day, she broke up with her boyfriend, who was Jewish but not religious, and started anew. Fear of God's judgment guided her religious orientation. She told me she kept trying to admonish girls who were making the same mistakes she had made. I last saw Katya in Israel in 2007, where she was studying in a religious Jewish girls' school. Knowing that I'd be going back to Odesa, she asked me to bring her mother a parcel of the head coverings that, she said, every married Jewish woman needed.

Leib (born in 1979), a newly observant Jewish man, had a mixed background, one similar to Vera's. He told me that after graduating from the Tikva religious boys' school, he took two years off from being Jewish: "I was interested in other things and just busy with life." Later, he started attending Migdal and going to weekly lectures given by a Jewish educator, Yosef. This greatly influenced his decision to become observant and follow the Chabad movement. "One day I just knew it was right for me," he said. Shortly thereafter, he adopted the Jewish name Leib. A great number of my Odesan friends born in the late seventies and early eighties and most students enrolled in Jewish schools had adopted Jewish names or used their birth names and Jewish names interchangeably.

While some newly observant Jews were motivated by a religious awakening, others were moved by witnessing a "miraculous" event that revealed God's power. Diana, born in 1982, whom we met in the previous chapter and who regarded herself as "traditional" but not religious, shared a story about her cousin and his gravely ill mother as an example. "They told him she only had two days to live. He spent all day in the synagogue praying for her recovery, and then he found out she was actually getting better. Once she was back on her feet, his previous interest in Judaism turned into a fanatically religious life."

Kostya, born in 1975, had recently returned to Odesa after living for about ten years in Israel. His life in Israel had been entirely secular, but some two years after his return, he became convinced that in Odesa one could only be Jewish through the prism of religion: "Everything else speaks of assimilation." Being drawn to Hasidism—specifically, to the Jewish mysticism he explored on one of his trips with the Chabad synagogue—Kostya found himself becoming more involved and observing many Jewish commandments. He was the only member of his family to incorporate Jewish religious practices into his daily routine.

For a number of my friends in Odesa, their religiosity was shaped by a romantic relationship with someone observant. A discrepancy in levels of observance could become an issue when dating or even after a couple was engaged to be married. David (born in 1981), who was introduced in the previous chapter, told me about dating Nastya (born in 1980), a young woman he met at Beitar camp, who started to become more and more religious, causing him to follow suit. But even after the relationship ended, David continued to lead a religious life, moving to Israel for a time. In 2008, he returned to live in Odesa and was still observant when we last met in 2019. Likewise, when Hannah was in her mid-twenties, she decided to become more religious after becoming engaged to Artur, a young yeshiva student from the neighboring city of Dnipro. Her religious "elevation," as she called it, was driven by her desire to be with Artur and to build a life with him.

For others, it was an interest in the Hebrew language and the discovery of their culture and history that initially attracted them to attend religious classes, lectures, or rituals. This evolved into adopting religious practices in everyday life. "Academic endeavor, with no interest in a religious life, originally brought me to study on my own," one young Jewish man explained, "and over time I started to put it into practice."

Most of the observant Jews I interviewed emphasized how secure they felt in their relationship with God, the almighty "protector" and "judge" of life. At the same time, they also valued the more practical comfort of belonging to an *obshchina* (communal group or community) and the support of other observant Jews. "Stability," "order," "assurance," "understanding life's path," and a sense of "belonging" were among the perceived benefits of living as observant Jews. When I asked Diana (mentioned above) what had persuaded friends in her circle to become "fully" observant Jews, she answered:

> Religious people have a lot of things in common. You get married right away, you have a wedding, holidays . . . lots of things to discuss and people to discuss them with. . . . Within the *obshchina*, people organize their own business . . . friends . . . holidays together . . . working together. . . . But if you're traditional, as most of us are, you start to feel pressure. It starts to feel uncomfortable to not put up a mezuzah if the rabbi offers . . . to not come to the synagogue for holidays . . . to not observe the holidays . . . for some, it's actually scary. Religion brings you comfort and the security that you're living the right life. . . . Others will praise you, understand you, and approve of your life choices . . . plus, there's a place for you after death. It's pretty. Also, it's nice to come to the synagogue and feel yourself *svoim* among *svoikh* [yourself among your own people].

Anthropologist Alexei Yurchak has written extensively about the term *svoi*, noting that this Russian word has no exact equivalent in English. Its closest translation may be "us," "ours," or "those who belong to our circle" and "share a particular ethic of responsibility to others."[26] I saw this sense of responsibility performed over and over during my time in Odesa, as families helped those newly observant Jews feel part of their "circle" by inviting them over for Shabbat meals and Jewish holidays. Similarly, when a congregant experienced hardship, other members would offer monetary, emotional, and practical support. Thus, beyond the trust and belonging embedded in a circle of *svoikh*, there was a shared responsibility to care for one another like kin. In *Solovyovo: The Story of Memory in a Russian Village*, anthropologist Margaret Paxson translates the term *svoi* (f. *svoia*, n.*svoe*) as "one's own" and notes that *svoi* is a marker for belonging of a wider range of types that "can mean being a member of an extended family, a covillager, a dear friend, a compatriot."[27]

Senya, a middle-aged physics professor who had no affiliation to the city's Jewish organizations and identified himself as a secular Jew, offered an interesting perspective on the "pull factor" toward religious life: "First, it's curiosity. Second, today we don't have the same system of organizations to entertain and improve our youth: *pionerskii lager'* [Communist youth camp], Komsomol [Communist Youth League], and others—none of those exist anymore, and nothing was introduced to replace them. Meanwhile, various new groupings have formed among new ethnic and national organizations. . . . Some people are attracted by the material benefits, then others get sucked into it. . . . I think these are the main factors, and not a call of blood." Though it might not be clear from these brief sketches, religious observance wasn't something that newly observant Jews simply folded into their lives. Most who spoke of their developing religious awareness mentioned a period of uncertainty as well as puzzlement and deflation. There was no inexorable progression from partial acceptance of and adherence to religious commandments leading to a complete dedication to a religious life. Indeed, from what I saw during my initial stay in Odesa, most Jews affiliated with synagogue life didn't go on to become observant—though more and more did after I completed my first extended fieldwork there.

For example, Vera told me that her attitude toward Judaism evolved as she traveled, matured, and grew older. She was maintaining a strict, observant life in Odesa when her status as a Chernobyl survivor made her eligible for a two-year program in Israel. While there, she chose to study at a religious women's seminary and discovered that the meaning of being religious depended more on context than she had anticipated. "For me, the period of fighting to express yourself as a Jew died when I left Odesa. There it had truly been a struggle, but in Israel, where it wasn't a problem to be a Jew, you suddenly realize that eating kosher and keeping Shabbat aren't acts of heroism, but just a way of life. I lost the sense of why I was doing what I was doing. It was more than that, though," she continued: "When you first learn about Jewish ideas as expressed in books, you expect religious people to always live according to those laws. But there are laws and there are people. And people are people. I was disappointed by some of the things I saw among religious people in Israel, and it [religious life] started to seem fake to me." That's when she rebelled at the religious training. "It was a serious crisis for me," she said. With an embarrassed laugh, she recalled blasting her stereo on Shabbat, even though using electricity was prohibited, and inviting female classmates to her room to take part in the Kiddush, the prayer traditionally conducted by men. She was quick to add that she'd never act like that today.

After returning from Israel, Vera eventually found her way back to her old routine of observance, largely because she wished to share her knowledge with other Jews in Odesa. Today, leading a life as a religious woman and Jewish educator, Vera described her early observance as "maximalist." Back in Odesa, she found the right balance between personal convictions and religious obligations: "It takes years for observance to become a natural part of you."

A number of those I met never gained that natural sense of conviction and obligation. Elena, a television producer who was then in her late twenties, told me she'd tried wearing a long skirt, keeping Shabbat, and keeping kosher, but she quickly realized it was not for her. After a short time, she said, "I was just fed up." But she didn't feel that she'd failed at being a "good Jew"; it was just that these religious observances infringed on her way of being and her freedom of choice. So it was with Miriam, a city guide in her thirties, who told me that she used to light candles on Shabbat but resented not being able to work on Saturdays, her busiest day for leading tours. Some Jews who'd previously experimented with religious observance said they still fulfilled some religious obligations, but others felt no duty to do so. I saw many of the younger Jews experiment with observance as they connected more deeply to Judaism, but it didn't feel natural for everyone to follow a formula of rituals they ultimately felt to be constraining. Several of the youth I met later made different choices regarding Jewish observance depending on their spouse and their mutual decision on how to raise their children. Miriam, for instance, became more observant when she married her partner, who observed Shabbat and kashrut, and when I saw her after her marriage her hair was covered with a discreet headscarf.

Negotiating Tradition: Challenging Orthodox Models of Judaism

During my initial stay in Odesa, I saw many friends selectively taking part in religious rituals. Because of their lack of "full" observance, these Jews didn't claim to be religious; rather, they saw themselves as *traditional*. After learning the proper conduct for Jewish holidays and rituals, many had adapted their own ways of acknowledging traditions, feeling comfortable enough to choose what suited them. Often, young parents passed on to their children Jewish traditions that they themselves hadn't experienced when growing up, giving their children what they called the "basics," such as circumcising a baby boy and giving him his first haircut at age three, an old Hasidic tradition called *upsherin* ("shear off" in Yiddish).[28] There were different reasons for not aspiring to be *wholly* religious—though some didn't rule it out as an eventual outcome.

Andrey and Lika, a young couple both born in the early 1980s, were each raised in a secular Jewish environment. They met at a Jewish camp run by Beitar and started dating.[29] "Beitar isn't a religious organization," said Lika, "but it is a Jewish organization, and it taught us a lot about Judaism." Neither remained active members of Beitar, but many of their close friends are linked to that period of their lives, as are their favorite stories. When they decided to marry, their parents didn't object to their desire to have a chuppah for the central ritual of their wedding vows, but the parents also wanted all the elements of a "traditional Russian wedding" to follow.[30] Lika and Andrey proudly told me

Figure 4.1. A Jewish bride awaits her groom before the chuppah ceremony. Photo by author.

they were the first in both their families to have a religious wedding. But while their parents didn't object, Lika said, they also didn't know what the ceremony would entail.

During the holiday of Pesach, I watched as Lika rid her home of all *khametz*, taking the traditional Passover observance seriously.[31] However, other Jewish holidays went almost unnoticed in their household. Of course, there's nothing particularly Odesan—or Jewish, for that matter—in the phenomenon of partial observance, of only recognizing a major holiday, be it Yom Kippur or Christmas. But the contemporary context gives new significance to partial observance: in Odesa, the meaning and content of High Holidays and other religious rituals were being shaped and reshaped as families and individuals explored different places on a "Jewish continuum."[32]

Choices about which Jewish religious holidays or rituals to observe paralleled choices about which customs not to observe when considering Soviet and Slavic holidays or old family traditions. Late one night, sitting with Lika and Andrey in their kitchen, I heard them debate whether to put up a New Year's tree—a tradition they'd both followed as children. Andrey thought it was wrong, citing the Israeli teachers who were advising him on proper Jewish domestic conduct in weekly classes at the synagogue: this tradition was pagan, Christian, and Soviet; it definitely wasn't Jewish. For her part, Lika thought it merely strange not to follow a family tradition. By the time I left, they'd settled on celebrating the New Year without a tree and decorating their house for Chanukah with garlands that they kept hanging throughout December.

For newly observant Jews, the New Year was most often reconsidered as a holiday celebration, but minor holidays also came under fire. Valentine's Day, for example, usually celebrated on February 14 after the American tradition, had gained great popularity in Ukraine, but it was seen as a Christian, and therefore not Jewish, tradition. Likewise, the old burial practices followed in Soviet times, now regarded as Christian in origin, were contested, compromised, or altogether abandoned and replaced by Jewish rituals.[33]

Negotiating traditions was a recurring topic of conversation among students at Jewish institutions; indeed, depending on the social setting, students faced different expectations and criteria for Jewish "membership." Vika and Masha, students at the Chabad school, explained that unlike the classmates they called "observant," they themselves only behaved "religiously" while at school. Neither of their fathers was Jewish, and at home, there were no dictates of a proper Jewish life. In fact, while all the students in religious Jewish schools had to stick to the rules ordained by teachers and sponsors, most students, Vika and Masha told me, abandoned those rules outside school: only two of the twelve girls in their class always observed religious laws. "The rest of us wear trousers, we eat nonkosher food, we don't observe Shabbat, or really anything." I asked if the nonobservant students were candid about this behavior—with each other and with the faculty. Both girls conceded that most students spoke to one another about it and that the teachers knew they were observant only within the institution.[34]

But religious education did have an influence on Vika and Masha. When I asked Vika how she'd feel about entering a Christian church, she replied: "Listen, when year after year you're drawn more into Jewish education, you get used to this type of Jewishness. We're not religious, we don't observe anything, we are as we are. But to be honest with you, somewhere deep inside me things have changed. . . . Before [studying at the Jewish school] I could easily have walked into a church; now it's not the same. It wouldn't feel right, for some reason."[35] Masha's response was different. Whereas Vika clearly defined herself as Jewish and therefore *not* Christian, Masha rejected the demand for such an exclusionary definition. "I belong to two religions," she told me. "I am baptized, I have a godfather and godmother, and I consider myself both Jewish and Christian."[36]

Proper behavior for observant Jews affiliated with the Orthodox community also involved reconciling the demands and discipline of religion and personal loyalties with local cultural norms, family, and upbringing. These negotiations could be seen in the forms of dress adopted by some observant women. The halakha requires married religious women to cover their hair, and most of the Israeli women emissaries appear publicly in Odesa wearing stylish wigs that are often hard to distinguish from natural hair. Such head coverings, often imported from Israel, were expensive at the time, so many women intent on following the dictate had to find cheaper options, such as scarf head coverings. For others, a hat or scarf simply felt more natural than a wig. Some women may have been willing to make concessions in response to the demands of observance but weren't willing to change their look. "Really, can you imagine me in a wig?" asked Maya. To her, one of the most difficult things as a Jewish religious woman was the obligation to cover her hair and wear modest clothing, such as knee-length or longer skirts. "I just feel more comfortable in trousers. I can't think straight in a skirt, it's not me." Growing up in Odesa, she was used to wearing casual summer clothes and going to public beaches. "I still have a hard time dressing religiously, and giving up public beaches and swimming in the sea. I'm from Odesa, after all, and the sea is part of who I am."[37]

Maya abandoned her casual style and covered her hair with a wig only for official gatherings or formal pictures with her congregation. She wasn't alone: other young and middle-aged women in Odesa identified themselves as religious without necessarily looking the part. But on my later visits to the city in 2014 and 2019, I saw that a number of Jewish women whom I knew to be "observant without looking the part" (Maya included) now appeared more religious, and most of the young observant women wore stylish wigs that they received as wedding gifts, hair wraps they purchased in Israel, or simple hats. Maya felt that because men had to be present at the synagogue daily, there was a firmer requirement for them to wear ritual dress, such as the tzitzit and kippah. But observant men had their own ways of sidestepping observant rules. The Israeli rabbis would avoid social settings such as theaters and concerts, where a woman's voice might be heard, and refrained from shaking hands or otherwise touching any women not in their immediate family. But many Orthodox men born and raised in Odesa held to their secular upbringing—they shook hands with women; they attended the theater, opera, and concerts without hesitation.

There were Jews in Odesa who had experimented with greater levels of observance for several years and then followed lesser or minimal observant practice, or none at all. In some instances, as with Vera, exposure to a different religious context—foreign in values and mentality—drove newly observant Jews away from the religious life they had previously romanticized. Others found that daily observance of rituals lost its meaning, becoming "burdensome," "unnecessary," and "tiresome."

Recall Dima, an Odesan native introduced earlier in this chapter who moved to Israel. When I met him, his head was shaven and uncovered, and he was dressed in gray cotton shorts and a sleeveless T-shirt. It was hard to believe that he'd once been a yeshiva student at an Orthodox Jewish institution in a city near Jerusalem. When he originally moved to Israel, he had been a devoted and observant Orthodox Jew affiliated with the Chabad movement. Dima described his drift away from religion this way:

> When I came here [to Israel], I was beaming with light from all directions. Here I was told that I could only glow in one direction, and a very narrow direction. In my yeshiva I met students who were not good people, and at first this shocked me. But, most important, the rabbis told me what I could and couldn't do, what I could and couldn't have, what I could and couldn't listen to or read. . . . To me this was awkward and constraining. I am the son of a hunter, and I am an artist. I grew up in Odessa, an open city. Before, I was used to a completely different balance in life. As you can understand, it wasn't a quick hop out for me. But over time, I started to see observance differently.

Among Dima's circle of friends were some whose departure from Jewish Orthodoxy was less dramatic, but they had similar stories about their choice to leave full observance behind.

Negotiating Values: The Dynamics of Family Relations

For Odesa's newly observant Jews, particularly the youth, observance was often adopted on an individual basis, with the rest of the family keeping a religious home only partially or not at all. Given the high rate of assimilation and intermarriage, religious observance by one family member often did not—or could not, in cases of intermarriage—bring the rest of the family closer to Judaism. I spoke to only a few families whose observance spanned as many as three generations.

I often heard parents express concern about sending their children to Jewish schools, as they believed it would increase the likelihood that the child would become more religious. Some parents voiced admiration for sons and daughters who taught them how to "do things right" by observing Jewish celebrations and rituals. Still others admitted they had little choice when it came to "getting used to" their children's new lifestyle; their common refrain was, "What am I to do? [*A chto mne delat'?*]"

I met Malka (born in 1978) during her visit home to Odesa from Israel. She was the only observant member of her family and described her parents as atheists who accepted her ways but were far from understanding them. When I asked Malka if her turn to Judaism had affected her parents' Jewish orientation, she responded, "I gave my father a small Torah book two years ago. When I was home recently, I saw it displayed on his bookshelf. Knowing him, that was a big deal." Malka's mother, Anna, told me her daughter had made the decision to start living a religious life entirely on her own. "My husband and I aren't religious people, and religion was never part of Malka's upbringing. She grew up with Jewish intelligentsia values, nothing more. I didn't even know that my daughter had taken a Jewish name for herself until I went to visit her in Israel."

In Hebrew, the name "Malka" means queen. I asked Anna whether she calls her daughter by her new name, and she told me she doesn't. "The name we gave her, Inna, starts with the same letter as my mother's name; it was given to her in memory of her grandmother. 'Malka' means nothing to me." It had at that time become fashionable among young Jewish families to give children traditional Jewish names rather than Russian or Ukrainian ones. This caused some consternation in several families I knew, with grandparents insisting that Hebrew names were unsuitable or too awkward to pronounce or lacked a connection to family history.

In a later conversation, Anna told me she saw her daughter as part of a larger shift in Jewish society. The new values prized and practiced by today's Jewish youth didn't stem from a knowledge of local Jewish history, art, literature, or music, she said, or from the works of Odesan Jewish writers, who wrote in Russian, Yiddish, and Hebrew. The notions of belonging to the Russian-speaking intelligentsia, of having an open orientation to the world and seeking to attain the highest levels of education and recognition, were no longer distinct markers of Jewish identity. This wasn't to say that the Jewish youth in Odesa no longer espoused such values and aspirations, she said, but these values and aspirations were no longer seen as markers of being a Jew. The historically cosmopolitan and secular way of "being a Jew" in Odesa was being displaced by a new, more potent association between being Jewish and identifying with Judaism as a religion in the Orthodox sense, emphasizing practice. At the same time, Anna acknowledged that the cosmopolitan basis of Jewish identity had already been radically undermined during Soviet rule, when most Jewish institutions—religious, cultural, educational, and Zionist—had been either closed, destroyed, or banned. Anna and other Jews of her generation had had no access to such institutions.

It was apparent that Anna herself was working to distinguish the different layers and modes of cosmopolitanism that existed in Odesa throughout its history and in relationship to the Jews. In contrast to the Orthodox model of Jewish identity, Anna differentiated between those Jews who relied on religious guidance and authority and those who espoused an older, more "open" identity—embodied, most likely, in a figure like Vladimir Jabotinsky (1880–1940), the journalist, writer, and Zionist leader who was born and raised in a secular Jewish family and possessed what she described as the "cosmopolitan outlook."

More than a half century after his death, Jabotinsky was still a presence in Odesa. His novel *Piatero* (*The Five*)—written in Russian in 1935 and published in 1936 in Paris—was widely read by many of the Odesans I knew who had either passed through Beitar, the Jewish self-defense league started by Jabotinsky, or through literary circles in Jewish Odesa. An English translation appeared in 2005, the year I first arrived in Odesa. Narrated by a person much like Jabotinsky, *The Five* recounts the story of a Russified, assimilated bourgeois Jewish family, the Milgroms, in *fin de siècle* Odesa. The title, as literary scholar Brian Horowitz notes, is a "double entendre" as it refers both to the five protagonists (the Milgrom children) and also to the revolution of 1905.[38] Through the story of the family's children, all of whom actually or symbolically die, Jabotinsky demonstrates how the dream of assimilation, or indifference to Zionism, had reached its limits. The Milgroms appear to be Russian in most senses of the term, except for their ability to negotiate a path through a society increasingly divided along national lines.[39] The narrator encourages readers to interpret the five main characters not as individuals but as typified characters who were part of the history of Russian Jewry, insinuating that the text is modeled on real life.[40] Literary critics have mostly interpreted *The Five* as a crypto-autobiography and "an epitaph mourning the decay of Odesa's Jewish life." But as literary scholar Mirja Lecke points out, the novel is a complex and ambiguous piece of literature that also depicts and praises the religious, ethical, and ethnic plurality (which can be identified as cosmopolitanism) of the city and thereby contradicts the nationalism visible in Jabotinsky's other writings.[41] There are many interpretations of the novel, and some suggest that the fates of the Milgroms imply Jabotinsky's condemnation of universalism, but as Brian Horowitz argues, by offering others a chance to contradict Zionism, Jabotinsky presented an intellectual portrait that is fuller and closer to the tenor of the age.[42]

On this note, Anna also acknowledged that despite the Soviet claim to a brotherhood of nations and Odesa's traits of cosmopolitanism and tolerance, Jewish organizations in Soviet times were eventually forced to end their operations. One might then say that the opening of Jewish organizations and the presence of religious Jews from Israel, and elsewhere, as well as the presence of Judaism supported by the Ukrainian state, spoke to yet another chapter of Odesa's cosmopolitan life, even as it lacked recognition by the secular Jewish population. Anna may well have been reacting to the limitations that came with strengthening Jewish identity through an association with Orthodox Judaism—thereby threatening the interaction of Jews with others and limiting the references and symbols that would define one as a Jew in that new Odesan context. That many young Jews recognized the halakha as the authority on Jewishness as presented by religious leadership was indeed far from the outlook of Jewish intelligentsia.

I asked Anna how she reacted to her daughter's observance of Shabbat and kashrut, two commandments that separate observant Jews from others. Anna told me that Malka often spent Shabbat with her friends. "There, they cook, sleep, and go to the synagogue together, as the synagogue is within walking distance. It's a life she mostly leads outside of our home." This was quite common among observant Jews; many adapted to their new lifestyle by finding a place to live that was close to a kosher grocery store, a Jewish school, a synagogue, and other observant Jews, even if it meant separating from their families.

Two of my other interlocutors, Maya and Vera, also had to work to balance family and religious obligations. Maya told me how their families had reacted to her and her husband's decision to become religious: "At first, they were against it—completely against it! Especially Slavik's family, and for some reason they were angry at me. They thought I was responsible for his religiosity. Then, after years passed, they calmed down. Time and our serious conviction did the job. They used to get very upset because we wouldn't eat at their houses. I had an easier time convincing my parents . . . but I think that's only because they were used to me making decisions from an early age." In Maya's view, "It was important for us to act in such a way that they knew it's not a joke but a serious life decision for us. And none of their fits and fusses would be able to turn everything back. It was difficult, but at the end of the day, they loved us."

As for Vera's process of integrating her faith and family, she said, "They were in shock. You must understand, back then the idea that 'religion is the opiate of the people' was embedded in everyone's heads. I think my family was trying to understand what had happened to their daughter . . . [and] the hardest thing for them was the fact that I had become *chuzhoi* ['other people's' or foreign] and they couldn't understand me. They couldn't even articulate what scared them so much. But time passed, and thank God I have a good family and we lived through this and more." By the time I met Vera, her religion had become a source of gentle teasing. Her dad would say, "I just don't understand how I, a Ukrainian man, could have fathered a Jewish daughter."

Marriage was another potential point of disagreement between younger generations and their families. On one occasion, my friend David took me along when he met his grandmother for their regular tea. A newly observant Jew, David did his best to evade her persistent questioning about when he was getting married. Eventually, he told her he was waiting to meet a nice Jewish girl. His grandmother replied: "You should want to marry someone because they're a good person, an intelligent person, a kind person. Marrying someone just because they're Jewish is nonsense. Our family has so many nationalities in it, so many wonderful people who have helped me throughout my days in Odessa. . . . Must you upset me with this kind of talk?" Referring to David's kippah, she demanded: "Why do you walk around in that funny hat? Must you tell everyone you're Jewish?" To this, David replied, "That is exactly the point."

Of course, not all families discouraged their newly observant young people. I encountered those who not only accommodated their children's choices but also embraced their developing an observant identity. For instance, Lera and Vadik's daughter and her family taught the sixty-year-old couple, who were raised in the Soviet Union, about observant Jewish life. Instead of resisting, the parents made sure they always had plastic dishes on hand to make their house kosher for family visits. I also talked to a man who wasn't Jewish himself but had a Jewish daughter through her maternal line. His daughter was observant, and out of respect for her choice, he had agreed to kasher his kitchen and to eat only kosher products and cuisine at home. I often saw nonobservant family members taking part in religious holidays and celebrations, even though they related to them only marginally. "I went to my grandson's bris," Emma, a sociologist in her early seventies, told me. "It was a nice celebration, but all these religious things . . . oh, not for me. I am a Soviet person."

There was a difference between the observant Jews who tried to smooth their own transition into a religious life for the sake of their nonpracticing or non-Jewish family members and those who dealt with the situation in a radical manner. Vera tried to gain her parents' approval by altering her life so rapidly they wouldn't have time to process the change she was going through—an approach she called "shock therapy." Others spoke of trying to talk their way through their new disposition. Mendy, a twenty-five-year-old city guide of Jewish Odesa who divided his time between Tel Aviv and Odesa, told me he explained everything to his mother and answered all her questions. "They're just not used to it," he said, meaning not only his parents but also their entire generation. "They grew up in a different time. We also have to understand that."

If becoming religious and observant sometimes exacerbated generational divides, the turn to religious practice fostered close bonds among those undergoing similar experiences—bonds that emulated those of family or close kin. In some cases, as with Malka, spending Shabbat away from home didn't just mean being able to walk to the synagogue; it also felt like "being in the right atmosphere." As one young Jewish woman explained, "When everyone's doing

Figure 4.2. Children at Migdal, the Jewish community center, get ready for the kapparah ceremony customarily done by Orthodox Jews on the eve of Yom Kippur. Photo by author.

the same thing, it's nice and you feel good about it. If you're the only one, it's lonely." Indeed, it was common for both Israeli emissaries and local observant Jews to invite religious newcomers to their homes for a Shabbat meal after the synagogue service, to make them feel part of the "family."

Both Orthodox synagogues held a Shabbat meal on the premises, free of charge to anyone wishing to partake. Attending Shabbat meals, whether in a private home or at the synagogue, was one of the first ways I was able to interact with the city's religious minority. The religious circles entered by newly observant Jews functioned as kin networks in many ways, offering care, attention, and love to new members of the community as if for their own children. Vera said, "Those with whom you share this experience often become like family."

Challenging Jewish Practice: The Politics of Jewish Observance

Religious practice allowed some of Odesa's observant Jewry to recognize one another as "kin." Pasha, an observant man working at the Chabad congregation, told me, "Only one or two percent of our greater community is religious."

He seemed to understand that the revival of observance would take time: "We're doing our job. We wish those numbers were higher, but for now that's where we stand." He explained the distinction between his sense of the truly religious and the rest this way: "Many people follow the customs that don't require repetition—Brit Milah, chuppah, Jewish burial. Far fewer observe the daily mitzvoth that require a greater level of dedication. For many, it takes time to become observant, and that's normal. I would be skeptical of anyone who turned religious overnight. They usually abandon this path as quickly as they come to it." To my question about his own commitment to Judaism, Pasha contrasted himself with those newly observant Jews who might prove to lack the necessary discipline, speaking succinctly and with another temporal definition: "I have been in Judaism for twenty-five years."

Such distinctions, however, generated a larger, ongoing debate—among those within and outside the religious minority—about what would constitute a "proper" Jew. At times, Odesa's Jews even questioned the authority of foreign religious leaders who differed in principles of observance. Members of one family told me that the Israeli families working in a congregation had refused to eat at the homes of some congregants, not trusting their kosher status. The family considered it blatant disrespect. The fact that Odesa's Jews had to rely on foreign rabbis was regarded by some religious families as a sad aftermath of Soviet rule. Other local Jews were heard to complain that some Israeli religious practices were more lenient than their own; on more than one occasion, they mocked the "guidance" from Israeli emissaries—such as "this is only expected of men"—and challenged it with a stricter observance of the commandment.

For others, the system of observance they'd internalized through Jewish education, provided mostly by the emissaries, served as their main frame of reference for judging whether they themselves or others were "good Jews." For example, ten-year-old Zhenya, a student in the Chabad Jewish school, stated, "I am Jewish and Ukrainian. My [Ukrainian] grandfather and my [Jewish] grandmother believe in Jesus." "And you?" I asked. "No, I do not," he replied. "But I'm not as good a Jew as [my friend] Haim. I don't keep my Saturday [Shabbat]; I watch T V. But at least I don't believe in Jesus." Because Haim followed one of the main obligations of Orthodox Jews, Zhenya judged him to be a "good" Jew, but he hesitated to grant himself this status. However, he considered himself a better Jew than his grandmother because she believed in Jesus. Like most students in Orthodox schools, Zhenya was immersed in different religious and cultural orientations at home and at school, but it was the official education that shaped his judgment on the contradictions he saw in his life.

While those who were religious practiced varying degrees of observance, many secular Jews rejected the belief that Jewish identity is defined by religious practice at all. Their own Soviet- and Odesa-formed notions of being Jewish were secular and linked to family history, education, knowledge, culture, a sense of growing up in that city's Jewish environment, a worldly outlook on life, and so on. Some were skeptical about religious Jews' practices, sincerity of belief, or level of morality. At times, secular Jews focused on religious Jews as individuals, but at other times, they saw them as representatives of imported efforts to "revive" Judaism as a way of life. The physics professor Senya expressed incredulity that a newly observant man he'd known as a *prorab* (simple laborer) but who was now employed by the synagogue could ever believe in anything more elevated than his wages. To Senya, the man's lack of education made him incapable of having a relationship with God; he questioned how a man who didn't live by the highest morals could claim to be religious. "I think that ninety percent of people who consider themselves religious have never even read the Bible," said Senya.

Evgeniy, the journalist mentioned in the previous chapter, believed that the Jewish life of the city wasn't what happened in the synagogues but rather what was seen in the Jewish newspapers and publications, the Jewish theater Migdal Or, the Odesa Literature Museum, and the work of Jewish artists and ordinary Odesan Jews. Such views were more often expressed by those closer to middle age and by members of the secular Jewish intelligentsia. Especially in the case of the elderly, being affiliated with a Jewish organization didn't necessarily imply religious commitment; as we've seen, many of them depended on the practical aid these organizations provided.

Many of the middle-aged Jewish Odesans I encountered were aware of Jewish activity in the city, often through their children. Most of them were neither involved in Jewish organizations nor observant of Judaism. The reasons they gave were multiple: time constraints, lack of interest, antireligious ideals. In many cases their orientation was similar to that of their parents and had been determined by their Soviet upbringing, though there might be different paths within one family. In the eyes of Jewish activists, middle-aged Jewish Odesans had an important responsibility: nurturing the Jewish knowledge their children received at school and in other centers of Jewish activity. As one middle-aged man described, "Jews are not those whose parents are Jewish but those whose children are Jewish." Many years later, I heard this line used to describe Ukrainian identity and to draw a parallel between Jews and Ukrainians. Despite these high expectations, I met few parents who'd made significant efforts to provide a religious context for their children, even if—as with the families of Vera, Hannah, and Maya—they occasionally showed support in such ways as accommodating kosher needs. Thus, it could not be said that these parents accepted any sense of an obligation to live their lives in accordance with religious laws. In many cases, the children explained that their parents' lack of enthusiasm was due to a mixed family background, where a non-Jewish parent would balk at accepting strict Jewish practices at home. In fully Jewish families, secular orientation or Soviet upbringing were among the major reasons that Jewish parents refrained from, or even objected to, religious practice at home.

I also came across young Jewish people who didn't associate Jewish identity with Judaism at all. Misha and Gosha, students in their twenties in the English class I taught at Migdal, both identified themselves as Jews "by nationality" (*po natsional'nosti*). Being Jewish was something they were born into, and like the generation who came of age in the Soviet era, they understood it as meaning a dedication to education, family history in Odesa, and secular Jewish culture as found in the works of Jewish writers and composers, plus a taste for Jewish cuisine. Both Misha and Gosha repeatedly insisted that being atheist didn't make them any less Jewish than the newly observant Jews, and both said they lacked the time and the interest to participate in Jewish organizations. In their teens, they'd been active in Migdal's programs, but they no longer took part. Like Misha and Gosha, most of Odesa's Jewish young people were not practicing (although some partially observed religious rituals in circles of Jewish organizations or at home). But to some degree or another, they were involved in some branch of organized Jewish life.[43]

The End of a Religious Revival?

In the immediate wake of the Soviet Union and its policy of secularization in the early phases of post-Soviet reforms, there was a sudden and widespread rise in "the number and variety of religious organizations."[44] By 1995, that rise had crested.[45] Generally, this pattern played out in Odesa. I was told that in the first decade after Ukraine's independence, many of the Jewish religious institutions and practices in Odesa appeared as new and inspiring. As I commenced my fieldwork in 2005, however, the novelty had worn off. For some, active involvement was a youthful phase they'd outgrown. Others changed focus under the pressure of providing for their families and building careers. A number of Odesan Jews I met suggested that because the once-new institutions and practices were now permanently established, their own desire for active participation had subsided. Moreover, some had participated in Jewish religious organizations mainly for the material support they offered, and as economic and social conditions improved, fewer of those in this category found it necessary to rely on that aid.

Leaders of the Jewish programs in Odesa acknowledge that emigration has meant fewer Jews recognized by the halakha and the Law of Return. Therefore, even as many secular and religious institutions have worked to regenerate Jewish awareness, there are demographic limits. As Misha, a young Jewish man in his twenties, told me: "There are more Jewish organizations [in Odessa] than there are Jews." Yulia, the Reform rabbi, expanded on this point when she explained that her congregation was so much smaller than those of the Orthodox communities because it had arrived "too late." By this, she meant that either a large number of Jews had already become affiliated with Chabad or the Litvak movement; or that they'd already tested the waters and, for one reason or another, had opted for partial or no religious affiliation; or that they were never interested in Jewish associations and had simply ignored the call of Jewish outreach. It is possible that, despite the active, highly visible outreach programs, some Jews were just unaware of the developments, perhaps because they lived far from any organized Jewish life.

Many social scientists have pointed out that Jews in the FSU who had definite plans for emigration often displayed heightened Jewish activism before they left.[46] This was true in Odesa. Many of the activists who took part in the early phases of the Jewish revival subsequently made their way abroad, to the United States, Israel, Germany, or elsewhere. Those who were left to run Jewish organizations couldn't compete with the economic means and opportunities offered by international actors. As Josef Zissels notes, the influx of foreign personnel with well-defined agendas represented a new stage of the "professionalization of Jewish life" that hadn't previously been seen in Ukraine.[47]

Observant Jews who remembered or knew of the local initiatives associated with Shaya Gisser in the early 1990s were well aware of what those initiatives had accomplished for the religious communities: a growth in infrastructure, an overall expansion, and a general strengthening, at least in numbers of congregants and the material sense. They accepted and even welcomed the new amenities brought by foreign funding, such as kosher grocery stores, Jewish programs supporting a religious way of life, and links to a wider network of observant Jewry. But some lamented the loss of a time when change was driven from "within"; now it was driven from "the top." As one middle-aged Jewish woman put it, "the [religious] *obshchina* [community] was nothing then. . . . We met in a small room and studied. . . . The classes didn't pay a stipend, and the rabbi didn't support us financially. . . . It wasn't easy, but it was real." Marking a comparison to other structures of organized Jewish life around the world, she noted that unlike many other places, in Odesa, the congregation doesn't pay the rabbi; the rabbi pays the congregation.

Comparing religious development to the process of building a house, Vera described those earlier moments of Jewish life as being like "living in a tent."

"When you're camping out, it's very romantic, but for some reason we always build ourselves houses with strong foundations and thick walls. At first it was groundbreaking to build anything, [and] we made big steps. . . . Today we see a different phase of construction. It reminds me of living with my neighbors, with all the pluses and minuses. . . . Whether we like it or not, such is the process." For all these reasons, many of Odesa's observant Jews and Jewish activists perceive the present-day religious Jewish life as the tail end of what some have described as Jewish rebirth (*evreiskoe vozrozhdenie*). But officially, the city's Jewish institutions all claim higher numbers of congregants on their respective websites and in personal communication, and the message of Jewish revival is still cited to describe their work.

Conclusion

This chapter has illustrated how religious adherence for Odesan Jews meant adopting a *new* way of life rather than a *return* to a code of social norms that previous generations had observed. As Jewish studies scholar Norman Solomon writes, "Europeans, east and west, who are 'returning to their roots' are not, and could not be, simply recreating the lifestyle of one or more Jewish communities of earlier times. . . . They are actually inventing new lifestyles, by selecting one or more past expressions of Judaism, and mixing these with other elements of Soviet, Russian, European and world culture."[48] Given what my interlocutors have shown, perhaps it's more appropriate to speak of "religious adherence" than a religious revival. This idea of adherence refers to a state of mind and a space for the formation of a spiritual life that leads some to a new or altered direction of Jewish belonging—without necessarily involving strict observance of religious laws. Religious adherence can apply to full, partial, short-term, or long-term dedication to Judaism, whether people seek it out as a complement to their previous convictions or as a replacement for them. It's also less laden with the implication of "newness" or "rebirth" and thus offers a better way to understand and discuss the attitudes and patterns of religious practice today. Religious adherence is a useful and appropriate term to describe and understand those religiously oriented Jews who test the parameters of Judaism and its institutions in a variety of ways—and who have brought about a permanent, if turbulent, change to the previous modes of Jewish practice in Odesa.

This chapter has also shown that binary definitions of Jewish belonging as either an ethnicity or a religion—*evrei* or *iudei*—are too simplistic to capture contemporary religious life anywhere, but particularly in Odesa. Separated by their diverse experiences and histories, Odesa's observant Jews are wildly differentiated by congregations, degrees of observance, paths into and out of religiosity, associations with different institutions, traditions, and the religious attitudes of their families. Moreover, while Judaism as a religion is undoubtedly one way for the people of Odesa to identify as Jewish, the concept has not gone unchallenged, from either within or outside, precisely because authenticity and authority are constantly questioned.

5

⁓⁓⁓

Asymmetric Cultural Encounters

Jewish Philanthropy Missions
and Revival on Display

During perestroika, Jews from the United States, Europe, and Israel began traveling to the Soviet Union. They were driven by a desire to learn family genealogies, to support aid projects organized by local Jewish communities, and to satisfy their curiosity by visiting both places and sites associated with their ancestors. Thus Jewish "heritage tourism" in the region began, and after the opening of the FSU, it intensified greatly.[1] The diaspora project—reclaiming a lost Jewish dimension in regions that had been closed off for generations—initiated a culture industry of museums, memorials, cultural centers, and other modes of exhibiting Jewish life.

The US and European congregations and organizations that sent philanthropists to the FSU did so following the Jewish commandment of tzedakah—the responsibility to give aid to those who need it, enacting a Jewish call to fix or repair the world (*tikkun olam*).[2] In this case, they mostly fell in line with the narrative that emphasized the need to revive Jewish life after the long period of communist repression. Indeed, for many Jewish philanthropists of Ashkenazi descent, making a charitable gift and connecting to their heritage and core Jewish values were combined: "Tzedakah has two aspects: one with the hand and one with the heart."[3] But their gifts were also doubled in terms of translating the experiences with new Jewish sites *abroad* into aiding Jewish communities at home, such as helping the elderly and giving tzedakah to less fortunate members of the Jewish family.[4]

The philanthropic missions that developed alongside the thriving Jewish heritage tourism (individuals seeking their "roots") profoundly affected Jews in these states. Foreign finance came to underwrite Jewish activity in Odesa and to dominate the institutions that shaped the social reproduction of Jewish life there. As we'll see, such financing has not been even and steady, leaving the local projects initially sponsored by international charities obligated to achieve greater financial independence.

In addition to the question of funding, there was the cultural encounter of foreigners and locals. The Jewish explorers searching for a lost past, and the organizations seeking to structure a Jewish revival, came to a place like Odesa looking for signs of their donations at work and evidence of Jewish life and living Judaism. In this dynamic, the local Jews would appear before the missions to "act out" their Jewishness and performatively express gratitude for the donations received from abroad. Put another way, when donations flowed in from outside, "the free gift is transformed into a heavily conditional gift when it reaches the ultimate recipient" and "there are in practice symbolic forms of reciprocity."[5] Even if local Jews occasionally joked about being the "poor relatives" of visiting Jews, they resented hearing others describe their presumed status in this way.

This chapter analyzes the encounters of philanthropists with Jewish recipients of aid and focuses on the cultural performances organized to greet foreign guests and their responses in turn. I concentrate on one of the largest donor events I followed over three days in July 2006, a philanthropic mission of the United Jewish Communities (UJC)—renamed in 2009 as the Jewish Federations of North America (JFNA)—that brought nearly two hundred Jewish donors from the United States to Odesa.[6] Most were middle- and upper-class Ashkenazi men and women ranging from middle-aged to elderly. By analyzing the tensions generated by the interplay of international donors and the Jews of Odesa, I'm seeking to engage the larger question of how differences in understandings of Jewish identity—in mentality, observance, values, and social status—manifested when foreign donors met with local Jews, creating what I call "asymmetric encounters."

In these encounters, we see how modes of Jewish outreach projects clearly relate to what anthropologist Mary Douglas, writing about Marcel Mauss's famous notion of the gift, describes as the wounding effects that reside within the virtue of charity.[7] As Douglas says, nothing is given for free, since "gift cycles engage persons in permanent commitments that articulate the dominant institutions."[8] Anthropologists Roderick Stirrat and Heiko Henkel draw parallels between Mauss's concept of the gift and the moral underpinnings of development NGOs, claiming that while "the gift is given in a way that attempts to deny difference and assert identity between the rich giver and the poor receiver, a gift in practice reinforces or even reinvents these differences."[9] In the minimal and often performative interactions between Jewish donors and the

Jews of Odesa who receive their donations, the unequal dynamics of power and influence demonstrated the painful side of charity.

What Is a Mission?

A Jewish mission can be seen as a form of Jewish tourism and heritage travel, insofar as it "offers its participants an emotional promise to renew their spirituality, their Jewish identity and their sense of place in a hostile world."[10] Organizers of Jewish outreach projects engage travelers on two levels. On the one hand, they presented the projects as a means of securing a bright and meaningful future for an afflicted Jewish population abroad. On the other hand, they designed the projects to be personally gratifying for those taking part. Philanthropists derived a heightened sense of "satisfaction," along with an elevated sense of moral achievement, from the accomplished mission of salvation.[11] As Naomi Leite points out through her research of tourism around Portuguese Morranos, behind the idea of traveling to meet "lost" or "isolated" Jews is a "pervasive presumption that it is good for Jews around the world to be in touch with one another," reinforcing the idea of a "Jewish *peoplehood*" who are seemingly interconnected and must aid one another.[12]

For the participants, Jewish missions abroad are as much about reflecting on the self as about seeing others. Describing the meaning of *missions* with regard to memorial tours in Poland, cultural anthropologist Jack Kugelmass suggests that the term is laden with a "time out of time" quality, a sense of liminality that visitors experience as they participate in activities they might avoid in everyday life, like eating kosher food, attending religious services, and so on.[13] Anthropologist Erica Lehrer, writing about Jewish trips to Poland, describes *mission* as a mindset, with "a single-minded pursuit of a particular experience" that is "advertised as a chance to make a difference, have a spiritual awakening, or undergo a life-changing experience."[14] Whereas the Poland that Lehrer describes is constructed by the organizers of mission tours as an anti-Jewish place, the organizers for tours in Odesa cast the city as a relic of a historically Jewish place and, frame the Jews there as extended kin—but kin in need of support, aid and rescue.

On the Odesa mission tour I attended, guides repeatedly asked visiting Jews to put themselves in the place of their "less fortunate brothers and sisters" or to imagine the faces of local Jews—strangers—as if they were the visitors' own parents who came from Odesa or somewhere similar. Like Leite's outreach activists who presents the Marranos they meet as "long-lost kin," organizers of mission tours in Odesa reinforce the idea of a Jewish "family."[15] Other

scholars of charity and philanthropy have pointed out how the process of giving serves to benefit the giver, allowing volunteers and aid workers to re-create
themselves as more virtuous and spiritual persons.[16] Indeed, anthropologist
Melissa Caldwell believes that the givers are the *main* beneficiaries of faith-
based charitable activity.[17] Judaism similarly teaches its followers that "donors
benefit from tzedakah as much or more than the poor recipients."[18] These
missions, similar to those Lehrer observes in Poland, attempted to "transform
communal ideology into embodied reality" and create "group memory."[19]
But anthropologist Jackie Feldman, describing Israeli youth tours to Poland,
reminds us that we need to see different layers of Jewish tourism and make
a distinction between the workings of the organizers and the sincere, real,
and deep sentiments of tour participants, who are often in "creative search of
personal identity."[20]

Travel to Odesa is imbued with narratives of the past and visions of the future that are often far from everyday reality and historical facts. The concept of
"the mission" clearly depicts the purposefulness of an interaction in which the
philanthropists and the international organization hold "expert knowledge."[21]
Although we're used to thinking of missions as a religious and historically
Christian phenomenon, the nature of the mission I witnessed is on the one
hand different, as both groups involved are of the same religion (Jewish), but
on the other hand similar, in that one group (the missionaries) seeks to elevate
the other's religious status for the well-being of the community and universal
values of religious freedom.

Aviv and Shneer conclude that such encounters are "less about sustaining
already existing connections and memories between individuals and communities" in the visited destination than they are about "inventing new relationships" between visiting Jews and other Jewish people and places.[22] In
a brochure of the Federation of Jewish Communities of the Commonwealth
of Independent States (CIS) printed in Russia in 2000, one can see Aviv and
Shneer's observations clearly:

> Our Generation has witnessed a miracle from G-d: With the fall of the
> Iron Curtain, Jews were given the right to leave the Soviet Union and, most
> importantly, the Jews who remained were finally free to learn about and
> practice what was so dear and important to them: their tradition. Today,
> we must celebrate this miracle by helping Russian Jews to become proud of
> who they are. This is the biggest challenge facing Russian Jewry today.
>
> The former Soviet Union is the only region in the world where poverty
> is both material and spiritual. Hundreds of thousands of Jews are so poor
> they cannot even put bread on their tables and take care of their basic needs.

At the same time, the lack of fundamental Jewish knowledge has deprived many Soviet Jews of their history, culture, and tradition. Let us not miss this opportunity to give these people a chance. The Soviet authorities once denied them their Jewishness. Now it is in our hands.

We must do all we can. Let our people know and let our people live![23]

The invented relationships described in this chapter use Odesa as a historical stage set for travelers seeking a meaningful Jewish experience—a place for creating new relationships on the basis of shared symbols of Jewish commonality (such as the Hebrew language, prayer, Israel, memory of the Holocaust, and Jewish traditions) and on the basis of a sentiment of belonging, experienced most profoundly by Jews of Ashkenazi descent. In these encounters, we see that even if those commonalties do coincide with local circumstances, "the fact that there are shared values does not necessarily mean that there is sameness," as sociologist Janet Poppendieck points out in her work on voluntarism in the United States.[24]

The philanthropic missions of the UJC/JFNA gave only select members— often those whose donations met a certain threshold—a firsthand experience of the impact of their donations and fundraising. They would get to meet local branch representatives of international partner organizations like the Sokhnut, the American Jewish Joint Distribution Committee (JDC or the Joint), or the Association for the Promotion of Skilled Trades (World ORT). More importantly, they were offered the chance to meet people who directly benefited from the programs administered by those organizations.[25]

According to the old UJC website, these missions offered donors a "heightened appreciation and connection to their Jewish identity." The goal of such a voyage was to cultivate experiences "imbued with meaning" as participants got a chance to visit with "members of their extended Jewish family and to come face to face with the shared heritage, traditions, and values that unite all Jewish people." The UJC website promised that travelers would come away with a new understanding of "where they've been and a vision of where they are headed." The site encouraged participants to "plant seeds for Jewish renaissance and renewal" and to "ensure the Jewish community never waivers on its commitment to provide human services." These trips would make Jews "feel good for doing good."[26]

Such missions were much welcomed by city authorities, who considered visits by foreign delegations to be an important part of Odesa's development at the time. The city made special arrangements to save these arriving donors from the usual travel hassles, offering them speedy transfer through passport control at the airport and luxury buses for transport around the city. Working

Figure 5.1. Children at the Tikva kindergarten demonstrate their knowledge of Shabbat to American visitors. Photo by author.

with these Jewish missions was also a high priority for organizers of Odesa's local Jewish institutions because the resulting donations, pledges of future support, and expanded sponsor lists helped sustain them.[27]

The missions were relatively short, lasting only two or three days with "fleeting encounters" similar to those Leite observes.[28] To guarantee that they ran smoothly, top representatives from the organization's operations team would fly in from the United States and Israel to guide the donors, taking them to observe the daily operations of the programs supported by their donations. Each group had about fifteen to twenty donors, and they were kept on a tight schedule. Local personnel were briefed on what the donors would want to see in the fifteen to thirty minutes they had to visit a facility and witness the program and its participants.[29]

These introductions to Jewish life in Odesa were undeniably theatrical. Certainly, Jewish life was on display—exhibited, narrated, and subsequently filtered through the ideals and perceptions of the visitors who served as an audience on the move. The Jewish organizations that were involved in these missions to Odesa concentrated their efforts on "designing, promoting and implementing programs with specific educational objectives based on the different ideologies and goals of organizational sponsors."[30] To strengthen their call for donations, the organizations created brochures, videos, and other materials that presented the image of Jewish Odesa as a place and a people *in need*. Stories and pictures of local Jews were carefully chosen to encourage giving based on specific project goal. Reports and pledge cards would often feature a black-and-white "before" picture of a needy child or a desolate Jewish place and an "after" picture of generated change in color.[31]

Each organization sought to exhibit a part of Jewish Odesa that was supported by its sponsored activities and to demonstrate these activities' efficacy at facilitating Jewish growth. This is what Aviv and Shneer called "diaspora business."[32] In this way, the complex richness of daily Jewish life in Odesa was stripped away in the interest of giving a local performance that reflected the international audiences' interests. For example, on a mission I attended with the Tikva Or Sameach Orthodox congregation, the donors followed a mapped tour of the city that omitted the presence of the other Orthodox (Chabad) congregation and the Reform community altogether. On another mission organized by Tikva, I saw visitors attend a performance at a religious kindergarten, where a four-year-old "couple" demonstrated their knowledge of Shabbat. The children set the table with the requisite objects, pretended to light Shabbat candles, and recited the appropriate prayers. Conversely, with Israeli-sponsored programs, children most often demonstrate their skill in speaking Hebrew and show their attachment to the "Jewish homeland" by reciting songs and sharing their stories of Taglit.[33]

My Odesa interlocutors told me these events aroused diverse, sometimes conflicting, feelings—from joy and excitement, to boredom, and frustration. In what follows, I try to contextualize these sentiments by concentrating on that July 2006 mission led by the UJC.

The UJC: Background and Structure

The United Jewish Communities (UJC)—again, renamed the Jewish Federations of North America (JFNA) in 2009—is an American Jewish umbrella organization representing 146 Jewish Federations and 300 independent Jewish communities across North America. Although the organization is also involved in advocacy work and lobbying, its core function remains raising and distributing funds "for social welfare, social services and educational needs."[34] As part of its outreach programs, UJC/JFNA protects and enhances the well-being of Jews in seventy countries through partnerships with the Jewish Agency for Israel (Sokhnut), the Joint, and World ORT.[35]

As an international organization, UJC focuses on serving the needs of Jews around the world, particularly where their lives as Jews are threatened. The motto of the Joint, its partner organization, is "Jews in need should be helped and should be helped to live as Jews."[36] UJC stated its commitment "to the principle that Jews should be helped to remain in countries of their birth rather than to immigrate to Israel."[37] The organization began to fund programs in Odesa in 1990, when it established an overseas partnership with the Odesa offices of the Joint and the Jewish Agency for Israel (Sokhnut). UJC described these groups as "the driving forces in developing re-emerging Jewish communities" in the FSU.

The UJC sponsors programs that provide relief and rescue and support religious observance (of all Jewish denominations), Jewish education, and Jewish culture and welfare to enrich Jewish life in Odesa. While most UJC-sponsored programs in Odesa at the time of my research were run by local Jewry, operational and budgetary concerns were handled primarily by its US representatives. As a result, UJC officials in Odesa felt that budget allocations were "not always well related to local needs." But participants in Jewish activities and organizers of various projects partly blamed those local officials for the misdirection of aid, saying funds were diverted for administrative or personal use.

Alternatively, programs run by the Jewish Agency (Sokhnut) in Odesa and elsewhere in the world are based on the assumption that "Israel stands at the heart of the Jewish future." The Jewish Agency for Israel (Sokhnut) initiatives in Odesa were, until recently, primarily focused on promoting aliyah. After emigration slowed from Odesa and the rest of the post-Soviet territory, the organization expanded its mission to strengthening the bonds of local Jews to their "homeland" by means of Zionist education and short-term study-abroad and internship programs, mostly focused on youth. These initiatives continue to support the ideology that Israel is the center of Jewish awareness, though most of the Jews who have become involved have chosen not to live there.

In Odesa, programs by the Joint and the Jewish Agency for Israel (Sokhnut) received most of their aid from the UJC, so their organizers devoted much attention to the missions of UJC members. Each year, the UJC would select one city where donors and activists could convene to take part in Jewish development projects firsthand, learn about fundraising and goal achievement, and improve their skills as philanthropists. During the time of my fieldwork, Odesa was selected as the destination for the UJC Annual Campaign Chairs and Directors Mission. As an English-speaking academic residing in Odesa, I was asked to brief the delegation on Odesa's Jewish history. This gave me the chance to follow the mission over its entire three-day stay in 2006, from July 10 to 12, observing and informally interviewing the participants.

Rehearsed Stories and "Professional Jews"

On the first day of the mission, fundraising workshops were held at the hotel. A welcome dinner featured speeches by the organizers and remarks about Odesa's Jewish history delivered by the city's Jewish mayor. On the second day, the UJC visitors separated into small groups to be escorted around Odesa by representatives of the Joint and the Jewish Agency for Israel (Sokhnut) while also learning about their initiatives. I was invited to join a group supervised by Shira, an energetic American Israeli woman in her forties who worked for the Jewish Agency for Israel (Sokhnut). With her was Olga Samburenko, then twenty-two and living in Israel; she was one of six Odesan natives paid by the organization to take part in the visit. Olga's travel expenses from Israel were covered in return for her role in a session called "My Odesa through the Sunglasses of an Israeli," set up to personalize the concept of aliyah. While showing our group "her Odesa," Olga repeatedly expressed her gratitude to UJC donors for helping her change her life by relocating to Israel.

When members of the delegation boarded the bus in the morning, each received a card describing Olga's story. Olga stood at the front of the bus and recounted the important details of her life. Born to a Jewish father and a Russian mother, she grew up in what she called an "international family": "We ate matzoh on Pesach, but I also went to church every Sunday with my mother." She explained that her decision to live "as a Jew" came directly from her participation in the Jewish Agency for Israel's (Sokhnut's) summer camp. She first heard about the program through a friend, and because she was considered a potential *oleh* (emigrant to Israel), her application was accepted. Her parents saw the camp as an opportunity for a nice "free vacation" and didn't initially object. Olga described the camp as an "injection of Jewishness." She spoke of her joy in meeting interesting people who "spoke the same language" and of feeling like "part of the Jewish family." On her return, she told her parents that she now considered herself Jewish and that she was no longer comfortable attending church with her mother. "My parents were shocked," she told the group. "They didn't know what had gotten into me." She continued to participate in the Sokhnut programs, at times hiding it from her parents, and returned to camp annually, later becoming a counselor.

Olga was careful to say that she didn't encourage her campers to go to Israel but that she did indicate it was an option.[38] She herself was prompted to move

to Israel by her evolving role in the Jewish Agency for Israel's (Sokhnut's) programs and a personal relationship with an Odesan-native Israeli she met at one
of the summer camps. Her plan to emigrate, she told them, was disrupted when
her parents moved to Germany, and as she was a teenager at that time, she had
to go with them. At this point, Shira noticed that some UJC visitors looked
surprised. She interrupted Olga's narrative to clarify why some ex-Soviet Jews
chose to migrate to Germany rather than "returning" to Israel. "They don't
have as bad an association with the country [Germany], because in the Soviet
Union they were never educated about the Holocaust." Shira also pointed out
the higher social benefits in Germany and the advantages of being part of the
European Union. Olga didn't volunteer her family's motivations for the move;
however, she later told me that her mother had suffered a stroke, so access to
"good medical care" had been a key reason for leaving Odesa. After two years
in Germany, Olga immigrated to Israel; at the time of our meeting, she lived
in Eilat with the man she'd met at the Jewish camp.

Shira presented Olga's story as one that embodied the promise of the Jewish Agency for Israel (Sokhnut's) programs. It was through the organization's
camp that Olga had recognized her Jewish connection and adopted it as her
permanent identity. Moreover, Olga had educated others in turn and had
then made the ultimate decision to live in Israel, setting the Zionist example
of a "good Jew." Where Olga cast her parents' move as pragmatic, Shira gave
Olga's story the plot of escaping a "hostile" Germany to find life in Israel—a
touching example of aliyah. Shira emphasized how the Sokhnut's efforts to
"reconnect Jews to their homeland" allowed people to leave the alienating,
repressive atmosphere of Odesa, and that Olga's story illustrated such a path.

But the story Olga told me later, away from the group, was much different. She and her partner had faced problems in Israel: Olga wasn't recognized
as Jewish by the halakha because her mother wasn't Jewish. This meant they
couldn't marry in Israel and had to travel to Cyprus for a civil ceremony that
would be recognized in Israel. Olga's decision to remain in Israel struck me
as rather more provisional than what she had presented to the group. "For
now, we're in Israel," she said, "and then we'll see." She added, "Odessa is very
nice to visit, but with my parents abroad I feel that I don't have much left here
anymore. . . . For now, Israel works for us."

When speaking directly with the UJC visitors, Olga placed Israel at the center of her Jewish identification. As a paid representative of the Jewish Agency for
Israel (Sokhnut), the Zionist organization that had sponsored her travel back to
Odesa, Olga told the personal story her audience expected to hear—minimizing
or passing over her struggles, her failure to be recognized as a Jew, and her
doubts about living in the "homeland." While she no doubt felt a connection

to the time she had invested in the Jewish Agency for Israel (Sokhnut), her professed feeling of obligation to the Jewish state and to those who had helped her emigrate was more of a performance than a reflection of her complex and confounding reality.

Mendy, introduced in the last chapter, was another participant in the "My Odesa through the Sunglasses of an Israeli" sessions. After the program ended, he and several others stayed on in Odesa to see family and friends. He explained that all the Odesan contributors were chosen because they could be counted on to relay the message of the Jewish Agency for Israel's (Sokhnut's) mission and answer any questions in the "right" fashion. These were the skills of what Mendy called "professional Jews."[39] He admitted that he himself had treated this as an opportunity to return home on a paid trip, stay in a nice hotel, and hang out with friends—an attitude he assumed all the participants shared. The terms *professional Jews* or *Jews by profession* used by the historian and writer Henryk Halkowsky are discussed in Magdalena Waligorska's ethnography of the klezmer music revival in Poland and Germany. They refer to non-Jews spearheading Jewish revival in places with little or no Jewish life.[40] Mendy's reference to "professional Jews" comes closer to anthropologist Olesya Shayduk's reference to Jews who "begin to position themselves as Jews" through their role in Jewish organizations or Jewish study-abroad programs rather than through their family upbringing.[41]

"Inappropriate" Narratives of Jewish Life

Next on the visitors' schedule was a visit with Olga's family. Since her parents were in Germany, Olga had arranged for us to meet her mother-in-law, Marina. A tall woman with short black hair and light hazel eyes, Marina was born in Moldova in 1950 and had relocated to Odesa with her husband and two children in 1983. The Soviet state gave them a small apartment on the outskirts of the city, and she started working as a baker at a small pastry shop, where she was still working when we met.

Marina was uncomfortable revealing her small apartment to foreign guests, so the meeting took place in a courtyard café near her home. Unlike Olga, who had prepared her talk, Marina appeared to be unsure what people wanted to hear. In addition to being unrehearsed, her story was further constrained by having to rely on Olga's translation. Still, the group was eager to hear about her family's experience during the Holocaust and Jewish life during Soviet rule. Marina's story focused on her father's struggles in the Soviet army while fighting the Romanian troops and her mother's fears during their evacuation to the Caucasus. She described how both parents were traumatized by the distance and uncertainty that separated them. When asked how she knew she was Jewish, Marina's response was simple: "I was born Jewish."

While Marina had been talking, the audience members had been leaning forward in their seats at the café, clearly expecting a longer tale of hidden Jewish activity or the pain felt for the lost world of Jewish traditions. At this response, they looked bewildered. For her part, Marina seemed uncertain how to explain "being Jewish in the Soviet Union," since to her, Jewishness was just a biological given. Feeling pressured to speak more, she elaborated, "I never paid attention to who was Jewish in Odessa; it's a Jewish city. . . . I never felt out of place or belittled because I was a Jew, and I can't say I ever experienced antisemitism. Everyone lived peacefully, and that's all that mattered." It is true that most Soviet Jews saw their Jewishness as an intrinsic component of who they were—one was "born Jewish."[42] But, their view of Jewish life in the FSU being shaped by Western stereotypes, the audience, mostly women, sat back in confused silence until one asked about Marina's participation in the Jewish organizations the mission was there to support. "I was never involved in Jewish organizations here or elsewhere," she said bluntly. "To be honest, I don't know anything about them. I always had my work, my home, and my children. Just work, home, and children."

During a pause, Shira pivoted and asked Olga to tell the group about her encounters with antisemitism. After Olga talked about being called a *zhidovka* in school, the UJC visitors again tried to place Marina's Jewishness within their own sense of what the identity entailed. They asked whether Marina's parents had ever done things that were "secretly Jewish," for as they understood it, anti-Jewish sentiment and persecution had been part of every Jew's life in the Soviet Union. "Did you light candles on Shabbat without being told what it was?" one woman asked. "Or maybe have a Jewish meal cooked by your mother?" "Matzo on Passover?" someone else asked. "Do you remember anything Jewish from your childhood?" a man from the back called out. After Olga translated these questions, Marina took a minute to think. Finally, she said she did recall the presence of matzoh at home. Olga announced this to the group with evident satisfaction.

One woman asked Marina why her son had decided to move to Israel. Marina answered without hesitation, "He met a girl at a Jewish camp, and they decided to move there together to try living on their own." Marina was referring not to Olga but to a previous relationship that had originally taken her son overseas. Her heavy breathing and tearful eyes made it clear that Marina worried about her son being so far from his family, especially during times of military operations in Israel. She added, "I only have one daughter here, and she recently got engaged, so soon I will have a son." A visitor asked whether her

Figure 5.2. UJC guests thanking Marina with a gift. Photo by author.

daughter's fiancé was Jewish. "He is not," she responded, "but he knows she is Jewish, and he's not bothered by it." In Marina's view, the fiancé's willingness to marry a Jewish woman spoke to his good character, while the fact that her daughter had revealed her Jewish roots made it clear she was proud of her family history and thus a good Jew.[43] Although Marina recognized Odesa's openness to Jews, her statements acknowledged that she knew marrying a Jew consti-tuted another level of proximity in the city. A woman in the group then asked what had changed in Marina's life since the fall of the USSR. Again, the answer was unexpected. "Everything got a lot worse," she said. "Prices are higher and everything is much more expensive today."

Again seeking to center the conversation on what mattered to her, Marina laid out photos of her children on the table. She admitted she missed her son profoundly, but she had no plans to move to Israel. She affirmed that her life is in Odesa; starting anew would be too difficult at her age. Shira spoke up to praise Marina for her strength and her support for Israel, on the basis of her son's aliyah. The women in the group saw Marina's story as that of a woman who'd lived a hard life as a Jew and was now having trouble "opening up" about her past. "We're grateful she even let us interview her," one woman said. "It can't be easy to think about everything she's lived through."

To my mind, Marina's heartaches came not from her Jewishness but from her struggles as a woman working long hours in a low-paying job, missing her

children, and dealing with all the changes involved in living in independent
Ukraine. Marina presented her Jewishness as unproblematic; she said she'd
always lived in cities where being Jewish was "part of the norm." From the visitors' perspective, however, Marina remained a "case unreached by outreach"—
neither affiliated with nor drawn to organized Jewish life. Shira used Marina's
story as a call for outreach and intervention. Marina's self-understanding was
seen as inadequate. Shira told the group that many Jews still needed help to
"remember their Jewishness, their connection to the Jewish people and their
homeland." Since Marina herself hadn't voiced any pressing need to live her
life in a more Jewish manner, I wondered what truly justified these initiatives.
If we take tzedakah as being "need oriented," where "you are commanded to
give according to the need of the other," we might ask why volunteers on philanthropic missions are so keen to elevate the Jewishness of those who don't
wish to follow that path, seeing them as a homogeneous group.[44]

Praise and Humiliation

We continued with Olga to the main office of the Jewish Agency for Israel
(Sokhnut), which Shira called "the heartbeat of the young generation." Having attended previous events there, I was struck by how different it appeared
on this day. There were twice as many participants and personnel as I'd seen
before. A few of the students I knew told me they'd been asked to come and
show support. For this, they were treated to a nice lunch at the synagogue.
Besides the usual displays of Israeli posters, plaques naming distinguished
donors, large images of the Hebrew alphabet, and pictures of Odesans in Israel, there were blue and white balloons and banners welcoming UJC donors
to Odesa.

Small groups of donors attended fifteen-minute sessions to learn about the
various programs sponsored by the UJC, such as Hebrew language classes,
study-abroad programs, a student club, contemporary dance classes, and a
Jewish choir. The sessions were held in classrooms where the visitors met local
participants and got a glimpse of Jewish life in Odesa. My group was invited to
join past and future participants of Na'ale, a study-abroad program that takes
youth under sixteen to Israel for a year; the aim is that their parents will follow
by making aliyah.

Inside the Na'ale room, some twenty young people sat facing the guests.
The students all wore "I love Israel" pins, and most looked exhausted from receiving group after group for the previous sessions.[45] Two of them were asked
to speak Hebrew to demonstrate the language skills they'd learned in Israel.
Two others who hadn't yet made the trip stood up to thank their sponsors

Figure 5.3. Shira introduces local youth to her delegation. Photo by author.

for the opportunity that awaited them. Beaming like the proud mother of well-behaved children, Shira asked the sponsors to give the students a round of applause. At the end of the session, she announced to the donors that this year, UJC money had bought these students brand-new backpacks decorated with the UJC and the Jewish Agency for Israel (Sokhnut) logos. "These students won't have to live through the embarrassment of carrying their books in plastic bags. Next school year, they'll have these wonderful backpacks, just like the rest of the Israelis."

To me, these young people didn't look economically deprived. I remembered a complaint once made by an Odesan friend: "Americans turn us into a third-world population." Carrying books in a plastic bag wasn't seen as unusual in Odesa, even among those who had other types of bags. Shira's comment struck me as condescending, but no one questioned the sponsored gifts of kindness. While it's common for Jewish missions to bring gifts, it sends an implicit message that local Jews are underprivileged. One might also question Shira's description of Odesa's Jewish youth as the "future of Israel." Most of the young people present planned to make a life in Odesa, not Israel, though they were willing to take advantage of free travel abroad. Most I met were happy to return home to Odesa and didn't entertain the idea of permanent emigration. When the economic situation worsened in Ukraine, or when young Jewish Odesans

Figure 5.4. UJC guests taking pictures of Migdal participants. Photo by author.

Figure 5.5. Migdal participants in traditional Ukrainian and Jewish dress pose for pictures as they welcome UJC guests. Photo by author.

felt they wanted to try living independently and grow from living abroad, those programs allowed them the possibility to try.

"Community Is Not a Given": Remapping the Contours of a Community

The rest of the tour was led by Rebecca, the Joint representative. She described her organization's role as providing the local Jewish population with basic social services and a sense of community. "In this part of the world," Rebecca declared, "community is not a given." When she led us to the entrance of the Migdal center, we saw four members dressed in Ukrainian embroidered shirts and Jewish attire that resembled Hasidic clothing of the late nineteenth century. It was the stuff of theater: traditional Ukrainian dress and what one might call costumes straight out of *Fiddler on the Roof*.

In his study of Kyrgyzstan, Mathijs Pelkmans describes a similar process of "folklorization" during church celebrations and fundraising events in Bishkek. There, dancers wear "traditional" costume while performing to traditional music played on a *komuz* (a string instrument like a lute).[46] For Pelkmans, "these displays had little significance in social life."[47] In Odesa, Jewish youth often reflected on how they felt about playing an expected role that had little or nothing to do with their lives. They were thus closer to Ruth Ellen Gruber's observation of a similar phenomenon in Krakow: Jews treated as museum pieces, there to be seen and photographed as relics of a Jewish past and living signifiers of a revived Jewish present.[48]

Playing their roles, the Migdal volunteers welcomed the UJC sponsors by offering them Ukrainian vodka and the braided challah bread made for Shabbat meals and Jewish holidays. Unlike the images of Israel and other Zionist markers of Jewish identification seen on the Jewish Agency for Israel (Sokhnut) visit, here the main display was the local Jewish culture—overacted, as if in a reenactment of some imagined Jewish shtetl.

Migdal was founded in the late Soviet period as the Jewish Theater Migdal Or. Its purpose was to educate Odesans about Jewish history, both local and biblical, and to raise awareness among locals and visitors about Jewish life in the city. Membership applicants are asked for papers proving their ethnic background, but the center has an open-door policy for visitors. A number of non-Jews work there and participate in its programs, use the library and computer lab, attend the school of Jewish art, and even learn Yiddish and Hebrew songs as well as Jewish dances.[49] Migdal also houses the city's first Jewish museum (located at a different address under the name the Museum of the History of Odesa Jews), with a wall dedicated to local Jewish heroes. Recall that the center is located inside the old butchers' synagogue officially owned by Chabad; when the current Chabad synagogue was being renovated in the 1990s, Migdal served as a prayer house.

All along Migdal's corridors, we saw proud moments in Odesa's Jewish history displayed in handcrafted posters, collages, postcards, letters, and old photographs. Its two floors were decorated with gifts from sister communities in Baltimore and Haifa. Unlike the religious education centers, in Migdal you would not see pictures of Anne Frank, unnamed Jewish Holocaust survivors, or other iconic images of Jewish history. Instead, the stories on display are rooted in Odesa.

During our visit to Migdal, the UJC sponsors saw children's dance troupes, a chess class, and classes in Jewish art. A group of Jewish ghetto survivors welcomed us with a song. As in the Sokhnut visit, all these activities were arranged so the guests could actively participate. Many Migdal members were there to represent the center's daily life. Clearly, the directors had made an effort to show the center as a lively place of Jewish activity. From their comments and smiling faces, I could tell that the UJC sponsors were highly entertained and touched by the level of enthusiasm and activity inside Migdal's walls. Many of the participants were proud to accept the visitors' praise and welcomed the brief exchange of ideas, opinions, and histories, which they described as "valuable." The young people generally appreciated the curiosity of these foreign Jews and were glad for the chance to practice their English, since some served as translators. As for the UJC guests, while they complimented Migdal's programs, they couldn't help but remark on the state of the building: chipped walls, decrepit bathrooms, and faded theater furniture stacked along the dim hallways. I wasn't the only one to notice their stares and whispered asides.

Later, while discussing the "mission day," my friend Gosha told me, "I don't understand these Americans. They come here as if they were coming to the zoo. I hear them talking about our lives as if it was a scary movie. Personally, it really irritates me." Gosha recalled how he used to be excited to see visiting Jewish groups—he, too, liked the opportunity to practice his English. But he remembered a number of incidents when, speaking with donors on missions, he and they would be talking at cross purposes on the subject of Jewish identity. "When they ask if I'm Ukrainian, I say, 'No, I'm Jewish.' They say, 'No, that's your religion. What is your nationality?' I explain that I'm not religious, I don't believe in God, but I'm Jewish by my nationality [ethnicity]."

In a conversation with my friend Diana, who also felt uncomfortable about the pity directed toward Odesa's Jews, she suggested that groups should spend a day outside the city, so the sponsors could understand that Odesans are living in comparative luxury. "There are places that really need help," she told me.

"Odessa is flourishing compared to them." On the whole, Diana was proud to say she lived in Odesa and not just another city in Ukraine. In her view, living in Odesa was a "privilege" she was happy to have been born into. As the famous Odesan comedian and musician Leonid Utesov used to say, "I was born in Odessa. You think I'm bragging? But it's really true. Many people would like to have been born in Odessa, but not everyone could."[50]

Philanthropy was a relatively new concept to most Odesans I met during my first visit to Odesa. As ex-Soviet Jewry became wealthier and more exposed to Western society, where philanthropy is widely practiced, they could, in practical terms, connect more with the idea of making donations for meaningful projects and supporting causes they valued. During the early phase of my fieldwork, I occasionally heard Odesan Jews describe visiting donors, who were mostly from North America, as "funny" and "naive" for the way they reacted to the local scene. In most cases, local Jews felt that visitors couldn't relate to Odesa because they only viewed it through the prism of their own experience. Sveta, a woman in her late thirties, told me:

> We simply don't get their mentality. I know some of them are here to see where their money goes, but I feel that a lot of them just come to see Jewish life in a third-world country. Sometimes, they bring things that are sentimental to them but have no value: something made by the hands of a child, that has traveled miles on an airplane and at times arrives broken. . . . Mostly they bring us cookies and sweets, sometimes even bags of diapers that have already been opened. Perhaps in Soviet days people found these gifts precious, but today things are different. But they don't see the change. They still treat us like Soviet subjects, deprived of basic needs.

I confess that initially, I found it hard to accept such comments. Having worked many years for nonprofit organizations, where fundraising never came easy, I was sympathetic to these sponsors who wanted to make Odesa a better place. When I shared these feelings with my respondents, their reactions were mixed. Some understood the donors' intentions and actions and appreciated their investment in Jewish futures; others even described Odesan Jews as spoiled by the system. On numerous occasions, I heard from Israeli teachers who explained that Jews in this part of the world expect to receive benefits, because that is the only model of Jewish community they know through continuous foreign support. Still other respondents saw the development of Jewish institutions and missions as problematic but necessary for sustaining Jewish life in the city. Gruber describes a similar attitude expressed by a Jewish activist in the Czech Republic, who said that while "we hate" the commercialization of Jewish places brought on by the international travel of foreign Jews, "it enables us to live."[51]

Over time, I started to understand how Odesan Jews struggled with the way these missions imposed various Jewish scenarios and ideologies that had no grounding in their own self-image. Among other things, their sincere pride in being citizens of Odesa was wounded when Jewish visitors failed to recognize their reasons for such pride or couldn't understand their reasons against emigration or aliyah, seeing them instead as being "frozen in [Soviet] time."

Imagined Community and Jewish Kin

The next stop on the group's tour was Gmilus Hesed, one of UJC's earliest programs in Odesa, set up to provide for elderly Jews and "righteous gentiles."[52] At the time of our tour, this program cared for more than eight thousand retired Jews and military veterans in the region. We entered through the courtyard, where Arkady, the newly appointed director, asked everyone to gather in a circle. "What you're about to see is not in any way rehearsed," he declared. "This is a typical day in the lives of our people." While everyone waited outside the door in suspense, Rebecca, the UJC organizer, addressed the group: "Your parents were fortunate enough to leave these parts of the world to make a better life in America. But you must remember, not everyone was given that chance. These Jews were not as fortunate as our families, who got to start their lives elsewhere. As you walk through the building, think about how these could be your parents if they hadn't left for America." Unlike the encounters of Portuguese Marranos and visiting Jews, where the language of kin is focused on "brothers and sisters" or "cousins," the UJC mission presented Odesa's elderly Jews as "parents" of American visitors. But in both cases, the framework of relatedness sent a strong message about the obligation of care for one another as a "family."[53]

The UJC sponsors then entered the old, run-down building, ready to see the programs that were said to be "operating as usual." At the entrance, Arkady pointed to a small folding table that held two types of food packages available to elderly Jews. The guests listened to a brief description of the various services provided and then proceeded to the main room, which had a small stage. Visitors and staff members sat down at several round tables, with a young translator at each. They all listened as the music coordinator, Nadya, played the piano while the Gmilus Hesed choir sang some Yiddish tunes. The American guests clapped and danced to the popular Yiddish melodies performed in their honor. Some even sang along, saying they remembered the songs from their parents' generation. The "tantalizing tension between familiar and exotic" that Leite describes and other anthropologists of Jewish tourism have picked up was clearly part of this encounter between the UJC mission and Odesa's elderly Jews.[54] That day, the UJC sponsors reflected on the points of commonality and difference between the two groups. But the elderly Jews I spoke with saw

Figure 5.6. The Gmilus Hesed choir sings for the UJC mission. Photo by author.

little in common with their audience, a distance perhaps heightened by their inability to communicate fluently with one another. Yiddish served as the link, but it wasn't a language that either group could converse in fluently.

The excursion to Gmilus Hesed stood out on that day's itinerary because it made the UJC sponsors recall their family history and prompted discussions about the idea of a more encompassing "Jewish family." Through her example of Jewish tours of the Marranos in Portugal, anthropologist Naomi Leite reminds us that "the description of the Jewish people as a 'family' is commonplace among Jews worldwide, likely stemming from centuries of liturgical emphasis on collective descent from the biblical patriarchs and matriarchs and the many holidays memorializing trials and triumphs of earlier generations."[55] Since many of the visitors were of Ashkenazi descent, the faces of Odesa's elder Jewry may well have evoked memories of their own relatives. However, Rebecca's effort to create an image of "relatives" who had been unable to immigrate to America denied the very real fact that these Jews had not failed to escape—instead, they had forged their own life histories, experiences, and attachments in Odesa. This distortion made the encounter between the American Jewish activists and Odesa's elderly Jews a kind of role play—one where the locals didn't get to tell their own stories but rather, by their sheer presence and performance, fulfilled an image already set by the organizers of the philanthropy tour to raise more money for those in need.

When done effectively, Jewish commentators explain, "tzedakah requires the donor to share his or her compassion and empathy along with money."[56] No doubt this tactic was thought to be useful in connecting visiting Jews to Odesa—a place unfamiliar to them—to boost their philanthropic efforts and their commitment to social justice and responsibility. As anthropologist Stephan Feuchtwang pointed out to me, the process of personalizing through identification is a common tactic in fundraising. It's part of a remembrance system deployed in other memorials where, for instance, a visitor is given a specific person's life to follow as a means of learning about a particular event and raising funds for a specific cause. Indeed, the UJC guests were deeply moved by their visit to Gmilus Hesed and expressed their support in terms of their obligation to Jews less fortunate.

Aviv and Shneer note that similar tours of eastern Europe "work to strengthen the allegiances and solidarity among Jews from different countries . . . to create a sense of a global nationhood."[57] Specifically, in the case of the Soviet Union, one must not forget the history of human rights activity led by Western Jewry to "Let My People Go." This movement raised an awareness among American Jews, among others, that Jews in this part of the world need saving. Visiting those who did not *go* is another asymmetry in the encounter of philanthropists and the people they support. Afterward, on the bus, Rebecca asked the visitors to tell their communities back home about the people they'd met—to help extend fundraising efforts for Odesa's Gmilus Hesed and other institutions.

Asymmetries of Encounter

As discussed in chapter 3, Odesa's new Jewish community center (JCC) Beit Grand met with much ambivalence from the local Jewish population upon its formation. But the facility built and furnished through donations provided by sponsors of the UJC was, of course, a main attraction during the mission. The UJC's organizers called it "the future of Odesa's Jewish community" and presented it as a clear sign of improvement in the local standard of living. Delegates had just seen the shabby facilities at Migdal and Gmilus Hesed, so the new JCC gave them a powerful "before and after" experience—another common fundraising tactic built into the mission.

Inside Beit Grand, guests walked through large spaces with clean, white, plastered walls, perhaps imagining the places they'd visited earlier rehoused inside such a facility—one that certainly resembled their impressive Jewish community centers back home. American donors would find it normal that the organizations housed inside the space were asked to pay rent and thus needed

Figure 5.7. A mission delegation tours the new Jewish Community Campus, Beit Grand. Photo by author.

to pass these costs on by raising participation fees. But Odesan Jews struggled with this new concept of becoming a "self-reliant group." Most of them did not donate to Jewish causes in their city. A number of well-to-do Odesan Jews had started to engage in local fundraising and charity, but their donations were small compared to those of the large international Jewish organizations. At this point, Odesan Jews were far from altering the local dependence on foreign funding and authority. The dominant mood was one of resistance to the self-reliance model, even as the impositions of that model—organizations that received outside funding should be moving to financial self-sufficiency—were growing stronger. As one of my interlocutors explained, "Here, unlike the West, Jews don't buy seats at their synagogues as a way of donating to their house of worship." In Odesa, she said, "Jews don't give to the rabbi; the rabbi gives to the Jews."

The aid organizations initially told Odesan Jews that they were receiving donations because they were Jewish. When the same authorities later tried to charge rents and participation fees, many were dismayed. The city's Jewish activists were concerned about being dependent on foreign leadership, but they didn't want to cut off foreign funds. When I asked Rebecca about the organizations being charged rent for use of the Beit Grand premises, she attributed the problem to program leaders' inability to consider the aid they received as just initial funding; instead, they expected permanent support for their operations. Rebecca had no concrete suggestions for resolving the financial issues created by this attitude.

The fact that the Beit Grand project was seeking to bring various organizations and programs sponsored by the Joint together under one roof also presented dilemmas. Because the organizations competed with one another—for funding, for Jewish participants, and for recognition—many were affected by internal politics. They didn't see themselves as sharing a common line of thought and being part of the same "community." As the Chabad school student Vika (introduced in the previous chapter) put it, referring to Migdal's current space, "At least here, nobody tells us what to do, and we don't feel like we're running a business and working under a landlord." For Vika and other Migdal staff, the pressures of digging up funds and relying on foreign representatives and agendas weighed against the upside of being located in a clean, modern space. The old Migdal building wasn't just the site of their activities; it was also a piece of the city's history, something that wasn't found in Beit Grand's freshly painted walls.

Memory and the Holocaust

The third day of the mission started in a somber mood. Across from the birch tree alley dedicated to righteous gentiles, and in front of one of the city's main Holocaust memorials, a crowd of nearly three hundred gathered to pay their respects to Odesa's victims of the Holocaust.[58] The event brought the American visitors together with representatives from most of the Jewish institutions that received funds raised through UJC initiatives, including children from the Chabad school, members of the Hillel Jewish youth club, Migdal members, local Holocaust survivors, and the Chabad rabbi, Avraham Wolf. He was the first to address the gathering, speaking briefly in Russian and then making the rest of his remarks in English. After Rabbi Wolf, a UJC guest delivered a short Holocaust-themed speech; the Jewish Agency for Israel (Sokhnut) choir sang Israel's national anthem, "Hatikvah"; and attendees recited the mourner's kaddish (prayer for the dead). Then everyone stood in silence as six Holocaust survivors, each paired with a teenaged Odesan, lit six torches in memory of the six million Jews who had been murdered. To conclude the ceremony, UJC sponsors placed small stones on a chalk inscription that spelled out the word "Remember." Some of the guests hugged; most said little.

The ceremony had emphasized the UJC mission's involvement in honoring local victims of the Holocaust, and Rabbi Wolf acknowledged the UJC for

Figure 5.8. Mission participants at the Holocaust memorial ceremony. Photo by author.

its work in rebuilding Jewish Odesa after the catastrophe. But apart from the UJC donor's short speech, little Odesan history was presented at this event. The Holocaust survivors themselves were asked only to light the six torches, not to address the group. For the most part, these survivors were reduced to being bystanders at an event dedicated to their experiences. As anthropologist Ulf Hannerz notes, the position of the tourist—as distinct from the cosmopolitan, who belongs to a place, in some ways—is typically defined as being limited to the role of spectator.[59] And yet during the ceremony, members of the UJC mission were given a stage on which to act out the ritual of Holocaust remembrance, all according to the universalized model of Jewish tragedy and solidarity: the Jewish prayer, the Israeli anthem, the lighting of six torches, and the imperative to remember.

Rebecca Golbert described a similar formula in Kyiv, at the Jewish Agency for Israel (Sokhnut) workshop on Holocaust Remembrance Day. There, the group was asked to re-create the setting of the Warsaw ghetto, the Auschwitz concentration camp, and Anne Frank's room, but specifically Ukrainian experiences were given little time. "An evocation of the ghetto and camp experiences rather than transmission of historical knowledge appeared to be the aim," Golbert concludes.[60] She notes that even though Ukraine certainly "had its share of ghettos and camps," it was the iconic sites of Poland and the Netherlands that were used to stand in for all places and memories in this thematizing of the Holocaust—itself a "generic model of Jewish suffering."[61] Poland, in particular, Erica Lehrer writes, has become an "epicenter of Holocaust abomination."[62]

A lot has changed on the level of memorialization in Ukraine since the time of Golbert's research, but according to scholar of Eastern European Studies and writer Nikolay Koposov, "attempts to develop the memory of the Holocaust in Ukraine has been the least successful in Eastern Europe to date."[63] Besides the general struggle between the particular and the universal that is visible in other places when memorializing the Holocaust, and the Soviet approach to seeing Jewish deaths in World War II through the prism of Soviet losses, in Ukraine the memorializing process was also tainted by the internal politics of victimhood between Jews, Ukrainians, and others.[64] In 2016, when President Petro Poroshenko and a group of Ukrainian and foreign leaders met on the site of Babyn Yar to commemorate the seventy-fifth anniversary of the massacre, the Israeli American journalist Sam Sokol noted that the memorial was submerged in national politics—Ukrainians and Jews taking part in "a game of victimhood."[65]

A dozen monuments to the various groups that died at Babyn Yar, including Jews, Ukrainian nationals, children, Roma, and others, manage to capture a piece of the tragic events that unfolded on this site but don't convey the significance of the larger events that the Babyn Yar deaths represent.[66] Several attempts to commemorate Babyn Yar in contemporary Ukraine have failed, including the proposed Babyn Yar Holocaust Memorial Center that was scheduled to go up in 2021 (the eightieth anniversary of the massacre).[67] Such failures are due to the internal politics of memory, ideological and practical issues, disputes about founders and funders, and, later, Russia's war in Ukraine.[68] Some Ukrainian historians were troubled that Babyn Yar would only be linked to the Holocaust and, as such, would only honor the Jewish and Roma victims, leaving out Ukrainian nationalists, Soviet prisoners, and others. They published a letter in March 2017 that stated: "We consider it a mistake to associate Babyn Yar only with the history of the Holocaust while ignoring other victims and other dramatic moments of its history. . . . This approach would only exacerbate the memory wars that have for many years been going on in the territory of Babyn Yar."[69] Others were troubled by the effort to assert a moral equivalence between Jews and others and found it offensive and incomparable to commemorate Jews and Ukrainian nationals together, given the history of collaboration of some members of the Organization of Ukrainian Nationalists and Ukrainian Insurgent Army.[70] And some Ukrainian Jewish activists and historians saw the proposed Holocaust memorial at Babyn Yar as a "paternalistic" project that highlighted the foreign origins of its backers, arguing that Babyn Yar is only partially about the Holocaust.[71]

For the Jewish youth in Kyiv whom Golbert describes, Babyn Yar repre-sented one of the most commemorated and grieved-over events in Ukrainian Jewish history. But most of my interlocutors (including the elderly Jews) fo-cused their Holocaust discussion on the Romanian Nazi occupation of Odesa and the horrific death of Jews in the ghettos and camps nearby.[72] Those were the memories displaced by the UJC mission ceremony, which didn't elaborate on the history of Jews during the Romanian occupation or commemorate days significant to local survivors, such as April 10, the anniversary of the Soviet liberation of Odesa in 1944.

Enacting a ritual purported to be about memory reinforced the idea of a "shared history" and a sense of "oneness" established on a foundation of Jewish pain. As with Golbert's example, the UJC ceremony ironed out most of the par-ticularities of place. The guests I spoke with said they felt a rush of emotion, but they'd learned little of what Jews in Odesa endured during World War II. The donors' performance and the survivors' spectatorship represent other aspects of the asymmetrical encounters that philanthropy missions represent. At this particular event, the stories of local Jews blended into the larger memory of the Jewish Holocaust, and the donors themselves became central to the narrative.[73] Lehrer notes that "descriptions of European Jewish life have tended to reflect the concerns and identity categories of American or Israeli Jewry rather than the lived realities of local Jews."[74] Though this ceremony took place in Ukraine, it was focused on a more recognized remembrance of the Holocaust rather than the specific experiences of survivors.

Responses varied among the locals who attended the Odesa commemora-tion. Daniel, a historian in his early thirties, remarked that the event was just another chapter in "the Holocaust industry," echoing the title of a book by po-litical scientist and activist, Norman Finkelstein.[75] A week later, when Daniel and I shared a train ride to Crimea, the topic turned to the people he called the "mitzvah [good deed] American Jews." Referring to the Holocaust memorial ceremony, he said,

Why did they [the organizers] need to bring children there, the elderly, and create all the commotion around people's personal lives, which these Americans couldn't relate to during this fake ceremony? I was very grateful to the rabbi, as he was the only one who said a few words in Russian to the crowd. Why didn't they have anyone translating the speeches to the people for whom it truly matters? I know, it's a mitzvah, but really most of the [Odessan] people aren't starving, they're not dying, and they don't need this huge Jewish cultural center they built. Why travel all this way to see how we live to feel sorry for us?

Daniel was upset that a local person hadn't been asked to speak to the crowd of Americans about Jewish Odesa. "Why give the task of describing Odesa's history to Rabbi Wolf, who's almost as foreign to the city as the visitors themselves? And why were you asked to give a welcome speech to this delegation, and not a local historian?" he asked me, point-blank.

Most of the young Jewish participants probably didn't notice anything out of the ordinary, nor would they have shared Daniel's critique. If they were involved with Jewish programs, they knew that the ceremony presented the Holocaust in a way that was similar to how it was done in many of those Jewish education programs and camps. These young people would have been able to follow the *kaddish* prayer and to recognize the occasion as one appropriate for the Israeli national anthem. In their minds, they would have had some vision of what they were being asked to "remember."

And what of the older participants, particularly those who had personally lived through the atrocities of the Nazi occupation? What do they make of such forms of remembrance in Odesa? The answer is perhaps not as straightforward as it might appear. In "the immediate aftermath of the Holocaust, many survivors simply wanted to forget and move on with their lives, while imploring the next generation to remember."[76] Moreover, the Soviet Union pushed an official state narrative of the Great Patriotic War—reinforced by Soviet media—that made no distinction between Jewish and non-Jewish suffering.[77] Furthermore, in many cases, at least prior to the death of Stalin, the Soviet state treated concentration camp survivors as "enemies of the state." For Jews who were old enough to have experienced the Holocaust period, the focus on forgetting could be profound.

Going against the grain of such pressures, many Odesan Jews who had seen the horrors of World War II did make a distinction between the experiences of the city's Jewish residents and those of others. Family stories shared privately with children and grandchildren spread knowledge of the killing of Jews; of their deportation, suffering, and imprisonment; and of those who survived. Elderly local Jews, like Nina (seen in chapter 2), also learned of the wider history of the Holocaust beyond Ukraine, thanks to global projects organized by Yad Vashem, the World Holocaust Remembrance Center and Museum. Nina's family story was recorded by Yad Vashem and included in publications on the theme of Nazi imprisonment. Other survivors, such as Nina's sister and mother, treated the subject with deep silence. Some, like Viktor (also in chapter 2), concentrated on other Jewish realities during the war, such as fighting in the Soviet Army, defeating the Nazis, and individual acts of bravery. Even members of the same family adopted different strategies for living with the past.

Exploration, research, and ways of commemorating the Holocaust are relatively new and evolving projects in Odesa, Ukraine, and across the FSU.[78]

Political scientist and scholar of Russian and Ukrainian Jewry Zvi Gitelman points out that "the word *holocaust* does not appear in Soviet literature; only in recent years have words such as 'catastrophe,' 'annihilation' (*unichtozhenie*), or 'kholokaust' (transliterated from English) been used."[79] As historians Ray Brandon and Wendy Lower point out, Ukraine was an ensemble of disparate territories partitioned among several neighboring powers from the mid-thirteenth century until the mid-twentieth.[80] For more than two generations, scholars and others discussed the Holocaust through the lens of the Soviet Union, Poland, Romania, or Hungary, because the Holocaust in Galicia is technically part of the Holocaust in Poland, the Holocaust in Transnistria is part of the Holocaust in Romania, and the Holocaust in Transcarpathia is part of the Holocaust in Hungary.[81] In more recent years, the politics of memory have also shaped issues such as nationalist collaboration in the Holocaust.[82]

In Odesa, not a single book on the subject was published prior to Ukraine's independence in 1991. Another decade passed before the Museum of the History of Odesa Jews mounted a permanent exhibition of Holocaust-related materials. A Holocaust conference held in 2006 served as an important platform for Odesa's intelligentsia to address the devastating history of the occupation. On June 22, 2009, the anniversary of the day Nazi Germany attacked the Soviet Union in 1941, the Holocaust Museum officially opened in Odesa. A satellite of the Regional Association of Jewish Ghetto Survivors, the museum is dedicated to victims of fascism and former prisoners of the ghetto and concentration camps. Research initiatives focused on the Holocaust were led by Odesa's expert on the subject, Leonid Dusman, and a cadre of young and middle-aged Odesan Jews, along with several survivors.[83]

In another step forward, the Museum of the History of Odesa Jews started its own YouTube channel in 2020 and in its first year posted more than a hundred short videos about Odesa's Jewish history, including the Holocaust. Meanwhile, former prisoners of ghettos and concentration camps were meeting regularly at Migdal for dance classes offered by the center's teachers. These gatherings were mostly social, celebrating birthdays and other personal events. But Migdal also organized public memorial ceremonies, and the center receives and administers—on behalf of the individual recipients—monetary compensation from the German government. Through these various routes, the subject of the Holocaust was slowly entering the public discourse, allowing for the memory, analysis, and commemoration of Jewish suffering, loss, and trauma in and around Odesa, and acknowledging the forms of Jewish survival and life that followed the war.

The UJC mission was not an event that contributed to that public discourse. After the Holocaust ceremony ended, the visitors were asked to imagine a

Figure 5.9. Sokhnut campers pose with UJC participants holding balloons in Israel's national colors. Photo by author.

bright Jewish future, and to think about the new generation of Jews they were connecting to Jewish life through their kind donations. The Jewish Agency for Israel (Sokhnut) summer camp would be their last stop before the mission flew to Israel.[84] The contrast between events—the Holocaust remembrance ceremony, followed by a meeting at the camp with young supporters of Israel, and then departure for Israel—reinforced "the traditional notion of diaspora and homeland" observed by Aviv and Shneer in other tours of eastern Europe and Israel that position Israel as "the center of Jewish life, and Eastern Europe as the center of Jewish death."[85]

As the mission's visit to Odesa ended at the Jewish Agency for Israel (Sokhnut) camp, UJC members were paired with local youth and gathered for a group photograph to be used in future UJC publications. Everyone received matching T-shirts and blue and white balloons; on the count of three, they all released the balloons and Israel's national colors rose into the Odesa sky.

Conclusion

The coordination exhibited in that symbolic balloon send-off and the mission's approaching flight to Israel was obviously not representative of the entire UJC visit to Odesa. The full three-day stay was indicative of many of the missions that became an element of the city's fabric. But as this chapter has illustrated, the foreign organizers who sought to draw Odesa's Jewish population into a greater, imagined Jewish community also perpetuated a system of inequality and division through the array of asymmetrical encounters.

I want to stress that such encounters are not merely awkward interpersonal interactions between strangers. They are illustrative in that they expose the differences in donors' and recipients' perceptions, priorities, understanding, and identification as Jews from different parts of the world. Those differences point to the unequally positioned stakes in their relationships, whose dynamics produce new cultural meanings, categories, objects, and identities.[86]

The divides between the international missions and the Jews of Odesa were sometimes subtle, sometimes stark. What ran through all the performances of Jewish identity, however, was the sheer fact that being "donated to" made a number of Odesan Jews feel they were seen as *less than*. Mission organizers tended to imagine a Jewish population that shared the traits, history, customs, and culture of the donors from abroad, while positioning that population's members as victims of Soviet oppression and dire economic conditions, and thus, in need of saving. This left little to no room for any details of the actual lives of Jews living in Odesa. Their role was reduced to providing quaint "local color" to motivate more donations and a greater investment in "saving" those Jews who were cast as merely *left behind*.

This example of a mission further illustrates how international agencies sculpt images of local Jewish life to further program goals in the region— images that reveal part of the reality but not *the* reality. The encounters created depend on local Jews playing the role of those in need of rescue and revival from alienation and poverty. This role may have some basis in the lived experiences of Soviet Jews who fought to stay connected to Jewish practices, but such families were among the first to leave the Soviet Union. While some Jews and others in Ukraine are certainly living in difficult material conditions, the suggestion of some typical Jewish poverty omits the stratification of the population across the whole of Odesa. In fact, many middle- and upper-class Jewish families certainly do not feel their lives need improving or saving, in any economic, social, or spiritual sense. Indeed, most Jews feel their lives are flourishing, and they are free to be Jewish in any way they choose.

The role of Jewish missions in Odesa and elsewhere should expand our understanding of how faith-based philanthropy works in independent Ukraine.[87] Scholars of Russian-speaking Jewry Valery Chervyakov, Zvi Gitelman, and Vladimir Shapiro label the process of Jewish revival in Russia and Ukraine a form of "cultural imperialism . . . the imposition of external agendas on people whose value hierarchy is different" from their own.[88] Indeed, the contributions of local Jews to the mission's discourse were minimal and even, in some instances, censored by the translators and mission leaders. If empowering the local population is a goal of development, then Jewish philanthropic organizations should approach ex-Soviet Jewry not as deprived subjects, but as Jews whose complex range of experiences and relation to Judaism can be instructive. They should approach them as equals.

Instead, the lives of younger generations are being shaped within an economy of aid. Beyond the critical analysis of cultural imperialism that is made vivid in religious revival, new models of fostering Jewishness have appeared through educational programs generated by local and international Jewish organizations. Jews in Odesa have internalized many of the transplanted models of Jewish identification introduced by the international agencies' educational programs and accepted them as their own. This is especially true among the young. What then of their path forward?

With foreign philanthropists funding most of the institutions serving Odesa's Jewish population, questions of sustainability come to dominate programs and agendas—the donations must continue.[89] For those who receive these donations, "underprivileged Jew" becomes an imposed position.

6

———~~———

"Jewish Is a Mode of Transportation"

Between Home, Homeland, and Diaspora

In the breakup of the Soviet Union, Israeli and American Jews helped facilitate one of the largest waves of Jewish emigration since nearly two million Jews of the Russian Empire fled political and social persecution, pogroms, and economic instability.[1] Human rights activists who had tried to pry open the cracks in Soviet restrictions had been motivated by the idea of helping Jews escape communist repression and state-sponsored antisemitism—a frame that, as the previous chapter demonstrated, came to define Jewish life in the FSU.[2]

But as we've seen in earlier chapters, the reality of Jewish life in the Soviet era and its immediate aftermath wasn't all that narrow in scope. Naturally, not everyone took up the opportunity to emigrate, and those in what was called the "stay-back" population baffled many of the activists who had long worked to free Jews from their supposed confinement behind the Iron Curtain. As one Russian scholar of Jewish studies, Mikhail Chlenov, recounted about his efforts to explain the real problems faced by Jews in the FSU during this time of unprecedented emigration: "An American colleague . . . said to me: 'Look, we don't have space in our mentality for the image you presented. We see only two scenarios: either they're hitting you on the head, or you're packing your belongings to go to Israel.' Such is the stereotypical image, but as with every stereotype, it's far removed from reality."[3]

Odesa's Jewish population certainly confounds the stereotype. While a large proportion of the city's Jewish population emigrated, some chose to stay in Odesa, and of those who emigrated at some point, some returned while others continued to travel between various cities that hold points of attachment for them (familial, cultural, social, or otherwise). Given these patterns, the central questions pursued in this chapter are as follows: What is the nature of this attachment to Odesa? What is the concept of "home" for those who left and for those who have since returned? Is the idea of the "homeland" for returnees still tied to Israel? And do the Jews of Odesa see themselves as part of a diaspora in ways that conform to traditional definitions of the term?

To begin, emigration—whether under Soviet rule or in the post-Soviet period—had definite consequences for the Jewish population that remained in Odesa.[4] It influenced how they defined their relationship to Israel and how they perceived the United States, Germany, and other destinations where many of their compatriots and family members had settled. To be Jewish in Odesa, in other words, was about much more than *being* in Odesa. Indeed, emigration had long been a variable of Jewish identity in the region—quite apart from the ways it was defined by the limitations imposed by Soviet policies and the push for emigration that came after the fall of the USSR. Though Odesan Jews have forged more intense attachments to the Israeli state in recent decades, the sociopolitical context influenced by patterns of Jewish emigration and communities abroad must be understood as multigenerational. Ideas of a distant "Jewish homeland" and an allegiance to a country of origin play out across myriad personal and family choices, ranging from pragmatic necessities— entrepreneurial, educational, and romantic—to the harder-to-define sense of feeling "at home." To grasp these distinctions of "home" and "homeland," we must pass the case of Odesan Jews and their patterns of migration through our understanding of the diaspora.

Jewish Emigration: The Historical Picture

The Odesa region witnessed many significant episodes of Jewish emigration in the nineteenth and early twentieth centuries. The pogroms in 1821, 1849, 1859, 1871, 1881, and 1905 drove Jews from Odesa and the rest of the Russian Empire (see chapter 2). From the 1880s onward, Zvi Gitelman writes, "no group of Jews has migrated as often, in as great numbers, and with such important consequences as the Jews of Russia and the FSU."[5] Between 1881 and 1912, an estimated 1,889,000 Jews moved abroad.[6] This immense outflow is usually portrayed as a flight from escalating social and political persecution.[7] Another line of scholarship has shown that large-scale Jewish emigration began a decade before the May Laws of 1882 (and the pogroms that followed). In this telling, Jews were escaping economic deprivation and population expansion.[8] In the early twentieth century, the upheavals surrounding the Bolshevik Revolution and both world wars also caused vast numbers of people to relocate.

During the early phases of Soviet rule, Jews made their way out of the country typically to join relatives abroad in what was referred to as "chain migration."[9] As emigration from the USSR became highly constrained, if not entirely eliminated, the shape and scale of Jewish emigration that did occur was molded by both external and internal factors. External factors included those surrounding Soviet-US relations, Soviet policies in and around the Middle East, and the increasing involvement of nongovernmental and human rights organizations. Internal factors included Soviet state ideology, local manpower requirements, and Soviet ethnic policies.[10] Such pressures were never monocausal. For instance, although the USSR didn't want emigration to undermine the world's image of the "happy Soviet citizen," such curbs on emigration also helped mitigate the country's labor deficits.[11]

For individuals who may have been tempted to emigrate, the obstacles were likewise multiple. Soviet policies ensured that would-be emigrants faced an "all or nothing" decision: the stated desire to leave the country and live elsewhere came with profound material and social costs, whatever the outcome. Emigrants were forced to renounce their citizenship, surrender passports, and resign from their workplaces.[12] Family members might pay the same price. I learned that in one family, after the son applied for an exit visa to Israel, the father was demoted from his high-placed position in the KGB. Indeed, many of my interlocutors spoke of being pressured to resign from their jobs. Peers and colleagues could interpret applying for an exit visa as an act of betrayal, and those who did so risked a permanent loss in status.[13] But the nature and orientation of one's work played an important role in how people reacted to another's plans to emigrate. Recall Nina, the artist in her early seventies: she told me that many of her colleagues were Jews who had openly contemplated leaving the USSR—"No one treated you negatively if you told them you would soon be living abroad. We all understood."

In the late Soviet period, political authorities did yield to international pressure by relaxing the quotas on Jewish exit visas. Jewish emigration during the Soviet era peaked in two periods: the 1970s and between the late 1980s and early 1990s. According to demographer Mark Tolts, nearly 300,000 Jews emigrated from the USSR in the first wave, compared to approximately 1,641,000 in the second wave, who left the FSU between 1989 and 2017.[14] The Jewish migrants of the early 1970s came mostly from peripheral areas where Jews were less assimilated, notably the Baltic States, western Ukraine, Moldova, western Belarus, and Georgia.[15] Some 164,000 Soviet Jews went to Israel in the early 1970s.[16] In the late 1970s, when most of the unassimilated Jews wanting to leave the USSR had either succeeded or been refused exit visas, the character of Soviet Jewish emigration changed.[17]

Until the mid-1970s, most of those who left the USSR went to Israel, but by the second half of the 1970s, "half of the total number of emigrants changed their destinations, mostly for the USA."[18] That change was significant, since

Jews who left the Soviet Union for Israel were granted exit visas only on grounds of "family reunification" or "repatriation," whereas Jews going to the United States and other Western countries were treated as "refugees" by virtue of overcoming Soviet restrictions.[19]

Those in this wave of Jewish emigration were also less likely to be inspired by Zionist ideology. They had more pragmatic reasons for leaving. They were driven not by aspirations of a "return" to the "homeland" but by the hope for a better life outside the USSR. So, while they may have left the country on Israeli exit visas, they were "dropping out" en route and heading for the United States or other Western countries.[20] Gitelman documents that after 1976, nearly 85 percent of Soviet Jews arriving in the United States were from Russia or Ukraine, and about 90 percent of those were from Moscow, Leningrad, Kyiv, or Odesa. As he concludes, most acculturated Jews were choosing America, not Israel, as their destination.[21] Many settled in Brighton Beach, a part of Brooklyn, New York, that became known as Little Odessa.[22] Smaller groups of Odesans moved to the San Francisco Bay Area, some to Chicago and Boston, and others chose areas with less concentrated populations of immigrants.

"Perestroika Migrants" and the Post-Soviet Period

The economic and political crisis that culminated in the disintegration of the Soviet Union in 1991 also generated the mass emigration that took place at this time.[23] In 1989, a total of 85,089 Soviet Jews were allowed to emigrate, compared to 22,403 recorded in the previous year.[24] In 1990, a record 205,000 Jews left the USSR (some estimates indicate nearly 230,000); almost 200,000 departed the following year.[25] These are referred to as the "perestroika migrants."

Many of the 1990s emigrants ascribed their flight to rumors of pogroms and uncertainty about the future. In this rendition of events, it's as if entire communities were seized with utter panic, and herd instincts (*stadnoe chustvo*) took over: "Everybody had left, and so we left too."[26] Sergey, a secular Jew born in 1955, described the times and events in a more measured way. "People were leaving because they finally could leave," he said, "not necessarily because they wanted to. They weren't sure if the opportunity would come again, so they wanted to go while the door was open." Given the historical vagaries of Soviet emigration policy, it wasn't unreasonable to expect exit visa regulations to change suddenly. Thus, as Sergey pointed out, many Jews took the chance when it became available, quickly saying their farewells to friends and neighbors. In total, between 1970 and 1997, an estimated 422,000 Jews emigrated from Ukraine.[27]

This wave of emigrants was further shaped by a change in US immigration laws in October 1989 that reduced immigration from the Soviet Union to a quota of forty to fifty thousand refugees a year.[28] Again, Israel became the primary destination for emigrating Jews, including a large number of Odesans. The United States remained the second-ranked receiving country until September 11, 2001, when US immigration policy was greatly curbed yet again. Surveys indicate that many Jews leaving the FSU in the 1990s were indeed choosing Israel not because it was their preferred country of settlement but because it had opened its doors more widely to ex-Soviet migrants.[29] Odesan Jews immigrating to Israel settled mainly in Netanya, Haifa, and Ashdod, attracted by those cities' proximity to the sea and large Russian-speaking populations. Many chose their destinations because of family connections or the advice of friends. No small number of early arrivals traveled from Odesa to Israel on a ferry that arrived in Haifa, and they settled in the very place where they had disembarked.

Another option emerged for Soviet Jews during this period: in 1991, Germany opened up to ex-Soviet Jews (and ethnic Germans from the USSR). As literary scholars Misha Belensky and Joshua Skolnik note, "The idea that a number of ex-Soviet Jewish emigrants, now pressured by new U.S. immigration regulations to choose Israel as their destination, would instead opt to go to Germany, of all places, clearly affronted Israel's self-conception as a natural home for Jewish refugees."[30] Nonetheless, tens of thousands opted for a life in Europe rather than the Middle East.[31] Hoping to accelerate adaptation, German state officials spread incoming ex-Soviet Jews throughout the country so as to avoid an unassimilated "Russian ghetto." From 2002 to 2004, "more emigrants went to Germany than to Israel."[32] But in 2005, Germany's policy became more restrictive, and Israel once again became the primary destination for ex-Soviet Jews. In all, between 1989 and 2017, an estimated 328,000 ex-Soviet Jews and their relatives moved to the United States, while 229,000 settled in Germany. "Jewish is no longer a nationality," many ex-Soviet Jews joked. "Now it's a mode of transportation."

Perspectives on Emigration

Aside from some who were elderly, most of the Jewish Odesans I met had at some point seriously entertained the idea of emigration. Some had taken steps toward it, such as exploratory travel, family discussions, researching information, learning a new language, and even going so far as to acquire refugee or returnee status—all without ever actually leaving. Often, their decision to stay was fraught with personal, familial, professional, economic, and social demands or obligations, which they weighed against the prospects of living abroad. A Brezhnev-era joke about migration seemed perpetually relevant in Jewish circles: "Among the Jews there are the brave and the very brave; the brave leave and the very brave stay."[33] On a number of occasions, however, stay-back Jews expressed much sympathy for their compatriots abroad: those Jews, having chosen to emigrate, were torn from their *dusha* (soul), so to speak.[34] When they left Odesa, the city of their family history and roots, they left the worldview and social relations they had known at home and *as home*.

For Odesans wanting to emigrate, the United States remained the first choice for most. Germany held appeal for its extensive social benefits, membership in the European Union, and proximity to Ukraine, which was reassuring to many who were considering starting life anew. But Israel was the easiest option. Legal channels for acquiring exit visas were available, and they would find a large Russian-speaking population (estimated at over one million) in their new country, with an extensive infrastructure of Russian-language institutions. Certainly, this was an important consideration for the elderly. On the other hand, the fear of living with Israel's continuous warfare, the difficulty of finding employment, an aversion to the climate, and a distaste for being isolated among other Russian speakers were among the many negative factors raised by my interlocutors.

Irina, who was in her midthirties and employed by an international Jewish organization in Odesa when we met, described her family's decision-making process this way: "My parents were seriously contemplating immigrating to the United States after my aunt and uncle left [Odessa] in the early 1990s. But my grandfather became ill, and we couldn't leave him on his own, so we stayed. When his health finally improved, some time had already passed, and we felt there was no longer a real need to leave, as things in Odessa had improved." Irina's statement echoed many other stories of those who may have considered leaving their city (notably during the 1990s) only to change their minds due to the improving social and economic situation.

Gosha, an IT specialist in his late twenties at the time of our meeting, told a similar story about his family. His father, a lawyer by training, was denied an exit visa in the 1970s (that is, he was a refusenik). As a consequence of his application, he'd been fired from his job. When emigration became more feasible in the early 1990s, Gosha's father considered moving his family to the United States, where they had relatives. But around this time he found a desirable job with a law firm. "We already had the refugee status to move to the US, but my parents decided that starting all over in another place would be too difficult,

so we decided to stay," Gosha explained. He didn't regret his family's decision, but he thought that living abroad might still be an option for him in the
future—but on his own terms, as a highly trained professional rather than as
an ex-Soviet Jewish refugee.

Other Odesans of Gosha's age shared his desire to one day work overseas.
But ex-Soviet Jews of his parents' generation and social class said they were
staying in Odesa to protect the comfortable lives they'd built, thanks to their
educational achievement and established careers. Emigration, they feared,
would mean learning a new language, few employment options, and general
downward social mobility. Emma, a woman in her early sixties, told me she'd
never felt the need to emigrate: she had a respectable, interesting job at Odesa
University; her family owned an apartment and a dacha; and their income met
their needs. No doubt, Odesans of Emma's stage in life would agree with her
sense of starting over in a new place: "I will be nobody there."

Emma was never registered as a Jew in her official documents and didn't
directly face discriminatory Soviet policies, but others did. Many very accomplished individuals acknowledged that they'd experienced antisemitism
in the Soviet era, typically in the form of quotas for Jews in universities and
most workplaces. As many of them pointed out, this was the everyday reality
that had made them strive for assimilation or work harder to achieve their
goals, but it hadn't swayed them to emigrate. Mila, who was in her mid-sixties
when we spoke, told me she'd been denied admission to Odesa University
seven times and was accepted only on her eighth try. Still, she proudly described herself as "Jewish" in all her documents and set her goals high. Being
Jewish, as she recalled, made it much harder to achieve her aspirations but not
impossible. In her view, the facts that Jews today held prominent positions in
Odesa, the city's mayor in 2006 was a Jew, and Jews no longer faced quotas
and were free to walk the streets in religious dress were all positive aspects
of contemporary reality. Mila was glad that Jews no longer felt they had to
hide their Jewishness and that some even proudly flaunted it. She confirmed
what we've seen here in previous chapters: many in the non-Jewish majority
of Odesans believed that Jews enjoyed privileged status because they were
eligible for better social services and emigration. She gave examples of non-
Jewish Odesans who forged a false Jewish ethnicity to access services or
married a Jew in order to leave the country. "Everyone wants to be Jewish
now," she concluded.

Indeed, most of my interlocutors were able to stay in Odesa because of their
somewhat privileged social status. Other Jews, perhaps those less established
and members of the working class, weighed the emigration option differently.

The prospect of making a decent living elsewhere or a loss of employment in Odesa was major motivation for seeking a life abroad.

Deciding to Leave

In chapter 2, we met Elena and her husband, Konstantin. They were among the few Odesans I encountered during my fieldwork who were in the process of immigrating to Israel. We'd been introduced by a mutual friend who knew of my research on return migration from Israel and hoped that I could explain to the couple why some former emigrants were returning to Odesa. Elena and Konstantin didn't need any briefing on the hardships of Israeli life, however. They had traveled there five times, and regular phone calls, letters, and emails with Elena's family in Beer Sheva kept them well informed about the life of Russian-speaking migrants in Israel. Still, I visited them regularly and looked forward to their invitations for meals, tea, and conversation.

As the months passed, Elena kept changing their departure date. She didn't want to leave Odesa before the summer, her favorite time of year, but then she didn't want to leave in the fall, which she also loved. Imagining her future life in Israel, she often comforted herself by comparing Odesa with Netanya, the coastal city where they expected to settle—after all, both were on the sea. Beyond such mental remedies for her already palpable nostalgia, Elena and her husband found a practical way to maintain their links to Odesa: they would hold on to their apartment, to make sure "the door remains open." They began seeing their move to Israel as just another trip abroad, albeit one for a whole year. "I'm not taking my books *this* time," Konstantin told me. "We'll leave them here in the apartment with our furniture, and when we're back next year, we'll decide what to do with it all." In this vision of emigration, there was a reassuring sense that *this* departure would be followed by the *next*.

Whatever their sentimental reasons for retaining the apartment, Konstantin confidently pointed out that owning property in Odesa was highly profitable—the rental income would pay for frequent trips home and even the possibility of a splendid summer vacation. "Some people own up to eight apartments in Odesa now," he said, "and they don't even live here." When November came, the couple finally found tenants for their apartment—fittingly, a family returning from Israel. At last, they booked their tickets to Tel Aviv, which were paid for by the local branch of the Jewish Agency for Israel (Sokhnut). Instead of a big farewell party, they just had a few close friends come for dinner. When people left in the early 1990s, it had been, seemingly, for forever. In 2006, when Elena and Konstantin departed, it seemed less permanent and less emotionally taxing, both for them and for their friends and family.

Yet despite the tentative nature of Elena and Konstantin's emigration discourse and behavior, other details spoke of something final. Shortly before
they left, Elena made a trip to Kherson, her mother's city of birth, to visit her
mother's grave. "I wanted to say my goodbyes properly," she told me. "I know
I'm planning to come back, but you never know what can happen." Concerned
about her own health and Israel's security issues, Elena could see that leaving
Odesa might be a more absolute choice than she'd recognized. When I asked
why she was going, I sensed that she found it hard to answer. "You know, we're
not getting younger. Konstantin is seventy-one now. Who will take care of us
if something happens to us here? We don't have medical insurance, and all the
good doctors have already [gone abroad]. We can't be a burden on our children,
and we don't want to be alone."[35] Reflecting her very positive outlook on life,
Elena also described the move to Israel as a new opportunity and a chance to
see the world. "Sometimes it's good to change things in life. It lets you meet
new people, see new things, and test yourself as a person."

Spending this time with Elena and Konstantin before their departure gave
me many insights into the present-day concerns of Odesans, both Jewish and
non-Jewish, about leaving their homes, and their thoughts about the meaning
of living abroad. At the same time, their departure plans showed me some of
the tactics used by Odesans to secure their socioeconomic links with their
departure city while residing elsewhere. Elena and Konstantin didn't seem to
feel rushed or pressured by their circumstances, though their age and necessary care had entered the calculations. Unlike those undergoing the "one-way
ticket" emigration of the Soviet era, they exemplified migrants who were able
to test their status abroad while maintaining their position at home in Odesa.

I found similar economic activity among a number of other migrants who
could afford to emigrate without selling their property and who owned property that could profitably be rented out. Having tenants at their places in Odesa,
or even in their dachas in the country, meant annual trips home to, at the very
least, collect the rent and check on their homes. Two of my friends lived in an
apartment owned by Odesans residing in Germany. Under their agreement,
my friends had to vacate the premises for a month every summer when the
owners returned on vacation. Some of the Odesans and other ex-Soviet immigrants I met abroad, who'd left before the privatization of the early 1990s,
expressed regret at having gone too soon: they'd missed this opportunity to
remain connected to their cities, and to enjoy the financial benefits reaped by
later migrants who'd come to own their homes.

In their dispersed family and transnational kin networks, Elena and Konstantin resembled many of the Jewish Odesans I met. Everyone had a relative
or friend abroad—in many cases, in more than one location. Odesa's Jewish

diaspora had come to span many countries and continents; by the late 1990s, it was larger than the number of Odesan Jews at home. Although Elena and Konstantin's story captured a certain age group and social class of Odesans, and specifically concerned migration to Israel, their case can nonetheless help us understand Jewish emigration as a challenge as much as an opportunity and a complex process when carried out by present-day Odesans.[36]

Visions of Israel

As a result of the last wave of Jewish emigration in the late 1980s and 1990s, Israel is now home to the largest number of ex-Soviet Jews outside the FSU. Almost as many Odesan Jews live there as in Odesa.[37] Many of my interlocutors had family members or friends who had moved to Israel in the 1990s and 2000s, or earlier. Most of these migrants had decided to remain in Israel, but others used Israel as a stepping stone for emigration to Canada, Australia, the United States, or elsewhere.[38] A few had returned to Odesa. I wanted to know how "stay-back" Odesans, who'd never left Ukraine, forged their ideas about Israel; I also wanted to know what returnees, mainly from Israel, thought about their relationship with Israel and with Odesa.

Middle-aged and elderly Odesan Jews who'd never moved abroad did not view Israel through a Zionist lens. Instead, they perceived it first and foremost through the filter of family and friends who had lived there. These interpersonal networks revealed what it was like to become a Russian-speaking Israeli in terms that reflected the daily rigors of social and economic life. Those who could afford it often chose to test their visions of that life by visiting kin. Personal attachments and practical considerations seemed to outweigh any ideological connections Jews might feel to their "homeland."

Mila, mentioned earlier in this chapter, lived in Odesa with her mother. Her only son, Mendy, had emigrated to Israel in 1997 and still lived there. Originally, Mila had thought that Mendy would return to Odesa. The thought of joining him in Israel had crossed her mind a number of times, she said, but "I feel much more at home in Odessa, where I was born and raised." Elaborating on her sense of identity, Mila said, "If someone asked me if I was part of the Russian *narod* [people] I would say yes, because I was raised in Russian culture and literature and I know it [Russian culture] much better than I know Jewish culture.[39] I know Israeli history, major holidays . . . but it's not the same thing."

Still, Israel was a familiar place. She connected it primarily with her son but also with her job at the Israeli Cultural Center. Before taking that job, she said she'd known little about Israel beyond the fact that it "existed." Even though Israeli life had become a regular topic of conversation at their house, it lacked the "nostalgic pull of a physical home."[40] That feeling was reserved for the city where they had grown up. "Odessa is a special place," Mila explained. "It's small, it's familiar, it's homey, it's mine. You can't compare it to other cities in Ukraine."

Mila's mother, in her late seventies, kept Israel in her peripheral vision only because her grandson lived there. She told me that at her age, she couldn't imagine leaving Odesa. Her husband and other family members were buried in Odesa's Jewish cemetery, to which she felt a personal responsibility. Both Mila and her mother relied on the fact that it was easier for Mendy to visit them, and they eagerly awaited his every return.

I met Mendy on one of his visits. Like many of his generation, he had been introduced to the idea of living in Israel through the Jewish Agency for Israel (Sokhnut) summer camp. This orientation was reinforced by his association with Beitar, where Zionist ideology was actively promoted. "This was something I only understood later," he said. "No one directly told you that you had to go to Israel, but everything pointed in that direction." He explained that his emigration to Israel at age eighteen was a natural move in identifying himself as a Jew, part of his search for a more meaningful Jewish life. While Mendy no longer stated his reasons for living in Israel in terms of the Zionist myth of return, he had other reasons for keeping Israel as his home, including work, friendships, and independence.

Given the nature of immigration to Israel, where a great many migrants were young people involved in religious or secular Zionist organizations who left their former homes on their own initiative, the scenario of leaving parents and grandparents behind in Odesa wasn't uncommon. In these circumstances, emigrants' families were often just as concerned with events in Israel as with Ukrainian news. Fear of terrorism loomed large and became all the more extreme when children or grandchildren were serving in the Israeli army or when conflicts arose.

A number of parents shared the image of Israel as a war zone where terrorism touches lives on a daily basis. These parents felt that their children had made a mistake in emigrating there. The same fear also led many parents to object to their children participating in Jewish organizations in Odesa, as they were concerned that it would persuade their children to move to Israel. In one extreme case, the parents of Roma forbade discussing any Jewish affairs at home, out of fear that their son might want to make aliyah.

Religious Jews who didn't wish their children to be brought up and educated according to what they saw as the excessively secular norms of Israeli society also kept the Zionist organizations at arm's length. Maya felt that Israel lacked the appropriate discipline, schooling, and personal relations that her son could experience in Odesa. Now that Odesa had all the institutions and conditions needed for living an observant Jewish life, staying was a comfortable option for many religious Jews.

Even Jewish youth who weren't participating in the Jewish Agency for Israel (Sokhnut) summer camp or Beitar's activities had personal networks with peers and family in Israel, just as their parents and grandparents did. Twenty-year-old Svetlana, whose sister lived in Tel Aviv, often spoke of her numerous visits to Israel and the hardships she witnessed in her sister's life. This direct contact with daily life there had left her with mixed feelings about living in Israel herself. Along with her parents, she often followed the television and radio news about Israel and expressed concern for her sister's well-being.

For those youth who did identify with Israel through institutional affiliations, the discourse was much different—more informational, more direct, and containing a more elaborate architecture of association and allure. In addition to what was taught at the secular institutions, Israel's biblical and contemporary history were part of the curriculum at religious Jewish schools, and the idea and place of messianic and ancient Israel were reinforced in daily prayer. The Litvak Orthodox movement sent many students to yeshivas and other religious institutions that offered programs of intense Jewish education in which the idea of aliyah is prominent. Another mode of contact with Israel was offered by the Israeli religious families who served as educators and spiritual leaders for many of Odesa's youth in the Jewish schools.

These institutions, whether secular, religious, or Zionist, invoked Israel not just as a place to live but as the place that represented Jewish people as a whole. However, that changed when youth traveled to Israel on study-abroad programs. These schemes, offered specifically to young people, were designed to promote aliyah. The short trips had become increasingly popular among Odesa's Jewish youth, who took the opportunity to visit Israel and to sample its social and political life without committing to immigration.[41] Among the most popular programs was Taglit, which many of my friends attended. A thirteen-day trip to take in Israel's most appealing destinations in the company of other young people left many young Odesan Jews with fond memories of "their" country and the wish to return. Recalling her own Taglit experience, nineteen-year-old Karina said, "When I landed at Ben Gurion [airport], it felt like I was coming home after some twenty years of being away. . . . You learn so much about it [Israel], you read all those books, you teach others about it, and when you finally get there it's such an overwhelming feeling of being in a familiar place. It's your imaginary castle built especially for you, where you feel like a princess. I couldn't wait to tell everyone about it." Pictures, music, necklaces with the Star of David, T-shirts with symbols of the Israeli army or Israeli flag, and tales of Taglit experiences were part of the shared discourse and material culture that linked past participants and motivated others to go. At the same time, many of Odesa's Jewish youth described having to defend their views on Israel to friends and family on their return. Karina's parents didn't understand how she could relate so closely to a country she'd visited only once; her friends half-jokingly accused her of having been "brainwashed."

For Karina, it took another, lengthier trip to Israel before she could make her decision about aliyah. "Israel is something special," she told me. "You can't compare it to other countries. But life [in Israel] isn't anything like it's described in the books." Karina recognized the distinction between tourism and emigration, as did many others who first experienced Israel as visitors. She ultimately based her decision on her longer stay in the country and the stories of the less prosperous migrants she knew. In general, I found that participants in extended Israeli programs expressed more diverse views on Israel—feelings of attachment, yes, but also displacement, and sometimes utter disappointment.[42]

Karina gave various reasons for her decision to stay, including her status as a nonhalakhic Jew and a Russian speaker, and the knowledge that other family members wouldn't consider immigrating to Israel themselves. In her family, she was the only one who favored Judaism over Russian Orthodoxy and held Israel close to her heart. (Her stepfather, a practicing Christian, was influential in the lives of Karina's mother and brother, who saw themselves as being "far from all things Jewish.") Moreover, Karina had a film career that was too important to her to sacrifice by emigrating. On the other hand, Karina's generation was the last in her family who would qualify for the Right of Return, and this meant that she bore the responsibility to secure a Jewish future for her future children and a connection with what she described as her "Jewish homeland." Like others who'd only recently learned of their Jewish links through Israeli-based organizations but who lacked the maternal link recognized by Israel's religious authorities, Karina also knew the limitations of her Jewish inheritance.

For other young people I met, the mere possibility of moving to Israel made them consider a different, independent mode of living. The Taglit trips fed into this. Discussing the opportunities for herself and her boyfriend, Daria said, "Misha and I are thinking of going to Israel. Through the Jewish Agency for Israel (Sokhnut) we can move there for free. Misha's grandparents live there, and they might help him find a job and let us stay with them. I'd like to go on Taglit just to see it; I've never been." Daria's family was similar to Karina's, and she knew that she'd probably be the only one in her immediate family to live in Israel—and that her family would disapprove. Israel thus functioned as the backdrop for a vision in which she and Misha could start a life of their own,

away from their parents' supervision. But even though the couple spent much
time foreseeing their new life, they never made concrete plans to leave.

In any one person's decision to live in Israel, a number of divergent motives
were at work. But during my fieldwork I met very few people who were finally
persuaded enough to relocate. Statistics from the Israeli Consulate support
this, showing a large drop in exit visas: in 1999, 4,041 visas were granted to
residents of the Odesa region, but by 2006, the number barely exceeded 300.[43]
However attached Odesan Jews may have felt to some idea of Israel, such sentiments didn't ultimately convince them to emigrate. The decision was no longer
"now or never," as it had been in the years after the Soviet breakup, and thus
many young people felt comfortable knowing they could hold on to the mere
possibility. "I feel that Israel will always be there," Igor said on his return from a
six-month study-abroad program. "No one's taking away my right to repatriate.
But for now, I don't want to be there."

Returnees, Transmigrants, and Long-Term Visitors in Odesa

To explore the subject of home and belonging, I reached out to returnees—
those who had tasted life in Israel and then chosen to leave it. During our
interviews, meetings, and interactions, I was keen to find out how their time
abroad had shaped their relationships with Israel, Ukraine, Odesa, and Jewish Odesa and whether it had changed their relationships with local Jews and
others upon their return. I also sought to explore how, after their return, they
viewed the new political and social order that affected both Jewish and non-
Jewish circles in Odesa.

The return migration of ex-Soviet Jews from Israel has received much
attention from politicians, scholars of Russian-speaking Jewish affairs, and
journalists around the globe.[44] A 2004 report from the Federation of Jewish
Communities of Russia stated that "for the first time in history, more Russian
Jews now migrate to Russia from Israel than the other way around."[45] In a
2007 survey of 4,214 Russian-speaking Jewish respondents, most of whom
(90 percent) resided in Israel, 81 percent said they'd considered leaving the
country.[46]

Taking a broader view, we know that of the nearly one million Jews who arrived in Israel after 1989, some 12 percent had left the country by the end of 2017.
Roughly half of those who departed kept moving, heading next to the United
States, Canada, or western Europe, while the other half went back to the FSU.[47]
The true depth of Jewish repatriation to the FSU is unclear. Official statistics
of the Russian and Ukrainian governments show 17,438 registered returnees to
the Russian Federation and 14,955 returnees to Ukraine from 1997 to 2009.[48]

But many returnees don't register with the local passport office; instead, they hold on to their Israeli passports.[49] This means that the unofficial tally of returnees is much higher. Moreover, many returnees travel frequently to Israel and therefore are automatically excluded from the statistics of out-migrants calculated by the Israeli state.

Israeli sociologists insisted that many of these returnees were not "failed cases of aliyah"—that is, individuals who were unable to adapt to the Israeli way of life—but rather individuals who, although young, well-educated, and capable, had skills that couldn't be accommodated in Israel's limited labor market and who had therefore reached a "glass ceiling."[50] Israeli state officials expressed concern about a possible "brain drain" to Russia, but specialists in Russian Jewish migration insist that, due to the nearly identical characteristics of emigrants *from* Russia to Israel and immigrants *to* Russia from Israel, these recent developments "do not cause a 'brain drain' in either place."[51] Regardless of the root cause, the outflow of Russian-speaking Jews, along with other groups of Israelis who choose to live outside Israel, can be seen as undermining the "Zionist assertion that Israel is the best place for Jews to live."[52]

Some journalists and their readers expressed surprise that Russian-speaking Jews would return to the FSU.[53] That surprise stemmed from the old narratives of Soviet repression that still prevailed.[54] In response, political scientist Evgeny Satanovsky has warned Western audiences not to read too much into this trend and to look beyond the Soviet days of repression: "There is no Iron Curtain any more, and that's what the phenomenon is . . . nobody is surprised when an American Jew goes to Nepal for a work contract and then returns to visit his aunt in New Jersey. . . . All these are simply signs that Russia is a normal country now."[55]

At the same time, new stereotypes were propagated in the media, asserting that returnees "galvanize Jewish community life" and "revive Jewish culture."[56] Those who have experienced life in Israel are thus perceived as active and knowledgeable Jews with something to teach stay-back Jews about Judaism and Jewish community.

Among the returnees I met were people who'd simply never managed to find their way in Israel. Facing economic, social, or personal constraints, they had decided to return to Odesa. Many of them were young Jews who'd set off on their own and found it difficult to survive without family support. In other instances, elderly Odesans in Israel found themselves too dependent on others for communication and everyday tasks. Some middle-aged migrants struggled to earn a living. There were also cases of well-to-do migrants who'd had no trouble acclimatizing but were lured back to Odesa by business opportunities. These "opportunity seekers" often traveled back and forth, dividing their time among multiple destinations with split business and family commitments, thus constituting a group I call *transmigrants*.

Education and community service opportunities also attracted both return-ees and other Israelis to Odesa.[57] I met returnees, transmigrants, and long-term visitors who weren't all originally from the city.[58] In some circumstances, re-turnees who grew up in other cities in the Soviet Union were drawn to Odesa by personal or professional connections. Although most ex-Soviet Jewish re-turnees chose to move to major cities in Russia and Ukraine, due to their eco-nomic growth, the Russian-speaking Israelis I met chose Odesa for a number of reasons. For some, it was the place they had left and longed to return to; others relied on the support of their local families and friends. In many cases, property ownership played a major role.

For many new arrivals, Odesa was both a familiar and a foreign place. A number of returnees from Israel said it reminded them of Tel Aviv and other coastal Israeli cities. Odesa's port atmosphere gave some returnees a sense of being part of the world and connected to their travel experiences. Returnees felt that its small, cozy feel, as well as its airy openness and grandeur, made it unique. "I love the fact that I'm able to see an opera or theater performance here, and I also love the market, where people speak to me as if they know me," one returnee shared.

Narratives of Returnees

Nina and her son Kostya were among the first returnees from Israel I met in Odesa. At that time, they didn't know of any others who'd returned.[59] Nina had left Odesa in 1989 and returned in 2000; her son came back a year later. She told me about their initial departure for Israel: "Many of my students left and were persuading me to go. You had to know what Odessa was like in those years [the 1990s].... It was very difficult to live here. There were no streetlights, darkness everywhere, extremely high prices, and nothing, absolutely nothing, in the grocery stores. People spoke of pogroms. Only later did I understand that it was just rumors. Unfortunately, I was one of those people who couldn't withstand social pressure."[60]

Nina left her apartment to her elder son, resigned from her job, and departed from her beloved city, believing she would never return. She didn't see her move to Israel as "going home." Quite the contrary: she spoke of her "difficult decision" to depart from what she loved and knew. But at the same time, she was comforted by the idea that she was going to a place where no one would ever call her *zhidovka*—and in that sense, to a place where she would be made to feel at home.

Back in Odesa, Nina reflected on her time in Israel with mixed emotions. At first, she was amazed at the generosity of the Israeli immigration and relocation personnel, who were dealing with an overwhelming number of ex-Soviet Jews. But she soon grew disillusioned with life in Israel.[61] "In Odessa, Israeli emissaries promised that I'd have no problem finding employment upon arrival. But no one told me that at my age [fifty-five], I was already considered retired. It was clear that they only wanted the young." For the first eleven months, Nina was given space in an art studio, and she and other immigrant artists made objects to sell at fairs. Eventually, all the artists were asked to leave, and she started teaching ceramics on her own initiative to a group of elderly, blind Israelis.

Nina struggled financially during the eleven years she spent in Israel. She and her son changed jobs, apartments, and cities in her efforts to make ends meet. She also suffered from the Israeli climate, especially the summers. And yet, she spoke of Israel as a "holy place" where she could feel history, see breathtaking landscapes, and take in the presence of God. In Israel, Nina started attending religious services, not in a synagogue but in a Russian Orthodox Church, which she described as being "culturally closer" to her. She recalled meeting a number of other Jews during services who were *vykresty* (baptized Jews).[62]

Though Nina had formed some attachment to Israel, in the end it wasn't enough to make her stay. Her great nostalgia for Odesa and Odesans strongly influenced her decision to return. She was one of the few returnees I met who, on coming home, opted to exchange an Israeli passport for a Ukrainian one. This allowed her to receive a pension and acquire a *propiska*.[63] When I asked Nina how others in the city had reacted to her return, she had little to say. "I don't tell many people about it," she said. "I don't want to brag about living abroad." Her shyness about her Jewish identity seemed bound up with a concern about having lived a life that others could not. One evening she told me about a painful incident when a neighbor called her a *zhidovka*. Nina insisted that the woman was simply envious. "She knew that I used to live in Israel. . . . I wish I'd never told her, because I could tell it aggravated her to know I had the chance to do something she can't." Nina was also convinced that no true Odesit would fling such an antisemitic slur; the neighbor's provincial behavior suggested she was a new arrival.

Kostya, Nina's son, hadn't met any negative reactions as a returnee. Rather, he said, "The people I told about Israel were always curious to know more." Soon after arriving in Israel, he'd been admitted to one of Tel Aviv's leading art institutes. He attended for several months but left because he couldn't afford to study without an income. Within a year of his arrival, he was drafted into the Israeli army. But after more than a decade in Israel, he hadn't managed to earn

a degree or gain fluency in the Hebrew language, which greatly limited his employment opportunities. He turned to intermittent manual labor. Despite these
struggles, Kostya considered his time in Israel to be extremely meaningful.
Four years after returning to Odesa, he still saw Israel as his homeland (*rodina*).

Kostya had held on to his Israeli passport, and he often spoke of eventually
going "home" to Israel—to his mother's apparent irritation. His long absence
from Odesa meant that he felt little connection to the city where he was born
and partially raised. Had he managed to find permanent employment back
in Odesa, or to forge meaningful friendships there, he might have felt more
rooted.[64] In the year before we met, Kostya had become more observant of Jewish religious laws and had started attending the synagogue regularly. Neither
had been part of his life in Israel, but back in Odesa, he found that he wanted
to combat "assimilation." Defining himself as an Israeli, he was also starting to
define himself as an *iudei*. In some cases, returnees became religiously observant during their time in Israel, but for Kostya and some others I met, it took
returning to Odesa, rather than moving to Israel, to develop the desire to be
in an organized Jewish community. Kostya felt a sense of connection within
Odesa's religious organizations, where he could practice his basic Hebrew and
discuss Israeli life.

Other returnees from Israel behaved similarly. Marat, a man in his midthirties at the time of our meeting, explained, "In Israel, I didn't do anything
Jewish; you don't need to. But when I came back, I started doing little things
with the Chabad congregation. Here I felt that it was nice to keep traditions."
He illustrated his participation in the religious congregation with an old joke:
"Rabinovich goes to the synagogue to talk to God, and I go to talk to Rabinovich." Speaking of Israel, Marat still referred to it as a homeland, though it hadn't
been his original choice for emigration and he acknowledged that immigrant
life there was difficult. When he finally resettled in Odesa in 2004, he and another Israeli returnee started a construction company. Marat enjoyed working
with pencil and paper rather than the manual labor he'd done in Israel. Though
he was back home, more religiously observant, and with a sense of knowing his
homeland, Marat kept his eye on the economy and his prospects. He wouldn't
return to Israel, he told me, but Canada or the United States, where his father
lived, weren't out of the question if Odesa's economic situation became too
difficult.

Homemaking and Jewish Organizations

The generational differences in affiliation to Jewish Odesa seen between Nina,
Kostya, and Marat weren't atypical among returnees. Older returnees tried to

ease back into their former lives almost unnoticed and usually avoided official membership (except for the sake of pensions and other benefits). The behavior of middle-aged returnees was largely determined by the nature of their employment and by family circumstances. Some, seeking career benefits, used Jewish organizations to network, especially for new clients; others saw no advantage in frequenting Jewish gatherings. For families with children enrolled in Jewish schools, occasional Jewish activity was the norm, and this sometimes led to more extended involvement; others lacked the time or interest. Most younger returnees strived to practice their Hebrew and to take part in Jewish holiday celebrations; some found employment in Jewish organizations. A minority chose to remain on the periphery of Jewish activities.

Nastya, whom we met in the previous chapter, returned to Odesa after nine years in Tel Aviv. She told me she couldn't relate to Jewish life in Odesa, given the public emphasis on religion—"too Jewish, narrow, and old-fashioned." Now in her late twenties, she'd moved back in 2006 to be closer to family. Her first encounter with Israel had been on a study-abroad program; then and there, she'd decided to emigrate. At age fifteen, she had made aliyah. Before the move, Nastya had been very involved in the Jewish life of Odesa, participating in programs offered by the Jewish Agency for Israel (Sokhnut) and Migdal. But her passion for being an active Jew faded during her time in Israel. As she saw it, when one moves to Israel, acting out one's Jewishness no longer seems important.

Returning to Odesa, Nastya hadn't opted to rekindle her old connections with the city's Jewish circles. She looked down on the Jewish Agency for Israel's (Sokhnut's) policy of "force-feeding Jews fairy tales" about their "home." In fact, nothing about the religious world struck a chord with her present Jewish identification. Lynellyn Long and Ellen Oxfeld, writing of returnees in general, point out that "as the act of returning unfolds, the specific experiences often contrast with the returnee's original dreams."[65] Other examples indicate that some returnees "feel that their own interests are more cosmopolitan and transcend [those of] the local community," which now appears "narrow."[66] This seems to have been Nastya's experience.

Moreover, Nastya spoke with some agitation about living with her parents. Having been independent, she wasn't used to answering to anyone, let alone sharing a room, as she now did with her sister. (Other young returnees also found family dynamics strained. Regina, a returnee from Haifa, told me it was hard to live with her mother-in-law, with whom she was forced to share an apartment.) Lacking the organizational ties to create a social circle, Nastya struggled to find her way, though she did manage to register for several classes at the Engineering Institute of Odesa. Most of her peers who'd stayed in Odesa had graduated from college and were working, and many of her old girlfriends were married and starting families. By contrast, Nastya was single, had "lost two years to the army," and despite her sustained efforts to work and study at the same time, she hadn't completed college in Israel. In Odesa, at least, education was still free of charge, though it often involved informal payments, such as bribes.[67]

Transmigrants

While some returnees intended their remigration to be permanent, others did not. This group of transnational migrants, or *transmigrants*, defined their relationship with Odesa as partial and intermittent.[68]

Galina, who was in her forties when we spoke, saw herself as living in two countries: "I arrive in Ben Gurion—I am home. I arrive in Odessa—I am home. Although I travel extensively, I experience this feeling of home only in these two places." Galina's sentiments are embedded in familial ties: her eldest son lives in Israel; her daughter from her second marriage lives in Odesa.

Dima, his wife, Luba, and their two children came to Odesa, where Dima grew up, after living in Israel for ten years. They had decided to move to Odesa to develop their business selling Israeli-made food supplements and skincare products. Dima and Luba traveled regularly to and from Israel, as well as across Ukraine, both for work and family reasons. They missed the food, music, and natural beauty of Israel. The couple had retained their Israeli citizenship, but they secured Ukrainian resident visas to get permission to work. Although their primary identification was as Israelis, Odesa was a convenient business base in the region. Dima's mother lived there and was available to mind their children, which made things easier. As Dima put it: "It's easy for me to come back to Ukraine, as opposed to moving to Canada, which is where my wife and I originally wanted to go once we decided to expand our business. In Odesa I know everyone I need to know for any given situation, and I feel free. In Israel, starting your own business is difficult, especially as an immigrant."

Other entrepreneurs I met had similar experiences of conducting business overseas. Vova, a returnee from Haifa, spoke of the troubles he faced. "You can't trust anyone in Israel. I had a business with a Moroccan guy, and he cheated me out of all my money." His motivation for coming to Odesa was straightforward, as were his plans for the future: "I am here to make money." Two months into his stay, he was working hard to open a hummus restaurant. He had attended a number of Jewish functions in the city and had approached the Chabad rabbi to ask for help in his entrepreneurial efforts. According to Vova, the rabbi knew many local businessmen who might provide funding.

Vova was originally from Saint Petersburg; his wife, Nadya, was born in Odesa. The deciding factor between the two cities was that Odesa had an apartment available for their use. Also, they'd visited Odesa many times during the years they lived in Israel. Nadya was confident she'd find a job in one of the city's Jewish organizations, where her Hebrew language skills would be in demand.

Like Nadya, many who considered returning from Israel made a number of preliminary visits to Odesa. Yulik, originally from the Ukrainian town of Dnipro and living in Israel, was making such an exploratory visit when I met him. Like Vova and Nadya, he was attracted to Ukraine for its business potential, in his case information technology. Though he'd been planning to relocate to Kyiv, Yulik began leaning toward a smaller city like Odesa or perhaps Dnipro, where the IT industry offered more opportunities and less job competition than the Ukrainian capital.

Yulik's family in Ukraine had offered to help him get started if he provided financing. But on a visit to his hometown, he'd found that Dnipro didn't feel like home. Having spent most of his life in Israel, he now felt like a foreigner back in Ukraine. He spoke Russian with a Hebrew accent, he didn't speak Ukrainian, and his diet, dress, and mannerisms all marked him as someone from abroad. Still, Yulik had been curious about living in a place that he was both close to and distant from. Odesa was a new adventure—though it wasn't a city he knew from his childhood, it was a familiar yet foreign place to be discovered.

This sentiment of encountering something known and unknown appears in the stories of many returnees. As anthropologist and migration scholar Anders Stefansson said of exiles, refugees, and emigrants who return to some place of origin, they find a home significantly changed, while they too have formed new habits and ways of thinking in the context of different resources and realities. Thus, homecoming often means not only the practical struggle of relocation but also "rupture, surprise, and perhaps disillusionment."[69]

A significant aspect of returnees' reintegration to life in Odesa was their approach to organized Jewish life in the city. Some, like Nadya, were looking to Jewish organizations for employment; others, like Kostya and Marat, became active participants in Jewish life. Some, even those of different generations, chose to remain on the periphery like Nastya and Nina.

For those returnees who became active in the Jewish life of the city, experiences differed. Neither Dima nor his wife put any importance on their own religious observance or that of their family, but they still sent their children to one of the Jewish Orthodox schools. Dima explained that he and his family didn't speak Ukrainian, now the language of instruction in most city public schools. At the Jewish school, their children could learn in Russian and still practice their Hebrew. Even so, Dima saw little in common between the ways he and his wife opted to raise their children as Jewish and the more religious approaches he found in Odesa on his return: "One of the teachers at Migdal complained to me that my children weren't paying attention to her lectures on Jewish traditions. I explained that for Israelis, this is natural. In Israel, most of the Russians aren't religious, and we don't mix with them [the religious Jews]. It's not a world I want [my children] to be in."[70] Although Dima's children had grown up in Israel knowing the Jewish calendar as a state-initiated agenda, he didn't accept that Judaism must be a crucial part of their identity, even if he did opt to enroll them in a religious school.

Conclusion

The migration trends visible in contemporary Odesa reflect the post-Soviet reality in Ukraine and the FSU. The Jews of Odesa have developed a web of attachments to places that for most were once far off and prohibited. Those places now stand as family members' homes, sites of new experiences and perspectives on religion, or locations of economic and material opportunity. Moreover, as migration moves in multiple directions, serving different roles for different generations, returning "home" becomes another stage of such movement— the arrival at a place that is understood and familiar but also changed and still changing.

As seen in this chapter, the experiences of Israeli Russian-speaking Jewish returnees in Odesa are especially helpful for understanding the limits and possibilities of what is meant by home, homeland, and diaspora. Their patterns of crossing international borders redraw the traditional model of Jews as a diasporic population connected to a distant homeland, the cradle of a people's identity. These returnees illustrate the innumerable, complicated, conflicted, and conflicting definitions of home and homeland, exile and return, foreigner and belonging. Diaspora, the "dispersion of any people from their traditional homeland," assumes a link between people and their *"proper* place."[71] Within diaspora studies, therefore, Jews serve as the "ideal type," since they're thought to embody the "classic 'old diaspora'"—that is, the ancient dispersal from Babylon, which serves as the root of the generalized term.[72]

Recent scholarship has challenged this connotation of diaspora-as-exile.[73] For instance, historian Daniel Boyarin and anthropologist Jonathan Boyarin have argued that "in a world grown thoroughly and inextricably interdependent," we must recognize "that peoples and lands are not naturally and organically connected."[74] Another version of this critique of assuming "a single center of a given community"—again, defined by a "natural bond" that people are said to have with their "native home"—stresses the notion of *multiple homelands* that exist for, and ultimately define, any one group of people.[75] No longer defined by places, "identities have become deterritorialized."[76] But for many of the Odesan Jews in this chapter, place remains a powerful frame of belonging and identity even if "home is a mental construct, not only a physical place."[77]

In many accounts of Jewish life outside Israel, we can see how the supposed diaspora countries and various cities within those countries are perceived and experienced as homelands, and how Israel—while still regarded as a place of spiritual, religious, and communal importance—can nonetheless lose the privileged status of "home" or "homeland" and thus be open to criticism, both for its claims as "the homeland" and for its politics in the name of such status.[78]

Russian-speaking Jews and other minority populations who faced difficulty adapting to Israeli society, where their cultural capital often wasn't recognized, have been instrumental in transforming the idea of Israel as a Jewish home.[79] Israelis who choose to live outside Israel demonstrate another ambivalent relationship between Jews and Israel—an ambivalence that's apparent in the literature on *yerida* (emigration from Israel).[80] Some returnees came back to Odesa expressing strong ties to Israeli culture. They retained their self-definition as Israeli through language, dress, music, food, worldview, and even, by way of their citizenship, the idea of an eventual return. But others can be seen as choosing their homes or other nearby locations because it was a familiar place, the site of professional activity and personal growth, as well as the place that gave them a sense of being rooted *there*. As for the transmigrants who shuttle between countries, it's less about a sense of home than pragmatic business demands, the need to use particular products and services available in a certain place. For some like Galina, whose children live in Tel Aviv and in Odesa, home is both.

Israel is undoubtedly regarded as an important place on the Russian-speaking and Ukrainian-speaking Jewish map, even for those who choose to leave it behind. It now has the largest Russian-speaking population outside the FSU, a growing Ukrainian-speaking community, and extensive economic, social, and political links with the global ex-Soviet population. Since the start of the Russian-Ukrainian war, language has become a sensitive and political topic. We are seeing a shift in belonging of some Ukrainian Jewish Israelis who are identifying more closely with Ukraine and the Ukrainian language. For many of the larger Jewish population in Odesa, including the returnees, the question of belonging in Odesa remains tied to the economic and social situations both at home and abroad—Israel offers a basis of comparison between the two places. To a large extent, the future for returnees will be dictated by the personal and professional opportunities that arise and by the economic and sociopolitical situation in the countries where they might settle. The ongoing war in the Donbas region and Russia's invasion of Ukraine have given rise to a new wave of aliyah and spurred the return of many Israeli citizens who'd been living in Ukraine.

Odesan Jewry is now part of the global Ukrainian Jewish population, spread across many continents and countries. They're as much part of the Russian-speaking and, more recently, Ukrainian-speaking diaspora as they are part of the Israeli, Ukrainian, and Jewish diasporas, whose "cultural [we can even add *religious*], geographic, and national boundaries are blurred and in flux."[81] The overlapping worlds that define ex-Soviet Jewish returnees and transmigrants through the process of migration and remigration account for multiple un-derstandings of home; ultimately, they transcend the working definitions in traditional diaspora discourse. Returnees, in effect, take up the role of being both transnational and Jewish, albeit in different ways.

The attitudes of Odesa's returning Jewish population toward "homeland" and "diaspora" continue to evolve. Like other migrant populations, their iden-tity as a "diasporic imagined community" is "constituted within the crucible of the materiality of everyday life."[82] As Stefansson points out, "After all, feelings of belonging do not rest on objective factors but are situated in the subjective realm."[83] Some emigrants had initially approached Israel as a place of belonging and their "historical homeland," but after suffering hardships in their new lives, they began to experience the place differently and saw themselves as living in the Russian-speaking diaspora. On the other hand, returnees coming back to a supposedly familiar place could also start seeing Odesa as more foreign, either because they were treated as foreigners there or because they encountered their unmet dreams in the place they'd once left behind.

Anthropologist Ruth Mandel writes about Turkish migrants in Germany who go back to Turkey on a permanent or temporary basis, saying that many "returnees suffer from disorientation" and are unable to "merge back into the Turkish mainstream" because they're judged by others, and by themselves, as "Alamancilar" (that is, German-like).[84] Moreover, sometimes the notion of "home" or "homeland" may be applied to more than one destination or, due to disorientation, may even cease to exist. This is particularly true for return-ees who shared the experience of living as members of a "Russian" diaspora in Israel and on their return viewed themselves, or were viewed by others, as "Israelis." As James Clifford notes, "at different times in their history, societ-ies may wax and wane in diasporism, depending on changing possibilities—obstacles, openings, antagonisms and connections—in their host countries and transnationally."[85] Thus, "home" and "diaspora" were not ideologically driven constants associated with a center (life in Israel) and a periphery (life outside Israel). Rather, they should be conceptualized as variable locations, infused with memories and attachments that social actors inhabit and relate to through everyday experiences and life circumstances, which in turn shape their imagined reality and senses of attachment. But notions of home and belonging are not stable entities; they can shift in the context of sociopolitical transformations and, as we are currently observing, a war.

If home, as Stephan Feuchtwang defines it, is "a reference to a territory of belonging," then ex-Soviet Jewish returnees have multiple and interconnecting homes that encompass their "cultural norms and individual fantasies" and bring together their diverse experiences as locals, migrants, repatriates, and returnees.[86] The examples of Odesan stay-back Jews and returnees discussed in this chapter enlarge and enrich the generalizations about diasporic traits by which Jews living outside Israel are classically represented. At the same time, they open new avenues for analyzing Jewish orientations and identities as embedded in culturally specific histories and locales.

7

Odesa

A Jewish City?

When I told my family and friends that I was doing fieldwork in Odesa, their first response was that it would be "exceptional," a one-of-a-kind place to study because it was the quintessential Jewish city. Then, inevitably, they'd pause and ask: "But how many Jews are left in Odessa? Is it *still* a Jewish city?" A similar duality plays out in two popular jokes about the place:

> "How many people live in Odessa?"
> —"One million."
> "How many Jews live in Odessa?"
> —"You already have your answer."[1]

> Two Odesans are walking down the street. One says to the other:
> "Look, here comes a woman! I think she might be Jewish."
> —"No, it can't be. All the Jews left in the nineties."
> "Still, I'll ask. Madam! Madam! I'm sorry to ask, but are you Jewish?"
> Woman: "I'm not Jewish; I'm just an idiot."

The first joke, from the early Soviet era, evokes a wholly Jewish Odesa. The second, post-Soviet, suggests an emigration so complete that only "an idiot" would have remained.

The theme of Odesa as a "Jewish city" has long been established in the public perception and imagination, both at home and abroad, through literature, music, stories, mass media, tourism, and local discourse. I argue that with Odesa, "Jewish" has served as a metonym—a figure of speech where the name of one element of something is used to represent the whole.[2] In other words, it is precisely the *Jewishness* of the place that stands in for the entire city. Jarrod Tanny writes that throughout history, some cities are branded as "Jewish" due to the sheer number of urban Jews living there.[3] Compared to the majority or near-majority of Jews in cities like Vilnius and Minsk at the turn of the twentieth century, Odesa was nowhere near as demographically Jewish. At its peak, in the 1920s, Odesa's Jewish population reached close to 40 percent. But in the 2000s, the city's Jewish population was less than a tenth of what it had been. If its image as a Jewish city has lived on, the meaning imparted by the adjective *Jewish* is neither clear nor stable. That meaning is kept in flux by the constellation of personalities, attitudes, and ideas about the social and cultural space that its residents inhabit and by the important perceptions they share or dispute concerning its character.[4] Ever-evolving and entwined discourses of myth, history, and individual realities both support and call into question the trope of Odesa's Jewishness.

I found that first and foremost, it was the local Jewish intelligentsia and religious leaders I met who defended the idea that Jews defined Odesa in a meaningful way. They were deeply invested in the claim that Odesa was, is, and always will be Jewish as a way to mark the city's diversity. This conception builds on the potent Odesa myth, which has cast the city as a unique and particular sphere within the Russian Empire, the Soviet Union, and present-day Ukraine, with distinct qualities that can at least partially be attributed to the influence of the city's Jews.[5] At the same time, the rhetoric of Jewishness in the daily life and conversations of ordinary residents is much more varied.

In what follows, I trace how these different internalized views manifested themselves in official or commercialized representations, such as tourism, and through the varieties of everyday life. I situate my analysis of Odesa's trope of Jewishness alongside the work of anthropologist Michael Herzfeld, who believes that stereotypes play an important role in both reproducing and contesting power relations at the local level.[6] Using Herzfeld's paradigm, I go beyond an analysis of whether Odesa should be considered a Jewish city today and focus on why and for whom the idea of a Jewish Odesa matters.[7] While Tanya Richardson has pointed out that "implicitly, contemporary representations of Jewish Odesa reinforce the idea that Odesa is situated in Russian cultural geographies but not Ukrainian ones," I later demonstrate that since the escalation of Russia's war with Ukraine, Jewishness has also become a powerful image for a new Ukrainian civic nation.[8]

History and Mythmaking: The Odesa Myth

According to a number of city chroniclers, Odesa was considered a famous Jewish city not only because of its impressively large Jewish population in the nineteenth and early twentieth centuries but also because that population was both well integrated into the cosmopolitan fabric of the metropolis and relatively empowered. Large numbers of Jews participated actively in the city's social, economic, political, and educational institutions and made significant contributions to its cultural and intellectual life (see chapters 1 and 2). But as Brian Horowitz points out, on the basis of his research on the Jewish intelligentsia in late imperial Odesa, the myth surrounding "Jewish" Odesa is full of paradoxes, contradictions, and uncertainty.[9]

In the twenty-first century, the city's cosmopolitan makeup includes a much smaller Jewish population but rising numbers of Ukrainians, Moldovans, Turks, Chinese, Koreans, Tatars, and other ethnic groups. In an age of a supposed Jewish revival, there's a concomitant growth in Christianity, Islam, and other religions. Today, Christian and Muslim populations represent a much higher percentage of Odesa's religiously observant population than do members of the Jewish faith.[10] The emergence of Ukraine as a nation-state also plays a significant role in perceptions of Odesa. That emergence has brought political, social, and economic pressures to make Odesa more Ukrainian—implementing changes at the level of language, politics, and education that grew in popularity as Ukrainian-Russian relations deteriorated.[11] Post-Maidan events (discussed in the conclusion and epilogue) have further solidified this process of nationalization and cast a new light on the imperial nature of the Odesa myth discussed further in this chapter. As Amelia Glaser asks, "How viable or lasting is the Odesa myth in the twenty-first century, particularly amidst a war between Ukraine and Russia?"[12] At the same time, some Ukrainian scholars, like Taras Maksymiuk, who conducted a tour of Ukrainian Odesa for Tanya Richardson during her fieldwork in the city, argued that Ukrainians had always contributed to the city's development and that people have often overlooked Ukrainian Odesa by not acknowledging the works of Russian-speaking Ukrainians and Russian-language Ukrainian publications on Ukrainian themes.[13] Literary scholars Mirja Lecke and Efraim Sicher remind us that from its early days, competing narratives of cultural ownership circulated in the various language communities and cultural groups.[14] The uniqueness and Jewishness of Odesa offered different points of contrast throughout its history. Rebecca Stanton notes how Odesa in early Soviet times presented a contrast to the "homogenizing impulse emanating from Moscow."[15] During the time of my fieldwork, the metonym "Jewish" also functioned to align Odesa with a minority culture versus the national (Ukrainian) culture. This alignment changed after Russia's invasion of Ukraine, as "supporters of the Kremlin have seized upon historical conflict between Jews and Ukrainians."[16] Not only was the idea of Odesa as a Ukrainian city solidified in the context of war, but the rhetoric of "Jewish" Odesa exhibited in various public and private conversations had also gained a political tone. The city was "Jewish" and therefore not "Russian."

History and demographics aside, Odesan natives and knowledgeable visitors relied on the Odesa myth to shape their image and experience of the city as well as their sense of self within its boundaries. In turn, their engagement with this myth perpetuated its existence. The myth I am referencing was built on an already-established picture of Odesa as "a multicultural, largely Jewish, urban, modern, and cheerful city" that stood for "alterity, nonorthodox ways of life, sin and a Southern *savoir vivre*."[17] Richardson describes the Odesa myth that followed as a "constellation of images and ideas" that originated in nineteenth-century Russian literature.[18] Efraim Sicher notes that Alexander Pushkin enthused about the multiethnic diversity of Odesa (although he excluded Jews) in the portions written for *Eugene Onegin* and "cemented Odesa into his vision of a European Russia."[19] To Pushkin and others, "most notably Kuprin, Balmont, and Bunin, Odessa represented a place whose very identity was bound up in 'otherness,' a place defined by its non-normative and nonmetropolitan status."[20]

Some scholars claim that "the myth of old Odessa *became* the city's history and Odessa's myth-makers became its leading historians."[21] Jarrod Tanny reminds us that the relationship of myth and history is indeed complex and fluid in many cities. It is pronounced in Odesa because many of the literary characters that helped give expression to the myth actually lived, the events described actually took place, and the humorous words were actually spoken.[22] Reinforcing the myth, a heterogeneous cohort of the city's mythmakers, writers, musicians, and actors have followed the same blueprint of rhythm, intonation, language, and themes that frame tales about the city since it first coalesced in the nineteenth century. Although the repression of the mid-1930s affected Odesan culture for the worse, Tanny argues that the myth "achieved hegemony and a near monopoly over the way the memory of old Odessa is publicly articulated, much as Marxism-Leninism previously governed the writing of history under Communism."[23]

In the early and mid-twentieth century, the image of the city was infused with new themes of Jewish humor and of the criminality and dark underside of city life, vividly portrayed in the works of Isaac Babel, Valentin Kataev, Ilya Ilf and Evegenii Petrov, Yury Olesha, and others.[24] These renowned Russian and Soviet writers, together with "local historians, film makers, poets, novelists, journalists, memoirists" and comedians, "extolled Odessa as a cosmopolitan, energetic oasis of freedom and beauty, and elaborated on the Odessa myth."[25] The overall effect was to "portray the city as a special place dominated by trade that seemingly sprang up from nowhere in the steppe, populated by people from different countries."[26]

Literary scholar Rebecca Stanton outlines the components of what came to be a standard repertoire for characterizing the city: "the sun, the sea, the dust;

the 'live varieties' of languages and nationalities, composed of sailors, traders, holidaymakers, Italian singers, Jewish fiddlers, and Russian poets, with a
steamy admixture of smugglers, gangsters, and exiled Russian malcontents."[27]
The multilayered myth of the city emerges from diverse impressions from literature, folklore, music, and art, that live in the minds of the city's inhabitants.[28]
The world created by Isaac Babel, especially in his *Odessa Tales*, is perhaps
the most widely cited as the representation of Old Odessa or *ta Odessa* ("that
Odessa"). Amelia Glaser writes, "No one has summed up the secular Jewish
condition quite like Babel, who described fantastical Jewish gangsters in his
Odessa stories at a time when the Bolshevik revolution had turned the world
upside down."[29] His work is credited with "popularizing the image of Odessa
as a city of swashbuckling Jewish swindlers."[30] Moreover, by putting Jewish
characters at the forefront of his stories, Babel helped counter the depictions of
Jews common in the work of Russian writers like Anton Chekhov and Maxim
Gorky, who tended to portray them as "small, bent, weak and pathetic" individuals who lived in fear of the next pogrom.[31]

Babel was popular, and his achievements as a writer elevated the status of
this imagined community of Russian Jewish intelligentsia. His descriptions
of Odesa generated an image of city life in which Jews "embodied the physical
strength, revelry and wit."[32] Babel's Odesa is "the most charming city in the
Russian Empire. If you think about it, it is a town in which you can live free and
easy. Half of the population is made up of Jews, and Jews are a people who have
learned a few simple truths along the way. . . . To a large extent it is because of
them that Odessa has this light and easy atmosphere."[33] Babel introduces areas
like Moldovanka, a neighborhood where immigrants settled, including new
Jewish "types" such as Benya Krik and his gang of "tough but honorable criminals."[34] In Babel's stories, Jewish people, affairs, practices, food, humor, and
language became vivid expressions of Odesa's reality for many. Tanny believes
that "with a few notable exceptions, most of Odesa's myth-makers and the legendary gangsters and musicians they have celebrated have either been Jewish
or have been significantly influenced by Jewish culture."[35] Thus, as writer and
literary scholar Sophie Pinkham, writing about the *blatnaia pesnia* (songs of the
underworld) of Leonid Utesov (1895–1982) and Arkadii Severnyi (1939–1980),
explains, Odesa's Jewishness in post-Stalin years became "detached from any
actual religious or ethnic identity" to "become strictly metaphorical."[36] The
symbol spread across the entire Soviet world, representing a "refuge from official culture"; "a category used to express otherness"; "rebelliousness, outsider
status, and freedom from the law of the state"—carried along in the popular
Soviet music depicting the criminal underworld.[37] While I agree that Jewishness was a fluid category in the world of culture and music, and often stood in
for other qualities of otherness, I would argue that it was not fully detached

from Jewish identity in the way Pinkham describes. Jewishness in Odesa was undoubtedly affected by Soviet policies, but its manifestations still drew on real Jewish experiences and identities of the time.

In the midst of waning Ukrainian-Russian relations and heightened political tension—and all the more after Euromaidan, Russia's annexation of Crimea in 2014, and Russia's invasion of Ukraine in 2022—some Odesans have followed the ideological transformation of the psychologist and poet Boris Khersonsky (born in 1950).[38] He switched to the Ukrainian language in solidarity with the Maidan "Revolution of Dignity" and in a 2019 interview noted that "the city's imperial past should take its proper place in history. But we should know that Odesa has another past: Turkish, Greek, etc. And most importantly, Odesa has a future. And this future is part of modern Ukraine. This means that the Ukrainian string in the city's past (and it was! and is!) should sound louder."[39]

While other Odesan artists and performers have spoken up against Russia's aggression, in some cases, their work has nonetheless perpetuated the Russian version of the Odesa myth that has been politicized. Writing about Mikhail Zhvanetsky, Amelia Glaser has pointed out that "his comedy perpetuates the trenchant cultural imperialism that Russia has sought to maintain in Ukraine which denies the significance of Ukraine in the Russian cultural landscape."[40] Khersonsky, who considers himself ethnically Jewish but belongs to the Christian faith, is not a popular figure among the general Jewish population or the leaders of the "Odesa cultural space." Still, his work is well known among literary circles outside the city and reviewed by scholars in and outside of Ukraine.[41] He has widely deconstructed and criticized the Odesa Myth for its hint of imperialism in what Amelia Glaser refers to, using Walter Mignolo's term, as Khersonsky's "critical cosmopolitanism."[42] Speaking against Odesa's claim to uniqueness, Khersonsky said in an interview with *Shoizdat* magazine, "If we admit that Odesa is more than a city, it is a country, then the (cultural) capital of this country is and will be Moscow."[43] While Khersonsky's view of the Odesa myth has been picked up by literary scholars, the Odesa myth still lives on in the popular culture of the place through the works of prominent cultural figures, the media, humor, tourism, and even fashion. For instance, the creation of Benya and Zubrick, a fashion brand of T-shirts and other clothing items that was started in late 2000 by two Jewish Odesans born in the late 1970s, has gained great popularity among Odesans and others by giving life to Jewish Odesan humor on apparel.[44]

Culture, Media, and Tourism

Historically, Odesa's Jewish image in popular culture was extended and enhanced through the satirical works of Mikhail Zhvanetsky; memoirs by Odesan locals and emigrants; films such as *The Art of Living in Odessa*, directed by Georgi Yungvald-Khilkevich in 1989; the television series *Likvidatsiia* (Liquidation), produced by Sergei Ursuliak in 2007, portraying the Odesa of the 1950s with Yiddishisms and humor; and the film *Odessa*, produced by Valery Todorovsky in 2017, depicting the internal drama of a Jewish family in Odesa during a cholera outbreak in the 1970s.[45] In his review of the 2005 film *Odessa . . . Odessa!* by the Israeli French director Michale Boganim (which I discuss later in this chapter), Tanny notes the film's grim picture of a contemporary Odesa from which significant numbers of "Jews have gone . . . taking the city's character with them." And yet, he writes, Odesa is a place "where Jewish integration was reciprocal: while the Jews became more Russian over the years, Odessa's Gentiles became more Jewish." Thus, in Tanny's view, Jewish contributions to Odesa's cultural landscape haven't been forgotten; they're actively commemorated today in the streets, parks, and museums. Even though "most of Odessa's Jews may be gone . . . Odessa remains a Jewish city."[46]

While Tanny's statements point to the Jewish out-migration that halved Odesa's Jewish population in the Soviet days, it also assumes that Jewishness in post-Soviet Odesa is not necessarily linked to the remaining Jews, but rather diluted in the general population of Odesa and the city culture. However, this type of Jewishness, tied to the Odesa myth, is still relevant today. Jewish Odesans and community leaders from abroad see themselves and their activity as key makers of Odesa's Jewishness. The new layer of Odesa's claims to being a "Jewish city," put forth by Jewish activists and institutions of Jewish life that operate in the city, is linked to the imagined community, but we must not forget about their real-life existence. Indeed, the city's defining features of Jewishness carry different meanings depending on who is applying the term and in what context.

In the digital sphere, blogs, websites, and online periodicals about Odesa help perpetuate the city's stereotypes and reveal their virtual and transnational force.[47] Various websites dedicated to Jewish travel describe Odesa as "one of Europe's Jewish capitals," often falling back on Babel's description of Odesa as a "city built by Jews."[48] But both historically and today, those making such claims share an understanding that in Babel's literary world (and, we can say, in modern-day Odesa), a "Jewish city" is not only "a reference to the sheer numbers of Jews in the city" but also a marker of the "general atmosphere, tolerant towards minorities."[49] Moreover, contemporary Odesa has an active Jewish life, not merely in terms of its marks of Jewish heritage but in actual Jewish presence, practice, observance, and public visibility.

Various Facebook groups linked to the topic of Jewish Odesa are some of the platforms dedicated to the topics of Jewish history and everyday life in the city. The English-language magazine *The Odessa Review*, published from 2016 to 2019 by Regina Maryanovska-Davidzon, an Odesan native who now resides in Paris, and her husband, Vladislav Davidzon, covered cultural events in Odesa (and greater Ukraine) and regularly featured stories about Jewish life there. For example, the October/November 2017 issue was dedicated to Jewish-Ukrainian relations; its cover showed a folkloric image of Hasidic men with long side curls and black frocks, dancing along with traditionally dressed Cossacks.

Large-scale events have been geared toward reaffirming the Jewish presence and associations with Odesa. In 2006, Migdal sponsored a weeklong, citywide Rainbow of Jewish Diaspora Festival with performances of Jewish plays, an exhibition of Jewish art, tours of Jewish Odesa, and various workshops and music concerts. That year, Odesa also celebrated a festival of klezmer music that, according to the organizers, was very successful in bringing Jewish and non-Jewish Odesans closer to Jewish, Yiddish, and Odesan culture. In October 2017, Odesa hosted its first Jewish Film Festival, screening both foreign and local productions.

In the 2010s, foreign media began to play a more prominent role in shaping an image of Odessa as a city that "throbs with Jewish life."[50] In 2018, *Haaretz* used the headline "Odessa, the Cradle of Israeli Culture, Enjoys a Jewish Renaissance" to explore Odesa's Jewish history and the qualities its contemporary culture shares with, and offers to, Israelis. The article's subhead announced, "The Ukrainian port city of Odesa, once home to hundreds of thousands of Jews, is experiencing a 'golden age'—with modern Israel proving an unlikely inspiration." The text and lavish photographs blended history and tourism promotion, mentioning the Holocaust as well as Israeli restaurants named after famous Jewish Odesans who helped build the state of Israel.[51]

Similar claims about Odesa's Jewish renaissance were streamed on the Israeli media channel ILTV in a short report entitled, "Odessa, Ukraine, Experiences Jewish Renaissance," followed by "Did you know that Odessa, Ukraine, was once home to one of the most Jewish communities on the planet?" The clip gave a broader vision of Odesa's historical importance (especially for the Zionist movement) and contemporary revival. In the segment, Rabbi Arie Rov, of the Litvak synagogue, says that "over the years, most Jews have immigrated to Israel, the United States, or Germany. But Odessa has remained a Jewish city." Recalling the long lines outside the synagogue for matzoh before Passover in 2018, Rabbi Rov points out that besides the active religious life many Jews lead, these changes are welcomed by the wider population. "Real Odessa locals," he claims, "know that when Passover comes, everyone goes to the synagogue to

Figure 7.1. Cover of the *City Guide of Jewish Odessa*, published in 2007. Photo by author.

buy matzoh." The footage showed the city's numerous Israeli restaurants named after famous figures (like Allenby, the British general who led the conquest of Palestine in 1917–19, and Dizengoff, the first mayor of Tel Aviv), reinforcing an image of twenty-first-century Odesa as a modern-day Tel Aviv. "It truly is a place that draws back Israelis and Jews who want to do business," concludes Rabbi Wolf, of the Chabad congregation.[52]

The visibility of Jews and Jewish places is part of the larger transformation of Odesa's urban terrain, where "new ethnic restaurants, cafes, and fast-food stalls—Turkish, Armenian, Georgian, Chinese and Arab," as well as Bulgarian, Greek, French, and Italian food establishments, are scattered throughout the city.[53] Vera Skvirskaja also reminds us about the less visible places of Odesa's ethnic diversity that are overlooked in social analyses of Odesa, such as the

Figure 7.2. An advertisement for Odessa Tours, including Jewish Odessa. Photo by author.

Seventh Kilometre market outside the city, populated by "Vietnamese currency dealers, Turkish leather goods traders, Afghan and Ghanaian show-sellers and Chinese selling a variety of goods."[54] But none of these groups have become immortalized in the Odesa myth the way the Jews have. The new aura of "Jewish cosmopolitanism" is no longer primarily the blend of Russian and Jewish orientations that Horowitz discussed in the Odesa of the early 1900s (see chapter 1). Rather, it is a combination of social, physical, and virtual spaces that bring together and display Jewish, Israeli, Ukrainian, Russian-speaking, and other international references, references brought in through the process of development, philanthropy, heritage travel, and the personal and professional connections of Odesa's historical and contemporary diasporas.

Not surprisingly, the tourism industry has picked up on this legendary myth of the city and turned Odesa's Jewishness into a "brand" in a tourist economy. Ruth Ellen Gruber describes a similar phenomenon across eastern Europe, where Jewish or "Jewish-style" expression (religious, cultural, pop-cultural, and other) was becoming part of the mainstream and a "recognized and recognizable commercial commodity that formed an off-the-shelf ethnic decorative and catering category alongside 'Chinese,' 'Japanese,' 'Indian,' 'Middle Eastern'

Figure 7.3. A display at the Museum of the History of Odesa Jews. Photo by author.

and even 'Wild West.'"[55] The street markets and souvenir shops I visited in
Odesa in the mid-2000s offered *matrioshkas* (wooden nesting dolls) decorated
with images of Hasidic households, and metal figurines of stereotypical Jewish jewelers and scholars (more positive images of old Jewish stereotypes than
the figurines of Jews clutching coins, as described by Ruth Ellen Gruber in
Kazimierz, Poland), alongside Cossack-style belts, decorative lacquered boxes,
and mock ID cards and passports that state the bearer's nationality as "Odesit."
Besides other official guides, the city released a *City Guide of Jewish Odessa*,
published in 2007 in Russian and English. It continues to be in print and is, according to the director of Migdal, "extremely popular." "Jewish Heritage Tours"
are advertised on posters near the open-air electric cars that can be rented for
excursions in the city center. But as Gruber points out, the new Jewish con-
structs, including souvenirs, "now form part of the Jewish (or 'Jewish') reality
of the post-Holocaust, post-communist world . . . and are integral parts of the
texture of living cities, with layer by layer, their own models, perspectives and
shorthand stereotypes that add to the palimpsest."[56] In Gruber's analysis, these
layers of city life form "new authenticities" of what she calls "real imaginary
spaces."[57] In her analysis of klezmer festivals, Waligorska also questions stable
realms of authenticity, criticizing a bipolar system of meaning where "'real'

Jewish heritage is understood as made by Jews and for Jews and simulated Jewishness as produced by non-Jews for non-Jews."[58] Rather, she suggests seeing these categories as constructed entities with unstable boundaries, and, I would add, a mixture of Jewish and non-Jewish audiences.

Odesa is different from Poland, Germany, and the parts of eastern Europe described by Gruber, Waligorska, and others, who depict a revival in places where Jewish life has been wiped out by the Holocaust and the Jewish heritage boom is driven by non-Jews. In Odesa there are different voices of authority that shape Jewish religious and cultural projects in the city and, similar to other places, questions around what defines Jewishness are intensively negotiated and redefined. But unlike the above-mentioned communities, in Odesa, the process of Jewish heritagization and revival—outside the tourist industry—involves mostly Jewish actors and live Jews.

Gruber raises important questions that are also relevant to our thinking about Odesa: What does it mean to say that something or, I would add, *someone* is Jewish? One can see how applying this adjective leads to myriad representations and interpretations. It's obvious that the souvenir figurines of Orthodox Jewish men in long coats and fur hats depict "Jewish" (such as an Orthodox Jewish man in scholarly pursuit, marked by a book in the figurine's hands), but the Jewish tours depict "Jewish" as part of the city's history and experience, based on relics and real-life expositions and visions of Jewish life.

Many Jewish historical and fictional characters are commemorated in statues throughout the downtown area. Two in the courtyard of the Literature Museum are dedicated to Odesa's humor, as personified by Sashka the Fiddler and Rabinovich, the Odesan character in many Soviet-era jokes. Farther up, on Odesa's main pedestrian thoroughfare, Deribasovskaya Street, are two more statues dedicated to Jewish Odesans—one of the comedian, singer, and writer Leonid Utesov, and the other of the missing "Twelfth Chair" from the 1928 novel by Ilf and Petrov. Utesov's music and performances celebrated "Odessa as a Jewish city of sin," and his memoirs "effectively constructed old Odessa as a Jewish city using Yiddish-inflected narrative style, pervaded with Jewish characters, fables, and witticisms."[59] This type of "implicit Jewishness" was used by other mythmakers in the city.[60] The first monument to Babel was erected in Odesa in 2011, across from his former apartment on the corner of Rishelevskaya and Zhukovskaya Streets. It depicts him "sitting next to a massive wheel of fate, scribbling in a notebook while gazing dreamily into the distance."[61] The monument was built with donations gathered by the International World Odesit Club from Odesans around the world. Odesans often cite these contributions as a testimony to their love for the city's history.

Borrowing the notion of a "Jewish space" from Diane Pinto, it might be said that the Jewish spaces of Odesa are indeed multiple, debated, and fluctuating;

layered with real, invented, imagined, remembered, re-created, and created realities; and touching on various stereotypes, real events, people, and mythical Old Odesa.[62] Like the contributors to *Jewish Topographies: Visions of Space, Tradition of Place*, I focus on the production of Odesa's Jewish spaces, what Brauch, Lipphardt, and Nocke term "doing Jewish space" or what I refer to as "lived Jewish spaces," which are defined by living Jews both within and outside Odesa.[63] And at the same time, I also engage with other Jewish spaces that exist in Odesa on virtual, textual, mythical, and metaphorical levels. Borders and definitions of different Jewish spaces often blur, converge, and overlap (as Gruber reminds us), and categories such as "Jewish," "non-Jewish," "authentic," and "inauthentic" (as Waligorska points out) are constructed entities whose boundaries are in flux.[64] This was particularly visible on the tours of Jewish Odesa and in the festivals and exhibitions that were organized by Jews but also drew in the surrounding society. In the early 2000s, Jewish tours were mainly organized by historians of Jewish Odesa and their students, but those tours grew in popularity; when I returned in 2014, I found many non-Jewish operators offering their versions of Jewish Odesa, which continue to be popular online events even in the current context of the war.

Language

The notion that there's an "Odessan dialect" is one of the city's most deeply rooted myths.[65] A mix of Russian, Ukrainian, and Yiddish, plus other foreign words, intonations, and case structures, the dialect has been called the linguistic equivalent of a Russian chopped beet salad (*vinegret*).[66] Literary critics in the early twentieth century looked down on Odesan slang as a "barbarization of the Russian language"; an Odesa newspaper published around 1912 "consistently referred to the city as *Iudessa* [Judaeo-Odessa]."[67] But today, tourists can acquire books on the Odesan language and collections of "Odessan anecdotes," many featuring the joker Rabinovich. Robert Rothstein writes that the Odesan language and music offer a way of approaching the "symbiotic relationship between and among nationalities."[68] In his article "How It Was Sung in Odessa," he shows how the Russian and Yiddish languages influenced each other in the public life of the city. He describes how the two were often used interchangeably in the context of songs and conversation. This was "life on the sidewalks of Odessa," where Jews regularly interacted with Russians, Ukrainians, Poles, Greeks, and others.[69] Anthropologist Abel Polese, who has long written about language politics in Odesa, reminds us that histories and cultures have always overlapped in this city and that its notion of cosmopolitanism depicts a reality "well beyond the dichotomy between Russian and Ukrainian cultures, identities, and nations."[70]

Today, the *vinegret* of Odesan Russian is far less colorful and mixed than it was in the past. Rothstein's studies are historical in nature, as indicated by his use of the past tense in the title of his article. He cites the title of a 1997 book published in Russian by Anatolii Kozak when he concludes that "Odessa doesn't live here anymore" (*Odessa zdes' bol'she ne zhivet*).[71] Indeed, Tanny suggests that people have mourned the passing of Odesa's golden age since the city's very inception.[72]

Rothstein attributes Odesa's changes partly to the processes of migration and globalization, both of which have affected the city's patterns of life. But, as Polese points out, "the languages of Odessa have constantly changed since its inception."[73] And yet Odesa hasn't lost all of its Yiddishisms. Many of my interlocutors commonly used words like *gesheft* (business), *maisa* (story), *schmuck* (fool), *sha* (quite!), and *mishpukha* (family). They also occasionally deployed such Odesan Russian phrases as *chtob ya tak zhil*, a translation of the Yiddish expression *zol ikh azoy lebn* (used to emphasize the truthfulness of something just said).

Besides the Yiddishisms, many Jewish Odesans—especially those who've spent time in Israel and those who lead religious lives—also use Hebrew in daily conversation. When some of my interlocutors send get-well messages on Facebook, they wish the sick "Refuah Shlema" (complete recovery), and follow it with a request for certain psalms (*tehilim*) to be read. As these messages travel across international borders and time zones, they create a support community for those in need. On the other side of the spectrum, "Mazl Tov" (good fortune or good luck in Hebrew) has become a common way to respond to a happy moment that someone has posted online or shared in real life. Many of the affiliated Jews also use their Jewish names on social media, along with or instead of their original names, revealing a stronger bond to their Jewish identity.

Individual Reflections on Odesa's Jewishness

Among those Odesans who believe their city to be Jewish is my friend Maya, who is devoted to preserving its historic character. After we spoke of the role played by Jews in the city's past growth, she moved to the present to say, "First, compared to other ethnic and religious groups, Odesa's Jewish *obshchina* [community] is by far the most active and involved in the life of the city." When I suggested that Odesa had many more Christians and Muslims than Jews, she quickly corrected my definition of "Jewish community," which was, implicitly, a religious definition. Religious Jews like herself were only a small portion of the Jewish population, but the Jewish national (ethnic) group was a more inclusive social structure.

To Maya, Jews' level of "activeness" was shown in the cultural programs they organized—festivals, classes, conferences, concerts, exhibitions, and publications. These often featured various strands of Jewish life in Odesa. She also referred to the positions held by local Jews in Odesa's political and economic structures: "Many of the city deputies are Jews," she pointed out, "and the mayor [Gurvitz] is Jewish. This couldn't happen in many other cities in the ex-Soviet world."[74] What's more, she said, Jews owned many local businesses and thus helped support the local economy. They were also well positioned to conduct business internationally because of the network created by all the Jewish Odesans now living in other countries as a result of migration. Though Maya highlighted the important roles played by Jews as politicians and entrepreneurs, she also recognized the rise of Jewish self-awareness, calling this process "strengthening your *evreikosti*," or "Jewish bones." She concluded, "There might be fewer Jews in the city today, but they have stronger *evreikosti*" because they now know Jewish history and traditions and they participate in the Jewish holidays and life cycle rituals.

Maya's notion of *evreikosti* highlights the bodily experience of Jewish identity. It also illustrates the transformation of one's understanding of what makes someone a Jew: once a biological given, it now means one who learns to do "Jewish" things. Jewish practices thus not only make the individual "stronger" as a Jew; they also make Odesa "more Jewish." Jewish influence in Odesa, as Maya saw it, has risen not only by the influence of Jews in society but also by the "quality" of the Jews who have become "stronger" through knowledge and self-awareness. This idea of strong Jewish bones connects the biological and performative nature of Jewishness, where the Jewish body becomes stronger as one learns Jewish history, traditions, and rituals and performs the commandments. Expanding on the process of religious education described by Alanna Cooper, where Jews "learn to do Jewish things," Maya also included knowledge of Jewish history, local and biblical.[75]

Maya judged Odesa's Jewishness by the extent to which Jews and their activities had been accepted and absorbed in the larger realm of city culture. In other words, the acceptance of Jewishness confirmed the city as a tolerant and cosmopolitan place.

More proof that Odesa was a "Jewish" city, in Maya's view, is that non-Jewish Odesans welcomed the Jewish festivals and celebrations, at times even participating in them. She added that some non-Jews send their children to the Jewish cultural centers as part of their upbringing.[76] And, Maya asked me rhetorically, didn't many Odesans of non-Jewish descent know a lot of Yiddish terminology? And weren't they familiar with the major Jewish holidays and with Jewish cuisine? Indeed, "gefilte fish is a dish everyone knows in all the restaurants in

Odessa," said Rabbi Arie Rov, of the Litvak synagogue, in a TV interview.[77] I met a number of non-Jews who were actively involved in Jewish organizations, some even playing leadership roles.[78] All this could be because the locals believe that, as a Ukrainian taxi driver once told me, "In Odessa, everyone's a little bit Jewish and a little bit everything else."

In a January 2021 interview in *Gazeta*, Chabad rabbi Avraham Wolf identified Odesa as a Jewish city judging by its successful and vibrant Jewish community, with its extensive programs and key Jewish institutions. He noted that of the thirty Ukrainian cities where Chabad operates, Odesa has the largest impact, reaching approximately thirty thousand Jews.[79] In another interview, Wolf noted: "The spectrum of programs (cultural, religious, educational, social and economic) that Odessa's Jewish community offers its members is unmatched.... My colleagues around the world don't have the success we have in Odessa in building synagogues, schools, etc., and having such a vibrant community. . . . Odessa gives its Jews 100 percent possibility to live by Jewish laws. Not in every city and country can you do that." Nonobservant Jews have a different sense of Odesa's Jewish space. As Elena, who was in her sixties when I met her in 2006, explained:

> Some twenty to thirty years ago, one could still have called Odessa a Jewish city—not so much for the number of Jews living there, but more because of the influence their presence had on all Odesans of all different nationalities, which you could sense. Undoubtedly, Yiddish and to a small extent Hebrew had an influence on the "Odessan language," by which Odessans were recognized by others and recognized one another in any corner of the Soviet Union. One can't overlook Jewish humor, *khokhmah* [Yiddish for wisdom], and of course Jewish food, which Odessans adopted in full as part of their cuisine.

Describing the Odesa she knew in the late 1960s, Elena said, "I remember seeing elderly and not-so-elderly women easily conversing in Russian and Yiddish on the street in a very natural fashion." While she acknowledged that Odesa was an international city, she insisted that its "Jewishness" was more pervasive than any other ethnic orientation.

However, Elena felt that once the borders opened after the breakup of the USSR and many Jewish Odesans left, the city was drained of its Jewish *kolorit* (tone, color, character, or carnivalesque or exotic quality). As another Odesan said, "Few of the Odessans with whom I grew up remain in Odessa today. At one time, they inhabited my city as the soul inhabits one's body. They have scattered, fragmenting Odessa into pieces, and these pieces are now making their mark on the streets of Israel, Australia, America, and Canada."[80] In recent

years, Elena said, different Jews had appeared in place of those Jews who departed: "Religious Jews, Israelis, people foreign to Odessa, incomprehensible
to Odessa, who do not know, and I think do not love Odessa the same way we
do. They have their own goals and missions, which have nothing in common
with the Soviet, jolly, easygoing and carefree, secular Jewish Odessa." Elena
did not blame the loss of Odesa's Jewish world solely on the outflow of Jews
from the city. Rather, as was common in other conversations, she pointed to
the influx of newcomers (*priezzhie*), especially those from rural villages and
small towns. Odesa during the current war is also experiencing a new influx of
newcomers—internally displaced refugees—whose presence has altered the
social landscape in new ways. Mila, who was in her fifties when we met in 2006
and working at the Israeli Cultural Center, expressed a similar view. "When I
came back to Odessa with my parents after the war, all but two families in my
courtyard were Jewish. Today, all but two are non-Jews. They're all *priezzhie*
who don't care about our city." Vera Skvirskaja has even argued that some urban
residents in Odesa have been "transformed into a new diasporic community in
their own city" as they have been "confronted by demands of the nation-state,
their social circle has emigrated, and new engagements have been blocked by
a form of tolerance marked by indifference."[81] But Mila's and Elena's reflections point out the important distinction Odesans make about belonging in
Odesa: between "true Odesans," who might have moved to the city later but
adopted an Odesan perspective and are touched by the departure of the Jews,
and "newcomers," who, in their eyes, are not knowledgeable about the city's
past or are indifferent to it.

According to Elena, Odesa's great reputation lives on, but those who created it are "long gone." "They live in Russia, the USA, Israel, even Australia—
but unfortunately, no longer in Odessa." She spoke of the nostalgia for this
"lost world," a nostalgia felt by many of its current inhabitants and by Odesans
abroad, Jews and non-Jews alike. The type of nostalgia Elena describes is not
only a nostalgia for a romanticized "once was" socialist past of "multiethnic
collectives"; it's also a nostalgia for sincere relations and a moral community
based on shared values and ideals that many ex-Soviets lament, as noted by
anthropologists working in postsocialist contexts.[82] Elena's reference to missing Jews is about the people who made Odesa a different city; their absence
is a reminder of the historic ruptures and the irrevocable change. Thus, their
departure is linked, also, to the dissolution of the Soviet Union. But unlike
some expressions of nostalgia associated with the process of modernization,
in Odesa, Tanya Richardson points out, expressions of nostalgia for the city's
kolorit speak of a longing for the city's other forms of modernity, prerevolutionary or Soviet.[83] Anthropologists Maya Nadkarni and Olga Shevchenko,

writing about the forms and practices of postsocialist nostalgia, note that the themes of spatial and temporal displacement are closely intertwined.[84] The nostalgia expressed here reminds us that nostalgia can also be experienced as social displacement by those who remain rooted but long for the people whose departure has altered the tone and character of the place.

Elena told me that Odesans love to sing songs about the city whenever they reunite with their compatriots, and many of those songs were written by Jews, speak about Jewish literary characters, and include a hint of Yiddish. Many like to read memoirs about the city or perhaps write them themselves. She made it clear that she wasn't just talking about Jewish Odesans. To illustrate her point, she told me this story: During a short trip to Odesa (from Israel) in 2008, she'd planned to spend her last day helping plant herbs at a new dacha her friend had rented for the summer. They arrived to find the homeowners still present, seated around a beautifully laid table in the midst of the May Day celebration. Elena and her friend were invited to sit and eat. Not wanting to be rude, they joined the company but said they couldn't stay long due to Elena's imminent departure.

When their hosts learned that Elena was headed back to Israel, the atmosphere suddenly changed. "They jumped up to kiss and hug me." Elena was somewhat surprised at this reaction. She told me that the congratulations quickly turned into a shower of kind words about Odesan Jews in general and about Israel. Reflecting on this incident, Elena said she'd never realized how much Odesans—*real Odesans*—missed the city's Jews and how grateful they were that Jews were still returning to visit their old city. "I think this was how they expressed their nostalgia—they longed for the Odesa they'd lost. Lost because of the mass migration of the Jewish population who, at one point in history, made Odesa—the city it was—loved by Jews and non-Jews alike."

When I sent a draft of this manuscript to literary scholar and city historian Anna Misuk to ask for her comments, she said, "It all sounds very serious, Marina. Here is something much lighter on the topic." She shared an animation of a song (sung in Russian) by Svetlana Nisilevich:

Зачем уехали евреи
И нас оставили сирот?
Без вас одесский мир беднее,
Все делаем наоборот

Наш дом - одесская тусовка
Она для жителей всех стран.
Одесса всех связала ловко,
Евреев не хватает нам!

Евреи, милые евреи!
Я потеряла вас, кошмар,
и так жалею!
В моей душе для вас
Всегда есть место,
Я ваша мама, тетя, тёща,
и невеста!

Зачем, скажите, вам Канада,
Зачем Австралия, Германия и США?
Евреи, может вам туда совсем не надо, а?
Ведь здесь живет ваша душа!

А у Одессы-мамы,
У Одессы-мамы,
А у Одессы-мамы,
Все мы хороши,
Не будьте так упрямы,
Не будьте так упрямы!
Евреи - вы же часть
Её большой души!

А для Одессы катастрофа:
Без вас осталась наша мать.
Грустит все время тетя Софа
И вас не хочет забывать!

Вы приезжайте, дорогие!
Не любит вас лишь идиот!
В иных краях вы все равно чужие,
А мама любит вас и ждет!

Why did the Jews leave
And leave us as orphans?
Without you the Odessa world has lost its wealth,
We can't seem to get it right since your departure.

Our house is the Odessa scene,
It's open to all around the world.
Odessa brought us all together,
But it's not the same without the city's Jews!

Jews, my dear Jews!
I lost you, what a nightmare,

I regret it deeply!
In my soul there is always a place for you,
I am your mama, auntie, mother-in-law,
And your bride!

Tell me, why do you need Canada,
Why do you need Australia, Germany and the USA?
Jews, maybe you don't need to go to those places, what do you say?
After all, your soul is in Odessa!

For Odessa-mama,
For Odessa-mama,
Oh, for Odessa-mama,
We are all good kids,
Don't be so stubborn,
Don't be so stubborn!
Jews, after all, you're all
Part of her big soul!

It's a disaster for Odessa:
Our mother is left without you all.
Aunt Sofia is so upset
And doesn't want to forget you all.

Please come and visit, my dears!
Only an idiot doesn't love you!
In other lands you're still a foreigner
But mama loves you and she is waiting.

This sense that the city's non-Jewish residents keenly felt the mass emigration of the Jews—and that many speak of their departure with regret—is borne out by the scholarship.[85] For example, "during the Humorina (Comedy) Festival in the late nineties," Richardson writes, "a friend saw a sign that read: 'Jews, come back to Odessa! We miss you—it's boring without you. If you can't come back, take us with you!'"[86] Among Odesan emigrants, there's a similar sentiment that their departure was the end of "the real Odessa." In his memoir *Est' gorod kotoryi vizhu vo sne* (*There Is a City I See in My Dreams*), David Shehter writes from Israel,

We Odessan Jews took with us not OUR Odessa, we took away ODESSA [emphasis in the original]. We took away all which made her a magical city so dear to millions of citizens of the USSR who loved not only her beautiful streets but her aura of freedom, blazing love of life, sparks of humor, something

so special which made Odessa not characteristic of a small Ukrainian city. . . .
Today, when the Jews have left Odessa, her streets are the same, I hear even
better, but Odessa became a very provincial city which it would not have been
if it were not for those citizens who spoke Russian but thought in Yiddish or in
Hebrew. Odessa's Jews have gone and so has Odessa.[87]

Not all the Jewish Odesans I met saw the Jewishness of today's Odesa
through the prism of nostalgia, particularly those in the younger generations.
Gosha, for example, told me that Odesa couldn't be considered a Jewish city
anymore: "Too few Jewish people are left in Odessa. . . . There's still something
in the air, but. . . . For instance, when I started school in 1988, five of my classmates were Jewish, [but] when I graduated, I was the only one. When I was
studying in Odessa Polytechnical Institute, I was the only Jew in my group."
While Gosha seemed to regret the changes that had taken place, he saw no
point in mourning the past; instead, he concentrated on his plans for the future.
He didn't think Odesa could ever become a Jewish city again, despite the efforts
of affiliated Jews and Jewish leaders.

Debating the character of her native city in a conversation that took place
in 2006, Diana (a woman in her twenties) emphasized the difference between
so-called public opinion and everyday life. There was the myth of Odesa's Jewishness, and there was the reality. Yes, Odesa could be viewed as "Jewish,"
but what was the point of assigning such a label? She said, "For me, the city
is *anational*. Despite the fact that it has a large number of Ukrainians, they're
all Odessans first and foremost. They don't open Ukrainian restaurants, they
don't speak Ukrainian, they don't wear embroidered shirts, they don't vote for
Yuschenko, and they don't fight with NATO or Russia. All that's Ukrainian in
them is the inscription in their passport; that's it. The same goes for the local
Russians, Germans, and others. They might each have their own religion, but
the mentality of the people is neutral."

Diana, who has since moved to Europe, has a very different rhetoric and
undoubtedly sees Odesa and herself as Ukrainian by different measures. Her
words of neutrality are a striking reminder of how much Odesa has been transformed by large-scale Russian aggression. Questions about Odesa's Jewishness
were often addressed in public conversation and debate. In April 2007, the
Museum of the History of Odesa Jews organized an exhibition entitled *Jews
of Odessa: Is It Only the Past?* Museum director Mikhail Rashkovetsky wrote
in the *Migdal Times*, "Many renowned researchers insist that Ukrainian Jews
are but a dried-up branch on the tree of world Jewry. But maybe Odessa can be
viewed as an exception? After all, Odessa was always unlike any other place.
That is how [Odessa] was thought of in the Russian Empire, that is how she

remained in the Soviet Union and throughout its history."[88] Rashkovetsky emphasized the museum's desire to portray Odesa as "an extraordinary place" in which "its Jews are not only mourning their legendary past but also awaiting their bright future." On the one hand, Rashkovetsky admitted, "Never in the history of its existence did Odessa have such a small Jewish population, except during the period between Spring of 1942 and Spring of 1944, when the city was 'Judenfrei' [Jew free]" during the German/Romanian occupation. On the other hand, Odesa is a city awaiting a bright Jewish future. "It is not [just] because of the collected materials about 'Jewish revival' that I make my claim about Odessa's bright future," he wrote. "The main point of optimism is some of the visitors to the exhibition—a group of parents and students from the Migdal center whose contribution to the future is already visible in the number of newborn babies among the group."[89]

Rashkovetsky doesn't focus the reader's attention on Odesa's Jewishness as an artifact of the past, but as a thread of continuation. Seeing Odesa as a Jewish city in the present and the future contributes to the claims of the city's Jewish intellectuals and activists that Odesa has been, and will continue to be, a Jewish city. It is the presence of Jews in the city and their connection to the historical tenets of Odesa's Jewish past that allow Rashkovetsky and other members of the intelligentsia to present Jewishness as an everlasting temporality of the place. Extracts from the museum's guest book, which appear in the same issue of the *Migdal Times* as Rashkovetsky's text on the exhibition, support the idea of Odesa's steadfast Jewish foundation. Those comments, inscribed in many languages, created a collage of affinity among visitors who came from Odesa, L'viv, Kyiv, Donetsk, Moscow, Minsk, New York, Baltimore, San Francisco, Tel Aviv, Jerusalem, London, Amsterdam, Sydney, and many other world cities. One pronouncement summarized the very point the exhibition was trying to make: "Jews were, are, and always will be in Odessa."[90] For the Odesans who believe that the aura of Jewishness is still alive in the city and extends to all periods of the city's history, today's Jewish revival signals the creation of a new post-Soviet chapter in the everlasting story of Odesa as a Jewish place.[91]

But others consider the city's Jewish identity to be on a downward trajectory—its essence diminishing and not replenishing over time. Among this group are some who believe that those elements that once made Odesa a Jewish city can never be re-created, and thus Odesa as a Jewish city remains alive only in the form of memory or "a legend in the making."[92] In this perspective, the efforts of "active" Jews in their city and the current Jewish visibility can't be seen as a continuation of something distinctively "Odesan," but only as a new import. Like Elena, many people make a distinction between the Jews now living in Odesa and the "real" Odesan Jews.

For all the debates, questions, and assertions about Odesa's Jewishness, there's also a persistent ideology in Jewish Odesan circles that might be called a neutral stance. In this view, Odesans are Odesans, period. No single ethnic group or religion can encompass the city and a people. Diverse people, processes, and interests are alive in Odesa's "urbanity."[93] This line of thinking doesn't dismiss the city's Jewish traits or consider them unimportant; rather, those traits are not privileged over the other ethnic elements that make Odesans a people of their city—on equal terms.[94]

Power, Politics, and the Jewish Stereotype

As I mentioned before, the Israeli-French director Michale Boganim's documentary *Odessa . . . Odessa!* focuses on the supposed twilight of Jewish life in the city. One summer evening in 2006, friends asked me to watch the film with others at their home. We'd barely made it through the first thirty minutes when our host, Anna, from the Literature Museum, stood up and turned it off. Many of those watching were already frustrated by the film's portrayal of Odesa and its Jews. Boganim begins by invoking dreams of a city that no longer exists. Then, as if filming in the faint light of a perpetual dusk, she conjures images of near-empty streets where solitary figures move slowly. These scenes are punctuated with interviews of elderly Yiddish-speaking Jews filmed in run-down, dimly lit Soviet-style apartments. The city of yore is cast as existing only in some nostalgic revelry; it now seems to be nothing but a gloomy and dying place.

In Anna's view, Boganim's selection of Yiddish-speaking Jews was based on an outdated sense of the city. Odesan Jews, she said, would typically speak to each other in Russian, maybe throwing in a few Yiddish words, but not speaking only in Yiddish as the film showed them. She and others that evening pointed out many things the film omitted. How could a collection of six elderly, lonely Jews and the single plangent theme of Jewish departure from this Black Sea port even begin to capture the essence of Jewish life in Odesa?

Interestingly enough, this group of viewers felt that the film showed their city as both too Jewish and not Jewish enough. Everyday Odesan conversations and local humor often used exaggerations like the ones shown in the film, but seeing these projected on screen by an Israeli director aroused a very different set of reactions. An outsider's view had invaded the intimacy of characterizing local Jewish culture. It was apparent that Jewish Odesans weren't inclined to accept any single interpretation of their city or to endorse a stereotype offered without their approval—even though they themselves often failed to agree on the character of the place.

Once we'd finished our discussion, Anna restarted the film. Soon she and her husband, Mark, were objecting to the portrayal of Odesans in the Brighton Beach neighborhood of Brooklyn, New York, and the Israeli city of Ashdod. Images of elderly Jews continued to dominate. In nostalgic gatherings on Soviet holidays, the longtime emigrants expressed their dream to return to Odesa. In response, my friends recited numerous success stories of Jews who'd made America or Israel their home, and of others who, like Mark and Anna, had stayed in Odesa without regret (though later they moved to Israel when old age approached, to be closer to their daughter and grandchildren). My friends' emotional reaction to the film prompted them to defend their social territory (a defense that may have been exaggerated by my presence). They despised being seen as victims, or as members of a dying breed whose destiny was limited to two bleak alternatives: death or emigration. It wasn't just the director's misreading of Odesa's Jewishness that my friends objected to, but also the fact that this misrepresentation came in the form of a widely circulated and easily accessible medium—a "locus of stereotype production"—that was beyond their control.[95] The film's vision might cause outsiders to see their city as a "Jewishless."

In his book on Odesa, Charles King notes that many cities balance on a thin line between historic moments of genius and periodic explosions of violence and misfortune. The latter are often left out of popular memory, as historiography overwrites the times when "urban civility fell victim to the stresses of cultural difference."[96] King's book ends with a plea for Odesans to acknowledge their city's dark times as well as the golden ages. Although Anna and Mark were well aware of the Jewish emigration from the city, and weren't trying to deny Odesa's darker periods, they still resisted the recasting of Odesa as a city dominated by the specter of a fading Jewish presence.

Likewise, some Odesans two decades after Ukraine's independence were troubled by attempts to cast their city as Ukrainian, especially on the level of language politics, which included Ukrainian language requirements and new standards and strictures in education, the press, and mass media. As Skvirskaja notes of Odesa in 2005, many ordinary Odesans described the government's political moves to "create a coherent pan-national Ukrainian identity" as Ukrainization (*Ukrainizatsia*) and "an attack on the city's old cosmopolitan orientation and linguistic aesthetics."[97] I spoke with some members of the Russian-speaking Jewish intelligentsia in the mid-2000s who pointed out the "absurdity of the legislation" as they objected to the idea of Pushkin being cast as a "foreign author" whose work needed to be translated into Ukrainian.[98]

Others I met, especially the younger Odesans, were not troubled by the new rules and knew well how to maneuver different situations, depending on the circumstances. Although Ukrainian is the only official language, anthropologist Abel Polese and colleagues remind us that there's a difference between language policies and language use: language politics are always negotiated between public and private spaces. In the Odesa I witnessed during my earlier fieldwork in 2005–7, people often switched between Ukrainian and Russian on a case-by-case basis, depending on their knowledge and habits—using Ukrainian, if they could and if required, in public spaces and Russian for personal and intimate conversations.[99] It was not uncommon for an official meeting, lecture, or even a conversation to start in Ukrainian and end in Russian. But amid the process of Ukrainization, the (Ukrainian) language that emerged from second-class status became fashionable for a younger sect to use.[100] The anti-Russian sentiment in Ukraine—caused by the resentment felt by many Ukrainians, Odesans included, after the 2013–14 events and even more so after Russia's invasion in 2022—influenced many Odesans to adopt Ukrainian as a statement of their loyalty to Ukraine, first and foremost in public spaces. In private spaces, many still rely on Russian since it is the language in which they feel more comfortable expressing themselves, but attitudes towards, and use of, Ukrainian has changed from a practical question to a political statement.[101]

At the same time, however, even those Odesan Jews who regularly spoke Ukrainian objected to the pressure they felt, even among some peers, to use it as proof of patriotism or loyalty as Ukrainian citizens.[102] In their view, language and geography could become the exclusive markers of Ukrainian identity.[103] Most of the younger Jewish Odesans who supported the popularization of the Ukrainian language believed that the development of such markers needed to come naturally, which would take time. From the mid-2000s, when I visited Odesa, to the early 2020s—as I write this book—none of my Jewish Odesan friends has switched from using Russian exclusively to using Ukrainian exclusively. Those who know Ukrainian well enough use it alongside Russian when appropriate. Some have made more of an effort to read or write in Ukrainian. Most understand and read both languages with ease, though some struggle to work and communicate in Ukrainian freely. But they all value the freedom to choose, recognizing some situations as appropriate for Russian and others for Ukrainian. Many Jewish Ukrainians denounce the claims that they are discriminated against as Russian speakers and argue that in instances when they are using Ukrainian, they are not acting out of fear or pressure from the state but, rather, are exercising their personal choice. Clearly, these choices are also supported by the legislation and infrastructure in place to support Ukrainian

Figure 7.4. The Ukrainian flag replacing the statue of Catherine II, January 2023. Photo by and courtesy of Igor Oks.

as the national language. Undoubtedly, as I discuss in Odesa-after-Maidan in the epilogue, more Jewish Odesans and others have developed a more positive attitude toward the Ukrainian language without abandoning Russian.

In 2007, some Ukrainian groups protested at the unveiling of a new monument to the Russian empress Catherine II (the city's founder). The new statue was part of Odesa's ongoing historic restoration, replacing the original one removed by Soviet authorities in the late 1920s. The activists petitioned the Security Services of Ukraine against the monument's resurrection, arguing that it would entrench interethnic hostility and provoke chaos and anarchy in Odesa.[104] Their protests invoked the heroism of the Cossack troops who died resisting the imposition of Russian imperialism and Catherine II's orders to liquidate the Zaporizhian Sich (a semiautonomous Cossack polity) in 1775. This violent rallying of Ukrainian nationalist forces was seen as a threat by some local Odesans, and its reverberations went well beyond that particular incident.[105] In December 2022, amid Russia's war on Ukraine, the monument to Catherine II was dismantled as part of Ukraine's campaign to clear public spaces of monuments to Russia. The decision of the city authorities was supported by the majority of the citizens who voted in an online poll, and the statue

of Catherine was moved to the Odesa Fine Arts Museum.[106] Most Ukrainian
Jews I discussed the event with thought that, as the monument was vandalized
numerous times and stirred up such emotional havoc, it was best the statue
be moved away from its prominent position and kept safe elsewhere. Others
clearly saw it as a relic of the Russian imperialism and colonialism they were
fighting in this war.

These sentiments stood in contrast to those I observed earlier, in 2005, when
some Odesans were concerned by Ukraine's nationalistic turn and objected to
the politicians trying to situate Odesa within this new Ukrainian project and,
in their minds, downplaying the city's international connections and inherent
links to Russia. People spoke of how politicians insisted on making fundamental distinctions between Russia and the Ukraine. In the words of Arcadiy,
a middle-aged cab driver I met in 2007, "I have relatives there [in Russia], and
I'm not going to turn my back on them because the politicians are having a
quarrel. We're all the same people when it comes down to it. We all grew up
on the same playground." While Putin's rhetoric of Russians and Ukrainians
as one people is rejected by Odesans and other citizens of Ukraine, many of
my earlier interviews reveal a sincere connection to Russian culture—a connection that has been troubled and, in many instances, undone by the ongoing
war. For example, after Russia's invasion of Ukraine in 2022, demands for the
legitimacy of Russian as a second language in Ukraine became taboo, and yet I
recall many of my older interlocutors interviewed in the mid-2000s complaining about old Soviet movies on TV being dubbed in Ukrainian. "They should
recognize the legitimacy of both languages," sixty-plus Inga said to me as she
raised issues with Ukrainian-dubbed films and her inability to fully understand
the dialogue.

In the current reality of war-scarred Odesa, I imagine that screening an old
Soviet film would raise different concerns and trigger a set of radically different responses.

Conclusion

This chapter has illustrated the interplay of local, national, and global forces
vying for the legacy of Odesa and thus shaping the character of Odesa as a city,
a cultural index, and a field of social relations, values, and imagination. Just as
in Soviet times—when "the mythical Odessa, cosmopolitan, Jewish, full of
witty, ironic tricksters like Ostap Bender, functioned as a counter-site to the
homogenizing influence of Soviet regime"—in the post-Soviet reality of the
twenty-first century, Odesa's Jews looked to the city's myth and its Jewishness
as a way to resist strong currents of national and religious revivals that could
threaten the city's unique qualities.[107] Ironically, after Russia launched a war on

Ukraine, Jewishness was used not to undermine Ukrainization but to support it and to undermine Putin's claims about Odesa being a "Russian" city. Thus, we can see how the new reality of war has transformed the image of Odesa from a Jewish city to a Ukrainian-Jewish city, but it has not shifted its image as an international and cosmopolitan place. Recognized by UNESCO in 2023 for its "outstanding universal value" visible through "its heterogenous architecture that reflects the diversity of its multicultural trading communities," Odesa also remains a place of "notable diversity" through its Jewish presence and multinational population, a symbol of an ethnically and religiously diverse Ukraine.[108]

Anthropologist Michael Herzfeld writes that stereotypes may function both to sustain and to struggle against configurations of power, "contesting and reproducing power relations on the local level."[109] The term "Jewish" as used by most of my interlocutors to describe their city in the mid-2000s goes beyond Herzfeld's interpretation of stereotypes as reductive and marginalizing. In actuality, the Jewish trope plays multiple roles. In calling their city Jewish, Jewish Odesans don't literally mean that only Jews live there or that they dominate the place in any significant way.[110] Rather, this self-stereotype stands in for other idiomatic ways of expressing what distinguishes Odesa—"cosmopolitan," "tolerant," and "international." These are ideas supported and expressed by the historical and continuing presence of Jews as an accepted ethnic and religious minority. It's also a way of crediting Jews with much of the special flavor of the city's dialect, cuisine, humor, music, and literature, and hence, with its feeling of being "truly Odesan." Understood this way, as a metonym for the city's famous attributes, the stereotype of Odesa as a "Jewish" city doesn't displace its other characteristics (or its other inhabitants). It was precisely this displacement that some Odesans interviewed in my early fieldwork feared might come to pass from a "Ukrainian" appropriation of the city's historical narrative, language, and culture.

This chapter therefore argues that the inconsistencies, contradictions, and complexities found in the "insider" discourse of the city's Jews exemplify how—following Herzfeld—stereotyping can be simultaneously a strategy of dominance, a tactic of resistance, a claim to some ownership of particular cultural traits, and a way to maintain long-distance ties between home and its many peripheries. Engaging in what Herzfeld calls "cultural intimacy," Odesans may be seen as internally questioning the real existence and measure of their city's Jewish stereotype, while externally supporting the stereotype when they feel it's needed to preserve the "special" status of the city and of themselves as its representatives.[111] Their attachment to the city's legacy serves as a strategy not just for living, but for living a life with distinction.

Conclusion

Negotiating Traditions

As we have seen throughout this book, Jewish identities in contemporary Odesa take many complex forms. Where once the Soviet state used "Jewish" to describe a broadly defined nationality, in the years after Ukraine's independence, new and competing senses arose of what it means to be a Jew, and these played out across categories of community, nationality, and religion. Concepts of Jewishness are shaped by the experiences of those who emigrated, those who stayed back, those who left only to return, and those who have built lives that move between Odesa and elsewhere. More discretely, the different forms of Jewish belonging at work in post-Soviet Odesa have been refined by the intricacies of language, kinship, education, political loyalties, local and international networks, and other variables of cultural capital. Undoubtedly, Odesa's Jewishness has also been shaped by geopolitical conflict and war. While I address these developments in the epilogue, the analysis and effects of the ongoing war on Odesa's Jewish life go beyond the scope of this book and are the subject of my subsequent study.

In this book, narrated life histories, informal conversations, interviews with Odesan Jews of various backgrounds and ages, and my own observations all demonstrate the wide range of experiences that have shaped Jewish life in Odesa two decades after Ukraine's independence. Through stories of prerevolutionary, Soviet, Nazi-occupied, and post-Soviet Odesa, as recounted by elderly Odesan Jews, and through the varied and unpredictable life trajectories of middle-aged and younger Odesans, I learned the processes by which Jewishness was constantly being remade and reshaped, developed from abroad and cultivated from within—in every case, with unexpected results.

This complex construction of Jewishness stands apart from the all-too-reductive image of Soviet and post-Soviet Jewry as a case of suspension and revival. While it was always far too simple to cast Jewish life under the Soviet period as a matter of state antisemitism and repression, we can trace how that image did in fact play a role in fueling projects of post-Soviet Jewish identity through the influence of international philanthropy and new forms of migration from, and to, Odesa. In turn, these variables created many forms of Jewish identification—with their different bases of affiliation, loyalty, and obligation—that made up Jewish realities at the time of my fieldwork. These forms of identification were neither static nor predictable. Crafted in the spheres of Odesa's particular urban climate, they are nonetheless influenced by the transformations affecting the Ukrainian nation-state and the global forces that impact its politics today. Therefore, the transitions of Jewish identification in contemporary Odesa—as witnessed on individual, familial, and communal levels—must be understood as ambiguous, contingent, sometimes contradictory, and always affected by greater societal and political pressures.

Odesa as a Place

Previous chapters have made clear that Odesa has never been a mere backdrop for the cultivation of Jewish identities: it has played a significant role in how Jews there have come to understand themselves. In turn, the city's Jewish history has molded its image as a cosmopolitan, tolerant, and unique space within the Soviet and post-Soviet worlds. The qualities that make Odesa so distinctive emerged from both its historical development and what we've seen as the Odesa myth. This elaborate sense of place shaped how local Jews now make sense of their reality and project themselves forward. When I observed the city from 2005 to 2007, it seemed that in every realm—past, present, and future—some Odesans defended the idea that their city represents something vitally different from the Russian Empire, from the USSR, and, at that time, from the rest of Ukraine.

But in more recent years, with the increased political tension and Russia's invasion of Ukraine in 2014 and larger assault in 2022, more and more Odesan Jews saw their city as a Ukrainian city (a point I return to in the epilogue). In the post-Maidan years, many of the Jewish Odesans I spoke with expressed a desire for Odesa to remain the city they knew—one that embraced rather than rejected ethnic and religious difference. Religious leaders of different faiths openly protested against Russia's aggression at the onset of Russia's full-scale invasion. On March 22, 2022, representatives of Odesa's largest Christian churches, along with one of the chief rabbis of Odesa, Chabad rabbi Avraham Wolf, and Deputy Imam Askar Olegovich Jasimov delivered a powerful address to Odesans that was streamed on the official channel of the Department of

Information and Public Relations of the Odesa City Council. In a plea to end
the war and support peace in Odesa, the religious leaders cited the fact that
Odesa has always harbored people of various nationalities and faiths who have
managed to coexist despite their differences. "Let this be a prayer for the city
as well as the world that Odesa represents to us all," said Archpriest Pavlo Po-
lenchuk (Orthodox Ukrainian Church—Moscow Patriarchate). The leader of
the Orthodox Ukrainian church, Father Teodor Orobets, spoke more directly
to the Russian aggressor, stating that "free people do not need liberation and
release. . . . The world that Russia brings is not peace, it is evil." Father Oleksandr Semrechinsky (Ukrainian Greek Catholic Church), chief chaplain of
the naval force in Odesa, said, "The city of Odesa is one big family. In this
family we are different, but we are one. We value everything that makes us
a family. We only need to be left alone to develop as a multireligious, multiethnic family, part of the Ukrainian land, the Ukrainian state, looking to the
future." Deputy Imam Jasimov added, "We are all united in the fight against
evil, and evil has no nationality." A prayer for the city was also voiced as a
prayer for the world of tolerance that Odesa represents and for all that is dear
to the city's residents. "I am proud to live in a city where I can speak in Russian
and everyone understands me and helps me," Rabbi Wolf said in conclusion.
"This is the most loyal city and country for any nation where you can work and
develop."[1] In this way, Odesa offers counterevidence to the recent antiessen-
tialist trend that questions the supposed bonds between people, culture, and
territory.[2]

By arguing for this interrelation of Jewishness to Odesa and Odesa to Jewishness, I'm not suggesting that all Odesans relate to their city in the same way,
or even see it as "Jewish." As mentioned before, Ukrainian, Greek, Turkish,
Moldovan, Italian, and other Odesas also exist in the city's popular culture,
imagination, and history. Even some places that are historically Jewish have
undergone transformations and produced an array of different memories. Students who played basketball in the Glavnaya (Main) Synagogue when it was
used as a sports hall in the Soviet period have their own connections and associations with that building. As modern Jewish studies scholar Barbara Mann
writes, "We create different, overlapping spaces, speaking about them in different languages, even calling the very same sites by different names."[3] Still,
there's no denying that the city's Jewish presence (both real and mythical)
provides crucial reference points for a larger, dispersed "imagined community" beyond the realm of the city's Jewish population. Indeed, the influence
of Odesa stretches far beyond its physical location, coming alive in memories,
photographs, memoirs, literature, art, discourse, songs, cuisine, and the rhythm
of everyday conversation. What it means to be an Odesan has changed with the

passage of time and the distance of its emigrants. But many feel that the city, or Odesa Mama, as some call it, has raised a unique type of person. Writing in kinship terms, historian Patricia Herlihy notes how "Odessa has always had a strong sense of its unique cosmopolitan history, priding itself on loose but real ties with the center" and earning a reputation among state rulers as an "enfant terrible" or the "slightly eccentric member" of a nation or family.[4] Indeed, Odesans see themselves as an urban kinship group, and others see them as a people defined by their city—always in positive, uplifting ways.

At the same time, the attachment to the city felt by Odesa's Jews has been affected by the migration of people and ideas, including the new constellations of ethnoreligious identities that have emerged, both Jewish and non-Jewish. In the world of Jewish development, for example, Odesa is just one among many post-Soviet cities categorized as "in need." As chapter 5 detailed, some philanthropic missions identified Odesa as a place of Jewish rebirth but also as a historical relic of Jewish suffering and oppression. Some local Jews felt that such projections offended their status as *Odesits*, while others willingly engaged with development projects, appreciating the visits and donations and even coming to rely on them. Many saw the arrival of foreign delegations, Jewish emissaries, and tourists from abroad as opportunities to connect with world Jewry and the wider world in general.

Thirty years after the collapse of the Soviet Union, Odesa's Jews have been introduced to a new symbolic vocabulary—the lingua franca of an international Judaism. And just as philanthropy has flowed in from outside, it has also been cultivated by ex-Soviet Jewry and those with connections to former Soviet states, as in the case of the Genesis Philanthropy Group and Limmud FSU, both set up as organizations that promote the growth and development of Russian-speaking Jewish culture.[5]

The opportunities for identification with the larger Jewish world have held particular sway over the younger generations of Odesa's Jews. They have come of age in a more religiously infused environment, where the traditions of Jewish faith and observance—daily prayer, wearing a kippah, observing Shabbat, eating kosher food, and so on—are taught and seen. The educational and international institutions that took root after the fall of the Soviet Union introduced these young people to some of the defining features of Jewish life. For example, consider the more than three hundred children being raised in the Tikva and Chabad orphanages run by the Orthodox congregations and the students in Jewish kindergartens and schools, including the boy who spoke to my father and me in the park (described at the start of this book). For those children, the sense of Jewish life in Odesa could hardly be further from the experiences of secular, unaffiliated, and older Jews.

Although some of the observant Jews I met had turned to Judaism before the development of organized Jewish life in Odesa, there's no question that the investments of international Jewish organizations have greatly raised the profile of religious observance and knowledge. Creating new institutions spreads religious values to the larger Jewish community, fuels philanthropic efforts, and thus brings in many Jews from abroad—both the tourists attracted by online advertisements selling Odesa as a Jewish destination and the philanthropists who weave Odesa into their understanding of an expanding Jewish world.

The Complexities of Odesa's Jewish Revival

Claims that Jewish life in Odesa had undergone a "revival" after the fall of communism suggest a past neatly recovered and triumphantly restored, as if the Soviet period had been cleanly swept aside. Chabad's website, for example, proclaims, "Jewish community activities are increasing day after day. Many new people come back to their roots, the heritage of their lost ancestors. They taste the sweet fruits of *Yiddishkeit* and learn more and more about the great culture and traditions of their people."[6] In the second decade after Ukraine's independence, Jewish life in Odesa is partly the product of those newly constituted religious institutions and the recently established organizations that have helped cultivate vivid signs of Jewish life throughout the city.[7]

In connecting Odesa's Jewry to a history of the Jewish people, Chabad's message and others like it portray a continuity between Odesa and the Jewish people that is bound by a common history, culture, and the traditions of Judaism. Such messages gloss over the more pragmatic reasons for Jews to turn to organized Jewish life, the multidirectional commitments to observance (including abandonment), and the diversity of Jewish traditions and people, presented previously as a singular entity. And thus, as I've tried to show in this book, understanding this Jewish "revival" means asking, What is being revived, and what is being created, and why? On what basis? By whom, and for whom?

My findings reveal the complexity embedded in the common assumption that within postsocialist societies, "a widening spectrum of individuals and organizations are looking to the sacred" and that religious affiliation is generally on the rise.[8] In fact, many individuals in post-Soviet settings weren't initially drawn to religious affiliation for the sake of the "sacred," even if this later became important to them. Within the affiliated community, and all the more outside it, Jews challenged one another on their motives for religious membership. Indeed, there were many reasons that brought Jews to organized Jewish life and to religion—and, as in the case of Nina and others, the reasons weren't always in the canon of Judaism.

It might be said that the young people turning to Judaism as religious practice and adopting a form of Zionist zeal are seeking out versions of prerevolutionary Jewish life. But we've seen that their motivation is often to *explore* the links to Jewish Odesa through the new institutions that emerged in the post-Soviet context. When young people joined a religious community, there was no certainty that they would remain adherent or keep following its practices. In fact, the religious "transformations" I witnessed in Odesa were far from complete: they were frequently multidirectional, sometimes fraught, and often shaped by ambivalence.

For those who do sustain their religious life, Jewish Odesa is now largely Orthodox. Community membership is thus mainly divided between the Litvak and Chabad congregations. Despite their different approaches, both groups agree that the Reform congregation "doesn't have the same vision of Judaism as the Orthodox movement."[9] The handover of the original Brody Reform Synagogue building to Chabad Lubavitch in 2016 proved to the Reform rabbi that Chabad's clout in Odesa (and in many other key former Soviet Union cities) is unassailable and will ultimately dominate the realm of Jewish authority.

The religious revivals led by Christians and Muslims in the former Soviet states are open to all and seeking converts, but Odesa's Jewish leaders have largely followed the strict criteria based on halakha that regulates access and recognition. These criteria are sometimes at odds with the previous markers of Jewish identification, whether specified by the state or culturally adopted. The Litvak and Chabad Orthodox congregations both grew larger; other Jewish congregations did as well, albeit more slowly. Since my initial departure from Odesa in 2007, I kept in touch with friends there, and I saw many of them become more observant of religious commandments and more engaged in organized Jewish life during my subsequent visits in 2014 and 2019. Several religious Jewish women started to dress more modestly and cover their hair. Those who'd already worn discreet head coverings moved on to wigs. Some of the men grew beards or sidelocks and adopted religious garments; some families suspended travel on Shabbat and abandoned habits like eating pork. In other words, as more Jews actively identified themselves as Jews, they did so through the strictures of Judaism. New congregations also formed, including a conservative Jewish congregation. It will be interesting to see how its presence might shift the polarized and politicized relations of the existing Jewish congregations, though I suspect that the more established Orthodox communities will continue to dominate.

Many of the stories in this book reveal radically different paths taken to reach those multiple forms of Jewish self-identification—ranging from a familiar immersion in Zionism to religiosity and to a secularism carried over from

the Soviet period. Chapters 4 and 6 map out how families and friends of different orientations negotiated these paths of identification. In the same chapters,
I highlight the contingent, partial, and sometimes impermanent nature of the
decision to become an *iudei*, a migrant, a Zionist, an Israeli, or an otherwise affiliated Jew. In practice, such categories weren't strictly defined: they were often
merged with other meaningful orientations, or contorted and compromised to
accommodate an individual's life.

The experiences of returnees and transmigrants added another dimension
to the development of the various Jewish identities, communities, and spaces
between home and diaspora that are all elements of this "revival."[10] My ethnography thus adds to the existing critiques of the binary home/diaspora model,
showing how Jews said to be living "in the diaspora" actually experience their
locale as their home, and extend this sentiment to other territories of belonging where family and friends reside, or with which they connect on the basis
of language, culture, and familial, entrepreneurial, and professional networks.
In this way, although Israel was one of the countries to which Odesan Jews
expressed an attachment, they thought of it in terms of personal relations. For
many of the Jews I met during my initial fieldwork, Israel wasn't a place they
intended to return to, either bodily or metaphorically, but as living conditions
deteriorated during the war, it became a real home to many who made aliyah.

Russia's 2022 invasion has created yet another seismic shift in identification
with place. The political conditions have driven more Jews to look to Israel as an
escape, even if many others have chosen to evacuate to neighboring countries,
including Poland, Hungary, Germany, and Moldova. Certainly, many hope to
return to Odesa eventually, but the future effects of these wartime evacuations
remain profoundly uncertain.

Jewishness and Contested Cosmopolitanism

One key theme in this book is the way a discourse of Odesa as a cosmopolitan
and Jewish city has shaped the identity politics among Odesa's Jewry and continues to inform their ideas about the city, their views on events unfolding in
the region, and their vision of their future. I have sought to demonstrate the
complexity and diversity of different people's engagement with this discourse.
I found that Jewish Odesans were experiencing multiple *cosmopolitanisms* that
called up different historical dimensions of the city's multicultural and ethnically diverse past, as well as links to the wider world through the networks
shaped by transnational organizations, tourism, and philanthropy.

It's too early to predict the full outcome of the current conflict, but we can
see that Ukrainian-Jewish solidarity speaks of a still newer cosmopolitan state

of mind for both groups. The ability to move beyond the painful episodes of Ukrainian-Jewish history exhibits the "capacity for openness and appreciation for others" described as a defining feature of cosmopolitanism by Caroline Humphrey and Vera Skvirskaja.[11] For the most part, Jews in Ukraine have pledged their loyalty to the Ukrainian state and the Ukrainian language as a stance against Russian aggression, but in taking this stand, they haven't abandoned their native Russian tongue—and many haven't abandoned friends from Russia who support them, either. The entanglements of Russian, Ukrainian, and Jewish heritage and culture are messy but real and need further research, especially in light of the current war.

Ukrainian Jewry who support the Ukrainian nation and feel an attachment to the state demonstrate a shift away from the extremely negative image of right-wing nationalist groups with antisemitic rhetoric and ideology to an all-inclusive model of Ukrainian nationalism—one defined by cosmopolitan values and virtues. Posting pictures of themselves in prayer on Facebook under the heading "An ordinary Monday of Ukrainian neo-Nazis in Odessa" (written in Russian), four young Jewish Odesans mocked Putin's claims that Ukraine is run by fascists—as well as the idea that either Jews or Russian speakers were persecuted groups in Ukraine. This post demonstrates their open practice of Judaism and their belonging in Ukraine. It also articulates a number of important points about identity politics, representing another layer of reality beyond the implicit binary of Russians versus Ukrainians, Jews versus Ukrainians, and Jew versus Jew that's visible in the popular press and alive in public perceptions. In fact, young Jews in Odesa feel free to identify themselves as Jews and as Ukrainians in any way they choose, without a noticeable contradiction linked to Soviet definitions of ethnicity or history. They are not reined back by historical memory or Russia's propaganda; in fact, they mock them with humor.[12]

We can say that the cosmopolitanisms Jews brought to Odesa are now connected with the idea of a plural Ukraine. Of course, the solidarity expressed for Ukraine has also fragmented many family units, friendships, and other collectives that are divided by individuals' stances on the war and by the stigma and hatred toward all things Russian. Diversity, as we know, does not always allow and compel the awareness of the cultural "other," nor does it guarantee peaceful relations.[13] This layer of reality also hinders lived cosmopolitanism in a major way and potentially threatens the "urbanity" described by Blair Ruble.[14]

The stark separation of politics from everyday life that Odesa maintained for much of its history has also been compromised since the Maidan protests and now the war with Russia. Ethnic, political, and religious conflicts have revealed the limits of Odesa's long-standing myth of peaceful, apolitical coexistence. But even before the collapse of Russian and Ukrainian ties,

Skvirskaja, describing the city in 2006, stated that "indifference, rather than engagement with difference" appears to be the "new mode of co-residence and coexistence in Odessa."[15] Comparing Odesa with other great cities, from Bukhara to Venice, Humphrey and Skvirskaja describe it as "post-cosmopolitan." They recognize that the inhabitants of Odesa and other comparable cities harbor "a sense that something precious has been lost, or sidelined, and that other less generous relations have taken its place."[16] In the view of these authors, the older diasporas that once defined the city—Greek, Jewish, and German—have passed from Odesa, while communities of new migrants from the rural hinterland and from Turkey, China, Chechnya, and other countries haven't blended into the larger social milieu.[17] I suggest that rather than thinking of urban cosmopolitanisms as beginning and ending in Odesa, we must think of cosmopolitanism as an ongoing, evolving process of contested interpretations.

For example, as we saw in chapter 7, many would agree that "Old Odessa" had already been eroded by an outflow of the city's Jews and the development of a Jewish community that was drawing stricter boundaries for membership based on Orthodox Jewish doctrine. This process, in the eyes of some older generations of Jewish Odesans, altered the engagement and exposure of Jews with others. To the younger generations, however, it was these processes that were opening the city to the wider Jewish world. This generational difference in outlook on the very idea of a cosmopolitan Odesa is why I believe that Jewishness still has a strong metonymic relationship to Odesa. Jews still stand for all the groups that the city has absorbed with tolerance throughout its history, however idealized this vision of Odesa may be.[18] And because the metonym is an idealized projection, the city's Jewishness doesn't entirely depend on the actual number of Jews residing there. Of course, a myth of tolerance and a cosmopolitan ethos aren't indestructible, and the actual practices and understandings of Jewishness and cosmopolitanism among Odesan Jewry are bound to be in flux.

This recalls the view put forth by historian Samuel Ramer and author and academic Blair Ruble in their collection *Place, Identity and Urban Culture: Odesa and New Orleans*.[19] They describe the unique qualities exhibited through the interaction of place and diversity in these two cities, both historically and today. For instance, Ruble emphasizes the specific qualities of Odesa and New Orleans as "model" cities for displaying multiculturalism in their streets—both are "urbane" insofar as they offer up the space and the pervasive willingness of their residents to engage with and accept the other. The authors point out that the mix of ethnicities, religions, and foreigners is facilitated by the layouts of both cities: pedestrian streets, parks and public squares, plentiful access to diverse cuisines, and colorful architecture. In each city, writes Ramer, the members of any one group may feel their minority status less acutely than they would in rural areas, and the distinctive sense of urban identity enhances the residents' sense of their personal identity as "special" and "significant."[20] Odesa's historical modes of coexistence are threatened, Ruble notes, by the homogenization that comes from Ukrainian nation building.

While Ruble is correct that homogenization of any kind threatens Odesa's lived cosmopolitanism, it's important to make a distinction. Ukraine's government policies after the Orange Revolution of 2004 were designed to create a coherent pan-national Ukrainian identity, and some Odesans saw aspects of these policies as "an attack on the city's cosmopolitan orientation and linguistic aesthetics."[21] But other Odesans welcomed them. And while language politics remained at the core of the argument voiced by Russian-speaking Odesans against Ukrainization, the same individuals accepted and supported other aspects of Ukrainian nationalism, including reorienting the country's geopolitical allegiances toward the West and away from Russia.

In different circumstances, the ethnic and religious boundaries observed in Odesa in the mid-2000s were fluid, and at times the categories of "Russian," "Russian-speaking," "Jewish," "Ukrainian," and even "Christian" merged. That was especially true in the powerful narrative of what it meant to be "Odessan" and thus "cosmopolitan," as well as in the context of ethnically and religiously mixed and bilingual families and of Jews like Nina, who saw themselves as ethnically Jewish but practiced a Christian faith. At the time of my fieldwork, Jewish identity was also entwined with those legacies of Soviet ideology and the meanings embedded in being "Russian," "Ukrainian," or "Odessan."

Complicating matters further, even though Odesan Jews were still very much tied to the larger Russian-speaking world, some were also becoming Ukrainian: learning Ukrainian history, literature, and culture; learning and using the Ukrainian language; and developing an affinity with Ukraine that they might have not experienced before. Various Jewish and Ukrainian organizations worked to build a dialogue and establish ties between Jews and Ukrainians. It was all part of their effort to overcome the aspect of Jewish history in Ukraine that's defined by pogroms and the Holocaust, and to learn about other dimensions of Ukrainian-Jewish relations.[22] These developments and conversations are extremely important for Ukrainians and Jews in the country as well as those in diaspora communities. They address historical traumas, facilitate healing, and teach new generations of Ukrainians and Jews about their shared history. They also break through the stereotyped image of Ukrainians as Nazi collaborators and antisemites, which has been spread in recent Russian propaganda and also remains alive in the perception of some Jews in and outside of Ukraine. Equally troubling for others is the remaking of historical narratives that overlook antisemitic atrocities. An honest conversation focused on a collaboration to see the past for all that it was, and also to make a distinction between then and now, is vital for developing a healthy and fruitful future for Ukrainian-Jewish relations. Discussing the historical parallels between Jews and Ukrainians, Amelia Glaser reminds us that we cannot pretend these groups have always gotten along. We need to see their history for all that it was: moments of solidarity but also periods of competition, scapegoating, and even competitive victimhood and betrayal.[23] We cannot collapse all time frames for a homogeneous picture of one sort or another. It's important to acknowledge the contradictions, changes, continuities, and developments that have always shaped Ukrainian-Jewish relations.

While ethnic, civil, and linguistic differences have become more politicized, Odesa's Jews find themselves as Russian-speaking and, increasingly, Ukrainian-speaking citizens of Ukraine, transcending many boundaries of separation. It wouldn't be surprising, then, for various threats of homogenization to stimulate the continuation of Odesa's discourse of cosmopolitanism, and for that discourse to become a means to subvert and resist the imposition of a strictly limited national and religious identity. In the context of war, the city's Jewishness, Ukrainianness, and cosmopolitan mix of the two are also powerful tools of resistance against the prevailing dominance of Russian imperialism.

The fight to maintain Odesa's designation as a Jewish place is, by extension, a battle for a historically constituted, if now weakened, process of cosmopolitanism—an antinationalistic ethos, international and open. It's hard not to think that if the leaders of national and religious movements in Odesa would adopt these sentiments and incorporate them into their visions of the city as a whole, they might achieve a greater level of integration, understanding, and prosperity for their own institutions.

Transforming Traditions

The decline of Jewish tradition in the Soviet Union had multiple causes: the destruction of religious institutions because of secularization, the catastrophe of the Holocaust, emigration, postwar grassroot antisemitism, and state antisemitic repression. As mentioned in the first two chapters of this book, some Jews voluntarily gave up their "traditions" as a way to "elevate" themselves above the shtetl. But when new Jewish traditions—Israeli, Litvak, Chabad, and others—were adopted, what remained of an old system of meaning was infused with new symbolism and differing ideologies, visions, and moralities.

The negotiations and contestations seen in Odesa's Jewish community are thus connected to larger processes of transformation that are visible across the former Soviet states.

Ethnic, religious, and national identities created new systems of meaning and were pitted against existing rubrics of moral standing, solidarity, and material wealth derived from the specific history of Soviet socialization. For the younger generations, life in the Soviet Union is but a faint memory or legend of the past, but for older Odesan Jews, it remains a key element of their identity—the ideological bedrock for how they perceive the cultural and political dynamics of their city postindependence. These generational divides fuel debates about authenticity that reveal the entanglements of secularism and religiosity, nationalism and cosmopolitanism, modernity and traditionalism, and the larger question of what it means to be a Jew. Indeed, different Jewish voices in Odesa appropriate, uphold, and challenge current developments in living Jewish practices as authentic, necessary, important, and progressive. The bottom-up approach to analyzing the religious revival in Odesa has offered us the perspective of members of different Jewish communities being involved at a local level. In the end, the discourse of community members and other unaffiliated local Jews—alongside the visions of Jewish leaders—paints a detailed and panoramic picture of the transformations seen at individual, familial, and community levels, inclusive of the contradictions, gaps, inconsistencies, and paradoxes of daily life.

Jewish practices and discourse in Odesa, like those Lara Deeb describes among practicing Muslims in Lebanon, "have been variously interpreted, debated, and authorized through its history."[24] In contrast with Deeb's example, however, a "break in continuity" occurred under Soviet rule, and thus it's questionable how much we can speak of continuation of practice. To establish their authority, Jewish religious leaders have constructed and presented "a community and a tradition . . . as unchanging and invariant."[25] The "social and cultural constructionism" observed by Galina Zelenina in the context of the Chabad movement in Moscow resonates with Odesa in many ways. Above all, it exemplifies the notion of an "invented tradition" extended to an "imagined community" of local Jewry.

The taxi driver we met in the introduction assumed that the observant families crossing the street near the synagogue were tourists, based on their black religious dress and head coverings. In other words, public religiosity still seems of place to some, while for many others, these symbols have been normalized and institutionalized, becoming an integral part of contemporary Odesa. Although most leaders of religious institutions in Ukraine are foreign,

Odesan Jews are starting to assume important roles in their community. As the Chabad rebbetzin Chaya Wolf said, "It used to be that all the teachers in the Jewish schools came from Israel, but now graduates of our own Jewish schools are coming back to teach here." Three local kolel graduates who received their rabbinic qualifications in Israel served as rabbis in Odesa before the war.[26]

In fact, Chaya's own case also demonstrates the complexity of the relations that religious emissaries build in the places they move to "on assignment" but come to regard as home. Born in Israel, Chaya has now spent more than half her life in Odesa. Although she speaks Russian with a heavy Israeli accent, she identifies with Odesa as the birthplace of her mother. Chaya's parents immigrated to Israel from the Soviet Union, but she grew up knowing little of their history or native tongue. Linking her role in Odesa with her family heritage, she sees it as her mission to repair a world that was broken for the Jews of her parents' generation. Her father was fired from his job and imprisoned after Stalin's death for practicing Judaism; today, Chaya is advancing Jewish practice as the norm. She admits that her mother can't believe how much attitudes have changed toward Jews or how much freedom Jews now enjoy in Odesa.[27] Along with her husband and other Israeli families, Chaya has helped integrate many traditional Jewish practices, such as kashrut, mikvah, chuppah, Brit Milah, Shabbat, and Jewish burial, as well as less obvious practices like seeking a rabbi's advice.[28]

While some elderly Odesan Jews believe that the return of these old traditions is undoing the "modernization" of the Soviet project, which took Jews out of their peripheral religious communities and brought them into the center of modern society, Rabbi Wolf and other religious emissaries view their work as the complete opposite: modernizing the secular. Indeed, many observant Jews involved in organized Jewish life see themselves as both modern *and* religious. Perhaps for those elderly Jews like Viktor and Olga, the creation of a Ukrainian Jewry linked to Judaism and Ukraine is undermining modernization on multiple levels. As Yohanan Petrovsky-Shtern reminds us, the dominant view perpetuated by Russian-oriented Jews was that Russia stood for Jewish modernization, whereas Ukraine, nicknamed Little Russia, did not.[29]

These sentiments aren't specific to Odesa or to Judaism. Sonja Luehrmann notes that religious revivals challenge the predictions of modernization theory, and Lara Deeb, writing about pious Shi'i Muslim women, points out that "public religiosities have emerged across the globe ... [and] have contributed to the collapse of the notion that religion and modernity are incompatible."[30] Although Deeb's examples include "Christian fundamentalists" and "ultra-orthodox

Jews," I think her statement can be applied to the larger insurgence of religion in public life due to many religious organizations, not just the ultra-orthodox or fundamentalists.

Throughout Jewish history, "there has been a constant redrawing of the cultural boundaries as a consequence of migrations, persecutions, and other fluctuations in Jewish social and economic fortunes."[31] Transformation in everyday religion, culture, communal life, and the representation of Jews isn't specific to Odesa or to the present day. It is part of Jewish history. In this book, however, I have strived to show those transformations and their dynamics through the perspectives of discrete lives. I saw individuals change their opinions, affiliations, attachments, and reasoning with regard to their own Jewish identifications and those of others. And of course, changes came in other, unavoidable ways as well. Most of my dearest elderly friends have passed away since the time of my fieldwork, and with them, their memories, stories, and experiences of Jewish life are gone as well.

Odesa is blessed with citizens who love the city and care deeply about its past. Before the outbreak of the war, two of my friends, a tour guide of Jewish Ukraine based in Tel Aviv and another young historian based in Odesa, were working with the Museum of the History of Odesa Jews on an online collection of memoirs and life histories of Soviet Odesans, one of the many heritage projects halted by the war. Once published, these oral histories, collected across the globe, will open the eyes of the world to a new layer of Soviet Jewish experiences and help us contextualize what it has meant to be Jewish in Odesa and what it means today.

History is one means by which Odesans have defended their Jewish values, progressive thinking, connections to the intelligentsia, unique humor and wit, and the openness, that Odesa has extended to Jews—and to people of all nations. In the more than thirty years since Ukraine's independence, Odesa has lost many of its Jewish residents. It has also recovered many of its Jewish spaces, welcomed new Jews and Jewish organizations, adopted new Jewish practices, and built a network of connections with world Jewry. Throughout these transformations, the city has retained its reputation as a unique place for Jews. It remains a powerful frame of belonging for Jewish Odesans at home and abroad. Here Jewishness doesn't stand in isolation from other practices, associations, or parameters of urban identity: Jewish institutions and community structures are tied into the local, national, and international geopolitical realms. Odesan Jews, especially the younger generations, see themselves as part of Ukraine's Jewish experience and larger world Jewish affairs in a way their parents and grandparents never did.

Odesa's Jewish features and lived cosmopolitanisms have changed throughout its days and continue their kaleidoscopic recombinations amid the new conditions of the war. Such changes give rise to new notions of what it means to be a Jew from Odesa, notions that will be formed, tested, and contested and then interwoven in the social imagination of the city. It is this complex but ongoing process of negotiating identities and traditions that defines Odesa as a Jewish and cosmopolitan space.

Epilogue

It is impossible to make conclusive statements about Odesa's Jewish identity in the years after Ukrainian independence without considering the political reverberations of the past decade: the 2013–14 Maidan protests, the subsequent Russian annexation of Crimea and incursion into the Donbas region, and Russia's invasion of Ukraine in February 2022. Nor can we predict the final outcomes of the current war and the eventual impact on Odesa, its Jewish population, and its cosmopolitanism, as the war of more than two years has no end in sight.

What occurred in 2014, however, is instructive for the ways it compelled Odesans to navigate distinctions between what is Ukrainian and what is Russian and the areas where the two intersect. In this epilogue, I focus on my visits to the city in 2014 and 2019 and on Odesa amid the political turbulence that started with Euromaidan and the fire that occurred in the city on May 2, 2014. On that day, street fighting broke out between pro-Maidan and anti-Maidan activists. Forty-eight were killed in a fire set at the Trade Unions House, where Russian supporters had taken refuge.[1]

The politics percolating throughout Ukraine at that time had an impact on Odesa and on the people I knew there, leaving scars that have no doubt been torn open by Russia's 2022 invasion. Both the city and the people I repeatedly spoke with became more political, a turn that was not predictable, definitive, or always enduring. Given what I've shown in these pages, this isn't surprising. Most Odesans I knew came to see themselves and their city as part of Ukraine in a way that hadn't been the case during my time there in the mid-2000s. Many of these individuals regarded Russia as the aggressor state waging a war on their home. Others drew a careful distinction between governments and people or between politics and reality. They blamed politicians on both sides of the Maidan conflict for creating narratives that stoked violence, including the waves of Russian propaganda that depicted a nationalist Ukraine driven by fascist and antisemitic Nazis.

Discussing the horrific fire at the Trade Unions House, some of my Jewish friends declared that there was no room for street violence and vandalism in their city, as such Manichean politics went against the grain of what Odesa stands for. Others refused to accept that native residents could be involved in the disturbances, claiming that the events were orchestrated by politicians and carried out by hooligans "from elsewhere." "I can't believe this is happening in my hometown," one woman told me. "The city is already crumbling, and these hooligans, without any thought, vandalized and broke everything." In her view, no "real" Odesans were involved in the fighting, because they would never damage their own city the way the protesters and police had done. But despite the speculations, real Odesans—Jews included—were undoubtedly part of the pro- and anti-Maidan camps involved in the chaotic attacks.[2]

In this way, Odesa did not change overnight, and its changes were not monolithic. Younger generations of Odesans grew up with a different mentality, constructed in post-Soviet society, and without the same exposure to the meta-narrative that Russification equals modernization. Until the escalation of Russia's aggression, many older Soviet-born Jews in Odesa and the eastern and southern parts of the country still regarded themselves as "Soviet people, firmly convinced of their connection with Russian culture and the primacy of this culture above others." In other words, all things Ukrainian were still perceived as second class, simple, and in many ways folkloric.[3] But in the context of an ongoing war between Russia and Ukraine, these perceptions greatly shifted. Much of the Ukrainian population born during and after the last decade of Soviet rule started to question others' attachments to Russia under the rhetoric of anticolonialism. The trauma of the war further intensified and politicized these views, and support of Russian culture or even neutrality toward Russia was regarded by some as a betrayal of patriotic allegiance. For them, the Ukrainian language, its symbolic vocabulary, and just being Ukrainian took on new positive associations, while identifying as Russian was increasingly linked with an aggressive and colonizing imperial power. Russian speakers in Ukraine, Jews included, were thus forced to navigate being viewed as "symbolic pawns" used by opposing sides to diminish the credibility of the other through accusations of discrimination and, in the case of Jews, antisemitism.[4] Some Jews were led to sever ties with friends and relatives, and families of mixed origin suffered the painful reality of this political rift and violence even more. Since the start of the Russia-Ukraine conflict, air travel has ceased between Russia and Ukraine, and the distance between the two nations is internalized by those with family members living across the border.

Tatiana Zhurzhenko has said that the Russian action in eastern Ukraine did what previous Ukrainian presidents had failed to do: it catalyzed the creation of a political nation.[5] Euromaidan and the events following it transformed Ukrainians' sense of individual and collective agency. Many of my close friends took a pro-Ukrainian stance. When I first met David in the mid-2000s, for instance, he was religiously observant. The last time I saw my friend, in 2014, he was wearing a bulletproof vest and carrying a pistol. I learned that he'd enrolled in a self-defense league and was heavily involved in the local operations that followed Russia's annexation of Crimea. "I'm not a Ukrainian patriot," he told me, "but if some filth wants to enter my city, I will fight till the end."

During that same visit to Odesa, I also saw large protests in support of Russia and signs asking the Russian state to save Slavs and protect them from Ukrainian nationalists. Many of my interlocutors speculated that the protesters were bused into the city and paid for their presence, but others recognized that the city residents were still divided on their stance toward Russia. One journalist, following the pro-Russian protests in 2014, noted the lack of support these gatherings had among real Odesans. A Jewish woman she met observing the mobs of people with pro-Russian symbols expressed outrage at these demonstrations, screaming, "What nonsense, Odessa is a Jewish city!" as she stormed away from the crowds.[6] For some, the battle took place on Facebook and other social media platforms where people engaged in heated arguments, "unfriended" those who took opposing views, and formed new alliances.

Seven years after the Odesa fire, Anna Misuk, a retired employee of the Odesa Literature Museum who now lives in Israel, acknowledged that the city's political atmosphere had changed—the historical and political pressures created opportunities for new loyalties among Odesans of her generation. She told me that many of her formerly apolitical friends had become involved in the conflict at the onset—whether by taking part in online debate or by protesting in the streets: "There are two extreme views among Odessan Jews and other citizens in the city. The first is called 'Ukrainian radicalism,' where individuals regard all things Russian as the enemy. The second is a pro-Russian stance among people who don't tolerate Ukrainization and regard an attachment to being 'Russian' as protection against Ukrainian right-wing nationalism. But most find themselves between the two extremes: they communicate in Russian but support Ukraine as a nation-state."

Others I spoke to in May 2014 and on my last visit in 2019 might have been pro-Ukrainian or anti-Putin, but they still spoke in Russian and still used the language in unofficial communication. Moreover, while claiming to support Ukraine, they criticized aspects of Ukrainian nationalism, decried the corruption and other ills of Ukrainian society, and took issue with some of the blatant displays of anti-Russian sentiment toward Russian speakers. While some Russian-speaking Jewish Ukrainians adamantly retained their use of Russian, due to their lack of proficiency or lack of desire to change their habits, others switched between Russian and Ukrainian with ease, depending on the circumstances. Several Russian-speaking Jewish Ukrainians told me that their knowledge of Ukrainian wasn't proficient enough for professional use, and although they could understand the language, they couldn't achieve fluency overnight. In one Jewish family I knew, the daughter spoke Russian with her father and Ukrainian with her mother. Most found a comfortable balance of using both languages, understanding when to switch to the appropriate choice of communication. More importantly, their language use did not translate into language identity as Volodymyr Kulik has argued to be true about the larger population of Russian speakers in Ukraine.[7]

As a native Russian speaker, I myself worried that these tensions could create a chasm in my friendships. But the political tension and later the war didn't separate us—presumably because I shared their political views. We continued to speak to one another in Russian, which was still the language on the streets and in the homes I visited. But the tenor of our conversation changed, since political topics commonly arose and, in some circumstances, divided people. Diana, who was born in 1984 in Odesa and moved to Moscow in 2015, told me her friends assumed she had become pro-Putin because she lived in Moscow. Heated arguments circulated online among her Beitar friends about Jewish participation in national conflicts. When we exchanged messages in October 2021, she explained that according to the philosophy of Beitar, debated by her friends, Jews are meant to be active in the political life of the state of Israel, but participating in political conflicts in other countries can only harm Jews.[8] The reasoning goes like this: taking a side in any conflict leaves Jews dangerously open to attack—communal responsibility dictates that they stay out of local politics except for specific Jewish concerns.

When I spoke with leaders of Jewish organizations in Odesa after the events of 2014, they tended to take a neutral stance, choosing not to discuss politics with their members. "We are a Jewish organization, not a political one," an activist explained. At the same time, leaders of global Jewish networks like Chabad and others in Russia and Ukraine were divided by the events and revealed their loyalties to their respective states. In a *New York Times* article entitled "Among Ukraine's Jews, the Bigger Worry Is Putin, Not Pogroms," Andrew Higgins wrote that Ukrainian Jews aren't falling for the propaganda of

Putin, who "described the ouster of President Viktor F. Yanukovych of Ukraine
as an armed coup executed by 'nationalists, neo-Nazis, Russophobes, and anti-
Semites' who 'continue to set the tone in Ukraine to this day.'"[9] Indeed, some
Jewish leaders blamed pro-Russian Ukrainians for antisemitic provocations
in Crimea, including graffiti that read "Kill the Zhids" spray-painted on a
synagogue.[10]

Many Jewish leaders wrote to Putin asking him to stop claiming that he
invaded Crimea "to save Jews." Some went so far as to state that the anti-
Jewish acts that broke out in Kyiv and other cities during and after the Maidan
protests were provocations by anti-Maidan forces seeking to prove that pro-
Ukrainian nationalism is linked to neo-Nazi movements and guided by
antisemitism—thus justifying Russian involvement in the crisis.[11] Other
leaders, like Baruch Fichman, founder and president of the Ukrainian League
Against Anti-Semitism, expressed concern that Ukrainian neo-Nazis were
emboldened by the success of the revolution and were indeed becoming
more dangerous.[12] In Odesa, such narratives were confounded by events on
the ground. After all, the right-wing Pravyi Sektor (Right Sector) Party supported Odesa's Jewish community by protecting Jewish property in the city
and by condemning antisemitism after a Holocaust memorial was defaced
with neo-Nazi graffiti.[13] Rabbi Wolf told me he couldn't believe that the same
organizations they once feared for their right-wing politics were now offering
them protection. But he also acknowledged that this move was a strategic alliance for both. Ukrainian groups like the Jewish Federation of Ukraine, the
largest umbrella organization representing Ukrainian Jewry, openly declared
their support for Ukraine's national project. Indeed, "strengthening Ukraine's
independence" is stated as one of the Jewish Federation's strategic tasks, along
with "development of the Jewish community, fighting anti-Semitism, memory
of the Holocaust and supporting the State of Israel."[14]

Four years after the 2014 disturbances, relations with Ukraine's right-wing
groups changed for the worse. When Tatiana Sorkina, head of Pravyi Sektor,
addressed a crowd of supporters during the 2018 March for Ukrainian Order,
held on the anniversary of the tragic events of May 2, she declared, "We will
restore order in Ukraine. Ukraine will belong to Ukrainians, not Jews and
oligarchs." I found this speech disturbing; however, it didn't make headlines
in the Jewish press, nor did it appear in any of my friends' social media posts.
When I raised this incident with Lika, a Jewish woman in her early forties,
she dismissed it. To Lika, Sorkina didn't represent Pravyi Sektor as it stands
today, and her antisemitic statements were out of touch. Her husband pointed
out that Sorkina was quickly removed from her post after her hate speech and
never seen again in the public eye. Through this example, he also underscored

Figure Epi.1. The president of Ukraine with Odesa's Rabbi Wolf (to his right) and other Ukrainian Jewish leaders. Photo copyright Chabad.org, used by permission.

Ukraine's stringent laws against antisemitism and the support the Ukrainian state offers to Jews today.

The 2019 election of Volodymyr Zelensky, who became the first Jewish president of Ukraine, was celebrated publicly; the media presented it as a victorious moment in Ukrainian Jewish history.[15] But at the time, Zelensky's election and his new status as president did little to diminish the anxiety felt by some Jews in Odesa about what was to come. Several of my elderly Odesan friends doubted that Zelensky really cared about his Jewish identity. "He never denied that he was Jewish, but he never advertised it, either," one said. Zelensky grew up in a Russian-speaking secular Jewish family, but he is not observant and is unaffiliated with Ukraine's cultural or religious Jewish organizations. His marriage to a non-Jewish woman and the baptizing of his children not only brought more suspicion about his Jewishness but also solidified his Ukrainian-ness. And because Zelensky's presidential campaign was widely known to have been financed by a Jewish oligarch, Igor Kolomoisky, many Jews were wary of the potential for continued corruption that could tarnish the image of Jews in the country and lead to a rise in antisemitism. Any impropriety by Zelensky, they feared, would reflect badly on all of the country's Jews. Similar concerns were expressed among older Jews in other cities, including the Dnipro district, where Zelensky was born.[16] But at the same time, as political scientist Olga Anuch and historian Henry E. Hale observe in their book, *The Zelensky Effect*, as a Russian speaker of Jewish heritage from the country's industrial southeastern heartland, Zelensky "embodies civic Ukrainian national identity" and is perfectly positioned to understand how the "'The Divide' was a kind of myth . . . that obscured the middle ground into which he tapped."[17]

David, my observant and armed Odesan friend, wasn't alone in 2014 in his fear that Putin would invade Odesa because of its strategic location as a port city with a coastline and a connection to the Danube.[18] The city's position next to the separatist, Moscow-backed region of Transnistria and its proximity to the northwest peninsula of Crimea made Odesa particularly susceptible to invasion.[19] David was unusual in taking an active part in physically defending his city. But others who chose not to take up arms at that time still volunteered to help the wounded, families affected by war, and the many refugees arriving in Odesa from the southeast part of the country.

Thus, we have seen how Odesa's tolerance and cosmopolitanism were tested and how its deep connection with Russian culture was jeopardized. And yet the reality of everyday life revealed that those lineages still remained, even if they were undergoing the kinds of historical transformations that I focus on in this book. For many Jewish Odesans, new bonds were formed and new allegiances created between Jews and Ukrainians. These added a fresh dimension to the Jewish and Ukrainian elements of Odesa's living cosmopolitanism—a cosmopolitanism that developed *with* rather than against Ukrainization. They referred to themselves as Ukrainian Jews and took pride in the Ukrainian language and culture in a way that hadn't been part of the social imaginings two decades before. Some spoke openly of themselves as patriots, while others used less political terms to describe their belonging in Ukraine. Commenting on the transformation of Jewish life in Ukraine, Joseph Zissel, head of the Association of Jewish Organizations and Communities of Ukraine, established in 1988, observed the same phenomenon. "Jews who always lived here in Soviet times were Soviet Jews," he said. "That is, they were very assimilated and knew almost nothing about their history or culture. Then, when the Soviet Union collapsed, fortunately, they became Jews in Ukraine. . . . And the third stage after the Soviets and Jews in Ukraine is Ukrainian Jews." As "Soviet Jews," their Jewishness was derided and placed them on the margins. Even as Russophiles and Russian speakers, they were never "Russians." The new identity of "Ukrainian Jews" recognizes the full citizenship and residency rights of Jewish people born and raised in Ukraine. They are part of Ukraine's *narod*, and by the same logic, they have obligations to serve Ukraine, as many now do in time of war.

In Ukraine headed by Zelensky, Ukrainians and Ukrainian Jews are co-creating their relationship as equal members of Ukraine's civil society. The current government has made great efforts to bring Jews within the framework of Ukraine's polity and culture. These joint initiatives are evident in the published media clips of Jewish leaders speaking Ukrainian and discussing their relationship with the Ukrainian state. One short clip, made with the sponsorship of the US Agency for International Development, appeared on Ukrainer.net and began with "Jews of Ukraine. Who are they?" In it, individuals like Zissel, who had been a political dissident and political prisoner, and Oleksandr Duhovnii, head rabbi of Progressive Judaism in Ukraine, describe their own Jewish and Ukrainian identities as intertwined. "I have always been close to Ukraine, but my core was always Jewish," said Zissel. "I will never be purely Ukrainian, but I have already become a Ukrainian Jew." Duhovnii speaks of Ukraine as a country that has learned how to fight antisemitism, racism, and xenophobia. He compares the Ukrainian state to a wreath made of different flowers woven together. "For me, Ukraine is the first Motherland. The first and last. I still have a historical homeland, but Ukraine is my land. I studied in London and I could stay there because my wife worked there, but it was very important for me to return to Ukraine."

I would argue that the larger process of Jews redefining their relationship with Ukraine, and Ukraine redefining its relationship with its Jews, stems not only from the turbulence of the current epoch but also from the public recognition of such historical atrocities as Babyn Yar and the Ukrainian collaboration with the Nazis during World War II and the closer look being made at historical moments of coexistence and coalescence between Jews and Ukrainians. In 2019, at an event commemorating the seventy-fifth anniversary of Babyn Yar, attended by then president Poroshenko, many Ukrainian and world Jewish activists expressed their commitment to bridging the gaps in Ukrainian-Jewish relations and forging more intimate ties.

In the last two decades, scholars have used a Ukrainian rather than a strictly Russian or Soviet lens to study Jewish history in the territory of present-day Ukraine. Growing initiatives to see, research, and analyze Jews in Ukraine as "Ukrainian Jews" are being made across academic and cultural sectors by important groups like the Ukrainian Jewish Encounter and the Jewish Confederation of Ukraine and by such publications as Yohanan Petrovsky-Shtern's *Anti-Imperial Choice: The Making of the Ukrainian Jews*. But the time period of the mid-2000s, which represents the core of this book, provides an important reminder of how Jewish Odesans lived prior to the current conflict and how reality has been transformed—and will only be further transformed—by living through war and the aftermath of this deep trauma.

NOTES

Preface

1. Leite 2017, ix.
2. Sapritsky-Nahum 2022.
3. Sapritsky-Nahum 2023.
4. Bringa 1995.
5. Tanny 2007.

Introduction

1. Throughout the manuscript I use the Ukrainian spelling of Odesa unless it appears differently in the original source. See the "Note on Transliteration and Translation" for more details.
2. A kippah is the skullcap worn by observant Jewish men.
3. Herlihy 1986, 241–43.
4. An example is the Bukharan Jewish younger generation, who no longer learn from the elders but are now teaching them (Cooper 2012, 195).
5. Wanner 1998.
6. In grassroots organizations like Migdal, the Jewish community center, and the Museum of the History of Odesa, Jews operated with the help of international Jewish organizations but also received funding from local donors for individual projects not covered by foreign grants. The Jewish Agency, the American Jewish Joint Distribution Committee (JDC or the Joint), Chabad Lubavitch, and Tikva were among the main players that shaped Odesa's Jewish spaces and offered funding for Jewish programs.
7. See Herlihy 1986 and Weinberg 1993.
8. Richardson 2008, 6; Cesarani 2002.

9. Benedict Anderson (1983) defined an "imagined community" as a group of people who will never know most of their fellow members as individuals, will never meet them or even hear of them, and yet the image of their community lives on in the mind of each member.

10. Richardson 2008, 5.

11. For an analysis of port culture among Jews, see Cesarani 2002.

12. Richardson 2004, 17; Skvirskaja 2010, 79.

13. Polese 2007.

14. Richardson 2008, 5.

15. Horowitz 2017, 40; Lecke and Sicher 2023, 2.

16. See Karakina 2007, 7.

17. Chervyakov, Gitelman, and Shapiro 1997, 289.

18. I am grateful to Zeev Volkov for pointing out this important distinction to me.

19. Tikva Children's Home, n.d.

20. Mark Tolts (2018, 217) identifies the "core" Jewish population as those who identify themselves as Jews or, in the case of children, are identified as such by their parents. This group doesn't include persons of Jewish origin who report another ethnicity in the census; the "enlarged" Jewish population, which includes household members of the core Jewish population; or the "Law of Return population," which includes Jews, children and grandchildren of Jews, and their respective spouses (Institute for Jewish Policy Research, n.d.)

21. In the 2001 state census, 83 percent of Ukrainian Jews declared Russian as their primary language (State Statistics Committee of Ukraine 2003–2004).

22. Richardson 2008, 227n5. Further legislation passed in 2019 under President Petro Poroshenko gave special status to the Ukrainian language and made fluency in Ukrainian a requirement for civil servants, soldiers, doctors, and teachers. The new laws also required 90 percent of the content on television and films distributed to be in Ukrainian and at least 50 percent of books to be printed in the Ukrainian language. Computer software also must have a Ukrainian-language interface (Polityuk 2019).

23. Herlihy 2008, 79.

24. The main basis for establishing citizenship in Ukraine following the collapse of the Soviet Union was the official registration of residency, a document called *propiska*. Other proofs of residency were also used, such as the testimony of witnesses who could assert that the person had permanently resided in Ukraine when the citizenship law came into force in November 1991 (Oxana Shevel, pers. comm., December 14, 2010). In other words, Ukrainian citizenship was extended to all who permanently resided in the territory of Ukraine at the time of the breakup of the Soviet Union, irrespective of their family roots. Thus, most Jews and others in Odesa are citizens of Ukraine.

25. Polese and Wylegala 2008, 792.

26. Skvirskaja 2010, 79.

27. Dmitry Khavin's film *Quiet in Odessa* demonstrates how for some Jewish activists, these loyalties changed places in the aftermath of the 2014 events.

28. Sylvester 2005, 5.

29. Magocsi and Petrovsky-Shtern 2016, 286.

30. It is difficult to establish exact numbers of congregants. Representatives of Tikvah claim to help more than three thousand men, women, and children through their community and education programs. Chabad Lubavitch cites comparable numbers but also claims twice as many for its newspaper subscribers. Congregants are often double-counted by many Jewish organizations, making it all the more difficult to establish reliable statistics.

31. Meir Dizengoff (1861–1936), the first mayor of Tel Aviv, lived in Odesa in the early 1880s and was active in the Hovevei Zion (Loving Zion) movement. Edmund Allenby, an English soldier and British imperial governor, was a prominent figure in the British conquest of Palestine.

32. Totally Jewish Travel, n.d.

33. Shabbat, the seventh day of the week, is the day of rest.

34. The Israel Institute for Advanced Studies, together with Hebrew University, had an ongoing research group and produced a conference in 2021 entitled "Cosmopolitanism in Urban Spaces: The Case of Odessa."

35. Lecke 2021.

36. Sylvester 2005, 5, 14.

37. Lecke 2021.

38. Horowitz 2023, 100–101.

39. Ibid.

40. Ibid., 114.

41. Sifneos 2018.

42. Humphrey 2012, 18–19.

43. Nathans 2002, 166.

44. Abbas 2000, 770.

45. Klier 2002, 175; Sylvester 2005, 13; Nathans 2002, 5.

46. Abbas 2000, 772; Cesarani 2002; Cesarani and Romain 2006; Cocco 2010; Sifneos 2018.

47. Lecke 2021.

48. Cohen 1992; Bhabha 1996; Malcomson 1998; Robbins 1998; Humphrey 2004.

49. Hannerz 1996, 103; Humphrey and Skvirskaja 2012, 2.

50. Abbas 2000, 771.

51. Mandel 2008, 47.

52. Ibid., 48.

53. Clifford 1998, 369.

54. Abbas 2000, 772.

55. Richardson 2004, 204.
56. Sicher 2023; Sifneos 2018.
57. Humphrey and Skvirskaja 2012.
58. Clifford 1992.
59. Mandel 2008, 48.
60. Humphrey 2012; King 2012.
61. Richardson 2008.
62. Mandel 2008, 47.
63. Aviv and Shneer 2005.
64. Wiesel 1966.
65. Golbert 2001a, 1. Edited volumes on Soviet and ex-Soviet Jewry, produced largely by Israeli and American social researchers (with limited contributions by Russian-speaking scholars), include Ro'i 1995; Lewin-Epstein, Ritterband, and Ro'i 1997; Ro'i and Beker 1991; Gitelman, Glants, and Goldman 2003; Gitelman and Ro'i 2007; and Ben-Rafael, Gorny, and Ro'i 2003. These books present a rather narrow picture of Soviet and post-Soviet Jewish reality and are heavily based on the sociological and statistical models of outside observers. Sociologist Larissa Remenick's 2012 updated volume, *Russian Jews on Three Continents: Identity, Integration, and Conflict*, tries to offset this by giving the perspective of a Russian Jewish sociologist whose research is based on participant observation. But Remenick's work is not an ethnography of everyday life in a specific urban context—which is what this book presents.
66. A great deal of literature has been produced about ex-Soviet Jewish communities abroad: in the United States (Markowitz 1993; Gold 1997; Rittenband 1997; Hegner 2000, etc.), Israel (Golden 2002; Markowitz 1997; Rapoport and Lomsky-Feder 2002; Fialkova and Yelenevskaya 2007; Remennick 2002, etc.), Germany (Bodemann 2008; Bernstein 2005 [also Israel]; Baraulina 2005, etc.), and other destinations. Work on ex-Soviet Jews in countries of the FSU is still scarce and is so far dominated by survey methods and by archival and statistical data. See, for example, Brym and Ryvkina 1994; Ryvkina 2005; Brym 1997; Tolts 2007; DellaPergola 2007; Gitelman 1988, (1988) 2001; and Chervyakov, Gitelman, and Shapiro 1997.
67. Goluboff 2003, 3.
68. See Cooper 2012.
69. Waligorska 2013, 12.
70. Bringa 1995, xii–xiii.
71. See Steinberg and Wanner 2008, 11.
72. Morris 2012, 254.
73. Ibid.
74. Biale et al. 2018; Loewenthal 2020.
75. Danzger 1989, 3; Myers 2014, 2.
76. Hobsbawm 1983, 4.
77. Zelenina 2018, 251.

78. Renato Rosaldo (1989, 21) emphasizes that social analysis must now grapple with the realization that its objects of analysis are themselves analyzing subjects who critically interrogate ethnographers—their writings, their ethics, and their politics.

79. My research was funded by an American Councils for International Education Title VIII grant, which required an official affiliation with a local university.

80. This was a branch of Migdal that sponsored a group for non-Jewish families to attend classes at the center for a small fee. For Jewish families, these classes were subsidized by sponsors of the Joint and by local donors.

81. Goluboff's 2003 synagogue study is predominantly based on the male informants with whom she interacted within and outside the synagogue, but I myself didn't encounter such leniency among Odesa's Orthodox congregants. It's possible that the later timing of my own fieldwork (2005–7) compared to Goluboff's (1995–96) indicates that the feasibility of such "transgressions" has declined.

82. Ries 1997, 2.

83. Ries 2000, ix.

84. Rosaldo 1989, 9.

1. Historical Background

1. Zipperstein 1999, 65.

2. Ibid.

3. Friedman 2013.

4. Petrovsky-Shtern 2009, 3.

5. Literature on Jews in the Russian Empire is extensive. Some key sources include Polonsky 2019; Polonsky 2013; Klier 1995; Veidlinger 2009; Rechtman 2021; Avrutin 2010; Nathans 2002; and Klier and Lambroza 1992. For books dedicated to Jewish experiences in the land of today's Ukraine, see Petrovsky-Shtern and Polonsky 2014 and Magocsi and Petrovsky-Shtern 2016, among others.

6. Petrovsky-Shtern and Polonsky 2014, 3.

7. Zipperstein 1999, 4; Bemporad 2013, 5. See also Nathans 2002 for a study of the Jews of St. Petersburg in late imperial Russia; Veidlinger 2000 for Moscow in the Soviet era; Goluboff 2003 for Moscow in the late 1990s; Meir 2010 and Khiterer 2017 for a study of Kyiv in its respective periods; and Kobrin 2010 for a study of Bialystok in the twentieth century.

8. Polonsky 2019, 3.

9. Markowitz 1993, 22.

10. Nathans 2002, 1.

11. Zipperstein 1999, 22.

12. Petrovsky-Shtern and Polonsky 2014, 2.

13. Polonsky 2019, 403.

14. Zipperstein 1999, 19.

15. Refuseniks were those who could not obtain exit visas in the Soviet period.

16. In her work on Jewish ex-Soviets abroad, Fran Markowitz (1995, 203) writes, "The majority of the people—at least those whom I interviewed during the mid- and late 1980s in New York, Israel, and Chicago—denied being modern-day Jewish heroes and stressed instead that they had really been striving for assimilation in the USSR and ultimately left when they—or their children— encountered insurmountable obstacles."

17. See Slezkine 2004; Yurchak 2006; Kotkin 1995; Humphrey 2004; and Steinberg and Wanner 2008.

18. Kotkin 1995, 154.

19. Steinberg and Wanner 2008, 3.

20. Humphrey 2004, 146.

21. Yurchak 2006, 8.

22. Slezkine 2004.

23. Nathans 2002, 2–3.

24. See Baron (1964) 1987, 2; Pinkus 1988, 2; Dubnow 1916–20, 1:1–13.

25. Petrovsky-Shtern 2014, 6.

26. Pinkus 1988, 3.

27. Petrovsky-Shtern 2014, 6.

28. Shapira 2014, 69, 76.

29. Magocsi and Petrovsky-Shtern 2016, 24.

30. Ibid.

31. Ibid.

32. Ibid., 29; Glaser 2015.

33. See Hanover 1983 for a Jewish account of the events and Magocsi and Petrovsky-Shtern 2016, 28–31, for a critique. Also see Glaser 2015 for a detailed description of the Khmelnytsky uprising from the vantage point of the Poles, Jews, Russians, and Ukrainians.

34. Polonsky 2013, 1.

35. In the first partition (1772), Russia annexed an area of Belarus, including Polotsk, Mogilev, and Vitebsk. In the second and third partitions (1793 and 1795), the Russian Empire incorporated almost the entire Grand Duchy of Lithuania, including major Jewish centers such as Minsk, Vilna, Grodno (today Hrodna), and Novogrudok and most of the right bank Ukraine, including Zhitomir, Bratslav, and Kamenets-Podolsky (Kamyanets-Podilsky) (Polonsky 2019, 322).

36. Petrovsky-Shtern and Polonsky 2014, 10. In addition to the large number of Jews, Catherine's dominions came to include millions of Poles, Lithuanians, Baltic Germans, and Tatars, whose faiths and cultures also influenced the cultural environments of the Russian Empire (Baron [1964] 1987, 14).

37. Polonsky 2019, 323. In 1820, Jews constituted nearly 3.5 percent of the empire's population of 46 million; by 1880, Jews made up 4.7 per cent of its total population of 86 million (ibid.).

38. Dubnow 1916–20, 1:261.

39. Petrovsky-Shtern and Polonsky 2014, 10–11; Baron (1964) 1987, 15–16. Under the Russian Empire, individuals who owned property worth more than 500 rubles could register as members of the merchant class, according to the following scale: the first guild, at least 10,000 rubles; the second guild, between 1,000 and 10,000; and the third guild, between 500 and 1,000. Those owning less than 500 rubles' worth of property were registered as townsmen. Jewish merchants were granted the privilege of admission to the guilds in 1780 (Pinkus 1988, 12).

40. See Rogger 1986 for a fuller description.

41. Polonsky 2013, 76.

42. Petrovsky-Shtern and Polonsky (2014, 11) point out that Russian authorities allowed Jews and other groups, including Old Believers, Muslims, and the Karaites, to administer themselves. The goal was to facilitate the incorporation of the borderland ethnicities into the monarchy.

43. Ibid.

44. Glaser 2012, xv, 4.

45. Pinkus 1988, 13.

46. For a fuller explanation of the restrictions passed during Catherine the Great's rule, see Pinkus 1988, 13, and Baron (1964) 1987, 13–17.

47. Pinkus 1988, 13; Polonsky 2019, 336.

48. Polonsky 2019, 328, 336.

49. Polonsky 2013, 79, 80.

50. Petrovsky-Shtern and Polonsky 2014, 11–12.

51. Polonsky 2019, 354, 356, 357. Polonsky points out that it was "in Nicholas's reign that the government began to intervene on a substantial scale in Jewish life, with the objective of 'molding the Jews in ways consistent with the emperor's overall aims and ideology' and turning them into loyal subjects of the tsar by establishing direct state supervision of the life and religious activity of the Jewish community and eliminating the traditional mediators between the state and the Jews." (356)

52. Petrovsky-Shtern and Polonsky 2014, 12. Men over eighteen served in the military for twenty-five years; younger recruits served in special cantonist battalions (army camp) until they were of age to transfer to the full service. While this legislation brought Jews into the military ranks of the Russian Empire and was implemented as part of the larger attempt to transform Jews into loyal Russian citizens, historians point out that religious freedom was disregarded during the time of service and conversion was openly encouraged, especially among the younger recruits who were taken to cantonist battalions. Some Jews were excluded from service, among them rabbis, members of the merchant estate, those educated in state-sponsored institutions, those in agricultural colonies, and, later, students from government-run Jewish schools (Polonsky 2019, 359). See Stanislawski 1983, 25, for a description of conversion in military service.

53. Nathans 2002, 4; Slezkine 2004, 105. All but 300,000 of Russia's Jews resided within the Pale. Those outside included 60,000 Georgian and Mountain Jews living in the Caucasus and 50,000 residents of central Asia and Siberia. The rest were mainly concentrated in urban areas; they made up the majority of the population in the cities of Belarus and Lithuania, and about 30 percent of Ukraine's city population (Gitelman [1988] 2001, 28–29; Nathans 2002, 4).

54. Zipperstein 1986, 13–14.

55. Ibid., 13.

56. Gitelman (1988) 2001, 8.

57. I am grateful to Marsha L. Rosenblit and Deborah Dash Moore for this point.

58. See Nathans 2002, 78–79.

59. Ibid., 45–79.

60. Polonsky 2013, 2.

61. Ibid.

62. Svirskii 1904, 169; quoted in Weinberg 1993, 9.

63. New Russia consisted of the provinces of Ekaterinoslav, Taurida, and Kherson (where Odesa is located), acquired by the Russian Empire in the eighteenth century. After 1828, New Russia also included Bessarabia (Weinberg 1993, 3).

64. Mazis 2004, 17.

65. Sifneos 2018, 99.

66. Herlihy 2018, 197.

67. Polonsky 2019, 326.

68. Skinner 1986, 209–11.

69. Zipperstein 1986, 32.

70. Herlihy 1986, 251; Rozenboim 2007, 33.

71. Ascherson 2007, 140. These statistics exclude bilingual Jews and others who spoke other languages.

72. Richardson 2004, 11. Imported goods were taxed at a much lower rate in Odesa than in other ports. As a result, it was cheaper to live in Odesa than anywhere else in Russia (Gubar and Rozenboim 2003, 80).

73. Weinberg 1993, 2.

74. Ibid., 4. See Herlihy 1986, 215–22, for a detailed description of Odesa's railroad and its effect on the local economy.

75. Zipperstein 1986, 39.

76. Sifneos 2018, 176.

77. For a detailed description of Jewish occupational ranks in Odesa, see Polishchuk 2002, 319–21.

78. Polonsky 2019, 177; Zipperstein 1986, 36.

79. Polonsky 2019, 177.

80. Zipperstein 1986, 39.

81. Rozenboim 2007, 34.

82. Mazis 2004, 25.

83. Polonsky 2019, 176.

84. Zipperstein 1986, 36–37.

85. This process of cultural transformation was not supported by all, nor was it without conflict. For example, Zipperstein (1986, 37) mentions a famous incident commonly cited by Odesan historians: In 1817, the city's rabbi, Berish ben Yisrael Usher of Nemirov, was beaten on the street by several Jews who were unhappy with his stringent approach to the observance of ritual law. Zipperstein describes how "traditional Jews" were opposed to the Odesa school administered by the maskilim, citing an incident when rocks were thrown at the school's students and teachers (48). In general, however, he characterized traditionalist opposition to Jewish reform as "muted" and "neutralized" (49).

86. Zipperstein 1986, 1.

87. Ibid., 37.

88. Ibid., 42; Polonsky 2019, 177.

89. Zipperstein 1986, 43; Gubar and Rozenboim 2003, 91.

90. Kravtsov 2002.

91. Zipperstein 1986, 55.

92. Ibid., 65–66.

93. Ibid.

94. Mazis 2004, 27.

95. Rubinstein 2023, 140.

96. Zipperstein, n.d.; Sicher 2023.

97. Gubar and Rozenboim 2003, 102.

98. Tanny 2007; Herlihy 1986, 240, 253.

99. Zipperstein 1986, 69.

100. Ibid., 131, 151.

101. Slezkine 2004, 124–25.

102. Ibid., 125.

103. Gubar and Rozenboim 2003, 91; Zipperstein 1986, 75.

104. See Veidlinger 2009.

105. Klier 2002, 175.

106. Simhah Pinsker, Perets Smolenskin, and Eliyah Werbel wrote in Hebrew; Joachim Tarnopol, in French; and Osip Rabinovich, Menashe Margulis, and Il'ia Orshanskii, in Russian. Other distinguished intellectuals included Mark Wahltuch, who translated Pushkin from Russian to Italian in 1855, and Maria Saker, a liberal Jewish educator who became the first woman to be published in the Russian Jewish press, among others.

107. Petrovsky-Shtern 2023; Zabirko 2023.

108. Klier 2002, 175.

109. Zipperstein 1986, 74.

110. Slezkine 2004, 128, 136.

111. Polonsky 2013, 276.

112. I am grateful for Marsha Rozenblit and Deborah Dash Moore for high-lighting this point.

113. Zipperstein, n.d.

114. Hrytsak and Susak 2003, 145.

115. Rozenboim 2007, 38. During the Soviet period, all but one of Odesa's synagogues were closed down and used for various nonreligious purposes, such as gym facilities and storage (Gubar and Rozenboim 2003, 70). The one that remained open didn't have regular prayer, but according to my informants, it did provide services for the major holidays. The other synagogue buildings only returned to their original purpose after the fall of the USSR in 1991.

116. Klier 2002, 173.

117. S. Katz 1996, 26.

118. Zipperstein 1986, 64.

119. Ibid., 105.

120. Ibid., 104.

121. Ibid., 57.

122. Polonsky 2019, 177.

123. Ibid.

124. Gerasimov 2003.

125. In 1908, Jews owned all of the thirty brothels in Kherson province, most of them located in Odesa (Zipperstein, n.d.).

126. Herlihy 1986, 251. Weinberg (1993, 20) links the decline of Odesa to a number of short-term events, such as bad harvests, and long-term trends, including recession, unemployment, decline of the port facilities, competition, and the effects of the Russo-Japanese War, which cut off maritime and trade connections with the Far East (see also Herlihy 1986, 295–96).

127. Klier 1992–1994, 178.

128. Herlihy 1986, 253.

129. Ascherson 2007, 140.

130. Herlihy 2018, 56.

131. Ibid.

132. Herlihy 1986, 254.

133. Petrovsky-Shtern and Polonsky 2014, 17; Herlihy 1986, 299; Sifneos 2018, 176.

134. Humphrey 2012, 23.

135. Weinberg 1992, 248. These official statistics undoubtedly underestimate the damage. Other sources report much higher figures: Dmitri Neidhardt, governor of Odesa during the pogrom, documented 2,500 casualties; the Jewish newspaper *Voskhod* reported more than 800 deaths and several wounded; and local hospitals reported treating at least 600 individuals for injuries sustained during the violent attacks of the pogrom (ibid.).

136. Historian Robert Weinberg (1992) presented a combination of long-term and immediate factors behind the 1905 pogrom. Among the long-term factors that contributed to the conditions for anti-Jewish violence over time was the economic competition between Jews and others in the city, long-standing ethnic and religious antagonisms, the prominence of Jews in the commercial affairs of Odesa, and the mistreatment of Jews as manifested in discriminatory legislation passed by the central government. The immediate factors have to do with the general course of political developments in 1905 and the polarization of pro- and antigovernment forces, the role of civilian and government officials promoting an atmosphere conducive to a pogrom, and the visible position of Jews in the opposition against autocracy (ibid., 250). Discussing the contradictory character of the accusations and rumors, Caroline Humphrey (2012, 42) explains that Jews could be attacked as both representatives of the exploitative bourgeoisie and as revolutionary activists.

137. Herlihy 1986, 258.

138. Petrovsky-Shtern and Polonsky 2014, 18.

139. Gitelman (1988) 2001, 18.

140. For more on Jabotinsky's life and time in Odesa, see Horowitz and Katsis 2016; Halkin 2019; Stanislawski 2001; and S. Katz 1996.

141. Oz 2004, 57; Misuk 2007, 52–54.

142. See Penter and Sablin 2020 and Guthier 1981, 175.

143. Petrovsky-Shtern and Polonsky 2014, 26.

144. Ibid., 27.

145. Petrovsky-Shtern and Polonsky 2014, 34.

146. Polonsky 2013, 275.

147. Guthier 1981, 166.

148. Petrovksy-Shtern and Polonsky 2019, 35.

149. Zipperstein, n.d.

150. Bemporad 2013, 5, 6.

151. Kotkin 1995, 356.

152. Bemporad 2013.

153. Ibid., 6.

154. For discussions of Soviet Yiddish popular culture, see Shternshis 2006 and Veidlinger 2000, 2009.

155. Polonsky 2019, 254.

156. Bemporad 2013, 176.

157. Slezkine 2004, 247.

158. Kulyk 2018, 123.

159. Hidden Jewish ancestry is common in many parts of the world. Stephan Feuchtwang (2007, 9) reveals a common thread in the history of Jewish assimilation in Germany, where even children of mixed marriages and Jews who had converted to Christianity were stigmatized.

160. Bemporad 2013, 5.

161. Manley 2009, 57.

162. The Nazi Nuremberg Laws of 1935 classified anyone with at least three "full-Jewish grandparents" as a Jew, and grandparents were "fully Jewish" if they belonged to the Jewish religious community (Pegelow 2006, 44). But in Odesa, as S. Y. Borovoi (2001, 23) explains, the local Nazi administration drafted an explanatory note of who, for the purpose of extermination, was considered a Jew: anyone with a Jewish ancestor in the maternal or paternal line (not specifying the generation), regardless of their religious belonging, or anyone practicing Judaism.

163. Gesin 2003, 128, emphasis in original.

164. Inber 1981, 79.

165. Arad 2009, 240.

166. King 2011, 202.

167. Ibid.

168. Deletant 2008, 157; see also Gesin 2003, 129.

169. Borovoi 2001, 19.

170. Gesin 2003, 129.

171. Charles King (2011, 213–14) writes that the ghetto was hastily organized and initially made up of a neighborhood of houses and apartment buildings, not a walled enclosure, where some Odesans managed to visit and sneak food to their Jewish neighbors. But later, full confinement followed.

172. King 2011, 213.

173. See Inber 1981, 89–91. Yad Vashem has recognized 2,185 Righteous among the Nations from Ukraine (Brandon and Lower 2008, 14).

174. See Gesin 2003, 139–40.

175. Ibid., 133.

176. King 2011, 215.

177. See Gesin 2003, 131–32, 136–39, 181 for detailed descriptions of Bogdanovka, Akhmetchetka, and Domanevka. Also see Yad Vashem, n.d.

178. King 2011, 218.

179. Ibid., 211.

180. The Museum of the History of Odesa Jews provided these estimates for the Odesa region. Other estimates range between 100,000 and 250,000 (see Gidwitz 1997; Borovoi 2001; Inber 1981, 83). Dennis Deletant (2008, 157) estimates that between 130,000 and 170,000 local Ukrainian Jews were murdered or left to die of disease in the region.

181. Gesin 2003, 137.

182. Fisher 1969, 122–23. The literature on the Holocaust in Ukraine is an emerging field. See Brandon and Lower 2008. For in-depth analysis and detailed accounts of the Holocaust in the Odesa region, see, among others, Gesin 2003, 126–50; Ofer 1993; Inber 1981; Fisher 1969, 120–25; Litani 1967, 135–54; Arad 2009, 240–45; and Dusman 2001.

183. Gesin 2003, 143.

184. Ibid., 263.

185. Inber 1981, 81.

186. Kruglov 2008, 284.

187. Deletant 2008, 157.

188. Friedberg 1991, 15.

189. Markowitz 1993, 40.

190. In 1949, a campaign was unleashed to expel "cosmopolitans"—80 percent of whom were Jews—from the communist party and banish them from public and scientific life. As Joshua Rubenstein (2016, 61) points out, "to accuse someone of being a 'cosmopolitan' was a crude way of questioning their loyalty to Soviet culture."

191. Rubenstein 2016, 85.

192. Gitelman (1988) 2001, 159.

193. Tanny 2011, 143.

194. Ibid.

195. Kotkin 1995, 154.

196. See also Friedberg 1991, 64–65.

197. Kotkin 1995, 155.

198. For more on the process of normalizing antisemitism, see Rapoport, Lomsky-Feder, and Hedider 2002.

199. Tanny 2011, 142. On Jewish life during the post-Stalin period (1953–1983) see, among others, Pinkus 1988.

200. Tanny 2011, 143.

201. Ibid.

202. Friedberg 1991, 1; see also Markowitz 1993.

203. Kotkin 1995, 216.

204. Richardson 2008, 4.

205. Richardson 2004, 42.

2. Remembering the Past and Making Sense of the Present

1. Mark Bassin and Catriona Kelly (2012, 8) remind us that "we need to combine the study of memory and the analysis of tradition—those habits, institutions, practices and linguistic formulas that characterized Soviet society" and here they concur, anthropologists (and sociologists) in particular can help us understand the deeper levels of collective belonging. See also Halbwachs 1992. The list of works on collective memory is immense. Some important contributions include Connerton 1989 and Ricoeur 2006, among others. The literature on oral history is just as extensive. Among other titles, see Ballard et al. 2007 and Thompson 2000.

2. Veidlinger 2013, xxv. See Ab Imperio Syllabus, n.d. Other important texts that reflect on how historians have struggled with methods of obtaining access

to the everyday lives of Soviet citizens include Bassin and Kelly 2012, Fitzpatrick 2000, Davies 1997, Kotkin 1995, and Kharkhordin 1999, among others.

3. Veidlinger 2013, xxvi.

4. Larson 2007, 80.

5. Cited in Sharpless 2007, 14.

6. Portelli 1997; Glaser and Strauss 1967; Larson 2007, 88.

7. See, for example, Wiesel 1966; Gitelman (1988) 2001. For Paul Ritterband (1997, 332), it was precisely the hostile atmosphere of the Soviet Union that intensified the sense of a Jewish self for many Soviet Jews.

8. Veidlinger 2013, xxii.

9. Grant 1995.

10. Lomsky-Feder and Rapoport 2002.

11. These images were supported in large part by Elie Weisel's influential book *Jews of Silence: A Personal Report on Soviet Jewry* (1966), but also by memoirs and biographies, including those by Emil Draitser (2008), Natan Sharansky (1998), and Saul Borovoi (1993).

12. Zipperstein 1999, 77.

13. A mezuzah is a decorative case containing biblical verses on a piece of parchment, fixed outside the front door of many Jewish homes. A menorah is a nine-branched candelabrum used for Chanukah.

14. Sheila Fitzpatrick and Yuri Slezkine (2000) describe how many Soviet women of that generation were reticent about personal matters, choosing instead to speak mainly about the public affairs of their time.

15. It was in that year, Viktor noted, that the Romanov family celebrated thirty years in power by granting amnesty to many deported "criminals," allowing them to return home.

16. *Goy* is a derogatory term for a non-Jew.

17. Bemporad 2013, 10.

18. Veidlinger 2013, 155.

19. Ibid., 80; Shternshis 2006, 17.

20. Veidlinger 2013, 80.

21. Polonsky 2013, 292.

22. Gitelman 1972, cited in Markowitz 1993, 19.

23. Shternshis 2006, 16.

24. The adjective *mestechkovye* is also used colloquially to indicate people who are considered backward in their ways and thinking.

25. See Inna Leykin's 2007 paper, which depicts narratives of achievement, pride, and victory still nurtured by Soviet war veterans in Israel.

26. Many elderly Jews emphasized a distinction between Soviet and Nazi antisemitism. They described Soviet antisemitism as state-sponsored discrimination against members of the Jewish nationality, which took the form of Jewish quotas in education and employment, anti-Jewish printed propaganda, the arbitrary refusal of travel and immigration visas, and unjust arrests and executions.

Such policies began to appear in the USSR in the late 1930s and increased after World War II. Nazi antisemitism, on the other hand, was directed against anyone of Jewish descent and expressed in arbitrary acts of brutality, destruction, and mass extermination.

27. King 2011, 230.

28. Soviet propaganda often portrayed Jews as creatures with horns and other animal features, such as a tail. See Gitelman (1988) 2001, 218.

29. For theoretical, historical, and empirical discussion of the concept of *intelligentsia*, see Malia 1960; Gessen 1997; Markowitz 1993, 125–36; Patico 2005, 484, 486; and Lissak and Leshem 1995, 20–36.

30. Rapoport and Lomsky-Feder 2002, 233.

31. Writing about the shift in values in post-Soviet Russia, Jennifer Patico (2005, 484) describes the increasingly dominant role of money, rather than social contacts, in the everyday life of Saint Petersburg residents in the late 1990s.

32. Zvi Gitelman (1988, 441) also notes that most Jews in Ukraine look on Russian culture as "higher" and "less provincial" or less "peasant" than Ukrainian culture.

33. Professor of Russian Studies Terry Martin describes the Soviet resolutions passed in 1937, which "made the Russian language a mandatory subject in all schools, liquidated national districts and village soviets, liquidated all non-Russian schools in the Russian regions of the USSR, and increased the number of Russian newspapers in Ukraine" (Martin 2001, 428). He notes that the Russian language was promoted in public propaganda and "Ukrainian nationalists were once again accused of attempts to 'divorce Ukrainian culture from fraternal Russian culture and orient the Ukrainian people on the capitalist west, on fascist Germany'" (ibid). In a series of newspaper articles written to promote the teaching of Russian language, this propaganda was visible. Martin gives the example of *Uchitel'skaia gazeta* for August 7, 1938, which states: "The great and mighty Russian language, the language of Lenin and Stalin, Pushkin and Gorky, Tolstoi and Belinskii, is profoundly dear to all citizens of the USSR, and is studied with love by children and adults . . . [which shows] the exclusive interest of all nationalities to study the language of the great Russian people, first among equals in the fraternity family of the peoples of the USSR" (Martin 2001, 428–29).

34. Other members of the intelligentsia, unlike Viktor and Olga, resisted the regime (see Rapoport and Lomsky-Feder 2002, 236, 240–41; Brym and Ryvkina 1994) and were highly critical of its institutions (Markowitz 1993).

35. It's a well-known fact, which Elena herself confirmed, that Intourist always had a large number of KGB workers in its various headquarters and that they would usually accompany travelers from abroad as translators and guides.

36. A combination of party membership and education offered the main route to advancement in Soviet society, as Sheila Fitzpatrick (1999 [2000], 16) has explained.

37. See Patico (2005) for a discussion of post-Soviet changes in taste, consumption, and values.

38. Elena didn't think that she herself "looked Jewish." Tamar Rapoport and Edna Lomsky-Feder (2002, 239) point out that their Jewish informants "took it as self-evident that Jews have a typical appearance and body language, and they all dealt with the issue of how their appearance reveals or does not reveal their ethnic belonging."

39. Today, leaders of Odesa's religious communities have adopted this ideology of difference, but now they view it as a positive trait. For them, the old Soviet joke would go: "Of course he doesn't drink! He's Jewish!"

40. According to Jewish law (halakha), cremation is a great sin and highly condemned. In the Soviet Union, however, cremation was a common practice among Jews and others. Today, it's still chosen by many citizens of the former Soviet Union, including Jews.

41. Zelenina 2012, 58.

42. The Purim festival commemorates the miraculous foiling of Haman's plot to kill all the Jews of Persia.

43. Serving as an official consulate of the state of Israel in Odesa, the Israeli Cultural Center also functions as an educational and cultural facility for those interested in Israeli life and culture.

44. Zissels 1999, 301.

45. See Richardson (2005) for a detailed description of this group.

46. Judith Deutsch Kornblatt (2003, 221), in her research on Jewish Christians in the former Soviet Union, writes that "many Jews in the Church are reluctant to identify themselves publicly for fear of discrimination from both Jews and Christians." Deutsch Kornblatt also notes that "Jews [like Nina] who converted to Christianity and then arrived in Israel under the Law of Return have legal fears as well" (221 n2).

47. King 2011, 208.

48. In various periods, Odesa's catacombs, tunnels carved in limestone, served as a "reliable sanctuary for the persecuted" (Gubar and Rozenboim 2003, 120).

49. Veidlinger 2013, 241.

50. Manley 2009, 262.

51. Michael Stewart (2004, 570) makes similar observations about the survivors of the Roma community in Romania. Following their return from Nazi concentration camps, they remained silent so as to gain readmission to their homes, villages, and towns.

52. Fitzpatrick (1999) 2000, 84.

53. The Sokhnut is an Israeli organization operating in the former Soviet Union to educate Jews about Israel and assist them in making aliyah.

54. In Israel, Jewish immigrants can acquire citizenship within three months of their arrival, or once a person turns eighteen years of age. An immigrant visa is needed before officially applying for citizenship.

55. Zelenina 2012.

56. Chervyakov, Gitelman, and Shapiro 1997, 281.

57. Krupnik 1994, 141.

58. Gitelman (1988) 2001, 271; Ritterband 1997, 332, 336.

59. Senderovich 2022, 6.

60. Gitelman 2012, 22–23.

61. Senderovich 2022.

62. The Institute of Judaica in Kyiv has made an important contribution to the history of Soviet Jewish life by collecting the life stories of Jews born before World War II and producing an archive of almost six hundred interviews conducted for two projects: "Witnesses of the Jewish Century" and "The Jewish Destiny of Ukraine."

63. Murav 2011, 9–11.

64. Gans 1956a.

65. Gans 1994, 579.

66. Markowitz 1993, 153.

67. Goluboff 2003, 6; see also Zelenina 2012, 2014; Golbert 2001a; and Cooper 1998, 2012. See Fran Markowitz's book *A Community in Spite of Itself* (1993, 52) for a different argument; she proposes that the overlapping of Russian and Jewish identities became possible only for those who immigrated to Israel and the United States.

68. Fialkova and Yelenevskaya 2007, 66.

3. Jewish Revival

1. A sukkah is a ritual outdoor booth or hut where Jews take their meals and sometimes sleep during the holiday of Sukkot. A *chanukiah* is a nine-branched candelabrum lit for the Chanukah festival. Chabad congregations usually display large *chanukiahs* in central parts of their cities. In 2007, I saw a twenty-foot-tall *chanukiah* erected in Odesa's most prominent square, above the Potemkin Steps.

2. Richardson 2008, 188.

3. City authorities, believing that Jewish buildings should belong in the Jewish community, offered the Brody Synagogue to the Chabad congregation. According to the secretary of Chabad congregation, however, no one in the city wanted the building, recognizing that it would take millions of dollars to bring it back to life. In my earlier interviews with Yulia Gris, the rabbi of the Shirat ha-Yam Progressive Jewish Congregation of Odesa, the story was, yet again, rather different. In her view, the strong political relationship between Chabad and local authorities played a role in the mayor's decision to return the building to Chabad. Nothing has been done since the building was handed over in 2016, as the state archives are still looking for new premises and currently have no plans for a move.

4. See Richardson 2008, 240 n18, for similar conclusions.

5. Gruber 2014, 335–36.

6. Klier 2002, 175.

7. Cited in Herlihy 2018, 62.

8. Zipperstein 1986.

9. Magocsi and Petrovsky-Shtern 2016, 283.

10. Ibid., 284.

11. Bassin and Kelly 2012, 9.

12. Ibid., 12.

13. Ibid., 7.

14. Ibid.

15. Hann and the "Civil Religion" Group 2006, 2. In Marxist-Leninist ideology, religion was the "opiate of the people," regarded as an irrational and potentially dangerous superstition. During the Soviet period, as Hann explains, "proselytizing and religious education in schools were prohibited and any display of religious commitment could prejudice not only one's own job but also the position and prospects of a wide circle of relatives and friends" (ibid.).

16. Golbert 2001b, 713.

17. See Friedman and Chernin 1999; Altshuler 2005.

18. Estimates for Odesa's Jewish population in 1989 range from sixty-five thousand to eighty thousand. See the introduction to this volume.

19. See Dragadze 1993, 146–56, for a discussion of the "domestication" of religious practice in the USSR.

20. Gidwitz 1997.

21. Chabad Lubavitch is a movement in Hasidism that is also thought of as a philosophy and an organization. The name Chabad is an acronym for *hokhmah* (wisdom), *binah* (comprehension), and *daa't* (knowledge). Lubavitch is the name of the town in White Russia where the movement was based. Today, the main headquarters of Chabad Lubavitch is in Crown Heights, New York, in the United States. Menachem Mendel Schneerson, the seventh rabbi, started a worldwide outreach movement to bring Jews back to Judaism. As part of this mission, he dispatched thousands of emissaries (*schlihim*) around the world. More than 3,800 emissary couples are stationed in forty-five US states and sixty-one foreign countries (Fishkoff 2003, 10). Particularly in the FSU, Chabad has become a dominant Jewish voice, "shaping the future of this newly emerging Jewish community in a way they have done nowhere else" (ibid., 8).

22. While a number of Israeli families have remained in Odesa since the first days of the community's operation, most stay only two to four years.

23. The Glavnaya (Main) synagogue was initially known as Beit Knesset Ha-Gadol. The original one-story building constructed in 1795 or 1796, was reconstructed in 1840 after a fire and eventually replaced in 1859 by a new two-story edifice in the Florentine style with Romanesque elements designed by the Italian Odesa architect Francesco Morandi. In 1899, the building was once again

reconstructed to the current structure (Zipperstein 1986, 57; Gubar and Rozenboim 2003, 67).

24. The Tikva Odesa Children's Home was set up in 1996 to serve the city's needy and homeless Jewish children. It's sometimes referred to as an orphanage, but some of the children have parents who are simply unable to care for them (see Fishkoff 2004a). In 2001, the synagogue and the children's home were combined into Tikva Or Sameach. Today, Tikva Odesa remains the main sponsor of the Tikva Or Sameach congregation, attracting Jewish philanthropists in the United States, Israel, Britain, and elsewhere who raise funds for its operation.

25. According to the organization's website, nearly 1,200 children benefit from the schools, homes, and university programs offered by Tikva. But I found the number of regular attendees at the synagogue to be significantly lower than the 1,000 mentioned by one employee of the congregation. The Friday night services I attended drew between thirty and fifty women and between sixty and eighty men. Holiday celebrations attracted greater numbers, including visiting Israeli families. For the Sukkot celebration I attended in 2006, nearly 350 guests were present.

26. Tikva Children's Home, n.d.

27. Bemporad 2013, 20. Litvaks—who followed a tradition of Jewish Orthodox practice that originated in Vilna, the capital of the Lithuanian Grand Duchy until 1791 and a hub of Jewish eastern Europe—were historically identified with highly intellectual Talmud study. Although the term *Litvak* technically means a Jew from Lithuania, it also includes Jews from Belarus and others who followed the Lithuanian tradition. The term has come to mean someone who is Orthodox but not Hasidic. Litvaks are frequently characterized as being more rationalist, dogmatic, and authoritarian than other branches of Ashkenazi Jewry. The movement is often closely linked to the teachings of Rabbi Elijah ben Shlomo Zalman of Vilnius (1720–97), known as the Vilna Gaon, who strongly opposed the development of Hasidism in eastern Europe. Opponents of Hasidim were called Mitnagdim (Bridger 1976, 192).

28. Hasidism (piety) is a Jewish religious movement that originated in the Polish-Lithuanian Commonwealth in the mid-eighteenth century. The name refers to not only the traditional virtues of piety espoused by the movement but also a new ethos of ecstatic joy and a new social structure: the court of rebbes (in Hebrew *tzaddikim* [righteous men]), and their followers, the Hasidim (formally meaning "pious men" but also "disciples"). Drawing on earlier texts of Kabbalah (Jewish mysticism) and other magical traditions, the tzaddikim were seen as intercessors between their followers and God, focusing primarily on prayer rather than study, as was previously believed to be the case in traditional Orthodox circles. Rather than withdrawal, they emphasized *simcha* (joy) and divine immanence, God's presence throughout the material world. Hasidism was more than an intellectual movement, it was also focused on bodily practices (praying, storytelling, singing, dancing, and eating, among other things). David Biale et al.

(2018) argue that the physicality of Hasidism played a major role in transforming it from an elite movement to a popular one. The founder of Hasidism, Israel
Baal Shem Tov, known as the Besht, "started to preach a living faith in which the
ordinary individual found comfort and a way to approach God" (Bridger 1976,
191). The movement aimed at bringing Judaism to every person, whatever their
level of education and literacy. In contrast to older forms of Orthodoxy, which
were text-centered and academic, Hasidism emphasizes personal piety, mysticism, and good deeds (mitzvoth) judged as individual merits. Ohr Avner is a
philanthropic foundation established in 1992 by Lev Leviev, an Israeli billionaire
of Bukhari Jewish background.

29. I occasionally saw women wearing nontraditional attire that some
would consider inappropriate, such as trousers or revealing shirts or skirts,
and families driving to service on Shabbat. When I asked about this, one of
my interlocutors said, "Wolf just closes his eyes to this." Perhaps Rabbi Wolf
extended an open invitation for any Jew in the city to attend his services and
feel welcome in his congregation, regardless of their level of observance or type
of dress. This could also explain why some violations of traditional Shabbat
practices were accepted.

30. Chabad Odesa, n.d.

31. Davidzon 2021, 9–10.

32. Each chief rabbi is designated as such by a municipal department that
has issued certificates and stamps (Gidwitz 1997). A number of local Jews were
disturbed by the fact that Wolf, the Chabad rabbi, drove an expensive car. I heard
two young students discussing this: one boy claimed that the car was a present to
the rabbi from one of his sponsors, and his friend responded, "Yes, I know those
types of gifts. Our rabbi [in Kherson, a neighboring city] also receives them."

33. Zipperstein 1986, 57.

34. Shneer 2007.

35. Ibid.

36. Zelenina 2018, 257.

37. See also Fishkoff 2004b.

38. See Polonsky 2013, 438–39.

39. "Floaters" were sometimes referred to as "prostitutes" for receiving benefits at both congregations.

40. See the websites of Tikva Children's Home (www.tikvaodessa.org) and
Chabad Odesa (www.chabad.odessa.ua).

41. Other scholars of religious movements in the FSU have pointed out that
with Christian and Islamic movements, the financial and material rewards attached to conversions are a factor in religious affiliation (Pelkmans 2006a, 36).

42. Caldwell 2005, 20, 22.

43. Odesa's Jews also receive aid from a number of nonreligious organizations, funded mainly by the JDC. I would guess that any Odesans of non-Jewish
descent who forged their documents did so not to explore Jewish life but rather

to gain access to all that's been offered to Jews by international Jewish organizations and donors. See Caldwell 2008 for a discussion of comparable Christian-based welfare in the former Soviet Union.

44. Similar attitudes are expressed toward ethnic Greeks and Germans in the FSU who have privileges tied to European citizenship, which many ex-Soviet citizens can't obtain (Eftihia Voutira, pers. comm., November 6, 2010).

45. Kotkin 1995, 152.

46. Chlenov 1994, 133. In the Russian language, children of mixed (Jewish and non-Jewish) origin were referred to as *polukrovok* (male) or *polukrovka* (female), which literally translates as "half-blood."

47. Gidwitz 2001, 4. Zvi Gitelman (2009, 258) notes that in 1988, 48 percent of Soviet Jewish women and 58 percent of Jewish men had married non-Jews. By 1996, the frequency of mixed marriages in Ukraine was 81.6 percent for Jewish men and 73.7 percent for Jewish women. In the Soviet Union, as Gitelman (ibid., 257) explains, interethnic marriages were presented in the media and the arts as a sign of progressiveness. On intermarriage among Soviet Jewry, see Altshuler 1998, 7, and Tolts 1992.

48. Of course, intermarriage, mixed ancestry, and the incidence of nonhalakhic Jews are widespread phenomena and not specific to Odesa. In the United States, for instance, the intermarriage rate recorded from 2005 to 2013 by the Pew Research Center is 58 percent (Sasson et al. 2017, 104). Reform Judaism welcomes the children of mixed marriages and the non-Jewish spouses of affiliated Jewry, even where the mother is not Jewish; in regarding them as Jews, it departs from the halakha.

49. Andrew Buckser presents a comparable scenario in Denmark, writing that "some members [of the Jewish community], following Orthodox guidelines, insist that only the children of Jewish mothers or formal converts count as true Jews; some others, noting the prevalence of intermarriage, include children of Jewish fathers as well; and still others recognize self-identification, rather than descent, as the proper criterion for Jewishness. . . . Some of these viewpoints have greater official standing than others—the Orthodox rabbi, for example, has the final word on official membership in the Community" (Buckser 1999, 194). High rates of intermarriage in Odesa and the legacy of Soviet nationality policy (which recognized a person as a Jew through either the maternal or paternal line) complicate boundaries of Jewish membership. The Reform approach to the question of who is a Jew opens the possibility of claiming Jewish identification through either line of descent. The open-door policy practiced by Temple Emanu-El, captured in the slogan posted on its original website, clearly relays a message of inclusivity for potential congregants: "If you are a Jew—come to us! If you are not quite a Jew—come to us!! If you have not yet decided who you are—come to us!!!" (the original website http://www.emanu-el.od.ua is no longer active).

50. Cooper 1998, 2012.

51. Ibid.

52. Such decisions, as Cooper notes, were influenced both by the notion that Islam, the major religion in central Asia, is transmitted through patrilineal lines of descent and by the fact that local Uzbeks follow patrilocal residential patterns.

53. Cooper 1998, 34.

54. In an earlier study of an immigrant enclave of Soviet Jews in Brighton Beach, New York, Fran Markowitz describes cases where boys were denied the bris procedure (circumcision) as a result of genealogical tracking conducted by American rabbis. She writes, "Boys who had considered themselves Jewish, and were considered Jewish in their native country, were told that they are, in fact, not Jews because of intermarriage a generation or two ago" (Markowitz 1993, 159). With compassion for these newly arrived immigrants and an evident distaste for the attitude of the rabbis who "were happy to have caught forgeries," Markowitz considers these cases truly upsetting, "leaving Soviet Jews with ambivalent feelings about their Jewish identity" (pers. comm., April 2004).

55. Cooper 2012, 192.

56. In the former Soviet Union, the Orthodox conversion process usually takes one to two years and entails strict observance of the Jewish commandments and learning an array of subjects such as Jewish history, the Hebrew language, prayers, rituals, and the Jewish calendar. For men, the process also involves circumcision. As conversion isn't an aim of the Jewish religion, rabbis initially discourage aspiring converts in order to test their sincerity and often deny applicants for having the wrong motives (wanting to marry a Jewish partner, for example, isn't considered adequate). Potential converts are also made aware that even after *giur* they may never be accepted as true Jews, since religious leaders are constantly challenging one another on the legitimacy of conversions. Adding to the sense of anxiety, in 2008 Israel limited its list of rabbis whose *giur* certificate is accepted as legitimate to those who work with state-run religious authorities, rejecting any private conversion (see Newman 2018). Odesa's Reform congregation also offered conversion classes, but few members of the congregation took advantage of the *giur* option, possibly because they already felt included without the formality of conversion. Yulia didn't insist on strict observance or try to discourage potential converts. While I was in Odesa, she used weekly study groups to teach interested individuals about Judaism within the framework of Reform ideology.

57. I don't mean to imply that only Jews were hired by Jewish organizations. In fact, many non-Jews worked in circles of Jewish activity (for example, at the Israeli Cultural Center, Museum of the History of Odesa Jews, and Migdal).

58. Kessel 2000, 10.

59. The Sokhnut is an international body representing the World Zionist Organization. Its purpose is to assist and encourage Jews worldwide to help develop and settle Israel. See *Encyclopaedia Britannica* 2023.

60. The Law of Return 1950 (section 1) simply states: "Every Jew has the right to immigrate to the country" of Israel, leaving the word "Jew" undefined. In 1970,

the Law of Return was amended to recognize as a Jew, for purposes of immigration, any person who was born of a Jewish mother or who has converted to Judaism (whether through an Orthodox or other process isn't specified) and is not a member of another religion. The amended law also grants the right to immigrate to the children and grandchildren of a Jew; the non-Jewish spouses of Jews; the non-Jewish spouses of children of Jews; and the non-Jewish spouses of non-Jewish grandchildren of Jews. "The purpose of this amendment is to ensure the unity of families, where intermarriage had occurred; it does not apply to persons who had been Jews and had voluntarily changed their religion." However, applications for immigration can be refused on other grounds, such as criminality, health, or national security. All immigrants admitted under the Law of Return are normally granted Israeli citizenship. Jewish Agency for Israel, n.d.

61. Levin 2021, 370–71.

62. Voutira 2006, 380, emphasis in the original.

63. Ibid., 393.

64. Fialkova and Yelenevskaya 2007, 3. Many immigrants from the former Soviet Union aren't considered Jewish in halakhic terms. Concerns about excessive numbers of "non-Jewish Russians" have been expressed by Israeli politicians, members of the religious *beit din* (rabbinic law court), and some ordinary Israeli citizens. They see the 1970 amendments to the Law of Return and nationality law as flawed legislation that's too broad in its parameters, especially in the consequent granting of citizenship. Negative stereotypes of Russian Jews as alcoholics, Mafiosi, prostitutes, and even Bolsheviks (see Lemish 2000) circulate endlessly in informal and formal settings of the Israeli media, press, and national dialogue (Fialkova and Yelenevskaya 2007, 5).

65. According to the Ministry of Absorption of Immigration in Israel, only 93 people immigrated to Israel from Odesa in 2006, compared to 6,703 in 1990 and 3,294 in 1991 (data emailed to me upon request by the Information Sector of the former Soviet Union Office of the Jewish Agency for Israel). Between 1989 and 1998, 770,000 people immigrated to Israel from the entire FSU. Between 1999 and 2016, the number of Jews and their relatives who emigrated from the FSU to Israel was estimated at 297,700 (Tolts 2018, 11).

66. "Repatriates" in the context of aliyah are treated differently than refugees and "are expected to integrate rapidly and easily due to their common ethnic and cultural roots" (Fialkova and Yelenevskaya 2007, 1). Yet the assumption that Jews would integrate more easily in Israel than in other destinations has been challenged by empirical studies showing that Jews coming to Israel often experience many of the same issues as Jews immigrating to other countries (Shuval and Leshem 1998; Voutira 2006).

67. The JCC offers a wide range of services, resources, and recreational programs for Jewish people of all ages and backgrounds. JCC members enjoy the benefits of Hebrew classes, lectures, films, athletic programs, and—most important—opportunities to communicate and interact with other Jews. See

Aviv and Shneer 2005 (164–71) for a description of the JCC's goals, functions, and history in the United States.

68. Golbert 2001b, 713, 715.

69. Bauman 2001, 506.

70. Broz 2009, 24. Broz describes adherents of Buddhism in Altai (southwest Siberia) who adopted a revivalist stance; they "emphasize the cultural proximity [referring to Mongolia and Tuva] and historical influence of Buddhism" on Altaian culture as they "claim to be dusting down a well-preserved Altaian tradition rather than proposing something new."

71. Bauman 2001, 506.

72. For further explanation of the word "Moriah," see Harris 2006.

73. Richardson 2008, 189.

74. Levin 2021.

75. Polonsky 2013, 437.

76. Hasidism (specifically Chabad) and the Litvak movement have undergone tremendous change through the last two centuries and have few remaining links to their earlier representatives in the city.

77. See YIVO Institute for Jewish Research, n.d. While Hasidic tzaddikim (righteous religious leaders) did visit Odesa periodically and had a following there, nineteenth-century Orthodox leaders acknowledged the general indifference to religion among the city's Jews; indeed, they "claimed that the fires of Gehenna burned seven miles around Odessa" (Klier 2002, 173; also Zipperstein 1986, 104–05).

78. Horowitz 2003, 124.

79. Pelkmans 2009, 2.

4. From *Evrei* to *Iudei*

1. Sapritsky-Nahum 2015.

2. Bauman 2001, 503.

3. Ibid.

4. Ibid., 506.

5. Ibid.

6. Gitelman 2009, 1. Cynthia A. Baker's 2017 book *Jew* offers an extensive historical analysis of this binary.

7. Deutsch Kornblatt 2003, 214.

8. Gitelman 2003, 50.

9. Leite 2017, 18.

10. Richardson 2006, 21 n10.

11. Chervyakov, Gitelman, and Shapiro 2003, 73.

12. Zelenina 2018, 251–52.

13. Pelkmans 2006a, 2006b, 34.

14. Pelkmans 2006b, 34.

15. Danzger 1989, 27.
16. Webber 1994b, 84.
17. Cooper 2012, xii.
18. Mathijs Pelkmans, pers. comm., January 21, 2022.
19. Ukraïner 2019.
20. A minyan is a quorum of ten men required for public prayer.
21. Eduard Gurvitz, Odesa's mayor at the time of my fieldwork, was generally shy about expressing any religious affiliation; he rarely spoke publicly of himself as a Jew. In 2008, however, he took part in a public celebration at the Chabad synagogue to honor the circumcision of his newborn son. The event was widely reported in the local press (see Runyan 2008).
22. *Ba'al teshuvah*, which means "master of return," is used to describe Jews who embrace Orthodox Judaism on their own initiative and often later in life, in contrast to Jews born and raised in Orthodox environments. The concept is most popular in the United States and Israel. See Danzger 1989 for an in-depth description of the contemporary revival of Orthodox Judaism in the United States.
23. Golbert 2001a, 209.
24. The bar mitzvah (for a boy) and bat mitzvah (for a girl) are ceremonies to celebrate the "coming of age" of young boys and girls and their willingness to accept the commandments that God requires of adult men and women.
25. A chuppah is a canopy under which the bride and groom stand during the wedding ceremony; it's symbolic of their shared future home. The term is also used to describe the wedding ceremony as a whole.
26. Yurchak 2006, 103, 109.
27. Paxson 2005, 53.
28. The ritual of the first haircut at age three, which dates back to the sixteenth century, has a number of explanations. Some scholars believe that it is related to the law in the Bible that states that one is not allowed to eat fruit from a tree during the first years after it's been planted. Thus, comparing human life to the life of a tree, waiting three years to cut a child's hair is like waiting three years to pick a tree's fruit, suggesting that the child will eventually grow tall like a tree and produce the fruit of knowledge, mitzvoth, and a family of his own. In the Hasidic tradition, this ceremony marks the transition in his education. The child's sidelocks are left intact, which signifies his first mitzvah. From this point on, a child is often taught to wear a kippah and tzitzit.
29. Beitar is a Zionist youth movement founded in 1923 by Vladimir Jabotinsky, based on principles of self-respect, military training, and defending Jewish life and property against antisemitic outbreaks.
30. Videos, pictures, and stories of other Jewish or mixed (Jewish and non-Jewish) wedding celebrations show a combination of Russian, Ukrainian, Jewish, and Soviet traditions in the ceremonies and receptions. Parents who weren't observant themselves often encouraged their sons and daughters who wanted a Jewish ceremony to include elements of Russian, Ukrainian, or Soviet customs

that would be familiar to the guests; this even happened in some cases where the parents were observant. The concern was to have a ceremony that wouldn't seem "foreign" to those unfamiliar with Jewish wedding rituals. A friend from Odesa had an Orthodox wedding ceremony in Dnepropetrovsk, the groom's home-town; the dinner reception included the Russian tradition of family toasts and the Russian toast, Gor'ko (bitter), which signals the bride and groom to please their guests with a public kiss. Both Russian and Ukrainian dishes were served.

31. *Khametz* refers to products made from any of five grains (wheat, barley, spelt, rye, or oats) that have gone through the process of fermentation; these are prohibited during Pesach.

32. Golbert 2001a, 210.

33. Although I never attended a burial ceremony in Odesa, I spoke with a number of local Jews about practices for the deceased, including cremation, prep-aration for burial, the actual ceremony, and the later markers of remembrance.

34. Religious leaders and teachers at religious schools cited the same phenom-enon when describing the limitations of their role in students' lives. An emissary from Israel said, "Many children faced the difficult task of living a religious life outside their schools, as their parents are not observant Jews—or in many cases are not Jewish."

35. During my interviews, other followers of the Chabad congregation also mentioned the discomfort of walking into a Christian church.

36. Masha said that Odesa Jews who were baptized knew one another, and on Russian Orthodox holidays, they were often absent from activities in school and Migdal. Surveys conducted in 1992 and again in 1997 show that the number of Jews in Ukraine who found Christianity to be the "most attractive" faith rose from 10.7 percent in 1992 to 15.5 percent in 1997 (Gitelman 2003, 195, 201–02; see also Deutsch Kornblatt 2003, 209–23).

37. According to Orthodox religious practice, swimming is allowed only on beaches segregated by sex.

38. Horowitz 2020, 222.

39. King 2011, 156–57.

40. Lecke 2012, 233.

41. Ibid., 330, 455.

42. Horowitz 2020, 226.

43. In many cases, younger members of this group participated at a higher level because they had more free time. University students and young adults were less active as they were concentrating on their studies, careers, or other realms of self-development.

44. Richardson 2006, 21 n10.

45. A survey conducted in 2003 by Pankov showed that 51 percent of respondents considered themselves believers, 32 percent could not answer, and 17 percent considered themselves nonbelievers. In 1995, the comparable figures were 51 percent believers, 19 percent difficulty deciding, and 28 percent

nonbelievers. While the proportion of believers identifying themselves as members of the Ukrainian Orthodox Church increased from 28 percent (in 1995) to 46 percent (in 2003), the numbers remained unchanged for adherents of Greek Catholicism, Roman Catholicism, Protestantism, Islam, Judaism, and other religions (each at 1 percent of the sample). Cited in Richardson 2006, 21 n10.

46. Chervyakov, Gitelman, and Shapiro 2003, 74.

47. Zissels 1999, 303.

48. Norman Solomon (1994, 97) describes meeting a group of young Jews in Leningrad (Saint Petersburg) in 1982 who had recently acquired tefillin and were praying according to the Orthodox requirements. His doubts about whether they were thus "returning to their roots" arose from the fact that the boys had been instructed about the rituals by a visiting Orthodox Jew, not by older Jewish residents of their native city; the boys feared that the latter had forgotten the "authentic" ways. This example makes Solomon wonder, "So in what sense were the young Jews of Leningrad returning to their roots? Certainly not in a sense of reclaiming the way of life of their grandparents or great-grandparents, but rather in fear of their altered standards" (87).

5. Asymmetric Cultural Encounters

1. Aviv and Shneer 2005, 61.

2. In Hebrew, tzedakah means righteousness, fairness, or justice. The root of the word, *tzedek*, implies that "social welfare is viewed as an economic and social justice matter and Tzedakah, giving, is part of Tzedek justice" (Shadmi 2019, 124).

3. Shadmi 2019, 125.

4. Aviv and Shneer 2005, 57.

5. Stirrat and Henkel 1997, 66.

6. To avoid confusion, I use the acronym UJC/JFNA to mark this change when necessary. Although the old UJC website has since shut down, I've kept some citations from it as they relate to the timing of the mission described here.

7. Douglas 1990, viii.

8. Ibid., ix.

9. Stirrat and Henkel 1997, 69.

10. Aviv and Shneer 2005, 57.

11. Poppendieck 1998.

12. Leite 2017, 177.

13. Kugelmass 1994; Leite 2017, 187.

14. Lehrer 2013, 57.

15. Leite 2017, 183.

16. Allahyari 2000; Craig 2005.

17. Caldwell 2008.

18. Shadmi 2019, 125.

19. Lehrer 2013, 57.

20. Feldman 2008, xviii, 20, 26.

21. Stirrat and Henkel 1997, 67.

22. Aviv and Shneer 2005, 52.

23. Chief Rabbi of Russia Berel Lazar's address to sponsors of the Federation of Jewish Communities of the CIS, printed in 2000.

24. Cited in Caldwell 2008, 199.

25. ORT was founded in Russia in 1880 to develop employable skills for Russia's impoverished Jews. In Russian, ORT is an acronym for Obshestvo Remeslennogo i zemledelchskogo Truda, meaning Society for Trades and Agricultural Labor. In the early 1990s, ORT began to support training programs in Jewish schools (World ORT, n.d.). ORT runs its own school in Odesa and provides computers and computer training programs to other Jewish schools in the city.

26. Poppendieck 1998, 185.

27. This description refers to the large fundraising missions conducted by nonprofit organizations. Smaller group and individual trips to the city rely on a wider range of resources and have other reasons for visiting. I met visiting Jews who had found resources through their synagogue, a travel agency, Jewish genealogy websites, friends who had previously visited the city, or local publications purchased abroad. They presumably experienced a somewhat different view of Odesa.

28. Leit 2017, 185.

29. In this context, "program" refers to particular projects designed to fulfill specified social needs.

30. Aviv and Shneer 2005, 56. Ruth Ellen Gruber (2002) describes the phenomenon of Jewish tourism and suggests that places and people are often presented (and even distorted) to suit specific organizational and individual needs.

31. Picturing Jews in the FSU, the old UJC website read, "Around the world, we help the needy and nurture Jewish life" (Jewish Federations of North America, n.d.-b), and the Joint's website spelled out, "We provide aid to vulnerable Jews" (JDC, n.d.).

32. Aviv and Shneer (2005, 52) describe diaspora business as "a broad institutional and organizational terrain that complicates the difference between home and abroad, centers and peripheries, in a shifting, increasingly compressed global world of capital, people, ideas, and national borders."

33. Taglit, also known as Birthright Israel, is a not-for-profit educational organization that sponsors free ten-day heritage trips to Israel for young adults (aged 18–32) of Jewish heritage.

34. See Jewish Federations of North America, n.d.-a.

35. See Jewish Federations of North America, n.d.-b.

36. O'Brien 1986, 128.

37. Ibid.

38. Others who worked in the Sokhnut programs called the organization's tactics "brainwashing." Based on their stories and those of others, I suspect that Olga wasn't typical—or perhaps her declaration was influenced by her role in the UJC/Sokhnut mission.

39. Markowitz 1993, 139. In the field, I often heard the term *professional Jew* in reference to Jews who worked for Jewish organizations, received work-related benefits, and treated their Jewishness as an attribute of their profession.

40. Waligorska 2013, 1–2; Halkowsky 2003.

41. Shayduk 2007, 3, 6.

42. Zvi Gitelman (2009, 248) also notes in his discussion of Jewishness in Russia and Ukraine that "Jewish" as a category "is based on biological descent and an ineffable feeling of belonging."

43. In surveys conducted in 1992 and 1997 by the Jewish Research Center and the Russian Academy of Sciences, respectively, "being proud of one's nationality" was the most frequent response to the question "What is the most important thing required of a person in order to be considered a genuine Jew?" (Gitelman 2009, 249).

44. Shadmi 2019, 125; Leite 2017, 181–82.

45. Leite describes a similar phenomenon among Marrano community members in a "rote performance," receiving group after group of tourists who start to "blur into one another" (2017, 177).

46. Pelkmans 2007, 892.

47. Ibid.

48. Gruber 2002, 132.

49. Migdal staff told me that documents are checked to assess which students can apply to programs in Israel (one of four grandparents must be Jewish), who can have a bar/bat mitzvah at the synagogue (the participant's mother must be Jewish), and so on.

50. Utesov 2006, 11. Leonid Utesov traveled around the Pale as an entertainer, combining comedy and improvised music. Writing about Utesov, Jarrod Tanny (2011) notes that "combining humorous lyrics and the celebrated chaos, crime and debauchery of old Odessa with the melodies and the wailing fiddles and clarinets of klezmer music, Utesov brought the Odessa Myth to the Soviet stage."

51. Gruber 2002, 145.

52. "Righteous gentiles" refers to gentiles who risked their lives to save Jews from the Holocaust.

53. Leite 2017, 194–200.

54. Ibid., 22.

55. Ibid., 17.

56. Shadmi 2019, 124–25.

57. Aviv and Shneer 2005, 52.

58. Three memorials commemorate Jewish suffering during the wartime occupation of Odesa. Two are located close to each other. The more recent one

(erected in 2004) depicts six life-size figures of naked Jews standing on what appears to be the edge of a cliff (symbolically the cliff of death). Below the terrified figures, a large inscription spells out "HOLOCAUST" in English, with "never again" underneath in smaller characters, in Russian, Ukrainian, and Hebrew. Another plaque says, in Russian, "We will never forget, we will never forgive." An earlier memorial, built in 1994, marks the starting point of the "Road to Death": in 1941, this was where the remaining Jews were assembled to be deported into Romanian-administered camps and ghettos in the Berezovka region, in Transnistria. The third memorial takes the form of a tall, semioval black stone with a hollowed-out Star of David. The inscription reads, in Ukrainian and Hebrew, "In the memory of Jewish victims who were burned and shot, 1941–1944." In 2009, the city's Holocaust Museum opened, an initiative of Odesa's Association of Jewish Ghetto Survivors Union. I'm grateful to Michael Rashkovetsky and Nusya Verhovskaya for detailed descriptions of the Holocaust memorials and museum.

59. Hannerz 1996, 105.

60. Golbert 2001a, 14.

61. Ibid., 146.

62. Lehrer 2013, 4.

63. Koposov 2018, 183. For a discussion of Holocaust remembrance linked to Babyn Yar, see, among others, Aleksandre Burakovskiy 2011; Hrynevych and Magosci 2016; and Dreyer 2018.

64. Sokol 2022, 197.

65. Ibid.

66. Tabarovsky 2018.

67. Babyn Yar is a ravine in a Kyiv oblast where the Nazis carried out a series of massacres during World War II. In one notorious mass killing, 33,771 Jews were executed in a single operation on September 29–30, 1941. It's estimated that more than 100,000 victims were murdered there, including Soviet POWs, communists, Roma people, Ukrainian nationalists, and civilian hostages.

68. The project's original funders were Victor Pinchuk, Mikhail Fridman, German Khan, and Pavel Fuks. All but Pinchuk had ties to Russia, which became an issue amid deteriorating Russian-Ukrainian relations and later the war. Holocaust Encyclopedia, n.d.

69. See the original of the letter at "Museum 'Babyn Yar': An Open Letter of Warning from Ukrainian Historians," 2017.

70. See Himka 2021.

71. Cited in Sokol 2022, 195.

72. As far as I'm aware, no public commemoration of Babyn Yar takes place in Odesa, but Richardson (2008, 62) notes that the topic is now included in the history curriculum of Odesa's public schools and is taught under the subject of the Holocaust.

73. I'm grateful to Mathijs Pelkmans for drawing my attention to the inverted aspect of this performance.

74. Lehrer 2013, 4.

75. Finkelstein 2000.

76. Findling 1999, 1; quoted in Aviv and Shneer 2005, 61.

77. Gitelman (1994, 140) gives a number of explanations for the fact that in the Soviet Union, "the Holocaust was not portrayed as a unique, separate phenomenon." He wrote that the Jewish population was "unable to press for broader and deeper treatment of the Holocaust." In addition, "no other country in the West lost as many non-Jewish citizens as did the Soviets," and thus elsewhere "the fate of Jews stands in sharper contrast to that of their co-nationals or coreligionists than it does in the USSR." Finally, "the Soviet authorities had explicitly political reasons for playing down the Holocaust." In the Soviet view, Gitelman explains, "the Holocaust was an integral part of a larger phenomenon—the deliberate murder of civilians—which was said to be a natural consequence of racist fascism, which is, in turn, the logical culmination of capitalism."

78. Regarding the Holocaust as a topic of study in Odesa's public schools in the early 2000s, Tanya Richardson (2008, 62) wrote, "although silence no longer enveloped the event, there was certainly a 'hush.'"

79. Gitelman 1994, 141.

80. Brandon and Lower 2008.

81. Ibid., 2.

82. Himka 2021, 15.

83. Employees of the Museum of the History of Odesa Jews give lectures in the public schools on the subject of the Holocaust. Their talks prompt Jewish and non-Jewish students alike to visit the museum and to write papers on related themes. The museum director told me that one lecturer runs a private bus tour around "Jewish Odessa" for the winner of the best project (Michael Rashkovetsky, pers. comm., December 12, 2010, and more recently Nusya Verhovskaya, pers. comm., January 27, 2021).

84. Golbert (2001a, 146 n77) presents other examples of American Jewish youth trips that tie the narrative of the Holocaust to the presence of the Jewish state. Organizers of some Jewish missions take participants to visit Auschwitz and other concentration camps, and then escort them to Israel (also see Gruber 2002, 149).

85. Aviv and Shneer 2005, 52.

86. Faier and Rofel 2014, 363.

87. Caldwell 2004; Patico 2002; Wanner 2003.

88. Chervyakov, Gitelman, and Shapiro 2003, 72; see also Caldwell 2008, 192, for a more recent confirmation of the same phenomenon.

89. Funding for projects directed by the Sokhnut and UJC was cut back in light of the economic crisis that began in 2007–8, thus reducing the influence of those groups in the region. It is not yet clear whether the philanthropic efforts of local well-to-do Jews (some of them returnees) will change these dynamics,

either in terms of financial dependency or in terms of outside cultural influences, particularly in the wake of Russia's invasion of Ukraine.

6. "Jewish Is a Mode of Transportation"

1. Gitelman 1997, 25.
2. Aviv and Shneer 2005, 29.
3. Chlenov 1994, 127.
4. Part of this material focused on returnees was published in Sapritsky-Nahum 2016, 2018.
5. Gitelman 1997, 23.
6. Ibid.
7. Gitelman 1997, 25; Zipperstein 1986, 20; Dubnow 1918, 2:373.
8. See, for example, Frankel 1981, 50.
9. Gitelman 1997.
10. Lewin-Epstein 1997, 3.
11. Siegel 1998, 3; Brym and Ryvkina 1994, 71–72.
12. See Golbert 2001a, 347 n228, for a detailed description of Ukraine's procedure for revoking the citizenship of emigrants leaving for Israel, the United States, or Germany.
13. Markowitz (1993) notes that "because one lost one's citizenship after submitting this application—and one's job as well—and because one never knew when or if the request to emigrate would be granted, submission of emigration documents was terrifying indeed" (265–66).
14. Tolts 2004, 58; Tolts 2020, 324.
15. Brym and Ryvkina 1994, 15; Gitelman 1997, 2.
16. Tolts 2004, 58; Tolts 2020, 324.
17. The most common reasons given for refusal of exit visas were possession of state secrets, state interest, unfulfilled military service, and the lack of any close relatives in Israel. The number of refuseniks—Soviet Jewish citizens denied exit visas—had surpassed eleven thousand by 1986 (Siegel 1998, 7, 63).
18. Tolts 2020, 324.
19. Rosenberg 2015.
20. Brym and Ryvkina 1994. Yehuda Dominitz (1997) and Fran Markowitz (1993, 265–67) offer close analyses of this "dropout phenomenon" among Jewish migrants from the USSR.
21. Gitelman 1997, 29; 1988, 444.
22. Markowitz (1993, 1) notes that about fifty thousand Soviet Jews settled in the greater New York City area between 1972 and 1984. As she explains, "The Council of Jewish Federations devised a plan to resettle Soviet Jews throughout the US in accordance with the proportion of Jews in each region. Thus, New York City, with about 45 percent of the nation's Jewish population, was allotted 45 percent of Soviet émigrés, followed by Los Angeles and Chicago" (267). Writing in

August 1991, she noted that since 1987, "the Soviet immigrant population of New York has almost doubled" (263).

23. DellaPergola 2002.

24. Polonsky 2013, 425.

25. Tolts 2007, 293; see also Polonsky 2013, 425.

26. Lebedeva 2001, 49. In Lebedova's survey of Jewish migrants in the 1990s, 65–72 percent of respondents offered this as one of the main reasons for their departure.

27. Polonsky 2013, 437.

28. Brym and Ryvkina 1994, 74; Gitelman 1997, 30. The 1989 change in US immigration law was carried out under pressure from the Israeli state, whose interests clearly lay in directing the large flow of Soviet Jews to Israel (Siegel 1998, 20). A number of my interlocutors speculated about Israel's involvement in US immigration laws. Similar conclusions were documented by Larisa Fialkova and Nina Yelenevskaya (2007, 45) during interviews conducted in Israel. They write, "Most of our interviewees admitted that they had planned to immigrate to America and eventually landed in Israel only because 'America had closed down.'"

29. According to Robert Brym and Rozalina Ryvkina (1994, 74), in September 1989, 97 percent of Soviet Jewish emigrants chose *not* to go to Israel. After the October 1989 US restrictions on immigration, the proportion fell to about 20 percent and remained at that level until 1991.

30. Belensky and Skolnik 1998, 30.

31. Misha Belensky and Jonathan Skolnik (1998, 30) note that although the West German government only started officially granting refugee status to Soviet Jews in 1991, including those arriving via Israel, Jews from the Soviet Union had been immigrating to Germany since 1989 and even before that. In the 1970s and 1980s, about 3,000 Jews arrived in West Germany. In the first few years after the implementation of Germany's 1991 Contingency Refugee Act, "about 200,000 Russian Jews migrated to Germany." But the law was amended in 2005 to "seriously restrict Russian Jews' admission into Germany" (Schoeps and Glöckner 2008, 144). The amendments introduced a points system for immigration and established other requirements for citizenship. The current position is that Germany openly welcomes Russian Jews who are young, skilled, and knowledgeable in the German language and who offer potential contributions to German society. But victims of Nazi persecution are still exempt from residency and other requirements for naturalization as German citizens.

32. Tolts 2020, 325.

33. Cited in Gozman 1997, 406.

34. This is reflected in the slogan of the International World Odesit Club: "Jews, Russians, Ukrainians, Greeks, and Moldovans! What else do you have but Odessa? Especially in your soul? She is your Mother!"

35. Victoria Hegner (2000, 5) documents the strong pull of family ties for elderly Russian Jews in Chicago, many of whom say that their sole reason for emigration was to follow their children (and not be left alone).

36. While I was in Odesa, I didn't meet or hear of anyone leaving for the United States or Germany. Besides Elena and Konstantin, I knew of only two others who immigrated to Israel while I was doing fieldwork. In my later visits, however, a number of the youth I knew were on Israeli study-abroad programs; I also met young people who had permanently relocated to Israel following an Israeli partner. Gosha, cited previously, was able to get a work contract as an IT specialist and moved to Israel in the way he had hoped.

37. According to statistics from the Israeli Ministry of Absorption of Immigration, 20,447 Jews and their families arrived from Odesa between 1989 and 2006.

38. From "New Promised Land for Russian Israelis: Canada," *Jewish Russian Telegraph*, February 2002, http://www.jrtelegraph.com/2007/02/new_promised _la.html (link no longer active).

39. A survey conducted by Brym and Ryvkina (1994, 80–81) indicated that 31 percent of respondents in Moscow, Kyiv, and Minsk who were planning to emigrate chose countries other than Israel because they felt that they would find it too difficult to live in an atmosphere of Jewish culture or to learn Hebrew.

40. Golbert 2001a, 378.

41. Ibid., 339.

42. See also Markowitz 1997.

43. Statistics provided by the Israeli Consulate in Odesa in 2007.

44. See Sapritsky-Nahum 2013.

45. "About fifty thousand Jewish former emigrants to Israel have returned to Russia since 2001. Over the same period, only about thirty thousand Russian Jews have left for Israel" (Osipovich 2004, 36, quoted in Aviv and Shneer 2005, 49).

46. Newsru.co.il. n.d. A smaller survey of more than one hundred Russian Israelis (residing either in Israel or elsewhere abroad) conducted by Evgenyi Finkel (2004, 327) on LiveJournal indicated that 20 percent of his respondents have left Israel: of those, 27 percent returned to their countries of origin; 24 percent left for the United States; 23 percent for Europe; 14 percent for Canada; and 7 percent for Australia. Another 25 percent of Finkel's respondents who have not left Israel have entertained the idea of doing so.

47. Khanin 2021.

48. Tolts 2009, 9.

49. Citizens of Ukraine need a visa for most destinations outside the FSU, and obtaining these can be time-consuming and costly. Israeli citizenship facilitates less restricted travel and an easier visa application process for travel worldwide. Former citizens of Ukraine are allowed to go back to Ukraine on their Israeli travel passports without a visa. Recent legislation allows certain foreigners to travel to Ukraine without a visa for a duration of three months: citizens of the FSU, the United States, and the European Union, including ex-Ukrainians who have acquired citizenship in these countries. But the rules can be manipulated. I

met Odesan migrants who'd managed to retain their Ukrainian passports after acquiring citizenship abroad, and they commonly exchanged one passport for another at the airport.

50. Author's notes from Russian-Speaking Jewry in the Global Perspective: Power, Politics and Community conference, Bar Ilan University, Israel, October 17–19, 2006; Finkel 2004.

51. Ash 2004; Tolts 2009, 15.

52. Gold 2004, 445.

53. See Friedgut 2007, 266. Extensive lists of articles dealing with ex-Soviet Jewish remigration from Israel to the FSU were posted on the following sites but are no longer available: http://www.ncsj.org/AuxPages/080404_return.shtml; http://www.jewishla.org/federationinforcus/html/apr05_jfishel.html; http://www.nysun.com/article14147. An article on returnees from the US was posted at http://www.businessweek.com/1997/25/b353252.html but is no longer available.

54. See, for example, "Return of the Jews: For Decades the Story of Russia's Jews Has Been One of Fear and Flight to Israel. Now Many Are Coming Home," *Newsweek International*, August 9, 2004; and "Once Desperate to Leave, Now Jews Are Returning to Russia, Land of Opportunity," *The Times*, April 28, 2005.

55. Cited in Osipovich 2004, 1.

56. *Los Angeles Times*, February 3, 2005; article no longer appears on the site.

57. During my earlier fieldwork, in 2005–7, Odesa was home to a number of Russian-speaking Israelis who had come to study medicine and other professions. In the synagogue, a number of religious families were also Israeli returnees, who had come back with the specific goal of aiding Odesa's Jewish community in religious education and practice. Most worked in the Jewish schools and other educational institutions. Sokhnut also sponsored Russian-speaking Israelis who usually held one- to two-year posts as counselors and educators for Jewish youth.

58. Nor were they all returning from the same country: many came from Israel, a smaller percentage from Germany, and a few from the United States. This pattern may be explained by the fact that "migration to the USA and Germany usually entails inter-generational families, rather than individual Jewish youth and young couples, as is frequently the case with Israel" (Golbert 2001a, 347). Also explaining the low frequency of returns from the United States are the greater distance and the cost of travel. While visits from Germany are very common, permanent returns are less frequent. Belensky and Skolnik (1998, 37) document that 92 percent of ex-Soviet Jews living in Germany have traveled back to their hometowns, compared with 9 percent of those living in the United States and 19 percent of those living in Israel. They provide no data on permanent returns from Germany to the FSU.

59. Returning Odesans didn't form any sort of organized network or community, unlike other major economic hubs of the FSU with larger communities of Israeli returnees, such as an estimated 50,000–60,000 in Moscow (Friedgut

2007, 266). Official statistics on return migrants are vague. Russian and Ukrainian authorities track return migrants based on their registration with the local passport office when they resume residence status in their country. According to these calculations, provided by Mark Tolts (2007, 297), in 2004 immigration compared to emigration was 37 percent in Russia and 30 percent in Ukraine. However, these statistics are of limited value since a number of returnees don't officially register with state authorities. Also, statistics provided by the Israeli government identify returnees as such only once they have remained outside Israel for more than one year, and thus "transmigrants" are excluded. Therefore, these statistics wouldn't account for the many Russian-speaking Israelis who frequently travel back to Israel for personal and work-related reasons.

60. Nina speculated that the pogrom rumors were spread by state representatives and others interested in seizing the property and belongings left behind by Jews who emigrated. She also hinted that Zionists working in the city were involved. At the same time, she acknowledged that local Jews themselves feared that instability in Ukraine might result in anti-Jewish sentiment, with Jews scapegoated for the troubles of the state. I met other families in Israel who spoke of similar rumors in Kyiv.

61. For similar accounts, see Siegel 1998, 92–99.

62. Another returnee, Oleg, had a comparable religious experience in Israel, where he realized the importance of having God in his life through his interaction with the Russian Orthodox Church. He was baptized when he returned to Odesa, and he recently had his son baptized. Oleg had returned traumatized, having survived a terrorist attack in Israel and losing a close friend.

63. In contemporary Ukraine, as in the rest of the FSU, citizens have two passports: an internal passport that's used for all domestic affairs and a travel passport for crossing international borders. Today, citizens of the Ukrainian state aren't legally permitted to hold dual citizenship. In general, citizenship was an issue mainly for people of the middle generations and older, who were concerned about having a *propiska*, which guarantees state benefits and authorizes renting and buying property.

64. Kostya would later return to Israel for another trial run in early 2007, even though he didn't yet have any specific prospects there. Kostya, and others who struggled to build a life in Odesa upon their return, did end up moving to Israel and staying there. Indeed, Israel was regarded as yet another fresh start for cases of unsuccessful returns, especially in cases of divorce or unsuccessful business ventures.

65. Long and Oxfeld 2004, 10.

66. Gmelch 2004, 213.

67. See Morris and Polese 2016.

68. Vladimir (Ze'ev) Khanin (2020, 96) describes a similar phenomenon in Austria among the Austrian-Russian-Jewish "business elite," or what he calls "reciprocal migrants." These individuals engage in repeated business trips between

the Commonwealth of Independent States (CIS) and Europe while their families live in Austria.

69. Stefansson 2004, 4.

70. As it happens, the teacher involved, Maya, had cited the same conversation when telling me that Israel wouldn't be her preferred place to raise her son, due to the vast gap between secular and religious culture.

71. Voutira 2006, 380, emphasis in original.

72. Safran 1991, 84; Levy and Weingrod 2005, 4.

73. Tye 2001, 3; Gruen 2002; Wettstein 2002, 2.

74. Boyarin and Boyarin 1993.

75. Aviv and Shneer 2005, 22; Voutira 2006, 380; Clifford 1994, 1997; Markowitz and Stefansson 2004; Levy and Weingrod 2005.

76. Cohen 2008, 2; see also Lavie and Swedenburg 1996.

77. Gitelman 2016, 15. Tanya Richardson (2008, 213) argues that in fact, the "cultivation and power of local senses of place" witnessed among Odesans is not unique to Odesa and can be observed elsewhere in Ukraine.

78. See, among others, Boyarin and Boyarin 1993; Aviv and Shneer 2005.

79. For the Russian case, see Siegel 1998; Fialkova and Yelenevskaya 2007.

80. *Yerida* is translated from Hebrew as "descent"; it refers to the "stigmatized path of Israelis who descend from the promised land into the Diaspora" (Gold 2004, 445). Emigrants from Israel are thus referred to as *yordim*.

81. Gershenson and Shneer 2011, 141.

82. Brah 1996, 183.

83. Stefansson 2004, 186.

84. Mandel 1990, 160.

85. Clifford 1997, 249.

86. Feuchtwang 2004, 7; Rapport and Overing 2007, 176.

7. Odesa

1. Richardson 2004, 3.

2. Tanya Richardson (2008, 115) describes how literary scholars have written about Isaac Babel's Moldovanka or Babel's Odesa, suggesting how the neighborhood at the heart of Babel's *Odessa Stories* has come to stand in for the whole of the place.

3. Tanny 2011, 17. Tanny notes that at the turn of the twentieth century, Warsaw was 33 percent Jewish, Vilnius had a Jewish population that made up more than 40 percent of its inhabitants, Minsk was 52 percent Jewish, Kishinev was 46 percent Jewish, and Odesa 33 percent Jewish.

4. Wirth (1928) 1998, 19.

5. Ramer 2008.

6. Herzfeld 2005.

7. I use the term "Jewish stereotype" as a shorthand way of referring to the idea of Odesa as a Jewish city. There have been many ways of giving context to Odesa's Jewishness, but what I'm emphasizing is the sheer assertion of Odesa's Jewishness and the role this plays in establishing Odesa as a distinctive, special, and "other" place. This, in turn, is highly bound up with the Odesa myth.

8. Richardson, 2008, 197.

9. Horowitz 2017, 39–40.

10. Today, the city's religious landscape is dominated by the Ukrainian Orthodox Church (UOC)–Moscow Patriarchate, with more than fifty communities and thirty churches (Richardson 2006, 219). Other Christian denominations include UOC–Kyiv Patriarchate, Russian Orthodox Church, Armenian Apostolic Church, Greek Catholic, Roman Catholic, and Protestant communities. One leader of the Muslim population, Imam Sheikh Usam, indicated that "there are some 40,000 Muslims in Odessa," a number that includes "Ukrainian citizens, permanent residents, students, and businessmen" (cited in Richardson 2006, 220).

11. Herlihy 2008; Bilaniuk 2005. Patricia Herlihy (2008, 20) noted that by the mid-2000s, 80 percent of the schools in Ukraine had changed the language of instruction from Russian to Ukrainian. A similar trend is also seen in university settings, where Ukrainian has been declared the official language of instruction and examination.

12. Glaser 2023, 302.

13. Richardson 2008, 198–99.

14. Lecke and Sicher 2023, 2.

15. Stanton 2012, 19.

16. Glaser 2023, 286.

17. Lecke 2012, 329.

18. Richardson 2004, 14.

19. Sicher 2023, 219.

20. Stanton 2003, 120.

21. Tanny 2008, 403; emphasis in original.

22. Tanny 2011, 3.

23. Tanny 2008, 404.

24. Other places have been portrayed as a "fabled city of thieves" (such as New Orleans and Shanghai), but Odesa alone "has been imagined as a *judeokleptocracy*, a city overrun and controlled by Jewish gangsters and swindlers" (Tanny 2008, 1). In the same passage, Tanny also writes that Odesa's "brand of humor," its "wit and irony," was "brought to the city from the shtetls of Eastern Europe," where it found a "new home" and "became the dominant mode for articulating the Odessa myth."

25. Gubar and Herlihy 2009, 139.

26. Naidorf 2001, 330; quoted in Richardson 2004, 14. Jarrod Tanny (2007, 2) emphasizes that the myth of Odesa "had been developing since the city's

founding in 1794." Moreover, he notes that the "passing of its golden age" was already "noted and mourned as early as the mid-nineteenth century . . . [and that] since then, successive generations of myth-makers have posited their own endings for old Odessa" (2).

27. Stanton 2003, 123.
28. Stanton, 2012, 3–4.
29. Glaser, n.d.
30. Tanny 2008, 2.
31. Safran 2002, 256; Stanton 2003, 122; Tanny 2008, 2.
32. Tanny 2008, 2.
33. Babel 2002, 71.
34. Ozick 2002, 12.
35. Tanny 2007, 14.
36. Pinkham 2014, 180–82.
37. Ibid., 181–82.
38. Glaser and Ilchuk 2022.
39. Kiva 2019.
40. Glaser 2023, 290.
41. See Glaser and Ilchuk 2022; Khersonsky and Khersonsky 2022.
42. Mignolo 2000; Glaser 2023.
43. Kiva 2019.
44. Benya and Zubrik, n.d.
45. Mikhail Zhvanetsky is the founder and director of the International World Odesit Club. In Levitin's (2005, 30–35) article "Ya Odessit" (I am an Odessan), he equates many of Odesa's distinctive qualities with the characteristics of Jews.
46. Tanny 2006, 24.
47. See, for example: Odesit, n.d.; Odesaglobe, n.d.; Ta Odesa, n.d.; Migdal 2014.
48. JGuideEurope, n.d.
49. Ibid.
50. Berger 2012.
51. Greig 2018.
52. ILTV 2019.
53. Skvirskaja 2010, 79.
54. Ibid.
55. Gruber 2014, 336.
56. Ibid., 340–41.
57. Ibid., 341.
58. Waligorska 2013, 7.
59. Tanny 2011, 155.
60. Ibid.
61. Davidzon 2011.
62. Pinto 1996.

63. Brauch et al. 2008; Lipphardt, Brauch, and Nocke 2008, 182.

64. Gruber 2014; Waligorska 2013.

65. Kotushenko 2007, 5.

66. Doroshevich (1895) 2007; reprinted in Kotushenko 2007, 7.

67. Savchenko 1996, 146; cited in Rothstein 2001, 784.

68. Rothstein 2001, 781.

69. Ibid., 782. Other languages such as Ukrainian, Polish, and Greek also penetrated the Russian used by Odesans, but Robert Rothstein (2001, 783) views these as less influential than Yiddish. He also notes that just as Odesan Russian is sui generis, so too is Odesan Yiddish. He points out that the *Great Dictionary of the Yiddish Language* (1961) has a specific entry for *odeser yidish* (Odesan Yiddish), which it describes as "full of Russian words" (cited in Rothstein 2001, 786).

70. Polese 2023, 253.

71. Rothstein 2001, 782.

72. Tanny 2007, 3.

73. Polese 2023, 254.

74. Rothstein 2001, 782.

75. On a number of occasions, Jewish Odesans expressed a reluctance to see Jews involved in local politics, believing it could contribute to the rise of anti-semitism. "Jews should stay away from power," one Odesan stated. "No matter how much good [Odesa's current mayor] Gurvitz does for the city, he will always be viewed from the side of the 'fifth line of his passport,' giving reason for anti-Semitic manipulation from the side of various structures and political parties" (http://www.migdal.ru/forum/18408, but link no longer active). In chapter 2, I discuss the concerns of elderly Jews who see the rise in antisemitism as a consequence of Jewish visibility; their view aligns with the claim made by Louis Wirth ([1928] 1998, 289): "when he [a Jew] is no longer seen, anti-Semitism declines."

76. Cooper 2012, 192.

77. Maya was referring to non-Orthodox Jewish organizations, which accept children of mixed families and have some non-Jewish participants, as well as the inclusive "Tolerance Program" organized for non-Jewish children by Mazl Tov, the early childhood development center.

78. ILTV 2019.

79. See "Eager Ukrainian Tests Hillel's Limits: He May Be Christian, but He's Addicted to Jewish Life," http://www.jewishaz.com/issue/printstory.mv?051202+ukrainian; see also Shayduk 2007.

80. Patlatuk 2021.

81. Kartsev 2001, 175; quoted in Tanny 2007, 14. Emil Dreitser (2003, 93) also states that Odesa as a "living city" is no longer in Odesa but rather in "the southernmost protuberance of Brooklyn," or Brighton Beach—otherwise known as "Little Odessa."

82. Skvirskaja 2010, 76.

83. Humphrey 2004, 146; Steinberg and Wanner 2008, 3; Yurchak 2006, 8.

84. Richardson 2008, 108.

85. Nadkarni and Shevchenko 2004, 496.

86. Richardson 2004, 21.

87. Ibid.

88. Cited by V. Serduchenko, http://www.pereplet.ru/kandit/156.html (site no longer active).

89. Rashkovetsky 2007, 3. Rashkovetsky moved to Israel in the mid-2010s, when his son needed emergency surgery that couldn't be performed in Odesa.

90. Ibid., 3–6.

91. Karakina (2007, 13) notes that Jewish tombstones found by archaeologists in Odesa confirm that Jews lived in the area long before the city was founded.

92. Dreitser 2003, 92–93.

93. Ruble 2008, 39.

94. See Glazer and Moynihan (1963) 1970 and Ramer 2008 for comparisons.

95. Herzfeld 2005, 208.

96. King 2011, 281.

97. Skvirskaja 2010, 79.

98. Polese et al. 2019, 272; see also Herlihy 2018, 78.

99. Polese et al. 2019, 272; Polese 2023.

100. Herlihy 2018, 76.

101. Polese 2023, 254–55.

102. Sapritsky-Nahum forthcoming.

103. Polese 2023, 80.

104. Ibid., 75.

105. Herlihy 2008, 19–20.

106. Solomon 2022.

107. Pinkham 2014, 180.

108. UNESCO 2023.

109. Herzfeld 2005, 205.

110. Karakina 2007, 7.

111. Ramer 2008, 4. Michael Herzfeld's (2005, 3; emphasis added) concept of "cultural intimacy" is only partially applicable here. While it captures the ways in which stereotypes are often put to use in power struggles, his emphasis on "those aspects of a cultural identity that are considered *a source of external embarrassment*" doesn't pertain to Jewishness for Odesans today.

Conclusion

1. See Dumskaya, 1, 2022 and also Religious Information Service of Ukraine 2022.

2. Gupta and Ferguson 1992; Lavie and Swedenburg 1996.

3. Mann 2012, 1.

4. Herlihy 2018, 80.

5. For example, the Genesis Philanthropy Group (GPG) was established by a Ukrainian-born, Russian-speaking Jewish businessman and philanthropist, Mikhail Fridman, who holds Ukrainian, Israeli, and Russian citizenship and now lives in London. GPG's goal is nothing less than to "strengthen [the] Jewish identity of Russian-speaking Jews worldwide." Likewise, Limmud FSU, a branch of the UK organization Limmud (from the Hebrew word "to learn"), aims to "bring together and empower Jews of all ages" in revitalizing Jewish communities and culture. Its 2019 meeting in Odesa celebrated the centennial of the ship *Ruslan*'s departure from Odesa carrying some six hundred settlers and dozens of Jewish cultural figures to then British-administered Palestine, where they sought to shape the intellectual life of the burgeoning Zionist movement (see Limmud FSU 2019). The act of highlighting Odesa's role in the Zionist project—and the role of Russian-speaking Jewish pioneers more broadly—offers Odesa's Jews a language and identity with which to transcend local, regional, and geopolitical conflicts, should they choose to do so.

6. See Chabad Odesa n.d. *Yiddishkeit* literally means "Jewishness" or a "Jewish way of life." The term is traditionally used by religious Yiddish-speaking Jews of eastern and central Europe to describe the "Jewish essence." See Wikipedia 2023.

7. A guide at the Museum of the History of Odesa Jews told me, "I use the words 'revival' [*vozvrozhdenie*] and 'renaissance' when I give my tours of Jewish Odesa. It's especially fitting when you're explaining contemporary Jewish life in the context of Soviet days and the Holocaust and making a link to today. Not every visitor understands this, but Jewish visitors from abroad do."

8. Steinberg and Wanner 2008, 17.

9. Slava Kapulkin, interview by the author, February 14, 2021.

10. See Sapritsky-Nahum 2016; 2018.

11. Humphrey and Skvirskaja 2012.

12. Sapritsky-Nahum 2023.

13. Ramer 2008, 4.

14. Ruble 2008.

15. Skvirskaja 2010, 88.

16. Humphrey and Skvirskaja 2012, 1.

17. Skvirskaja and Humphrey 2007.

18. Tolerance is a deeply ingrained part of the city's influential myth, but the pogroms, events of World War II, and more recent instances of antisemitism are also part of Odesa's reality. These can't be ignored when examining local notions of coexistence and sociality. The intolerance shown by local Jews and others to newly arrived migrants also reveals the limits of tolerance in the city.

19. Ramer and Ruble 2008.

20. Ibid., 5.

21. Skvirskaja 2010.

22. Collaborative organizations such as the Ukrainian Jewish Encounter work to develop a "shared historical narrative" of Jewish-Ukrainian relations through dialogue with scholars and experts in the field.

23. See Glaser and Veidlinger 2022.

24. Deeb 2006, 21.

25. Zelenina 2018, 254.

26. Patlatuk 2021.

27. Ibid.

28. Rabbi Wolf once told me, "Following a very old Jewish tradition, Jews in Odessa now come to the rabbi as they once used to for all questions in life."

29. Petrovsky-Shtern 2009.

30. Luehrmann 2011, 1; Deeb 2006, 4.

31. Webber 1994b, 74.

Epilogue

1. For discussions on the Odesa fire, see Carey 2017, 86–91; Pomerantsev 2019, 129–33; and Amos 2015.

2. See also Richardson 2014, and Dmitriy Khavin's film, *Quiet in Odessa*.

3. Portnikov 2017, 16–17.

4. Tracy 2014.

5. Zhurzhenko 2014.

6. Levchuk 2022.

7. Kulyk 2023.

8. Beitar, the Zionist youth movement mentioned in chapter 4, became a popular Jewish organization across the FSU. Thus many young Jews I met in Odesa participated in Beitar camps and were exposed to the Zionist ideology embedded in the core of Beitar's activity.

9. Higgins 2014.

10. Pfeffer 2014.

11. Liphshiz 2014.

12. Ibid.

13. Cohen 2014.

14. Jewish Confederation of Ukraine, n.d.

15. Margolin 2019.

16. See Higgins 2019.

17. Onuch and Hale 2022, 23–24.

18. Richardson 2019, 264.

19. Ibid.

BIBLIOGRAPHY

Abbas, Ackbar. 2000. "Cosmopolitan Descriptions: Shanghai and Hong Kong." *Public Culture* 12 (3): 769–86.

Allahyari, Rebecca Anne. 2000. *Visions of Charity: Volunteer Workers and Moral Community*. Berkeley: University of California Press.

Altshuler, Mordechai. 1998. *Soviet Jewry on the Eve of the Holocaust: A Social and Demographic Profile*. Jerusalem: Hebrew University and Yad Vashem.

Altshuler, Stuart. 2005. *From Exodus to Freedom: A History of the Soviet Jewry Movement*. Lanham, MD: Rowman & Littlefield.

Amos, Howard. 2015. "'There Was Heroism and Cruelty on Both Sides': The Truth behind One of Ukraine's Deadliest Days." *The Guardian*, April 30, 2015. https://www.theguardian.com/world/2015/apr/30/there-was-heroism-and -cruelty-on-both-sides-the-truth-behind-one-of-ukraines-deadliest-days.

Anderson, Benedict. 1983. *Imagined Communities: Reflections on the Origin and Spread of Nationalism*. London: Verso.

Arad, Yitzhak. 2009. *The Holocaust in the Soviet Union*. Lincoln: University of Nebraska.

Ascherson, Neal. 2007. *Black Sea: The Birthplace of Civilisation and Barbarism*. London: Vintage Books.

Ash, Lucy. 2004. "Israel Faces Russian Brain Drain." *Crossing Continents*. BBC Radio 4, November 25, 2004.

Ashwin, Sarah. 1999. "Redefining the Collective: Russian Mineworkers in Transition." In *Uncertain Transitions: Ethnographies of Change in the Postsocialist World*, edited by Michael Burawoy and Katherine Verdery, 245–72. Lanham, MD: Rowman & Littlefield.

Aviv, Caryn, and David Shneer. 2005. *New Jews: The End of the Jewish Diaspora*. New York: New York University Press.

Avrutin, Eugene M. 2010. *Jews and the Imperial State: Identification Politics in Tsarist Russia*. Ithaca, NY: Cornell University Press.

Babel, Isaac. 2002. "Odessa." In *The Collected Stories of Isaac Babel*, edited by Nathalie Babel, 71–75. New York: W. W. Norton.

Baker, Cynthia M. 2017. *Jew*. New Brunswick, NJ: Rutgers University Press.

Ballard, Leslie Roy, Lois E. Myers, Rebecca Sharpless, and Thomas L. Charlton. 2007. *History of Oral History: Foundations and Methodology*. Lanham, MD: Altamira Press.

Baraulina, Tatiana. 2005. "Russians or Germans? Migrants or Nationals? Local Redefinition of National Belonging: The Case of the Russian Germans." Paper presented at the Conference on Russians in Israel and Beyond: The Meaning of Culture in Discourse and Practice, Van Leer Jerusalem Institute, Jerusalem, June 8–9, 2005.

Baron, Salo W. (1964) 1987. *The Russian Jew under Tsars and Soviets*. New York: Schocken Books.

Bassin, Mark, and Catriona Kelly. 2012. *Soviet and Post-Soviet Identities*. Cambridge: Cambridge University Press.

Bauman, Richard. 2001. "Tradition, Anthropology of." In *International Encyclopedia of the Social and Behavioral Sciences*, edited by N. J. Smelser and B. Baltes, 503–7. London: Pergamon.

Belensky, Misha, and Jonathan Skolnik. 1998. "Russian Jews in Today's Germany: End of the Journey?" *European Judaism* 31 (2): 30–44.

Bemporad, Elissa. 2013. *Becoming Soviet Jews: The Bolshevik Experiment in Minsk*. Bloomington: Indiana University Press.

Ben-Rafael, Eliezer, Yosef Gorny, and Yaacov Ro'i, eds. 2003. *Contemporary Jewries: Convergence and Divergence*. Leiden: Brill.

Berdahl, Daphne, Martha Lampland, and Matti Bunzl, eds. 2000. *Altering States: Ethnographies of Transition in Eastern Europe and the Former Soviet Union*. Ann Arbor: University of Michigan Press.

Berger, Paul. 2012. "Odessa Still Throbs with Jewish Life." *Forward*, May 21, 2012. https://forward.com/news/156496/odessa-still-throbs-with-jewish-life/.

Bernstein, Julia. 2005. "Russian Food Stores as a Transnational Enclave? Coping with Immigration Realities in Israel and Germany." Paper presented at the Conference on Russians in Israel and Beyond: The Meaning of Culture in Discourse and Practice, Van Leer Jerusalem Institute, Jerusalem, June 8–9, 2005.

Bhabha, Homi. 1996. "Unsatisfied: Notes on Vernacular Cosmopolitanism." In *Text and Narration: Cross-Disciplinary Essays on National and Cultural Identities*, edited by Peter Pfeiffer and Laura Garcia-Moreno, 191–207. Columbia, SC: Camden House Publishing.

Biale, David, David Assaf, Benjamin Brown, Uriel Gellman, Samuel Heilman, Moshe Rosman, Gadi Sagiv, and Marcin Wodzinski, eds. 2018. *Hasidism: A New History*. Princeton, NJ: Princeton University Press.

Bilaniuk, Laada. 2005. *Contested Tongues: Language, Politics and Cultural Contestation in Ukraine*. Ithaca, NY: Cornell University Press.

Bodemann, Michal Y. 2008. *The New German Jewry and the European Context: The Return of the European Jewish Diaspora*. New York: Palgrave Macmillan.

Borovoi, Saul I. 1993. *Vospominaniia*. Moscow: Evereiskii universitet v Moskve.

———. 2001. *Gibe'l evreiskogo naseleniya Odessy vo vremia fashiskoi okkupatsii* [Catastrophe of Odessa's Jews during the Fascist Occupation]. In *Pomni! Ne povtori!* [Remember! Never Repeat!], edited by Lionid Dusman, 17–41. Odessa: Druk.

Boyarin, Daniel, and Jonathan Boyarin. 1993. "Diaspora: Generation and the Ground of Jewish Identity." *Critical Inquiry* 19 (4): 693–725.

Brah, Avtar. 1996. *Cartographies of Diaspora: Contesting Identities*. London: Routledge.

Brandon, Ray, and Wendy Lower. 2008. *The Shoah in Ukraine: History, Testimony, Memorialization*. Bloomington: Indiana University Press.

Brauch, Julia, Anna Lipphards, and Alexandera Nocke. 2008. "Introduction: Exploring Jewish Space an Approach." In *Jewish Topographies: Visions of Space, Traditions of Place*, edited by Julia Brauch and Anna Lipphardt, 1–23. London: Routledge.

Bridger, David. 1976. *The New Jewish Encyclopedia*. West Orange, NJ: Behrman House.

Bringa, Tone. 1995. *Being Muslim the Bosnian Way: Identity and Community in a Central Bosnian Village*. Princeton, NJ: Princeton University Press.

Broz, Ludek. 2009. "Conversion to Religion? Negotiating Continuity and Discontinuity in Contemporary Altai." In *Conversion after Socialism*, edited by Mathijs Pelkmans, 17–37. New York: Berghahn Books.

Brubaker, Rogers, and Frederick Cooper. 2004. "Beyond Identity." In *Ethnicity without Groups*, edited by Rogers Brubaker, 28–63. Cambridge, MA: Harvard University Press.

Brym, Robert. 1997. "Jewish Emigration from the Former USSR: Who? Why? How Many?" In *Russian Jews on Three Continents: Migration and Resettlement*, edited by Noah Lewin-Epstein, Paul Ritterband, and Yaacov Ro'i, 177–93. London: Frank Cass.

Brym, Robert, and Rozalina Ryvkina. 1994. *The Jews of Moscow, Kiev and Minsk: Identity, Anti-Semitism, Emigration*. New York: New York University Press.

Buckser, Andrew. 1999. "Keeping Kosher: Eating and Social Identity among the Jews of Denmark." *Ethnology: An International Journal of Cultural and Social Anthropology* 38 (3): 191–210.

Burakovskiy, Aleksandr. 2011. "Holocaust Remembrance in Ukraine: Memorialization of the Jewish Tragedy at Babi Yar." *Nationalities Papers* 39 (3): 371–89.

Burawoy, Michael, and Katherine Verdery, eds. 1999. *Uncertain Transition: Ethnographies of Change in the Postsocialist World*. Lanham, MD: Rowman & Littlefield.

Cahan, Abraham. 1993. *The Rise of David Levinsky*. London: Penguin Classics.

Caldwell, Melissa L. 2004. *Not by Bread Alone: Social Support in the New Russia*. Oakland: University of California Press.

———. 2005. "A New Role for Religion in Russia's New Consumer Age: The Case of Moscow." *Religion State and Society* 33 (1): 19–34.

———. 2008. "Social Welfare and Christian Welfare: Who Gets Saved in Post–Soviet Russian Charity Work?" In *Religion, Morality and Community in Post-Soviet Societies*, edited by Mark Steinberg and Catherine Wanner, 179–214. Washington, DC: Woodrow Wilson Center Press.

Carey, Matthew. 2017. *Mistrust: An Ethnography Theory*. Chicago: HAU Books.

Carsten, Janet, ed. 2007. *Ghosts of Memory: Essays on Remembrance and Relatedness*. Oxford: Blackwell.

Cesarani, David, ed. 2002. *Port Jews: Jewish Communities in Cosmopolitan Maritime Trading Centres, 1550–1950*. London: Frank Cass.

Cesarani, David, and Gemma Romain, eds. 2006. *Jews in Port Cities London: 1650–1990*. London: Vallentine Mitchell.

Chervyakov, Valery, Zvi Gitelman, and Vladimir Shapiro. 1997. "Religion and Ethnicity: Judaism in the Ethnic Consciousness of Contemporary Russian Jews." *Ethnic and Racial Studies* 20 (2): 280–305.

———. 2003. "E Pluribus Unum? Post-Soviet Jewish Identities and Their Implications for Communal Reconstruction." In *Jewish Life after the USSR*, edited by Zvi Gitelman, Musya Glants, and Marshall I. Goldman, 61–75. Bloomington: Indiana University Press.

Chlenov, Mikhail A. 1994. "Jewish Communities and Jewish Identities in the Former Soviet Union." In *Jewish Identities in the New Europe*, edited by Jonathan Webber, 127–38. London: Littman Library of Jewish Civilization.

Clifford, James. 1992. "Traveling Cultures." In *Cultural Studies*, edited by Lawrence Grossberg, Cary Nelson, and Paula Treichler, 96–116. New York: Routledge.

———. 1994. "Diasporas." *Cultural Anthropology* 9 (3): 302–38.

———. 1997. *Routes: Travel and Translation in the Late Twentieth Century*. Cambridge, MA: Harvard University Press.

———. 1998. "Mixed Feelings." In *Cosmopolitics: Thinking and Feeling beyond the Nation*, edited by Pheng Cheah and Bruce Robbins, 362–71. Minneapolis: University of Minnesota Press.

Clifford, James, and George E. Marcus. 1986. *Writing Culture: The Poetics and Politics of Ethnography*. Berkeley: University of California Press.

Cocco, Emilio. 2010. "Performing Maritime Imperial Legacies: Tourism and Cosmopolitanism in Odessa and Trieste." *Anthropological Notebooks* 16 (1): 3–57.

Cohen, Josh. 2014. "Why Jews and Ukrainians Have Become Unlikely Allies." *Foreign Policy*, May 7, 2014. https://foreignpolicy.com/2014/05/07/why-jews-and-ukrainians-have-become-unlikely-allies/.

Cohen, Mitchell. 1992. "Rooted Cosmopolitanism." *Dissent* 39 (4): 478–83.

Cohen, Robin. 1997. *Global Diasporas: An Introduction*. Seattle: University of Washington Press.

———. 2008. *Global Diasporas: An Introduction*. London: Routledge.

Cooper, Alana E. 1998. "The Bukharan Jews in Post-Soviet Uzbekistan: A Case of Fractured Identity." *Anthropology of East Europe Review* 16 (2): 27–33.

———. 2003. "Feasting, Memorializing, Praying and Remaining Jewish in the Soviet Union: The Case of the Bukharan Jews." In *Jewish Life after the USSR*, edited by Zvi Gitelman, Musya Glants, and Marshall I. Goldman, 141–51. Bloomington: Indiana University Press.

———. 2012. *Bukharan Jews and the Dynamics of Global Judaism*. Bloomington: Indiana University Press.

Cornish, Flora, Karl Peltzer, and Malcolm MacLachlan. 1999. "Returning Strangers: The Children of Malawian Refugees Come Home." *Journal of Refugee Studies* 12 (3): 264–83.

Craig, David M. 2005. "The Give and Take of Philanthropy." In *Good Intentions: Moral Obstacles and Opportunities*, edited by David H. Smith, 57–84. Bloomington: Indiana University Press.

Danzger, M. Herbert. 1989. *Returning to Tradition: The Contemporary Revival of Orthodox Judaism*. New Haven, CT: Yale University Press.

Davidzon, Vladislav. 2011. "Monument to Isaac Babel Erected in Odessa." *Forward*, September 13, 2011. https://forward.com/schmooze/142758/monument-to-isaac-babel-erected-in-odessa/.

———. 2021. *From Odessa with Love: Political and Literary Essays from Post-Soviet Ukraine*. Washington, DC: Academica Press.

Davies, R. W. 1997. *Soviet History in the Yeltsin Era*. New York: St. Martin's Press.

Deeb, Lara. 2006. *An Enchanted Modern: Gender and Public Piety in Shi'i Lebanon*. Princeton, NJ: Princeton University Press.

Deletant, Dennis. 2008. "Transnistria and the Romanian Solution to the 'Jewish Problem.'" In *The Shoah in Ukraine: History, Testimony, Memorialization*, edited by Ray Brandon and Wendy Lower, 156–89. Bloomington: Indiana University Press.

DellaPergola, Sergio. 2002. "World Jewish Population 2002." *American Jewish Yearbook* 102 (2002): 601–42.

———. 2007. "The Demography of Post-Soviet Jewry: Global and Local Contexts." In *Revolution, Repression, and Revival: The Soviet Jewish Experience*, edited by Zvi Gitelman, and Yaacov Ro'i, 313–30. Lanham, MD: Rowman & Littlefield.

Deutsch Kornblatt, Judith. 2003. "Jewish Converts to Orthodoxy in Russia in Recent Decades." In *Jewish Life after the USSR*, edited by Zvi Gitelman, Musya Glants, and Marshall I. Goldman, 209–23. Bloomington: Indiana University Press.

Dominitz, Yehuda. 1997. "Israel's Immigration Policy and the Dropout Phenomenon." In *Russian Jews on Three Continents: Migration and Resettlement*, edited by Noah Lewin-Epstein, Paul Ritterband, and Yaacov Ro'i, 113–27. London: Frank Cass.

Doroshevich, V. (1895) 2007. "Odesskii iazyk" [Odessan Language]. In *Iaazyk Odessy: Slova i frazy* [The Odessan Language: Words and Phrases], edited by Konstantin Katushenko. Odessa: Optimum.

Douglas, Mary. 1990. "Foreword: No Free Gifts." In *The Gift*, edited by Marcel Mauss, ix–xxiii. London: Routledge.

Dragadze, Tamara. 1993. "The Domestication of Religion under Soviet Communism." In *Socialism: Ideals, Ideologies, and Local Practice*, edited by Chris Hann, 148–56. London: Routledge.

Draitser, Emil. 2003. *The Supervisor of the Sea and Other Stories*. Riverside, CA: Xenos Books.

———. 2008. *Shush! A Memoir Growing Up Jewish under Stalin*. Berkley: University of California Press.

Dreyer, Nicolas. 2018. "Genocide, *Holodomor* and Holocaust Discourse as Echo of Historical Injury and as Rhetorical Radicalization in the Russian-Ukrainian Conflict of 2013–18." *Journal of Genocide Research* 20 (4): 545–64.

Dubnow, Simon M. 1916–20. *The History of the Jews in Russia and Poland from the Earliest Times until the Present Day*. 3 vols. Philadelphia: Jewish Publication Society.

Dunham, Vera S. 1976. *In Stalin's Time: Middle-Class Values in Soviet Fiction*. New York: Cambridge University Press.

Dusman, Leonid. 2001. *Pomni! Ne Povtori!* [Remember! Never Again!]. Odessa: Druk.

Etinger, Iakov. 1995. "The Doctors' Plot: Stalin's Solution to the Jewish Question." In *Jews and Jewish Life in Russia and the Soviet Union*, edited by Yaacov Ro'i, 103–24. Ilford, UK: Frank Cass.

Faier, Lieba, and Lisa Rofel. 2014. "Ethnographies of Encounter." *Annual Review of Anthropology* 43:363–77.

Feldman, Jackie. 2008. *Above the Death Pits, Beneath the Flag: Youth Voyages to Poland and the Performance of Israeli National Identity*. New York: Berghahn Books.

Feuchtwang, Stephan. 2004. "Theorising Place." In *Making Place: State Projects, Globalisation and Local Responses in China*, edited by Stephan Feuchtwang, 3–30. London: UCL Press.

———. 2007. "Belonging to What? Jewish Mixed Kinship and Historical Disruption in Twentieth Century Europe." In *Ghosts of Memory: Essays on Remembrance and Relatedness*, edited by Janet Carsten, 150–71. Oxford: Blackwell.

Fialkova, Larisa, and Nina N. Yelenevskaya. 2007. *Ex-Soviets in Israel: From Personal Narratives to a Group Portrait*. Detroit: Wayne State University Press.

Findling, Deborah. 1999. "A Hermeneutic Exploration of the Past as Present and Future: The March of the Living as Text." PhD diss., University of San Francisco.

Finkel, Evgeny. 2004. "Na dvuh stul'iakh" [On Two Chairs]. Otechestvenie
    Zapiski 4 (19): 324–56.
Finkelstein, Norman G. 2000. The Holocaust Industry: Reflections on the Exploita-
    tion of Jewish Suffering. London: Verso.
Fisher, Julius S. 1969. Transnistria: The Forgotten Cemetery. London: Thomas
    Yoseloff.
Fishkoff, Sue. 2003. The Rebbe's Army: Inside the World of Chabad-Lubavitch. New
    York: Schocken Books.
———. 2004a. "At Risk in Odessa: Young Jews Getting Aid Where Elderly Were
    Focus." Jewish Telegraph Agency, August 20, 2004.
———. 2004b. "Tales from the Pale If I Were a Rabbi: Jewish Women Struggle
    for Acceptance in Ukraine." Jewish Telegraph Agency, August 13, 2004.
    https://www.jta.org/archive/tales-from-the-pale-if-i-were-a-rabbi-jewish
    -women-struggle-for-acceptance-in-ukraine.
Fitzpatrick, Sheila. (1999) 2000. Everyday Stalinism: Ordinary Life in Extraordi-
    nary Times: Soviet Russia in the 1930s. Oxford: Oxford University Press.
Fitzpatrick, Sheila, and Yuri Slezkine. 2000. In the Shadow of Revolution: Life
    Stories of Russian Women from 1917 to the Second World War. Princeton, NJ:
    Princeton University Press.
Frankel, Jonathan. 1981. Prophecy and Politics: Socialism, Nationalism, and the
    Russian Jews, 1862–1917. Cambridge: Cambridge University Press.
Friedberg, Maurice. 1991. How Things Were Done in Odessa: Cultural and Intellec-
    tual Pursuits in a Soviet City. Boulder, CO: Westview Press.
Friedgut, Theodore H. 2003. "Nationalities Policy, the Soviet Regime, the Jews and
    Emigration." In Jewish Life after the USSR, edited by Zvi Gitelman, Musya Glants,
    and Marshall I. Goldman, 27–45. Bloomington: Indiana University Press.
———. 2007. "The Problematics of Jewish Community Development in Con-
    temporary Russia." In Revolution, Repression, and Revival: The Soviet Jewish
    Experience, edited by Zvi Gitelman, and Yaacov Ro'i, 239–72. Lanham, MD:
    Rowman & Littlefield.
Friedman, George. 2013. "Ukraine: On the Edge of Empires." Forbes, December
    17, 2013. https://www.forbes.com/sites/stratfor/2013/12/17/ukraine-on-the
    -edge-of-empires/.
Friedman, Murray, and Albert Chernin. 1999. A Second Exodus: An American
    Movement to Free Soviet Jews. Brandeis Series in American Jewish History,
    Culture, and Life. Waltham, MA: Brandeis University Press.
Gans, Herbert J. 1956a. "American Jewry: Present and Future. (Part I: Present)."
    Commentary 21 (1): 422–30.
———. 1956b. "The Future of American Jewry. (Part II)." Commentary 21 (2):
    555–63.
———. 1979. "Symbolic Ethnicity: The Future of Ethnic Groups and Cultures
    in America." Ethnic and Racial Studies 2 (1): 1–20. Reprinted in On the Making
    of Americans: Essays in Honor of David Riesman, edited by H. Gans, Nathan

Glazer, Joseph R. Gusfield, and Christopher Jencks. Philadelphia: University of Pennsylvania Press.

———. 1994. "Symbolic Ethnicity and Symbolic Religiosity: Towards a Comparison of Ethnic and Religious Acculturation." *Ethnic and Racial Studies* 17 (4): 577–92.

Gerasimov, I. V. 2003. 'My ubivaem tol'ko svoikh': prestupnost' kak marker mezhetnicheskikh granits v Odesse nachala XX veka (1907–1917 gg.). *Ab Imperio* (January): 209–60.

Gershenson, Olga, and David Shneer. 2011. "Soviet Jewishness and Cultural Studies." *Journal of Jewish Identities* 4 (1): 129–46.

Gesin, Michael. 2003. "Holocaust: The Reality of Genocide in Southern Ukraine." PhD diss., Brandeis University.

Gessen, Masha. 1997. *Dead Again: The Russian Intelligentsia after Communism*. London: Verso.

Gidwitz, Betsy. 1994. *Visit to Jewish Communities in Ukraine and Moldova.* Report. https://docplayer.net/62024611-Visit-to-jewish-communities-ukraine-and-moldova.html.

———. 1997. *Travel to Jewish Popular Centers in Ukraine.* Report.

———. 2001. "Jewish Life in Ukraine at the Dawn of the Twenty-First Century: Part One." *Jerusalem Letter* 451:1–14. Report. www.jcpa.org.

Gilman, Sander L., and Milton Shaim. 1999. *Jewries at the Frontier: Accommodation, Identity, Conflict.* Champaign: University of Illinois Press.

Gitelman, Zvi. 1972. *Jewish Nationality and Soviet Politics: The Jewish Sections of the CPSU, 1917–1930.* Princeton, NJ: Princeton University Press.

———. 1988. "Contemporary Soviet Jewish Perceptions of Ukrainians: Some Empirical Observations." In *Ukrainian Jewish Relations in Historical Perspective*, edited by Peter Potinchnyi, and Howard Aster, 437–57. Edmonton: Canadian Institute of Ukrainian Studies.

———. (1988) 2001. *A Century of Ambivalence: The Jews of Russia and the Soviet Union, 1881 to the Present.* 2nd ed. Bloomington: Indiana University Press.

———. 1994. "The Soviet Politics of the Holocaust." In *The Art of Memory: Holocaust Memorials in History*, edited by James E. Young, 139–48. Munich: Prestel.

———. 1997. "From a Northern Country: Russian and Soviet Jewish Immigration to America and Israel in Historical Perspective." In *Russian Jews on Three Continents: Migration and Resettlement*, edited by Noah Lewin-Epstein, Paul Ritterband, and Yaacov Ro'i, 21–41. London: Frank Cass.

———. 2003. "Thinking about Being Jewish in Russia and Ukraine." In *Jewish Life after the USSR*, edited by Zvi Gitelman, Musya Glants, and Mrashall I. Goldman, 49–60. Bloomington: Indiana University Press.

———. 2009. "Jewish Identity and Secularism in Post-Soviet Russia and Ukraine." In *Religion or Ethnicity? Jewish Identities in Evolution*, edited by Zvi Gitelman, 241–66. New Brunswick, NJ: Rutgers University Press.

———. 2012. *Jewish Identities in Postcommunist Russia and Ukraine: An Uncertain Ethnicity*. Cambridge: Cambridge University Press.

———. 2016. "Introduction: Homelands, Diasporas, and the Lands in Between." In *The New Jewish Diaspora: Russian-Speaking Immigrants in the United States, Israel and Germany*, edited by Zvi Gitelman, 1–19. New Brunswick, NJ: Rutgers University Press.

Gitelman, Zvi, Musya Glants, and Marshall I. Goldman, eds. 2003. *Jewish Life after the USSR*. Bloomington: Indiana University Press.

Gitelman, Zvi, and Yaacov Ro'i, eds. 2007. *Revolution, Repression, and Revival: The Soviet Jewish Experience*. Lanham, MD: Rowman & Littlefield.

Glaser, Amelia. 2012. *Jews and Ukrainians in Russia's Literary Borderlands: From the Shtetl Fair to the Petersburg Bookshop*. Evanston, IL: Northwestern University Press.

———, ed. 2015. *Stories of Khmelnytsky: Competing Literary Legacies of the 1648 Ukrainian Cossack Uprising*. Stanford, CA: Stanford University Press.

———. 2023. "Reading Babel in Post-Maidan Odessa: Boris Khersonsky's Critical Cosmopolitanism." In *Cosmopolitan Spaces in Odessa: A Case Study of an Urban Context*, edited by Mirja Lecke and Efraim Sicher, 273–304. Boston: Academic Studies Press.

Glaser, Amelia, and Yuliya Ilchuk. 2022. "'Every Hut in Our Beloved Country Is on the Edge': Contemporary Ukrainian Poetry by Boris Khersonsky." Literary Hub, March 11, 2022. https://lithub.com/every-hut-in-our-beloved-country-is-on-the-edge-contemporary-ukrainian-poetry-by-boris-khersonsky/.

Glaser, Amelia, and Jeffrey Veidlinger. 2022. "A Conversation on Yiddish Studies, Jewish Studies, and Ukraine." *In Geveb: A Journal of Yiddish Studies* (blog), June 28, 2022. https://ingeveb.org/blog/a-conversation-on-yiddish-studies-jewish-studies-and-ukraine.

Glaser, Barney, and Anselm Strauss. 1967. *The Discovery of Grounded Theory: Strategies for Qualitative Research*. Chicago: Aldine.

Glazer, Nathan, and Daniel P. Moynihan. (1963) 1970. *Beyond the Melting Pot: The Negroes, Puerto Ricans, Jews, Italians and Irish of New York City*. 2nd ed. Cambridge, MA: MIT Press.

Gmelch, George. 2004. "West Indian Migrants and Their Rediscovery of Barbados." In *Coming Home? Refugees, Migrants, and Those Who Stayed Behind*, edited by Lynellyn D. Long and Ellen Oxfeld, 206–23. Philadelphia: University of Pennsylvania Press.

Golbert, Rebecca. 2001a. "Constructing Self: Ukrainian Jewish Youth in the Making." PhD diss., Oxford University.

———. 2001b. "Transnational Orientations from Home: Constructions of Israel and Transnational Space among Ukrainian Jewish Youth." *Journal of Ethnic and Migration Studies* 27 (4): 713–31.

Gold, Steven J. 1997. "Community Formation among Jews from the Former Soviet Union in the US." In *Russian Jews on Three Continents: Migration and Resettlement*, edited by Noah Epstein-Lewin, Yaacov Ro'i, and Paul Ritterband, 261–83. London: Frank Cass.

———. 2004. "The Emigration of Jewish Israelis." In *Jews in Israel: Contemporary Social and Cultural Patterns*, edited by U. Rebhun, and C. Waxman, 445–64. Waltham, MA: Brandeis University Press.

Golden, Deborah. 2002. "Belonging through Time: Nurturing National Identity among Newcomers to Israel from the Former Soviet Union." *Time and Space* 11 (1): 5–24.

Goluboff, Sascha. 2003. *Jewish Russians: Upheavals in a Moscow Synagogue*. Philadelphia: University of Pennsylvania Press.

———. 2008. "Communities of Mourning: Mountain Jewish Laments in Azerbaijan and on the Internet." In *Religion, Morality and Community in Post-Soviet Societies*, edited by Mark D. Steinberg, and Catherine Wanner, 149–78. Washington, DC: Woodrow Wilson Center Press.

Gozman, Leonid. 1997. "Is Living in Russia Worthwhile?" In *Russian Jews on Three Continents: Migration and Resettlement*, edited by Noah Lewin-Epstein, Paul Ritterband, and Yaacov Ro'i, 406–14. London: Frank Cass.

Grant, Bruce. 1995. *In the Soviet House of Culture: A Century of Perestro'ikas*. Princeton, NJ: Princeton University Press.

Greig, Rebecca. 2018. "Odessa, the Cradle of Israeli Culture, Enjoys a Jewish Renaissance." *Haaretz*, August 14, 2018. https://www.haaretz.com/world -news/europe/2018-08-14/ty-article-magazine/.premium/odessa-the-cradle -of-israeli-culture-enjoys-a-jewish-renaissance/0000017f-f562-d044-adff -f7fbdeb00000.

Gruber, Ruth Ellen. 2002. *Virtually Jewish: Reinventing Jewish Culture in Europe*. Berkeley: University of California Press.

———. 2014. "Beyond Virtually Jewish: Monuments to Jewish Experience in Eastern Europe." In *Jewish Cultural Studies*, vol. 4, edited by Simon J. Bronner, 335–56. Oxford: Littman Library of Jewish Civilization.

Gruen, Erich S. 2002. "Diaspora and Homeland." In *Diasporas and Exiles*, edited by Howard Wettstein, 18–46. Berkley: University of California Press.

Gubar, Oleg, and Patricia Herlihy. 2009. "The Persuasive Power of the Odessa Myth." In *Cities after the Fall of Communism: Reshaping Cultural Landscapes and European Identity*, edited by John Czaplicka, Nida M. Gelazis, and Blair A. Ruble, 137–65. Washington, DC: Woodrow Wilson Center Press.

Gubar, Oleg, and Alexander Rozenboim. 2003. "Daily Life in Odessa." In *Odessa Memories*, edited by Nicolas V. Iljine, 49–122. Seattle: University of Washington Press.

Gupta, Akhil, and James Ferguson. 1992. "Beyond 'Culture': Space, Identity, and the Politics of Difference." *Cultural Anthropology* 7 (1): 6–23.

Guthier, Steven L. 1981. "Ukrainian Cities during the Revolution and the Inter-
    war Era." In *Rethinking Ukrainian History*, edited by I. L. Rudnitsky, and J. P.
    Himka, 158–79. Edmonton: Canadian Institute for Ukrainian Studies.
Halbwachs, Maurice. 1992. *On Collective Memory*. Chicago: The University of
    Chicago Press.
Halkin, Hillel. 2019. *Jabotinsky: A Life*. New Haven, CT: Yale University Press.
Halkowsky, Henryk. 2003. *Zydowskie zycie (Jewish Life)*. Kraków: Austeria.
Hann, Chris, and the "Civil Religion" Group, eds. 2006. *The Postsocialist Reli-
    gious Question: Faith and Power in Central Asia and East-Central Europe*. Berlin:
    Lit Verlag.
Hann, Chris, Caroline Humphrey, and Katherine Verdery. 2002. "Introduction:
    Postsocialism as a Topic of Anthropological Investigation." In *Postsocialism:
    Ideals, Ideologies and Practices in Eurasia*, edited by Chris Hann, 1–30. London:
    Routledge.
Hannerz, Ulf. 1996. *Transnational Connections: Culture, People, Places*. London:
    Routledge.
Hanover, Nathan. 1983. *Abyss of Despair*. London: Routledge. Originally pub-
    lished in 1653 in Venice.
Harris, Robert. 2006. "Examining the Word Moriah." Torah Commentary.
    https://www.jtsa.edu/torah/examining-the-word-moriah/.
Hegner, Victoria. 2000. "Preserving Heritage in the Face of Change: Russian-
    Jews and the Gentrification of Uptown." In *Perspectives on Civil Activism and
    City Life*, vol. 1. Center for Cultural Understanding and Change. Chicago:
    Field Museum.
Herlihy, Patricia. 1986. *Odessa: A History, 1794–1914*. Cambridge, MA: Harvard
    University Press.
———. 2005. *Cultural Intimacy: Social Poetics in the Nation State*. New York:
    Routledge.
———. 2008. "How Ukrainian Is Odesa? From Odessa to Odesa." In *Place, Iden-
    tity, and Urban Culture: Odesa and New Orleans*, edited by Samuel C. Ramer
    and Blair A. Ruble, 19–26. Washington, DC: Woodrow Wilson International
    Center for Scholars.
———. 2018. *Odessa Recollected: The Port and the People*. Boston: Academic
    Studies Press.
Herzfeld, Michael. 1992. *The Social Production of Indifference: Exploring the Sym-
    bolic Roots of Western Bureaucracy*. Chicago: University of Chicago Press.
Higgins, Andrew. 2014. "Among Ukraine's Jews, the Bigger Worry Is Putin,
    Not Pogroms." *New York Times*, April 8, 2014. https://www.nytimes.com
    /2014/04/09/world/europe/ukraines-jews-dismiss-claims-of-anti-semitism
    .html.
———. 2019. "Ukraine's Newly Elected President Is Jewish. So Is Its Prime Min-
    ister. Not All Jews There Are Pleased." *New York Times*, April 24, 2019. https://

www.nytimes.com/2019/04/24/world/europe/volodomyr-zelensky-ukraine
-jewish-president.html.

Himka, John-Paul. 2021. *Ukrainian Nationalists and the Holocaust: OUN and
UPA's Participation in the Destruction of Ukrainian Jewry, 1941–1944*. Vol. 12 of
Ukrainian Voices. Stuttgart: Ibidem.

Hobsbawm, Eric. 1983. "Introduction: Inventing Traditions." In *The Invention of
Tradition*, edited by Eric Hobsbawm and Terence Ranger, 1–15. Cambridge:
Cambridge University Press.

Horowitz, Brian. 2008. "How Jewish Was Odessa? The Society for the Promotion
of Enlightenment as an Innovative Agent of an Alternative Jewish Politics." In
Place, Identity, and Urban Culture: Odesa and New Orleans, edited by Samuel C.
Ramer and Blair A. Ruble, 9–18. Washington, DC: Woodrow Wilson International Center for Scholars.

———. 2017. *The Russian Jewish Tradition: Intellectuals, Historians, Revolutionaries.*
Boston: Academic Studies Press.

———. 2020. *Vladimir Jabotinsky's Russian Years, 1990–1925*. Bloomington: Indiana University Press.

———. 2023. "Elitism and Cosmopolitanism: The Jewish Intelligentsia in Odesa's School Debates of 1902." In *Cosmopolitan Spaces in Odesa: A Case Study of
an Urban Context*, edited by Mirja Lecke and Efraim Sicher, 100–117. Boston:
Academic Studies Press.

Horowitz, Brian, and Leonid Katsis. 2016. *Vladimir Jabotinsky's Story of My Life.*
Detroit: Wayne State University Press.

Horowitz, Martin. 2003. "The Widening Gap between Our Model of Russian
Jewry and the Reality (1989–99)." In *Jewish Life after the USSR*, edited by Zvi
Gitelman, Musya Glants, and Marshall I. Goldman, 117–26. Bloomington:
Indiana University Press.

Hrynevych, Vladyslav, and Paul Robert Magosci. 2016. *Babyn Yar: History and
Memory*. Kyiv: Dukh I litera.

Hrytsak, Yaroslav, and Victor Susak. 2003. "Constructing a National City: The
Case of Lviv." In *Composing Urban History and the Construction of Civil Identi-
ties*, edited by J. J. Czaplicka and Blair A. Ruble, 140–64. Washington, DC:
Woodrow Wilson Center Press.

Humphrey, Caroline. 2004. "Cosmopolitanism and *Kosmopolitanizm* in the Political Life of Soviet Citizens." *Focaal: European Journal of Anthropology* 44:138–52.

———. 2012. "Odessa: Pogroms in a Cosmopolitan City." In *Explorations of the
Post-Cosmopolitan City*, edited by Caroline Humphrey and Vera Skvirskaja,
17–65. New York: Berghahn Books.

Humphrey, Caroline, and Ruth Mandel. 2002. "The Market in Everyday Life: Ethnographies of Postsocialism." In *Markets and Moralities: Ethnographies of Postsocialism*, edited by Ruth Mandel and Caroline Humphrey, 1–16. Oxford: Berg.

Humphrey, Caroline, and Vera Skvirskaja. 2012. *Post-Cosmopolitan Cities:
Explorations of Urban Coexistence*. New York: Berghahn Books.

Iljine, Nicolas V., ed. 2003. *Odessa Memories*. Seattle: University of Washington Press.

Inber, Vera. 1981. "Odessa." In *The Black Book: The Ruthless Murders of Jews by German-Fascist Invaders throughout the Temporarily-Occupied Regions of the Soviet Union and the Death Camps of Poland during the War of 1941–1945*, edited by Ilya Ehrenburg and Vasily Grossman, 77–91. New York: Holocaust Library.

Jessa, Pawel. 2006. "Religious Renewal in Kazakhstan: Redefining Unofficial Islam." In *The Postsocialist Religious Question: Faith and Power in Central Asia and East-Central Europe*, edited by Chris Hann and the "Civil Religion" Group, 169–90. Berlin: Lit Verlag.

Karakina, E. 2007. "Jews Always. . . ." In *City Guide of Jewish Odessa*, edited by Elena Karakina, Anna Misuk, and Alexander Rozenboim, 6–13. Odessa: Studio Negotsiant.

Kartsev, Roman. 2001. *Maloi, sukhoi, i pisatel: Zapiski prestarelogo sorvantsa* [Small, shriveled and a writer: Notes of an elderly rascal]. Moscow: Vagrius.

Katz, Jacob. 1986. "Orthodoxy in Historical Perspective." In *Studies in Contemporary Jewry, Vol. 2*, edited by Peter Y. Medding, 3–17. Bloomington: Indiana University Press.

Katz, Shmuel. 1996. *Lone Wolf: A Biography of Vladimir (Ze'ev) Jabotinsky*. Vol. 1. New York: Barricade Books.

Kessel, Barbara. 2000. *Suddenly Jewish: Jews Raised as Gentiles Discover Their Jewish Roots*. Waltham: Brandeis University Press.

Khanin, Vladimir (Ze'ev). 2020. "'Russians', 'Sephardi' and 'Israelis': The Changing Structure of Austrian Jewry." In *Being Jewish in Central Europe Today*, edited by Olaf Glukner, Haim Fireberg, and Marcela Zoufalá, 73–101. Berlin: De Gruyter.

———. 2021. *From Russia to Israel—And Back?: Contemporary Transnational Russian-Israeli Diaspora*. Berlin: De Gruyter.

Kharkhordin, Oleg. 1999. *The Collective and the Individual in Russia: A Study of Practices*. Berkeley: University of California Press.

Khersonsky, Boris, and Luidmila Khersonsky. 2022. *The Country Where Everyone's Name Is Fear*, edited by Katie Farris and Ilya Kaminsky, 2–65. Sandpoint, ID: Lost Horse Press.

Khiterer, Victoria. 2017. *Jewish City or Inferno of Russian Israel? A History of the Jews in Kiev before February 1917*. Boston: Academic Studies Press.

King, Charles. 2011. *Odessa: Genius and Death in a City of Dreams*. New York: W. W. Norton.

Kirshenblatt-Gimblett, Barbara. 1998. *Destination Culture: Tourism, Museums, and Heritage*. Berkeley: University of California Press.

Kiva, Iya. 2019. "Boris Khersonsky: 'Одеса—це завжди життя в подвійному просторі' [Odesa is always about living in a double spaces]. Shoizdat, April 12, 2019. https://shoizdat.com/boris-khersonskii-odesa-tse-zavzhdi/.

Klier, John D. 1992–1994. "'Popular Politics' and the Jewish Question in the Russian Empire, 1881–2." *Jewish Historical Studies* 33 (1992–1994): 175–85.

———. 1995. *Imperial Russia's Jewish Question 1855–1881*. Cambridge: Cambridge University Press.

———. 2002. "A Port, Not a Shtetl: Reflections on the Distinctiveness of Odessa." In *Port Jews: Jewish Communities in Cosmopolitan Maritime Trading Centres, 1550–1950*, edited by David Cesarani, 173–79. London: Frank Cass.

Klier, John D., and Shlomom Lambroza. 1992. *Pogroms: Anti-Jewish Violence in Modern Russian History*. Cambridge: Cambridge University Press.

Kobrin, Rebecca. 2010. *Jewish Bialystok and Its Diaspora*. Bloomington: Indiana University Press.

Koposov, Nikolay. 2018. *Memory Laws, Memory Wars: The Politics of the Past in Europe and Russia*. Cambridge: Cambridge University Press.

Kotkin, Stephen. 1995. *Magnetic Mountain: Stalinism as a Civilization*. Berkeley: University of California Press.

Kotushenko, Vasily. 2007. *Yazik Odessy: Slova i frazy* [Odessan language: Words and phrases]. Odessa: Optimum.

Kravtsov, Sergey. 2002. "Brods'ka Synagogue in Odessa." Series Byzantina, 6. http://seriesbyzantina.eu/wp-content/uploads/2022/04/06.-Brodska _Odesa20222.pdf.

Kruglov, Alexander. 2008. "Jewish Losses in Ukraine, 1941–1944." In *The Shoah in Ukraine: History, Testimony, Memorialization*, edited by Ray Brandon and Wendy Lower, 272–90. Bloomington: Indiana University Press.

Krupnik, Igor. 1994. "Constructing New Identities in the Former Soviet Union: The Challenge for the Jews." In *Jewish Identities in the New Europe*, edited by Jonathan Webber, 139–49. London: Littman Library of Jewish Civilization.

Kugelmass, Jack. 1994. "Why We Go to Poland: Holocaust Tourism as Secular Ritual." In *The Art of Memory: Holocaust Memorials in History*, edited by James Young, 175–84. New York: Prestel.

Kulyk, Volodymyr. 2018. "Shedding Russianness, Recasting Ukrainianness: The Post-Euromaidan Dynamics of Identification in Ukraine." *Post-Soviet Affairs* 34 (2–3): 119–38.

Kunin, Seth D. 2002. "Judaism." In *Religions in the Modern World*, edited by P. Fletcher, H. Kawanami, and D. Smith, 128–52. New York: Routledge.

Kuzio, Taras. 1998. *Dynamics of Post-Soviet Transformation: Contemporary Ukraine*. London: M. E. Sharpe.

Laitin, David. 1999. *Identity in Formation: The Russian Speaking Populations in the Near Abroad*. Ithaca, NY: Cornell University Press.

Larson, Mary A. 2007. "Research Design and Strategies." In *History of Oral History: Foundations and Methodology*, edited by Thomas L. Carlton, Lois E. Myers, and Rebecca Sharpless, 78–101. Lanham, MD: AltaMira.

Lavie, Smadar, and Ted Swedenburg. 1996. *Displacement, Diaspora, and Geographies of Identity*. Durham, NC: Duke University Press.

Lebedeva, N. 2001. "Russkaia Emigratsiia v Zerkale Psikhologii" [Russian emigration in the mirror of psychology]. In *Emigratsia i repatriatiia v Rossii* [Emigration and repatriation in Russia], edited by V. A. Iontsev, N. M. Lebedeva, M. V. Nazarov, and A. V. Okorokov, 104–224. Moscow: Popechitel'stvo o nuzhdakh rosiiskikh repatriantov.

Lecke, Mirja. 2012. "Odessa without Dogma: Jabotinsky's The Five." *Ab Imperio* 1:325–50.

———. 2017. "The Street: A Spatial Paradigm in Odessan Literature." *Slavonic and East European Review* 95 (3): 429–57.

———. 2021. "Opening remarks for the Odessa, Cosmopolitanism, Modernism Conference." June 21, 2021. https://www.youtube.com/watch?v=JT_qTyZioD 4&list=PLTn74Qx5mPsTvwYBo78GgPW1jdjumYYMe&index=1.

Lecke, Mirja, and Efraim Sicher. 2023. "Introduction." In *Cosmopolitan Spaces in Odesa: A Case Study of an Urban Context*, edited by Mirja Lecke and Efraim Sicher, 1–20. Boston: Academic Studies Press.

Lehrer, Erica T. 2013. *Jewish Poland Revisited: Heritage Travel in Unquiet Places*. Bloomington: Indiana University Press.

Leite, Naomi. 2017. *Unorthodox Kin: Portuguese Marranos and the Global Search for Belonging*. Oakland: University of California Press.

Lemish, Dafna. 2000. "The Whore and the Other: Israeli Images of Female Immigrants from the Former USSR." *Gender and Society* 14 (2): 333–49.

Levin, Zeev. 2021. "Religious, National or Cultural? A Case Study of Framework of Jewish Education in Post-Soviet Central Asia." *Central Asian Survey* 40 (3): 368–81.

Levitin, Michael. 2005. "Ia Odesit" [I am an Odesan]. *Okyiabr'* 7:30–35.

Levy, Andre. 2004. "Homecoming to the Diaspora: Nation and State Visits of Israelis to Morocco." In *Homecomings: Unsettling Paths of Return*, edited by Fran Markowitz and Anders Stefansson, 91–108. Lanham, MD: Lexington Books.

———. 2005. "A Community That Is Both a Centre and a Diaspora: Jews in Late Century Morocco." In *Homelands and Diasporas: Holy Lands and Other Places*, edited by Andre Levy and Alex Weingrod, 68–96. Stanford, CA: Stanford University Press.

Levy, Andre, and Alex Weingrod. 2005. "On Homelands and Diasporas: An Introduction." In *Homelands and Diasporas: Holy Lands and Other Places*, edited by Andre Levy, and Alex Weingrod, 3–26. Stanford: Stanford University Press.

Lewin-Epstein, Noah. 1997. "Introduction." In *Russian Jews on Three Continents: Migration and Resettlement*, edited by Noah Lewin-Epstein, Paul Ritterband, and Yaacov Ro'i, 1–18. London: Frank Cass.

Lewin-Epstein, Noah, Paul Ritterband, and Yaacov Ro'i. 1997. *Russian Jews on Three Continents: Migration and Resettlement*. London: Frank Cass.

Leykin, Inna. 2007. "Men of War: National Heroes or Local Retirees: WWII Veterans, Immigrants from the FSU and Israeli National Discourse." Paper presented at the Association of Studies of Nationalism Conference, Columbia University, New York, 2007.

Liphshiz, Cnaan. 2014. "Ukrainian Jews Split on Support for Russian Invasion." *Times of Israel*, March 5, 2014. https://www.timesofisrael.com/ukrainian-jews -split-on-support-for-russian-invasion/.

Lipphardt, Anna, Julia Brauch, and Alexandra Nocke. 2008. "Exploring Jewish Space: An Approach." In *Jewish Topographies: Visions of Space, Traditions of Place*, edited by Julia Brauch and Anna Lipphardt, 1–24. Burlington, VT: Ashgate Publishing.

Lissak, Moshe, and Eli Leshem. 1995. "The Russian Intelligentsia in Israel: Between Ghettoization and Integration." *Israel Affairs* 2:20–37.

Litani, Dora. 1967. "The Destruction of the Jews of Odessa in the Light of Ruma-nian Documents." In *Yad Vashem Studies Volume VI*, edited by Nathan Eck and Aryeh Leon Kubovy. Jerusalem: Yad Vashem.

Loewenthal, Naftali. 2020. *Hasidism beyond Modernity: Essays in Habad Thought and History*. London: Litman Library of Jewish Civilization.

Lomsky-Feder, Edna, and Tamar Rapoport. 2002. "Intelligentsia as an Ethnic Habitus: The Inculcation and Restructuring of Intelligentsia among Russian Jews." *British Journal of Sociology of Education* 23 (2): 233–48.

Long, Lynellyn D., and Ellen Oxfeld. 2004. "Introduction: An Ethnography of Return." In *Coming Home? Refugees, Migrants and Those Who Stayed Behind*, edited by Lynellyn D. Long and Ellen Oxfeld, 1–15. Philadelphia: University of Pennsylvania Press.

Luehrmann, Sonja. 2011. *Secularism Soviet Style: Teaching Atheism and Religion in a Volga Republic*. Bloomington: Indiana University Press.

Magocsi, Paul Robert, and Yohanan Petrovsky-Shtern. 2016. *Jews and Ukrainians: A Millennium of Co-Existence*. Toronto: University of Toronto Press.

Malcomson, Scott L. 1998. "The Varieties of Cosmopolitan Experience." In *Cosmopolitics: Thinking and Feeling beyond the Nation*, edited by Pheng Cheah and Bruce Robbins, 233–45. Minneapolis: University of Minnesota Press.

Malia, Martin. 1960. "What Is Intelligentsia?" *Daedalus* 89 (3): 441–58.

Mandel, Ruth. 1990. "Shifting Centers, Emergent Identities: Turkey and Germany in the Lives of Turkish Gastarbeiter." In *Muslim Travellers: Pilgrim-age, Migration and the Religious Imagination*, edited by Dale Eickelman and James Piscatori, 153–71. London: Routledge.

———. 2008. *Cosmopolitan Anxieties: Turkish Challenges to Citizenship and Belonging in Germany*. Durham, NC: Duke University Press.

Manley, Rebecca. 2009. *To the Tashkent Station: Evacuation and Survival in the Soviet Union at War*. Ithaca, NY: Cornell University Press.

Mann, Barbara E. 2012. *Space and Place in Jewish Studies*. New Brunswick, NJ: Rutgers University Press.

Markowitz, Fran. 1993. *A Community in Spite of Itself: Soviet Jewish Émigrés in New York*. Washington, DC: Smithsonian Institute Press.

———. 1995. "Emigration, Immigration and Cultural Change: Towards a Trans-National Russian Jewish Community?" In *Jews and Jewish Life in Russia and the Soviet Union*, edited by Yaacov Ro'i, 403–13. Ilford, UK: Frank Cass.

———. 1997. "Cultural Change, Border Crossings and Identity Shopping: Jewish Teenagers from the CIS Access Their Future in Israel." In *Russian Jews on Three Continents: Migration and Resettlement*, edited by Noah Lewin-Epstein, Paul Ritterband, and Yaacov Ro'i, 344–63. London: Frank Cass.

———. 2004. "The Home(s) of Homecomings." In *Homecomings: Unsettling Paths of Return*, edited by Fran Markowitz and Anders Stefansson, 21–33. Lanham, MD: Lexington Books.

Markowitz, Fran, and Anders Stefansson, eds. 2004. *Homecomings: Unsettling Paths of Return*. Lanham, MD: Lexington Books.

Martin, Terry. 2001. *The Affirmative Action Empire: Nations and Nationalism in the Soviet Union, 1923–1939*. Ithaca, NY: Cornell University Press.

Mazis, John Athanasios. 2004. *The Greeks of Odessa: Diaspora Leadership in Late Imperial Russia*. Boulder, CO: East European Monographs.

McBrien, Julie. 2006. "Extreme Conversations: Secularism, Religious Pluralism, and the Rhetoric of Islamic Extremism in Southern Kyrgyzstan." In *The Post-socialist Religious Question: Faith and Power in Central Asia and East-Central Europe*, edited by Chris Hann and the "Civil Religion" Group, 47–73. Berlin: Lit Verlag.

McBrien, Julie, and Mathijs Pelkmans. 2008. "Turning Marx on His Head: Missionaries, Extremists and Archaic Secularists in Post-Soviet Kyrgyzstan." *Critique of Anthropology* 28 (1): 87–103.

Meir, Nathan M. 2010. *Kiev Jewish Metropolis: A History, 1859–1914*. Bloomington: Indiana University Press.

Mignolo, Walter. 2000. "The Many Faces of Cosmopolis: Border Thinking and Critical Cosmopolitanism." In *Cosmopolitanism*, edited by Carol Brecken-ridge, Sheldon Pollock, Homi Bhabha, and Dipesh Chakrabarty. Durham, NC: Duke University Press.

Misuk, Anna. 2007. "The Gate of Zion." In *City Guide of Jewish Odessa*, edited by E. Karakina, 52–55. Odessa: Studio Negotsiant Publishing House.

———. 2010. *Kuda by Vas Poslal Klassik* [Where a classic would send you]. Odessa: Midal.

Morris, Jeremy, and Abel Polese. 2016. "Informal Health and Education Sector Payments in Russia and Ukraine Cities: Structuring Welfare from Below." *European Urban and Regional Studies* 23 (3): 481–96.

Morris, Mike. 2012. *Concise Dictionary of Social and Cultural Anthropology*. Malden, MA: Wiley-Blackwell.

Murav, Harriet. 2011. *Music from a Speeding Train: Soviet Yiddish and Russian-Jewish Literature of the Twentieth Century*. Stanford: Stanford University Press.

Myers, David N. 2014. "Introduction: At the Border: David Ellenson and the Study of Modern Judaism." In *Between Jewish Tradition and Modernity:*

Rethinking and Old Opposition, edited by Michael A Meyer and David N. Myers, 1–15. Detroit: Wayne State University Press.

Nadkarni, Maya, and Olga Shevchenko. 2004. "The Politics of Nostalgia: A Case for Comparative Analysis of Post-Socialist Practices." *Ab Imperio* 2:487–519.

Nathans, Benjamin. 2002. *Beyond the Pale: The Jewish Encounter with Late Imperial Russia*. Berkeley: University of California Press.

Newman, Marissa. 2018. "European Rabbis to No Longer Recognize Private Israeli Conversions." *Times of Israel*, November 26, 2018. https://www .timesofisrael.com/in-deal-with-rabbinate-european-rabbis-to-reject-private -israeli-conversions/.

O'Brien, Lee. 1986. *American Jewish Organizations and Israel*. Washington, DC: Institute for Palestine Studies.

Ofer, Dalia. 1993. "The Holocaust in Transnistria: A Special Case of Genocide." In *The Holocaust in the Soviet Union: Studies and Sources on the Destruction of the Jews in the Nazi-Occupied Territories of the USSR, 1941–1945*, edited by Lucjan Dobroszycki and Jeffrey S. Gurock, 133–55. London: M. E. Sharpe.

Onuch, Olga, and Henry E. Hale. 2022. *The Zelensky Effect*. London: Hurst & Company.

Onuch, Olga, and Gwendolyn Sasse. 2016. "The Maidan in Movement: Diversity and the Cycles of Protest." *Europe-Asia Studies* 68 (4): 556–87.

Orbach, Alexander. 1980. *New Voices of Russian Jewry: A Study of the Russian Jewish Press of Odessa in the Era of the Great Reforms, 1860–1871*. Leiden: Brill.

Osipovich, Alexander. 2004. "Reverse Exodus: Why Are So Many Jews Returning?" *Russian Profile* 4:36.

Oz, Amos. 2004. *A Tale of Love and Darkness*. London: Vintage Books.

Ozick, Synthia. 2002. Introduction to *The Collected Stories of Isaac Babel*, edited by Nathalie Babel, 11–15. New York: W. W. Norton.

Patico, Jennifer. 2002. "Chocolate and Cognac: Gifts and the Recognition of Social Worlds in Post-Soviet Russia." *Ethnos* 67 (3): 345–68.

———. 2005. "To Be Happy in a Mercedes: Tropes of Value and Ambivalent Visions of Marketization." *American Ethnologist* 32 (3): 479–96.

Patlatuk, Irina. 2021. "Дівчинка завжди ходить із телефоном, бо мати обіцяла подзвонити" [A girl is always walking around with her phone because her mother promised she would call]. *Gazeta Po Ikrainsky*, January 20, 2021. https://gazeta.ua/articles/people-and-things-journal/_divchinka-zavzhdi -hodit-iz-telefonom-bo-mati-obicyala-podzvoniti/1008640?fbclid=IwARow41 ZPR.

Paxson, Margaret. 2005. *Solovyovo: The Story of Memory in a Russian Village*. Bloomington: Indiana University Press.

Pegelow, Thomas. 2006. "Determining 'People of German Blood', 'Jews' and 'Mischlinge': The Reich Kinship Office and the Competing Discourses and Powers of Nazism, 1941–1943." *Contemporary European History* 15 (1): 43–65.

Pelkmans, Mathijs. 2006a. "Asymmetries on the Religious Market in Kyrgyzstan." In *The Postsocialist Religious Question: Faith and Power in Central Asia
and East-Central Europe*, edited by Chris Hann and the "Civil Religion"
Group, 29–46. Berlin: Lit Verlag.
———. 2006b. *Defending the Border: Identity, Religion and Modernity in the
Republic of Georgia*. Ithaca, NY: Cornell University Press.
———. 2007. "'Culture' as a Tool and an Obstacle: Missionary Encounters in
Post-Soviet Kyrgyzstan." *Journal of the Royal Anthropological Institute* 13 (4):
881–99.
———. 2009. "Introduction: Post-Soviet Space and the Unexpected Turns of
Religious Life." In *Conversion after Socialism*, edited by Mathijs Pelkmans,
1–16. New York: Berghahn Books.
Penter, Tanja, and Ivan Sablin. 2020. "Soviet Federalism from Below: The Soviet
Republics of Odessa and the Russian Far East, 1917–1918." *Journal of Eurasian
Studies* 11 (1): 40–52.
Petrovsky-Shtern, Yohanan. 2009. *The Anti-Imperial Choice: The Making of the
Ukrainian Jew*. New Haven, CT: Yale University Press.
———. 2014. *The Golden Age Shtetl: A New History of Jewish life in East Europe*.
Princeton, NJ: Princeton University Press.
———. 2023. "The Ukrainian Odes(s)a of Vladimir Jabotinsky." In *Cosmopolitan
Spaces in Odesa: A Case Study of an Urban Context*, edited by Mirja Lecke and
Efraim Sicher, 37–69. Boston: Academic University Press.
Petrovsky-Shtern, Yohanan, and Antony Polonsky, eds. 2014. Introduction to
Jews and Ukrainians, 3–64. Vol. 26 of *Polin: Studies in Polish Jewry*. Oxford:
Littman Library of Jewish Civilization.
Pfeffer, Anshel. 2014. "Apprehension Grips the Crimean Jewish Community."
Haaretz, March 10, 2014. https://www.haaretz.com/jewish/.premium-crimea
-jews-apprehensive-1.5331285.
Pinkham, Sophie. 2014. "Making Deals in the Paradise of Thieves: Leonid
Utesov, Arkadii Severnyi, and Blatnaia Pesnya." *Ulbandus Review* Hearing
Texts 16:177–97.
Pinkus, Benjamin. 1988. *The Jews of the Soviet Union: The History of a National
Minority*. Cambridge: Cambridge University Press.
Pinto, Diane. 1996. *A New Jewish Identity for Post-1989 Europe*. Policy Paper No. 1.
https://www.bjpa.org/content/upload/bjpa/a_ne/A%20New%20Jewish%20
Identity%20For%20Post-1989%20Europe.pdf.
Polese, Abel. 2007. "Where Marx Meets Ekaterina (the Great): The Dichotomy
between National and Plural Identities in Odessa." Paper presented at the As-
sociation of Studies of Nationalism (ASN), Columbia University, New York,
April 2007.
———. 2023. "The Ukrainization of Odes(s)a? On the Languages of Odesa and
Their Use." In *Cosmopolitan Spaces in Odesa: A Case Study of an Urban Context*,

edited by Mirja Lecke and Efraim Sicher, 252–72. Boston: Academic Studies
Press.

Polese, Abel, Rustamjon Urinboyev, Tanel Kerikmae, and Sarah Murru.
2019. "Negotiating Spaces and the Public-Private Boundary: Language
Policies versus Language Use Practices in Odessa." *Space and Culture* 22 (3):
263–79.

Polese, Abel, and Anna Wylegala. 2008. "Odessa and Lvov or Odesa and Lviv:
How Important Is a Letter? Reflections on the 'Other' in Two Ukrainian
Cities." *Nationalities Papers* 36 (5): 787–814.

Polishchuk, Michail. 2002. *Evrei Odessy i Novorosii: Sotsial'no-politicheskaia
istoriia evreev Odessy i drugikh gorodov Novorosii 1881–1904* [Jews of Odessa
and Novorossiya: Sociopolitical history of Jews of Odessa and other cities of
Novorossiya 1881–1904]. Moscow: Mosty Kul'tury.

Polityuk, Pavel. 2019. "Ukraine Passes Language Law, Irritating President-
elect and Russia." Reuters, April 25, 2019. https://www.reuters.com/article
/us-ukraine-parliament-language/ukraine-passes-language-law-irritating
-president-elect-and-russia-idUSKCN1S111N.

Polonsky, Antony. 2013. *The Jews in Poland and Russia: A Short History.* London:
Littman Library of Jewish Civilization.

———. 2019. *The Jews in Poland and Russia.* Vol. 1, *1350 to 1881.* London: Littman
Library of Jewish Civilization.

Pomerantsev, Peter. 2019. *This Is Not Propaganda: Adventures in the War against
Reality.* London: Faber and Faber.

Poppendieck, Janet. 1998. *Sweet Charity: Emergency Food and the End of Entitle-
ment.* New York: Penguin Books.

Portelli, Alessandro. 1997. *The Battle of Valle Giulia: Oral History and the Art of
Dialogue.* Madison: University of Wisconsin Press.

Portnikov, Vitaly. 2017. "Ukrainian Jews after the Maidan." *Odessa Review* 11:
10–12.

Ramer, Samuel C. 2008. "Meditation on Urban Identity: Odessa/Odesa and New
Orleans." In *Place, Identity, and Urban Culture: Odesa and New Orleans,* edited
by Samuel C. Ramer and Blair A. Ruble, 1–8. Washington, DC: Woodrow
Wilson International Center for Scholars.

Ramer, Samuel C., and Blair A. Ruble, eds. 2008. *Place, Identity and Urban
Culture: Odesa and New Orleans.* Occasional Papers, 301. Washington, DC:
Woodrow Wilson International Center for Scholars.

Rapoport, Tamar, and Edna Lomsky-Feder. 2002. "Intelligentsia as an Ethnic
Habitus: The Inculcation and Restructuring of Intelligentsia among Russian
Jews." *British Journal of Sociology of Education* 23 (2): 233–48.

Rapoport, Tamar, Edna Lomsky-Feder, and A. Hedider. 2002. "Recollection
and Relocation in Immigration: Russian Jewish Immigrants Normalize Their
Anti-Semitic Experiences." *Symbolic Interaction* 25 (2): 175–78.

Rapport, Nigel, and Jaonna Overing. 2007. *Social and Cultural Anthropology: The Key Concepts*. London: Routledge.

Rashkovetsky, Mikhail. 2007. "Tol'ko li Proshloe?" [Is it only the past?]. *Migdal Times* 84: 3–6.

Rechtman, Abraham. 2021. *The Lost World of Russia's Jews: Ethnography and Folklore in the Pale of Settlement*. Bloomington: Indiana University Press.

Reid, Anna. 1997. *Borderland: A Journey through the History of Ukraine*. Boulder, CO: Westview Press.

Remennick, Larissa. 2002. "Transnational Community in the Making: Russian Jewish Immigrants of the 1990s in Israel." *Journal of Ethnic and Migration Studies* 28 (3): 515–30.

Richardson, Tanya. 2004. "Odessa, Ukraine: History, Place and Nation-Building in a Post-Soviet City." PhD diss., Cambridge University.

———. 2005. "Walking Streets, Talking History: The Making of Odessa." *Ethnology* 44 (1): 13–33.

———. 2006. "Living Cosmopolitanism? 'Tolerance,' Religion, and Local Identity in Odessa." In *The Postsocialist Religious Question: Faith and Power in Central Asia and East-Central Europe*, edited by Chris Hann and the "Civil Religion" Group, 213–40. Berlin: Lit Verlag.

———. 2008. *Kaleidoscopic Odessa: History and Place in Contemporary Ukraine*. Toronto: University of Toronto Press.

———. 2014. "Odessa's Two Big Differences (and a Few Small Ones)." Eurozine, September 1, 2014. https://www.eurozine.com/odessas-two-big-differences-and-a-few-small-ones/.

———. 2019. "The Regional Life of Geopolitical Conflict: The Case of Odes(s)a Oblast." *Soviet and Post-Soviet Review* 46:263–303.

Ries, Nancy. 1997. *Russian Talk: Culture and Conversation during Perestroika*: Ithaca, NY: Cornell University Press.

———. 2000. "Foreword: Ethnography and Postsocialism." In *Fieldwork Dilemmas: Anthropologists in Postsocialist States*, edited by H. G. De Soto and Nora Dudwich, ix–xi. Madison: University of Wisconsin Press.

Ritterband, Paul. 1997. "Jewish Identity among Russian Immigrants in the US." In *Russian Jews on Three Continents: Migration and Resettlement*, edited by Noah Lewin-Epstein, Paul Ritterband, and Yaacov Ro'i, 325–43. London: Frank Cass.

Robbins, Bruce. 1998. "Comparative Cosmopolitanisms." In *Cosmopolitics: Thinking and Feeling beyond the Nation*, edited by Pheng Cheah and Bruce Robbins, 246–64. Minneapolis: University of Minnesota Press.

Rogger, Hans. 1986. *Jewish Policies and Right-Wing Politics in Imperial Russia*. Berkeley: University of California Press.

Ro'i, Yaacov, ed. (1991) 2003. *The Struggle for Soviet Jewish Emigration, 1948–1967*. Cambridge Russian, Soviet and Post-Soviet Studies 75. Cambridge: Cambridge University Press.

———. 1995. *Jews and Jewish Life in Russia and the Soviet Union*. Ilford, UK: Frank Cass.

———. 1997. "Soviet Policy towards Jewish Emigration: An Overview." In *Russian Jews on Three Continents: Migration and Resettlement*, edited by Noah Lewin-Epstein, Paul Ritterband, and Yaacov Ro'i, 45–67. London: Frank Cass.

———. 2003a. "Religion, Israel, and the Development of Soviet Jewry's National Consciousness, 1967–91." In *Jewish Life after the USSR*, edited by Zvi Gitelman, Musya Glants, and Marshall I. Goldman, 13–27. Bloomington: Indiana University Press.

———. 2003b. "Soviet Jewry from Identification to Identity." In *Contemporary Jewries: Convergence and Divergence*, edited by Eliezer Ben-Rafael, Yosef Gorny, and Yaacov Ro'i, 182–93. Leiden: Brill.

———. 2007. Introduction to *Revolution, Repression, and Revival: The Soviet Jewish Experience*, edited by Zvi Gitelman, and Yaacov Ro'i, 1–12. Lanham, MD: Rowman & Littlefield.

Ro'i, Yaacov, and Avi Beker, eds. 1991. *Jewish Culture and Identity in the Soviet Union*. New York: New York University Press.

Rosaldo, Renato. 1989. *Culture and Truth: The Remaking of Social Analysis*. Boston: Beacon Press.

Rosenberg, Victor. 2015. "Refugee Status for Soviet Jewish Immigrants to the United States." *Touro Law Review* 19 (2): Article 22. https://digitalcommons.tourolaw.edu/cgi/viewcontent.cgi?article=1563&context=lawreview.

Rothstein, Robert A. 2001. "How It Was Sung in Odessa: At the Intersection of Russian and Yiddish Folk Culture." *Slavic Review* 60 (4): 781–801.

Rozenboim, Alexander. 2007. "Old Odessa: Community and City Life." In *City Guide of Jewish Odessa*, edited by E. Karakina et al., 33–37. Odessa: Studio Negotsiant.

Rubenstein, Joshua. 2016. *The Last Days of Stalin*. New Haven, CT: Yale University Press.

Rubinstein, Anat. 2023. "The Cosmopolitan Soundscape of Odesa." In *Cosmopolitan Spaces in Odesa: A Case Study of an Urban Context*, edited by Mirja Lecke and Efraim Sicher, 139–64. Boston: Academic University Press.

Ruble, Blair A. 2008. "New Orleans and Odesa: The Spaces in Between as a Source of Urbane Diversity." In *Place, Identity, and Urban Culture: Odesa and New Orleans*, edited by Samuel C. Ramer and Blair A. Ruble, 35–42. Washington, DC: Woodrow Wilson International Center for Scholars.

Ryvkina, Rozalina. 2005. *Kak zhivut evrei v Rosii: Sotsiologicheskii analiz peremen* [How Jews live in Russia: Sociological analysis of change]. Moscow: Dom Evreiskoi Knigi.

Safran, Gabriella. 2002. "Isaak Babel's Eliia Isaakovitch as a New Jewish Type." *Slavic Review* 61 (2): 253–72.

Safran, William. 1991. "Diasporas in Modern Societies: Myths of Homeland and Return." *Diaspora* 1 (1): 83–99.

Salitan, Laurie P. 1992. *Politics and Nationality in Contemporary Soviet-Jewish Emigration, 1968–1989.* New York: St. Martin's Press.

Sapritsky-Nahum, Marina. 2012. "Negotiating Cosmopolitanism: Migration, Religious Education and Shifting Jewish Orientations in Post-Soviet Odessa." In *Explorations of the Post-Cosmopolitan City,* edited by Caroline Humphrey and Vera Skvirskaja, 65–93. New York: Berghahn Books.

———. 2013. "Returnees or Immigrants: Anthropological Analysis of 'Russian' Israelis in Odessa." [In Russian.] Special Issue, Israeli Diasporas: Where, How and Why. *Diaspora* 2013 (2): 47–66.

———. 2015. "От евреев к иудеям: поворот к вере или возврат к ней?" [From *Evrei* to *Eudei*: Turning or Returning to Faith?] [In Russian.] Special Issue, Judaism after USSR: Old and New, Religious and National. *State, Religions and Church* 3 (33): 224–55. http://www.religion.ranepa.ru/sites/default/files /GRC_3-2015_final++.pdf.

———. 2016. "Home in the Diaspora? Jewish Returnees and Transmigrants in Ukraine." In *The New Jewish Diaspora: Russian-Speaking Immigrants in the United States, Israel and Germany,* edited by Zvi Gitelman, 60–74. New Brunswick, NJ: Rutgers University Press.

———. 2018. "Between a Home and a Homeland: Experiences of Jewish Return Migrants in Ukraine." In *Travelling towards Home,* edited by Tom Selwyn and Nicola Frost, 55–76. New York: Berghahn Books.

———. 2022. "Germany Wants Jews." *Tablet,* April 26, 2022. https://www .tabletmag.com/sections/news/articles/germany-wants-jews.

———. 2023. "Fragmented Lives and Fragmented Histories in Odesa." In *Dispossessions: Imperial Legacies and Russia's War on Ukraine,* edited by Catherine Wanner. London: Routledge.

———. Forthcoming. "Russian-Speaking but not Svoi: Linguistic Entanglements of Ukrainian Jewish Refugees in Europe." Special Issue, Ukraine. *Sociolinguistic Studies.*

Sasson, Theodore, Janet Krasner Aronson, Fern Chertok, Charles Kadushin, and Leonard Saxe, 2017. "Millennial Children of Intermarriage: Religious Upbringing, Identification, and Behavior among Children of Jewish and Non-Jewish Parents." *Contemporary Jewry* 37 (1): 99–123.

Satanovsky, Evgeny. 2009. "Russian Jews: The Variants of the Future." *Euro-Asian Jewish Congress.* http://jewseurasia.org/page34/news14038.html.

Savchenko, Boris. 1996. *Estrada retro: Iurii Morfessi, Aleksandr Vertinskii, Iza Kremer, Petr Leshchenko, Vadim Kozin, Izabella Iur'eva* [Popular music: Iurii Morfessi, Aleksandr Vertinskii, Iza Kremer, Petr Leshchenko, Vadim Kozin, Izabella Iur'eva]. Moscow: Iskusstvo.

Schoeps, Julius H., and Olaf Glöckner. 2008. "Fifteen Years of Russian-Jewish Immigration to Germany: Successes and Setbacks." In *The New German Jewry and the European Context: The Return of the European Jewish Diaspora,* edited by Michal Y. Bodemann, 144–57. New York: Palgrave Macmillan.

Senderovich, Sasha. 2022. *How the Soviet Jew Was Made.* Cambridge, MA: Harvard University Press.

Shadmi, Erella. 2019. "The Jewish *Tzedakah* (Gifting) Community." *Canadian Women's Studies* 34 (1–2): 123–31.

Shapira, Dan. 2014. "The First Jews of Ukraine." In *Jews and Ukrainians*, edited by Yohanan Petrovsky-Shtern and Antony Polonsky, 66–77. Vol. 26 of *Polin: Studies in Polish Jewry*. Oxford: Littman Library of Jewish Civilization.

Sharansky, Natan. 1998. *Fear No Evil: Classic Memoir of One Man's Triumph over the Police State.* New York: Public Affairs.

Sharpless, Rebecca. 2007. "The History of Oral History." In *History of Oral History: Foundations and Methodology*, edited by Thomas L. Carlton, Lois E. Myers, and Rebecca Sharpless, 13–31. Lanham, MD: AltaMira.

Shayduk, Olesya. 2007. "The Construction of Jewish Identity of Youth under Institutional Influence: The Case of St. Petersburg." Paper presented at the Association for the Study of Nationalities World Convention, Columbia University, New York, 2007.

Shneer, David. 2007. "Shvitz Exclusive: Why Chabad Excels in Russia, and Why Reform Judaism Doesn't." Jewcy, April 16, 2007. https://www.jewcy.com/post /shvitz_exclusive_why_chabad_excels_in_russia_and_why_reform_judaism _doesnt/.

Shokin, Samantha. 2001. "To Ukraine with Love." *Tablet*, August 17, 2021. https://www.tabletmag.com/sections/community/articles/to-ukraine -with-love.

Shternshis, Anna. 2006. *Soviet and Kosher: Jewish Popular Culture in the Soviet Union, 1923–1939.* Bloomington: Indiana University Press.

Shuval, Judith T., and Elazar Leshem. 1998. "The Sociology of Migration in Israel: A Critical View." In *Immigration to Israel: Sociological Perspectives*, edited by Elazar Leshem and Judith T. Shuval, 3–50. Vol. 8 of *Studies of Israeli Society*. New Brunswick, NJ: Transaction Publishers.

Sicher, Efraim. 2023. "The End of Cosmopolitan Time: Between Myth and Accommodation in Babel's Odessa Stories." In *Cosmopolitan Spaces in Odesa: A Case Study of an Urban Context*, edited by Mirja Lecke and Efraim Sicher, 193–221. Boston: Academic University Press.

Siegel, Dina. 1998. *The Great Immigration: Russian Jews in Israel.* New York: Berghahn Books.

Sifneos, Evrydiki. 2018. *Imperial Odessa: People, Spaces, Identities.* Leiden: Brill.

Silber, Michael K. 1992. "The Emergence of Ultra–Orthodoxy: The Invention of a Tradition." In *The Uses of Tradition Jewish Community in the Modern Era*, edited by Jack Wertheimer, 23–85. Cambridge, MA: Harvard University Press.

Skinner, Frederick W. 1986. "Odessa and the Problem of Urban Modernization." In *The City in Late Imperial Russia*, edited by Michael F. Hamm, 209–49. Bloomington: Indiana University Press.

Skvirskaja, Vera. 2006. "A Post-Cosmopolitan City? Changing Dynamics of Coexistence in Odessa, Ukraine." Paper presented at the Research Seminar on Anthropological Theory, London School of Economics and Political Science, London, March 10, 2006.

———. 2010. "New Diaspora in a Post-Soviet City: Transformations in Experiences of Belonging in Odessa, Ukraine." *Studies in Ethnicity and Nationalism* 10 (1): 76–91.

Skvirskaja, Vera, and Caroline Humphrey. 2007. "Odessa: Skoľzkii gorod i uskoľzauchii kosmopolitism" [Odessa: Slippery city and slipping cosmopolitanism]. *Acta Eurasia* 1 (35): 87–116.

Slezkine, Yuri. 2004. *The Jewish Century*. Princeton, NJ: Princeton University Press.

Smolar, Boris. 1971. *Soviet Jewry Today and Tomorrow*. New York: Macmillan.

Sokol, Sam. 2022. *Putin's Hybrid War and the Jews: Antisemitism, Propaganda, and the Displacement of Ukrainian Jewry*. 2nd ed. Oxford: ISGAP.

Solomon, Norman. 1994. "Judaism in the New Europe: Discovery or Invention?" In *Jewish Identities in the New Europe*, edited by Jonathan Webber, 86–98. London: Littman Library of Jewish Civilization.

Solomon, Tessa. 2022. "Ukrainians in Odesa Dismantle Monument to Russia's Catherine the Great." ARTnews, December 29, 2022. https://www.artnews .com/art-news/news/ukraine-odesa-catherine-the-great-monument -removed-1234652206/.

Stanislawski, Michael. 1983. *Tsar Nicholas I and the Jews: The Transformation of Jewish Society in Russia, 1825–1855*. Schöningh: Brill.

———. 2001. *Zionism and the Fin de Siècle: Cosmopolitanism and Nationalism from Nordau to Jabotinsky*. Berkeley: University of California Press.

Stanton, Rebecca. 2003. "Identity Crisis: The Literary Cult and Culture of Odessa in the Early 20th Century." *Symposium* 57 (3): 117–26.

———. 2004. "Odessan Selves: Identity and Mythopoesis in Works of the Odessa School." PhD diss., Department of Slavic Languages and Literatures, Columbia University.

———. 2012. *Isaac Babel and the Self-Invention of Odessan Modernism*. Evanston, IL: Northwestern University Press.

Steenland, Robert. 2018. "Ukraine's Unity and the Euromaidan's Legacy." *New Eastern Europe*, November 22, 2018. https://neweasterneurope.eu/2018/11/22 /ukraines-unity-euromaidans-legacy-divisions-east-vs-west-no/.

Stefansson, Anders H. 2004. "Homecomings to the Future: From Diasporic Mythographies to Social Projects of Return." In *Homecomings: Unsettled Paths of Return*, edited by Fran Markowitz and Anders Stefansson, 2–20. Lanham, MD: Lexington Books.

Steinberg, Mark D., and Catherine Wanner. 2008. "Introduction." In *Religion, Morality and Community in Post-Soviet Societies*, edited by Mark D. Steinberg and Catherine Wanner, 1–21. Washington, DC: Woodrow Wilson Center Press.

Stewart, Michael. 2004. "Remembering without Commemoration: The Mnemonics and Politics of Holocaust Memories among European Roma." *Royal Anthropological Institute* 10 (4): 561–82.

Stirrat, R. L., and Heiko Henkel. 1997. "The Development Gift: The Problem of Reciprocity in the NGO World." *The Annals of the American Academy of Political and Social Science* 554:66–80.

Svirskii, A. I. 1904. "Iz putevogo denvika." *Knizhki 'Voskhoda'* 7:166–72.

Sylvester, Roshanna P. 2001. "City of Thieves: Moldovanka, Criminality and Respectability in Pre-revolutionary Odessa." *Journal of Urban History* 27 (2): 131–57.

———. 2005. *Tales of Old Odessa: Crime and Civility in a City of Thieves*. Dekalb: Northern Illinois University Press.

Tabarovsky, Izabella. 2018. "Is Ukraine's Holocaust Memorial at Babi Yar in Trouble?" *Tablet*, January 25, 2018. https://www.tabletmag.com/sections /news/articles/holocaust-memorial-babi-yar.

Tanny, Jarrod. 2006. "The Myth of 'Odessa Odessa.'" *Odeskiy Listok* 133:24.

———. 2007. "The Many Ends of Old Odessa: Memories of the Gilded Age in Russia's City of Sin." Paper presented at the Association for the Study of Nationalities World Convention, New York.

———. 2008. "City of Rogues and Schnorrers: The Myth of Old Odessa in Russian and Jewish Culture." PhD diss., Department of Philosophy and History, University of California, Berkeley.

———. 2011. *City of Rogues and Schnorrers: Russia's Jews and the Myth of Old Odessa*. Bloomington: Indiana University Press.

Thompson, Paul. 2000. *The Voice of the Past: Oral History*. Oxford: Oxford University Press.

Tolts, Mark. 1992. "Jewish Marriages in the USSR: A Demographic Analysis." *East European Jewish Affairs* 22 (2): 3–19.

———. 2004. "The Post-Soviet Jewish Population in Russia and the World Jews." *Russia and Eastern Europe* 1 (52): 37–62.

———. 2007. "Post-Soviet Jewish Demography, 1989–2004." In *Revolution, Repression, and Revival: The Soviet Jewish Experience*, edited by Zvi Gitelman, and Yaacov Ro'i, 283–312. Lanham, MD: Rowman & Littlefield.

———. 2009. "Post-Soviet Aliyah and Jewish Demography Transformation." Paper presented at the Fifteenth World Congress of Jewish Studies, Jerusalem, August 2–6, 2009.

———. 2016. "Jews in the Post-Soviet World: New Demographic Material." [In Russian]. *Demoskop Weekly* 693–694:1–22. https://www.demoscope.ru /weekly/2016/0693/tema01.php.

———. 2018. "Post-Soviet Jewish Demographic Dynamics: An Analysis of Recent Data." Institute for Jewish Policy Research Report. https://archive.jpr .org.uk/download?id=3486.

————. 2020. "A Half Century of Jewish Emigration from the Former Soviet Union." In *Migration from the Newly Independent States, Societies and Political Order in Transition*, edited by Mikhail Denisenko, Salvatore Strozza, and Matthew Light 323–44. New York: Springer.

Tracy, Marc. 2014. "What the Crisis in Ukraine Means for Its 70,000 Jews." *New Republic*, March 4, 2014. http://newrepublic.com/article/116855 /ukrainian-russia-jews-respond-anti-semitism-crimea-crisis.

Tye, Larry. 2001. *Home Lands: Portraits of the New Jewish Diaspora*. New York: Henry Holt and Company.

Utesov, Leonid. 2006. *Spasibo, Sertse* [Thank you, my heart]. Moscow: Vagrius.

Veidlinger, Jeffrey. 2000. *The Moscow State Yiddish Theatre: Jewish Culture on the Soviet Stage*. Bloomington: Indiana University Press.

————. 2009. *Jewish Public Culture in the Late Russian Empire*. Bloomington: Indiana University Press.

————. 2013. *In the Shadows of the Shtetl: Small Town Jewish Life in Soviet Ukraine*. Bloomington: Indiana University Press.

Vladimirsky, Irena. 2021. "From the Black to the Yellow Sea: 'Port Jews' and Cosmopolitanism across the Borders (the Case of the Soskin Family)." Paper delivered at the Odessa, Cosmopolitanism, Modernism Conference June 21, 2021. https://www.youtube.com/watch?v=U2EB56YR4QA.

Voutira, Eftihia. 2006. "Post-Soviet Diaspora Politics: The Case of Soviet Greeks." *Journal of Modern Greek Studies* 24 (2): 379–414.

Waligorska, Magdalena. 2013. *Klezmer's Afterlife: An Ethnography of the Jewish Music Revival in Poland and Germany*. Oxford: Oxford University Press.

Wanner, Catherine. 1998. *Burden of Dreams: History and Identity in Post-Soviet Ukraine*. Philadelphia: Pennsylvania University Press.

————. 2003. "Advocating New Moralities: Conversion to Evangelicalism in Ukraine." *International Journal of Phytoremediation* 21 (1): 273–87.

————. 2007a. *Communities of the Converted: Ukrainians and Global Evangelism*. Ithaca, NY: Cornell University Press.

————. 2007b. "Missionizing Eurasia: The Global Networks of Ukrainian Evangelicals." Paper presented at the Annual Soyuz Symposium, Princeton University, Princeton, NJ, April 27–29.

Webber, Jonathan, ed. 1994a. *Jewish Identities in the New Europe*. London: Littman Library of Jewish Civilization.

————. 1994b. "Modern Jewish Identities." In *Jewish Identities in the New Europe*, edited by Jonathan Webber, 74–85. London: Littman Library of Jewish Civilization.

Weinberg, Robert. 1992. "The Pogrom of 1905 in Odessa: A Case Study." In *Pogroms: Anti-Jewish Violence in Modern Russian History*, edited by John Klier and Shlomo Lambroza, 248–89. Cambridge: Cambridge University Press.

————. 1993. *The Revolution of 1905 in Odessa: Blood on the Steps*. Bloomington: Indiana University Press.

Wettstein, Howard. 2002. "Introduction." In *Diasporas and Exiles*, edited by Howard Wettstein, 1–17. Berkley: University of California Press.

Wiesel, Elie. 1966. *The Jews of Silence*. New York: Holt, Rinehart and Winston.

Wigoder, Geoffrey, Fred Skolnik, and Shmuel Himelstein. 1989. *The New Encyclopedia of Judaism*. New York: New York University Press.

Wilson, Andrew. 2002. "Elements of a Theory of Ukrainian Ethno-National Identities." *Nations and Nationalism* 8 (1): 31–54.

Wirth, Louis. (1928) 1998. *The Ghetto*. New Brunswick, NJ: Transaction Publishers.

Young, James, ed. 1994. *The Art of Memory: Holocaust Memorials in History*. New York: Prestel.

Yurchak, Alexei. 2006. *Everything Was Forever, Until It Was No More: The Last Soviet Generation*. Princeton, NJ: Princeton University Press.

Zabirko, Oleksandr. 2023. "Where the Steppe Meets the Sea: Odesa in the Ukrainian City Text." In *Cosmopolitan Spaces in Odesa: A Case Study of an Urban Context*, edited by Mirja Lecke and Efraim Sicher, 222–51. Boston: Academic University Press.

Zborowski, Mark, and Elizabeth Herzog. (1995) 2009. *Life Is with People: The Culture of the Shtetl*. 5th ed. New York: Schocken Books.

Zelenina, Galina. 2012. "'Tsirk, kotoryi mnogim stoil zhizni': Obrezanie u sovetskikh evreev i ego posledstviya v gody voiny" [Circus that caused many their lives: Circumcision of Soviet Jews and its ramifications during the war years]. *Religioveniye* 2:56–67.

———. 2014. "'One's Entire Life among Books': Soviet Jewry on the Path from Tanakh to Library." *State, Religion and Church* 1 (2): 86–111.

———. 2018. "'Our Community Is the Coolest in the World': Chabad and Jewish Nation–Building in Contemporary Russia." *Contemporary Jewry* 38 (2): 249–79.

Zemtsov, Ilya. (1991) 2001. *Encyclopedia of Soviet Life*. New Brunswick, NJ: Transaction Publishers.

Zhurzhenko, Tatiana. 2014. "From Borderlands to Bloodlands." *Eurozine*, September 19, 2014. https://eurozine.com/from-borderlands-to-bloodlands/.

Zipperstein, Steven J. 1986. *The Jews of Odessa: A Cultural History, 1794–1881*. Stanford, CA: Stanford University Press.

———. 1999. *Imagining Russian Jewry: Memory, History, Identity*. Seattle: University of Washington Press.

Zissels, Josef. 1999. "The Jewish Community of Ukraine: Its Status and Perspectives." In *Jewish Roots in Ukraine and Moldova: Pages from the Past and Archive Inventories*, edited by Miriam Weiner. Jewish Genealogy Series. Miriam Weiner Routes to Roots Foundation.

Websites

Ab Imperio Syllabus. n.d. "Soviet Subjectivity." Accessed December 3, 2023. https://sites.google.com/view/ai-syllabus/keywords/soviet-subjectivity.

All Ukrainian Population Census. n.d. Accessed December 19, 2023.
http://www.ukrcensus.gov.ua/eng/.

Benya and Zubrik. n.d. "Odessa-fashion." Accessed December 3, 2023.
https://benyaizubrik.com/shirts.

Chabad Odessa. n.d. Accessed January 8, 2023. https://www.chabad.odessa.ua
/templates/articlecco_cdo/aid/1744856/jewish/English.htm.

Dumskaya, 1. 2022. "Звернення духовенства Одеси" [Address of the Clergy
of Odessa]. YouTube, March 16, 2022. https://www.youtube.com/watch
?v=cCyseJyAbdg.

EJAC. n.d. Accessed December 21, 2023. https://eajc.org/en/home/.

Encyclopaedia Britannica. 2023. "Jewish Agency." Last updated October 5, 2023.
https://www.britannica.com/topic/Jewish-Agency.

FJC. n.d. "Stars." Accessed December 21, 2023. https://fjc-fsu.org/department
/students-youngsters/stars/#:~:text=STARS%20is%20a%20contact%
2Dgroup,current%20events%20and%20everyday%20life.

Glaser, Amelia. n.d. "Secular Jewish Literature in Ukraine." My Jewish Learning
website. Accessed December 3, 2023. https://www.myjewishlearning.com
/article/secular-jewish-literature-in-ukraine.

Holocaust Encyclopedia. n.d. "Mass Shootings at Babyn Yar (Babi Yar)."
Accessed December 3, 2023. https://encyclopedia.ushmm.org/content/en
/article/kiev-and-babi-yar.

ILTV. 2019. "Odessa, Ukraine Experiences Jewish Renaissance." https://www
.youtube.com/watch?v=lbHVE8zGhqo.

Institute for Jewish Policy Research. n.d. "Ukraine." Accessed December 3, 2023.
https://www.jpr.org.uk/countries/how-many-jews-in-ukraine.

Israel Institute for Advanced Studies. 2021. "Cosmopolitanism in Urban Spaces:
The Case of Odessa (Online Webinar)." Hebrew University of Jerusalem.
https://iias.huji.ac.il/event/cosmopolitanism-urban-spaces-case-odessa.

JDC. n.d. "Our Work." Official organization website. Accessed December 3,
2023. https://www.jdc.org/our-work.

Jewish Agency for Israel. n.d. "Official Website." Accessed December 3, 2023.
https://archive.jewishagency.org/first-steps/program/5131/.

Jewish Confederation of Ukraine. n.d. "About the Confederation." Accessed
December 3, 2023. https://jcu.org.ua/en/about-confederation.

The Jewish Federation of Greater Los Angeles. n.d. "Explore." Accessed December 21, 2023. www.jewishla.org/federationinforcus/html/apr05_jfishel
.html.

Jewish Federations of North America. n.d.-a. "About." Accessed December 3,
2023. https://www.jewishfederations.org/about-jfna.

The Jewish Federations of North America. n.d.-b. "Building Flourishing Jewish
Communities in Your Home Town and Around the World." Accessed
December 21, 2023. www.ujc.org.

Jewish Federations of North America. n.d.-c. "How We Help." Accessed December 3, 2023. https://jewishfederations.org/how-we-help/global-jewry.

JGuideEurope. n.d. "Ukraine/From Kiev to the Black Sea: Odessa." Fondation Jacques et Jacqueline Lévy-Willard, Fondation du Judaïsme Français. Accessed December 3, 2023. https://jguideeurope.org/en/region/ukraine /from-kiev-to-the-black-sea/odessa/.

Kulyk, Volodymyr. 2023. "Myths and Misconceptions about the Language Situation in Ukraine." University College London, January 16, 2023. https://www.ucl.ac.uk/ssees/events/2023/jan/myths-and-misconceptions -about-language-situation-ukraine.

Levchuk, Olga. 2022. Пол-Оборота №27 Ігор Окс (Half-Turn, Interview with Igor Oks) "єврейське питання, деформація українців, антисемітизм" [The Jewish question, deformation of Ukrainians, anti-semitism]. https://youtu.be /oIDooe6AnwY.

Limmud FSU. 2019. "Limmud FSU Ukraine in Odessa Attracts More Than 600 Participants." March 4, 2019. https://www.limmudfsu.org/hp-newsagragation /limmud-fsu-ukraine-2019.

Margolin, Dovid. 2019. "First Jewish President of Ukraine Holds 'Historic' Meeting with Rabbis." Chabad.org News, May 7, 2019. https://www.chabad .org/news/article_cdo/aid/4377198/jewish/First-Jewish-President-of-Ukraine -Holds-Historic-Meeting-With-Rabbis.htm.

Migdal. 2014. Website forum. January 22, 2014. http://www.migdal.ru/forum.

The Mikvah Project. n.d. Accessed December 21, 2023. http://www.mikvah project.com/china.html.

"Museum 'Babyn Yar.' An Open Letter of Warning from Ukrainian Historians." Special Project: The Holocaust. March 28, 2017. https://www.istpravda.com .ua/articles/2017/03/28/149652/.

National Coalition Supporting Eurasian Jewry. 2018. "NCSEJ Condemns Anti-Semitic Remarks at M2 Demonstration in Odessa, Ukraine." Press release, May 3, 2018. https://app.robly.com/archive?id=e97597a25e4a4b63fdd8589fde9 602aa&v=true.

Neumann, Jeannette. n.d. "What Dermatologists Really Think about Those Anti-Aging Products." *Bloomberg Businessweek*. http://www.businessweek .com/1997/25/b353252.html.

Newsru.co.il. n.d. "Survey: Departure from Israel; Pros and Cons." Accessed April 8, 2018. http://www.newsru.co.il/info/bigpoll/yerida2007.html.

Odesit. n.d. "Portal of Ukraniain Community of Odessa." Accessed December 4, 2023. http://www.odesit.com.

Odessaglobe. n.d. Accessed December 4, 2023. http://www.odessaglobe.com.

Religious Information Service of Ukraine. 2022. "We Don't Need to Be 'Liber-ated,' Go Home!—The Appeal of Representatives of Different Religions and Confessions of Odesa." October 17, 2022. https://risu.ua/en/we-dont-need-to

-be-liberated-go-home---the-appeal-of-representatives-of-different-religions
-and-confessions-of-odesa_n127290.

Runyan, Tamar. 2008. "Circumcision Makes History in Odessa, Ukraine."
   Chabad.org News, March 13, 2008. https://www.chabad.org/news/article
   _cdo/aid/650316/jewish/Circumcision-Makes-History-in-Odessa-Ukraine
   .htm.

State Statistics Committee of Ukraine. 2003–2004. "About Number and Composition Population of Ukraine by All-Ukrainian Population Census 2001 Data."
   All-Ukrainian Population Census 2001. http://2001.ukrcensus.gov.ua
   /eng/results/general/language.

Ta Odessa. n.d. Tourism and recreation in Odessa website. Accessed December
   3, 2023. http://www.ta-odessa.com/.

Tikva Children's Home. n.d. "History of Tikva." Accessed February 20, 2021.
   https://www.tikvaodessa.org/about-us/history-of-tikva.

Tikva Odessa. n.d. Accessed December 19, 2023. https://www.tikvaodessa.org.

Totally Jewish Travel. n.d. "Hotels in Odessa, Ukraine." Accessed December 3,
   2023. https://www.totallyjewishtravel.com/kosherhotels-TJ891-Odessa
   _Ukraine-Observant_Friendly_Accommodation.html.

Ukraïner. 2019. "The Jews of Ukraine. Who Are They?" December 20, 2019.
   https://ukrainer.net/the-jews-of-ukraine/.

UNESCO. 2023. "The Historical Center of Odesa." https://whc.unesco.org/en
   /list/1703/.

Wikipedia. n.d. "Karaite Judaism." Accessed December 21, 2023. https://en
   .wikipedia.org/wiki/Karaite_Judaism.

Wikipedia. 2023. "Yiddishkeit." Last edited June 18, 2023. https://en.wikipedia
   .org/wiki/Yiddishkeit.

World ORT. n.d. Official website. History timeline. Accessed December 3, 2023.
   https://ort.org/en/about-ort/history/.

Yad Vashem. n.d. "Transnistria." Shoa Resource Center. Accessed December 3,
   2023. https://www.yadvashem.org/odot_pdf/Microsoft%20Word%20-%20
   5883.pdf.

Yad Vashem—The World Holocaust Remembrance Center. n.d. Accessed
   December 19, 2023. https://www.yadvashem.org.

YIVO Institute for Jewish Research. n.d. "Odessa: Community Institutions."
   Accessed December 3, 2023. http://epyc.yivo.org/content/19_3.php.

Zchor. n.d. "Babi Yar: Killing Ravine of Kiev Jewry—WWII." Accessed
   December 21, 2023. http://www.zchor.org/BABIYAR.HTM.

Zipperstein, Steven. n.d. "Odessa." YIVO Encyclopedia of Jews in Eastern
   Europe. Accessed December 3, 2023. https://yivoencyclopedia.org/article
   .aspx/odessa.

INDEX

Abbas, Ackbar, 16
acculturation, 29, 30, 37, 42–43, 68
Ahad, Ha'am (Asher Ginsberg), 44
Akhmetchetka concentration camp, 51
Albanians, 38, 109
Aleichem, Sholem (Solomon
　Naumovich Rabinovitch), 43, 67
Alexander I, Tsar, 36
aliyah (Jewish migration to Israel),
　47, 81, 150–51, 162; "failed cases" of,
　189; Law of Return and, 105, 106;
　Litvak Orthodox movement and,
　186; "repatriates" and, 193, 273n66;
　Russian invasion of Ukraine and,
　198, 234
Anderson, Benedict, 6, 252n9
And Quiet Flows the Don
　(Sholokhov), 67
anthropology, 18, 22, 110–11, 216
*Anti-Imperial Choice: The Making of
　the Ukrainian Jews* (Petrovsky-
　Shtern), 250
antisemitism, 13, 154, 244, 248,
　292n18; in Crimea, 247; "Jewish"
　as synonym for being different,
　72, 266n39; Jewish identity hidden
　in response to, 68, 72, 83; Jewish

visibility and, 290n75; Nazi versus
　Soviet, 264n26; in postwar Soviet
　Union, 62; quotas for Jews in
　universities and workplaces, 49, 52,
　63, 85–86, 119, 181; religious revival
　and, 90; right-wing Ukrainian
　nationalist groups and, 235;
　sanctioned by the Soviet state, 56,
　119, 175, 229; of Stalin, 52; *zhid/
　zhidovka* epithet, 71, 81, 109, 154, 190,
　191. *See also* Holocaust; pogroms
Antonescu, Ion, 50, 51
Anuch, Olga, 249
Argentina, Jewish emigration to, 46
Armenians, 10, 38, 62
Art of Living in Odesa, The (film, dir.
　Yungvald-Khilkevich, 1989), 206
assimilation, to Russian/Soviet
　culture, 19, 32, 43, 56–57, 85, 181,
　256n16; religious Jews' rejection of,
　66; religious observance and family
　relations in context of, 131; return
　migrants from Israel and, 192
Association of Jewish Organizations
　and Communities of Ukraine,
　118, 249
atheism, 61–62, 70, 72, 73

Jewish Research Center, 279n43

"Jewish revival," xii, 4, 19, 23, 141, 202, 221; complexities of, 232–34, 292n7; as "cultural imperialism," 173–74; emigration and, 140; international projects of, 3, 20, 26; non-Jews and, 153; Odesa as Jewish city and, 221; philanthropy and, 144; as restoration of "lost" Jewishness, 89–90; revival as questionable concept, 116. *See also* religious revival, post-Soviet

Jewish Street, 8, 12

Jewish studies, 17, 98, 117, 141, 175, 230; on relation between tradition and modernity, 21; Soviet and post-Soviet research, 18

Jewish Theater Migdal Or, 138, 159

Jewish Topographies: Visions of Space, Tradition of Place, 212

Jewish–Ukrainian relations, xi, 11–12, 207, 293n22; cosmopolitanism and, 234–35, 237, 238; formalization of, 249–50; old paradigms of conflict and hostility, 31

Jews: American, 13, 32, 157, 163, 164; Ashkenazi, 143, 144, 147, 163, 269n27; commercial culture and, 39; connections to global Judaism, 5; "core" Jewish population, 10, 253n20; in early Soviet period, 46–49; identification with Russian-speaking culture, 11; internal displacement of, xi; local politics and, 214, 290n65; in military ranks of Russian Empire, 257n52; as percentage of Odesa population, 10, 39, 45, 46–47; in Polish-Lithuanian Commonwealth, 34–35; in poverty, 45, 173; privilege of admission to guilds, 35, 257n39; in professions, 43; Soviet war veterans, 62, 70, 264n25;

Ukrainian names adopted by, 52, 80

Jews, newly observant, 54, 120, 277n48; adoption of religious names, 132; compared to new language learners, 110; doubts about sincerity of, 84, 114; evolving attitude toward Judaism, 126; motivated by "miraculous" events, 123–24; negotiation of tradition as challenge to Orthodoxy, 127–31; politics of Jewish observance and, 136–39; relations with secular family members, 114, 131–39, 276n34; self-image as pioneers, 121; younger Jews' experimentation with observance, 127. *See also* religious revival, post-Soviet

Jews of Silence: A Personal Report on Soviet Jewry (Wiesel, 1966), 264n11

JFNA. *See* UJC/JFNA

Joint, the. *See* JDC (Jewish Distribution Committee; the Joint)

journalists, 45, 53

Judaism, xii, 5, 20, 27, 86; as defining feature of Jewish identity, 116; first post-Soviet encounters with, 93; *giur* (formal conversion) to, 103, 272n56; global, 18; international, 231; motivations and paths from secularism to, 120–27; redefined relationship to, 114. *See also* Orthodox Judaism; Reform (Progressive) Judaism

Kabbalah (Jewish mysticism), 269n28

kaddish (prayer for the dead), 166, 170

kapparah ceremony, 136

Karaism/Karaits, 33–34, 62, 63, 257n42

Karakina, Elena, 291n92

kashrut (Jewish dietary laws), 60, 65, 116, 119, 240

Kataev, Valentin, 203

MARINA SAPRITSKY-NAHUM is a social anthropologist based in London. She is Honorary Research Fellow at University College London and Visiting Fellow at the London School of Economics and Political Science. She is also affiliated with the European Center for Jewish Music in Hannover, Germany, where she is currently conducting research on Ukrainian Jewish cultural heritage in Europe and writing more broadly about the effects of war on Jewish life in Ukraine.

For Indiana University Press

Tony Brewer, Artist and Book Designer
Dan Crissman, Editorial Director and Acquisitions Editor
Gary Dunham, Director and Acquisitions Editor
Anna Francis, Assistant Acquisitions Editor
Brenna Hosman, Production Coordinator
Katie Huggins, Production Manager
Nancy Lightfoot, Project Editor and Manager
Dan Pyle, Online Publishing Manager
Pamela Rude, Senior Artist and Book Designer
Stephen Williams, Marketing and Publicity Manager